£40.00

THE UNIVERSITY OF
WINCHESTER

Martial Rose Library
Tel: 01962 827306

-5 APR 2013

To be returned on or before the day marked above, subject to recall.

Reading Gothic Fiction

Reading
Gothic Fiction
A Bakhtinian Approach

JACQUELINE HOWARD

CLARENDON PRESS · OXFORD

Oxford University Press, Walton Street, Oxford OX2 6DP
Oxford New York
Athens Auckland Bangkok Bogota Bombay
Buenos Aires Calcutta Cape Town Dar es Salaam
Delhi Florence Hong Kong Istanbul Karachi
Kuala Lumpur Madras Madrid Melbourne
Mexico City Nairobi Paris Singapore
Taipei Tokyo Toronto
and associated companies in
Berlin Ibadan

Oxford is a trade mark of Oxford University Press

Published in the United States
by Oxford University Press Inc., New York

© Jacqueline Howard 1994
First published 1994

British Library Cataloguing in Publication Data
Data available

Library of Congress Cataloging in Publication Data
Howard, Jacqueline.
Reading Gothic fiction:
a Bakhtinian approach/Jacqueline Howard.
Includes bibliographical references and index.
1. Horror tales, English—History and criticism—Theory, etc.
2. Bakhtin, M. M. (Mikhil Mikhaïlovich), 1895–1975.
3. Gothic revival (Literature)—Great Britain.
4. Feminism and literature—Great Britain.
5. Women and literature—Great Britain. I. Title.
Pr830.T3H69 1994 823'.0872909—dc20 93–5220
ISBN 0-19-811992-5

3 5 7 9 10 8 6 4 2

Printed in Great Britain
on acid-free paper by
Ipswich Book Co Ltd, Ipswich

Acknowledgements

I would like to thank Ian Reid, John Frow, Ken Ruthven, Vijay Mishra, and Judith Barbour for reading and providing advice and encouragement regarding various aspects of an earlier version of the manuscript. I am also deeply grateful to Les Howard who not only offered encouragement but gave up many hours of his own time to assist with word-processing. Finally, for their personal help and support during times of pressure and fatigue, my thanks go to my mother, Edna Mawet, my daughter, Anthea Howard, and my friends, Alexandra Dixon, Christine Thompson, Lorraine Ragless, Betty Szilagyi, Annette Jarrett, and Michael Walsh.

JACQUELINE HOWARD

January 1993

p 54
intro

pi

women
inferor
in life
?... in
lit

Contents

Introduction

HOW ANY READER or critic reads the Gothic depends to a large extent on his or her assumptions about genre. For those who conceive of the Gothic primarily as a system of codifiable conventions, there are difficulties in giving sufficient recognition to historical variability and change. The reader is caught in the hermeneutically circular process of interpreting a text in such a way as to produce the generic frame against which the text is being read. From this in turn can flow aesthetic judgements which deny a text's specifically historical, social, cultural, or political meaning and significance.

This study sets out to show the relevance of Mikhail Bakhtin's concept of dialogism in the novel for theorizing the Gothic, and to reconstruct the intertextual relations of selected works of Gothic fiction written between 1760 and 1820. My object has been to situate Gothic texts historically, socially, and culturally by examining how they construct and define themselves in relation to prior discourses, both literary and non-literary. In drawing attention to the plural dimensions of reading in relation to the Gothic, I have also indicated its historically changing generic structure as it has continued to fascinate readers with its peculiar order of being, one which, as John Frow puts it, 'emphasizes the subjective apprehension of a threatening environment'.[1]

Novels, romances, and tales commonly labelled 'Gothic' have varied considerably in their modes of production, reception, and reproduction. Between those examined here we can perceive marked differences in the registers on which they draw, the complexity of their artistic arrangement, and the subject positions and imaginative spaces which they offer to readers. Yet too often studies of Gothic fiction which purport to be historical are so broad in the sweep of their theses that

[1] John Frow, *Marxism and Literary History* (Oxford: Blackwell, 1986), 167.

they seem static and homogenizing. Concern with synchronic elements and evaluative comment overtakes interest in the historical, social, and cultural specificity of individual texts and leads to a suppression of awareness of the interpretative process itself. Indeed, for all the studies which have been made of the Gothic, to date there have been few written within the context of post-structuralist theories of narrative and reading. Given the more or less fixed nature of many received views—about the rise of the novel and realism as its dominant form, about the marginal role and status of women writers, about the nature of genre itself and the Gothic as a 'popular' form with predictable textual properties—situating Gothic texts with greater precision against the dominant literary canon and other cultural texts seems an important task.

The value of approaching interpretation of the Gothic with Bakhtin, on the side of history, lies in the quite different orientation to genre which his dialogism implies. While there is recognition that, in social intercourse, texts guide interpretation and signal their kinds by familiar conventions or allusions, there is resistance to classifying and systematizing isolated features as generic essences. Certain conventions may become institutionalized within a culture as recurring generic features, but this is a contingent business, subject to change. Hence, for our purposes in reading the Gothic, there is no requirement to abstract predictable structural and stylistic features and insist on a dialectic of finalization or closure. Bakhtin's notion of 'heteroglossia' or 'multi-voicedness' in the novel takes us away from holistic notions of genre and allows us to acknowledge freely the disparate discursive structures we perceive in the Gothic. In 'Discourse in the Novel' the novel is seen as 'orchestrating its themes . . . by means of the social diversity of speech types'. Heteroglossia enters the novel through such 'compositional unities' as 'authorial speech, the speeches of narrators, inserted genres, the speech of characters'.[2] Although Bakhtin's dialogic view of language has been properly criticized for its lack of precision and ultimate dissolution of

---

[2] Mikhail Bakhtin, *The Dialogic Imagination*, ed. Michael Holquist, trans. Caryl Emerson and Michael Holquist (Austin and London: University of Texas Press, 1981), 264. Further references appear in the text.

all conceptual distinctions,[3] and various appropriations of his work continue amid much debate,[4] his view of genre as performance or practice within a socio-historically specific context is a fruitful one, opening up areas of genre criticism which to date have not been explored sufficiently.[5] For Bakhtin, the novel is inserted into an already existing discursive space as a response to both what has been and what might be said. In thus orientating itself, it can be conceived of as representing 'the social and ideological voices of its era'—the competing, often contradictory discourses which give meaning to social reality. Given this interaction of perspectives, we can examine whether and how the Gothic's folk-tales, fairy-tales, superstitions, myths, discourse of the sublime, everyday 'common sense', and fragments of discourses drawn from non-literary realms are simply reproduced or actually transformed, and in whose interests, as they are incorporated in new contexts. Recognition of modes of subjectivity offered to the reader through the conflict of realities produced in the inter- and intra-textual patterning of a novel or tale enables us to assess the degree to which that text's dominant discourse and its associated moral code may be confirmed or subverted in reading.

Gothic fiction has long attracted comment from some that it is a 'revolutionary' or subversive genre. More recently, however, the preponderance of female-authored Gothic has received considerable attention from feminist critics who claim that Gothic fantasy has been appropriated differentially by

[3] Robert Young, 'Back to Bakhtin', *Cultural Critique*, 2 (Winter 1986), 85–6.
[4] See 'Introduction: Rethinking Bakhtin', in Gary Saul Morson and Caryl Emerson, eds., *Rethinking Bakhtin: Extensions and Challenges* (Evanston, Ill.: Northwestern University Press, 1989), 1–60, and Gary Saul Morson and Caryl Emerson, *Mikhail Bakhtin: Creation of a Prosaics* (Stanford, Calif.: Stanford University Press, 1990). Also Ken Hirschkop and David Shepherd, eds., *Bakhtin and Cultural Theory* (Manchester and New York: Manchester University Press, 1989); David Danow, *The Thought of Mikhail Bakhtin: From Word to Culture* (New York: St Martin's Press, 1991); and Dale M. Bauer and S. Jaret McKinstrey, eds., *Feminism, Bakhtin, and the Dialogic* (Albany: State University of New York Press, 1991).
[5] Evelyn Cobley, 'Mikhail Bakhtin's Place in Genre Theory', *Genre*, 21 (Fall 1988), 321–88.

men and women and is subversive of patriarchal norms. These claims are usually based on perceived patterns of repeated duplicity and images of confinement in Gothic writing by women, an approach which frames out issues of class and history as well as generic differences both within and between Gothic texts. My aim has been, without eliding such issues, to treat questions of gender as complex political constructs which are recontextualized in different ways in the novels. In so doing, I have sought to eschew Saussurean and post-Saussurean, gender deterministic formulations of woman as 'other'. Moreover, unlike some proponents of Bakhtin's theories, I do not see discursive tension or ambiguity in fiction, Gothic or otherwise, as *inherently* subversive, 'carnivalizing' an official ideology. The political force of particular discourses is contingent upon their interaction with others in the process of reading. The meanings and significance of texts change continually as they are read in new contexts.

In reconstructing the intertextual relations of the Gothic and examining its differential reception, then, I have not claimed any fixity or finalization of given textual properties or relationships between texts and readers. Nor have I attempted to map the generic differences between, say, Radcliffe's *Udolpho* and Lewis's *Monk* on to gender differences in any generalized way. Rather, I have attempted to describe how a variety of subject positions are constructed by each novel's appropriations or transformations of discourses in circulation at the time of writing. The privileging by readers of one or another of a text's identifiable discourses leads to conflicting interpretations, all of which can only ever be partial. In as much as any particular framing resists or transcends dominant social and cultural codes which are also offered by the text, the interpretation can be said to constitute an 'oppositional' or 'subversive' reading.

Two aspects of the interpretative process are relevant here. First, there is the matter of the plural, often contradictory, meanings which each of our Gothic texts could have generated for readers at the time of their initial publication. Secondly, there are the discursive structures which have actually been perceived by different readers over time to constitute each text's organizing principles. Here we are considering matters of reception, the ways in which contemporary and subsequent readers have chosen to frame the texts in the process of reading. A check on a text's potential for subversion is its differential reception as it is reproduced over time in different social and cultural formations. Where possible I have attempted this.

Chapter 1, 'Theories of the Gothic', first of all states the usefulness of Bakhtin's theory of dialogism for an understanding of the structure of the Gothic, which is often considered to be an inferior genre because of its lack of structural and/or thematic unity. This is followed by a consideration of the main issues or problems in recent discussions of the Gothic's thematic and structural dimensions. In the process I take up suggestions by Marxist critics that eighteenth-century Gothic narratives can be read as part of a process of cultural mythmaking and that 'fantasy' elements provide the Gothic's potential for subversion. With reference to the work of Tzvetan Todorov, Rosemary Jackson, and Gerhard Hoffmann, I discuss how we are to theorize the literary fantastic and its place in Gothic fiction. In the final section of the chapter, I outline Bakhtin's concepts of dialogism, heteroglossia, stylization, and intentionality as presented in *The Dialogic Imagination*, in order to suggest an approach to reading Gothic texts which foregrounds their hybrid nature and enables us to reconstruct some of their semantic potential for the readers to whom they were addressed.

In Chapter 2, 'Women and the Gothic', I examine critically some current feminist positions *vis-à-vis* the Gothic and describe the construction in critical discourse of 'female Gothic', before situating the rise of Gothic fiction in relation to eighteenth-century discourses of sensibility, the sublime, originality, and genius. My argument here is that, because these discourses privileged lack of classical learning and 'female' sensibility, they were, for a time, in an important respect enabling ones for aspiring women writers. As novelists, women appropriated discourses about sensibility and 'original genius' to bring the Gothic romance to its position of dominance in the 1790s. The final section of this chapter rehearses important particulars of the discussion in Chapter 1 of the plural dimensions of reading, and discusses the usefulness of Bakhtin for feminists constructing politically effective readings while acknowledging their partiality.

Chapter 3, 'Gothic Sublimity: Ann Radcliffe's *The Mysteries of Udolpho*', attempts to illustrate the Bakhtinian argument more fully. It describes how *Udolpho*, with its setting in the ancestral past, participated in socio-political mythmaking about issues of class and gender during the 'revolutionary' decade in England. I show how Radcliffe's recontextualization in this novel of late eighteenth-century discourses of sensibility, taste, and the sublime, together with elements of the fantastic, renders it distinctly ambiguous. While *Udolpho* condemns 'excess' of all sorts, including extreme sensibility and flights of fancy, and stresses bourgeois values of restraint, reason, benevolence, obedience, and fortitude, such 'everyday legality' is in turn relativized by the privileging of an uncanny prescience and aesthetic or romantic sensibility in artistic women.

In *The Mysteries of Udolpho*, the discourses of sensibility and taste function to establish aesthetic and moral norms: familial affection, obedience, appreciation of nature and art, creativity, retirement from worldly values, benevolence towards the poor, harmony and order in the family and society—all of which are reasserted at the end of the novel. Sensibility, however, is also repeatedly criticized by the narrator for its dangerous potential to destabilize and weaken individuals, particularly women, making them susceptible to every fleeting emotion. At the same time, working dialogically against such criticism, is the recontextualization of superstitions, folklore, and a discourse of the sublime which operates as a more or less unproblematic extension of the 'real', and encourages belief in the uncanny and the perceptional powers and sublime feelings of Emily St Aubert. Readers readily identify with Emily's intense imaginings and presentiments. And although there is strong narratorial emphasis on the need for 'common sense' and 'fortitude', Emily's perceptions of uncanny coincidence and the supernatural cannot be wholly subordinated to the didactic frame which cautions against excessive sensibility. One reason for this is that Emily's terrors and illusions of the supernatural are not always satisfactorily explained; another is that, given the events which do actually occur, her reactions are not altogether inappropriate.

So, for many readers there is a persistence of the impressions of strangeness and disorder abroad and of the accuracy of Emily's anxieties and projections. Moreover, her 'romantic passion' and 'enthusiasm' are vindicated in the continual allusions to the richness of her sublime responses to nature which give rise to her poetry. To the extent that Radcliffe's use of the fantastic and the poetization of her romance are felt to reproduce and reinforce fears of male domination and to give authority to women's assertiveness, perceptional and creative powers, *Udolpho* can be said to disturb unquestioning acceptance of an upper-middle-class patriarchal, social, and cultural order.

In Chapter 4 'Gothic Parody', I discuss the difference between Bakhtin's concepts of parody and stylization and indicate the relationship of parodic to other forms of dialogic utterance. I then situate and read Eaton Stannard Barrett's burlesque, *The Heroine*, and Jane Austen's posthumously published *Northanger Abbey* as responses to *Udolpho* and other Gothic fiction of the 1790s. While there is little doubt for modern readers that Barrett's parodic satire of both novels and female readers tends towards monologism in its desire to suppress alternative ways of speaking and reproduce official norms, Austen's parody of Gothic conventions is dialogic, pluralizing meanings and transforming official norms. Having argued that both Radcliffe and Austen recontextualize aesthetic and other discourses in ways which question and challenge official, patriarchal codes, I summarize the discursive tensions which my situational analyses of both *Udolpho* and *Northanger* bring to light. These analyses are then considered against other, non-historicizing readings in order that I might explicate more clearly my own procedures and theoretical position. Although the perceived inter- and intra-textual patternings of a text can guide interpretation to the point where it seems feasible to generate hypotheses about authorial intention, we cannot on that basis postulate a single, authorial 'voice' or individuality. We may wish to frame a text in a particular way for strategic reasons, but our readings are always partial, in both senses of the term. There remain all those other textual 'voices'—meanings which are surplus to any particular framing of a text we may desire to make.

Having reconstructed the intertextual relations of two Gothic novels by women, in Chapter 5, 'Anticlerical Gothic', I describe the ways in which Matthew Lewis's novel, *The Monk*, can be said to define itself against *Udolpho*. In brief, it does this by expropriating discourses of sensibility, taste, and the sublime in a minimal, sometimes cynical way and by interpolating and transforming English, German, and other European folk-tales, ballads, fragments of novels, and scenes from anticlerical and other drama. Given *The Monk*'s Preface and the sensationalism of stretches of its narrative, I hypothesize that Lewis's expropriation of *Sturm und Drang* sentiments both stakes his (male) claim to authorship in opposition to Radcliffe and mocks strict, middle-class codes of conduct. Despite its anticlerical, 'Protestant' stance, *The Monk* can be read as a rewriting of the myth of Gothic ancestry in terms of a fantastic, amoral universe. Its blatant use of the supernatural through its appropriation of German spirit-ballads, folk-tales, drama, and ancient myth undermines belief in 'everyday legality' in a more radical way. Indeed, such is the pervasiveness and sensational unpredictability of the diabolical in Lewis's romance, that its anticlericalism goes beyond exposing the supposed hypocrisy and moral corruption of the Catholic Church to suggest that no justice or succour can be had from a divine, supernatural realm at all. Moreover, far from being morally normative or ideal, the sensibility and rationalism which construct Lorenzo's 'Protestant' virtue render him vulnerable to the demonic. The novel's construction of female sexuality is also questionable, as Antonia's sensibility and innocence, too, not only construct her as weak and naïve, but are presented as in some sense bogus, veiling a susceptibility to demonic passion within. Furthermore, *The Monk*'s narratorial commentary is cynical of moral sensibility; and female characters who display it are treated with a voyeuristic and sadistic harshness. The positive, visionary, and creative aspects of sensibility which are so prominent in *Udolpho* are virtually absent, displaced by burlesque and lewd description. Essentialist and often cynical statements about women's nature by the narrator place women in inferior and passive roles as objects of male desire. Thus it is difficult to argue that Lewis's romance is potentially subversive of patriarchal codes governing women's sexuality and freedom from societal restraint. On the other hand, *The Monk's* perceived appropriation of German Gothicism, anticlericalism, lubricity, and blasphemy offended many critics who saw it as subversive of Christian morals and authority. After describing how the novel's profound moral and epistemological ambiguities led to its wide reception as morally and politically subversive, I conclude the chapter with a brief examination of the double-voiced nature of Ann Radcliffe's response to Lewis in *The Italian*.

Finally, in Chapter 6, 'Pseudo-Scientific Gothic', the discussion turns on how, in the early nineteenth century, Gothic fiction moved away from the 'explained supernatural' and 'accepted supernatural' of the earlier Gothic of Walpole, Reeve, Radcliffe, and Lewis towards the use of pseudo-scientific explanation which still leaves room for doubt and fear. Tales such as *Frankenstein* introduce and maintain the fantastic in such a way that the strange and disturbing events of the narratives cannot be explained with any certainty as having either supernatural or natural causes. Combining supposedly scientific discourse with the marvellous and uncanny in first-person narrations, such texts present us with extreme states of consciousness which could be taken for either paranoid delusion or demonic possession. Because *Frankenstein* utilizes the fantastic in this way and also tends towards prose realism, it represents a new development in, and revitalization of, the Gothic, while demonstrating the continuing reliance of the genre on folk-tales, ballads, legends, and myths for its effects.

I begin the discussion of *Frankenstein* with the ways in which early nineteenth-century discursive tensions enter Percy Shelley's 1818 Preface, Mary Shelley's 1831 Introduction, and the 1818 narrative. As this novel has been the site of many critical and theoretical disputes, several competing frames for interpretation are discussed. To these I add a further reading: that Mary Shelley's appropriation, in her 1831 Introduction, of Romantic discourses about the imagination, constitute a celebration of her imaginative creation of *Frankenstein*. I then show that the novel's pattern of narration, with its combination of balladry and elements of scientific discourse, generates uncertainty about more than the reliability of the narrator. The immutability of everyday reality and the morality of 'male' scientific and artistic endeavour are put in question as well. On the other hand, the avowed value of a 'feminine' realm of sensibility and 'domestic affection' is also interrogated when its inability to contain or accommodate heroic striving, passionate desires, and irrational fears is exposed.

While the main focus of this work is a reader-orientated reconstruction of each text's intertextual relations with literary and non-literary texts which are chronologically prior, it does not eschew all interest in authorial intentionality for a number of reasons.

First, Bakhtin himself allows that writers re-inflect language, attempting to bend it for their purposes, making it compete with other inflections. The difference between his concept of intentionality and authorial intention as it is commonly used in critical discourse is addressed in the final section of Chapter 1. Secondly, it is difficult to examine how particular discourses have been appropriated and perhaps transformed in a potentially subversive way without hypothesizing at some point about the author's intention. Thirdly, such hypotheses may in any case be politically useful, particularly in the task of rereading women's writing and constructing a feminist literary history.

For instance, in making partial readings of *Northanger Abbey* as a parodic novel which mocks and exploits Gothic conventions and also satirizes the moralizing interpretations of female-authored novels by contemporary male critics, it is virtually impossible not to use an evaluative terminology and imply intentionality. Moreover, from a feminist perspective, there is no reason why we should want to avoid hypothesizing about Austen's intentions, provided that we remember that the ambiguous meanings of *Northanger Abbey* cannot be contained by this hypothesis.

Similarly, I claim that discourses of sensibility and taste not only partially construct the subjectivity of the characters in *Udolpho* but also make a bid for the authority of the writer of the novel *qua* author. The Introduction to *Frankenstein*, too, I argue, appropriates 'already said' fragments of discourse about the imagination in order to celebrate Mary Shelley's 'monstrous progeny'. Once such claims are made, Radcliffe and Shelley can be seen as engaged in the discursive struggle regarding the status of the novel and of women writers during the period examined. Again, the burlesque and representation of so many German genres which introduce the 'accepted supernatural' in *The Monk* can lead us to hypothesize that Lewis was attempting to displace sensibility as the mark of the author for a *Sturm und Drang* paradigm of genius, that is, of a writer who is given to boldness and risk-taking and driven by extraordinary passions and revolutionary (masculine) energy.

Finally, in demonstrating the multi-voicedness of these Gothic texts, I am not suggesting that this leads or should lead to a *comfortable* pluralism of readings. For Bakhtin, dialogical 'voices' represent specific semantic or socio-ideological positions. They are not conceived as being somehow equal; nor are they considered to be permissively tolerant of each other.[6] Thus, in making these hypotheses about authorial intention while acknowledging their partiality, I aim to intervene in various discussions and debates in the hope of provoking further dialogue.

[6] Iris M. Zavala, 'Bakhtin and Otherness: Social Heterogeneity', *Critical Studies*, 2, 1/2 (1990), 85.

I

Theories of the Gothic

The Gothic as an Indeterminate Genre

When what is generally accepted to be the first Gothic novel, *The Castle of Otranto*, first appeared on Christmas Eve, 1764, it proclaimed itself to be simply 'A Story' translated from 'the purest Italian' of a sixteenth-century monk, Onuphrio Muralto. However, lest the tale's supernatural happenings be thought too wild, its pseudonymous translator asked his wise and rational eighteenth-century readers to excuse its *'air of the miraculous'*.[1] Not until *Otranto* had proved successful did Horace Walpole come into the open as author and criticize what he saw as a lack of imagination in the modern novel. In a new preface for the second edition—now boldly subtitled 'A Gothic Story'—he both laid claim to his work and attempted to theorize its form. *Otranto*, he explained,

was an attempt to blend two kinds of romance, the ancient and the modern. In the former all was imagination and improbability: in the latter, nature is always intended to be, and sometimes has been, copied with success. Invention has not been wanting; but the great resources of fancy have been dammed up, by a strict adherence to common life. (p. 43)

Thus, at its inception, there existed the idea that Gothic fiction is not a 'pure' genre, but a combination of styles, including a fantastic discourse which might be unsettling to the reader.

Far from being the homogenous 'blend' which Walpole said he hoped later authors would achieve, the many disparate narratives which were labelled 'Gothic' after *Otranto* con-

---

[1] Horace Walpole, *The Castle of Otranto*, in Peter Fairclough, *Three Gothic Novels*, with an introductory essay by Mario Praz: contains also *Vathek* by William Beckford and *Frankenstein* by Mary Shelley (Harmondsworth: Penguin Books, 1978), 40.

tinued to participate in varying degrees in several genres. In the late eighteenth- and early nineteenth-century novels of Radcliffe, Lewis, Maturin, and Mary Shelley, for example, we find not only different uses of supernatural, sublime, and uncanny elements but also interpolated poems, letters, folktales, and snatches of discourses from non-literary fields.

Yet, for all the modern histories and critical accounts we have of Gothic fiction, Walpole's notion of the Gothic as a combination of styles has rarely been explored further. And, with few exceptions, contemporary critics have been slow to bring the Gothic into conjunction with post-structuralist literary theory which treats literature as discourse and regards genres paradoxically as not pure but mixed.[2]

Recent studies of Gothic fiction have drawn on literary psychoanalytic, Marxist, and feminist theory to offer a wide range of interpretation and assessment of the Gothic's social and political significance. However, as in the past, many of these studies have tended to proceed by cataloguing and codifying the literary conventions perceived to be common to the form. We find, for example, references to the setting of a remote castle, monastery, or gloomy house with its confining crypts, vaults, and underground passage-ways. There is also discussion of particular character types such as the persecuted heroine, tyrannical parent, villainous monk, Faustian overreacher, or vampire-like apparition, and of plot devices such as dreams, mysterious portents, animated portraits and statues, magic mirrors, and the like. Again, we have analyses of narrative techniques such as framed and embedded stories, letters, diaries, or broken-off manuscripts, which allow forgotten information or secrets from the past to re-surface disturbingly in the present.

Undoubtedly these conventions are utilized by the genre and do cue readers in particular ways, often arousing suspense and terror or horror—what Ann B. Tracy calls 'a chronic sense of apprehension and the premonition of impending but unidentified disaster'.[3] They also go far in enabling psychoanalytic

[2] See e.g. Jacques Derrida, 'The Law of Genre', trans. Avital Ronell, *Critical Inquiry*, 7 (Autumn 1980), 65–6.
[3] Ann Blaisdell Tracy, *The Gothic Novel 1790–1830: Plot Summaries and Index to Motifs* (Lexington: University Press of Kentucky, 1981), 3.

critics and theorists of the Gothic to construct a 'fixed' or synchronic form, monomyth, or archetypal structure against which to read their favoured texts. Feminists, too, focus on the Gothic as a 'female' genre which, through its imagery, conventions, and structure, registers the confinement of women in pre-ordained social, sexual, and authorial roles. However, problems arise with such ahistorical and homogenizing approaches, as they impose a 'monologic' structure or closure— that is, a single 'authoritative' reading which disallows a text's semantic richness and suppresses alternative ways of speaking. Thus we find strong, mutually exclusive political claims being made for the Gothic. For one theorist it is a subversive genre while for another it is conservative.

More specifically, formalist, structuralist, and many psycho-analytic approaches suppress not only the differences of texts from one other, but also the ways in which each text differs from itself, for stylistic ambiguities, gaps, silences, and inconsistencies are either missed, ignored, or dismissed as authorial failings. For example, one of the Gothic's most recent critics, Elizabeth Napier, argues that the significance of late eighteenth- and early nineteenth-century Gothic novels has been overblown; that they have been 'subjected to overreading'; that the genre is in fact superficial and formulaic, but uneven, unstable, and 'at cross purposes with itself'. This 'generic instability', which results from mixing genres such as 'fairy tale, romance, Jacobean drama, and the novel of manners', is perceived as naïvely producing 'unintentionally humorous instances of collision'. The authors of Gothic fiction must have suffered from a 'profound uncertainty about both its generic status and intent', she explains. Thus its 'failure', which is defined in moral and aesthetic terms, is laid at the door of the authors, who were unable or unwilling to resolve moral and aesthetic problems.[4] Such a view is based on the belief that the novel, at its best, is a unified, seamless whole. It also ignores the role of the reader in interpretation and denies a text's potential to mean differently in different historical and social

---

[4] Elizabeth R. Napier, *The Failure of the Gothic: Problems of Disjunction in an Eighteenth-Century Literary Form* (Oxford: Clarendon Press, 1987), pp. xii–xiii, 4–7, 67.

contexts of reading. We need to remember that Gothic fiction, like any other genre, carries much that is culturally specific— ideological, aesthetic, and literary norms, which are received and interpreted or 'rewritten' by readers on the basis of their own interests, their own cultural and institutional, as well as personal, history.

Even George Haggerty's *Gothic Fiction/Gothic Form* (1987), despite its positive acknowledgement of Gothic indeterminacy, pays scant attention to the concrete social and historical environments in which successive writers and readers have operated. Taking issue with Elizabeth Napier for her negativity, Haggerty argues that the 'formal muddle' she perceives has in fact been fruitful over time in prompting the evolution of the Gothic tale as 'affective form'. By this term he means the 'shift in sensibility', 'new perception of things', or external objectification of an imaginative world which can leave the reader unable to distinguish what is real—a notion which, as we shall see later, is close to Todorov's definition of the fantastic. For Haggerty, Gothic devices are 'metaphorical vehicles' which have 'the power to objectify subjective states of feeling'. However, they must remain of indeterminate meaning, because 'they can only be expressed by each reader in his or her private terms'. Thus this critic attributes the Gothic's range of interpretative possibility to its formal properties, such as its setting, supernatural elements, and the nature of each tale's subjectivity and narrative technique. In terms of the reader's implication in the subjective and the personal, he argues, 'Gothic *tales* succeed where Gothic *novels* fail' and the former 'resolve the inconsistency and incoherence of many Gothic novels'. Ultimately, he posits the Gothic as a form which evolves by disentangling itself from the novel to reach its apogee in Henry James's fantastic tale, *The Turn of the Screw*.[5] This argument is thus tendentious both in delimiting the novel as an essentially realist form and in suggesting that the Gothic is anti-novelistic.

Such attempts to read the Gothic synchronically as a system of certain unifying stylistic and structural features are bound

[5] George E. Haggerty, *Gothic Fiction/Gothic Form* (University Park and London: Pennsylvania State University Press, 1987), 4, 8, 10, 11, 167–8.

to see the form as flawed.[6] My contention is that it can most satisfactorily be viewed in a Bakhtinian way as a *plural* form, that is, as a novelistic genre which draws on and recontextualizes or transforms prior discursive structures, fragments of 'the already said', both literary and non-literary. As such, it is constituted by numerous speech genres which have arisen from historically concrete situations of social interaction. These ways of speaking can include professional jargons (medical, legal, pedagogical, aesthetic, theological discourses, for example) and more everyday communicative practices such as lists, letters, diaries, anecdotes, travel accounts, folk-tales, songs, and superstitions. As Maria Shevtsova explains, these speech forms

are not used exclusively in the novel by characters and narrators, and by the author, or posited author, whose voice is heard, so to speak, between the lines, when it does not intercede as such in the narrative. They are all-pervasive, as audible in expository or descriptive passages, which do not come intentionally from the mouths of designated characters and narrators (or the author or posited author), as in dramatized events, in which characters and narrators may be implicated, but which are not directly constructed out of the evaluative tones—the particular points of view—indicative of designated characters and narrators (or the author or posited author). Because speech genres are the very stuff of language, we may say, glossing Bakhtin, that they cannot avoid being the essential structuring feature of the novel. Consequently, the form of any novel is determined by the various speech genres that are written into it.[7]

This study will maintain that the Gothic novel is a type in which the propensity for multiple discourse is highly developed and that it is *dialogic* because of its indeterminacy or its open structure. The Gothic only plays at being totalized or closed, as its supposed 'unity' encompasses 'several heterogeneous stylistic unities, often located on different linguistic

[6] For a formalist analysis which examines several Gothic novels in the framework of Romanticism and, like Napier, views their lack of formal unity negatively, see Robert Kiely, *The Romantic Novel in England* (Cambridge, Mass.: Harvard University Press, 1972), 1–2.

[7] Maria Shevtsova, 'Dialogism in the Novel and Bakhtin's Theory of Culture', *New Literary History*, 23/3 (1992), 751.

levels and subject to different stylistic controls'.[8] Although discourses are 'subject to an artistic reworking' as they enter the novel and there is a synthesizing voice, no one voice is the novel's decisive voice. What we have is 'a structured stylistic system that expresses the differentiated socio-ideological position of the author amid the heteroglossia of his epoch' (Bakhtin, p. 300). Or, as Patricia Yaeger puts it, the novel's 'heteroglossia' is 'barely constrained by the shifting framework of the author's intentionality'.[9] This characteristic gives readers much scope for interpretation; and more so, as novels traverse different cultures over time.

The consequences of Bakhtin's concept of multiple, interpenetrating and mutually transforming languages in the novel are far-reaching and will be addressed in the last section of this chapter and again in Chapter 2 when we consider feminist appropriations of the Gothic. For the moment, suffice to say that Bakhtin's theory of dialogism in the novel allows us to situate individual Gothic romances, novels, and tales with a greater degree of historical, social, and cultural specificity and to reflect on ways in which different interpretations can be, and have been, generated. By demonstrating the 'multi-voicedness' of Gothic texts, we can affirm that any aesthetic or political claims made for the genre are closely dependent on which discursive structures are privileged in the reading process.

However, in arguing that the Gothic is best viewed dialogically, I do not wish to deny the value of previous treatments of the genre, despite their often essentializing, thematic nature. If, as Ian Reid argues, 'genre is uncategorical: it is a shifting semiotic space where a certain range of textual possibilities may be framed in order to interact meaningfully',[10] then, by their various framings, past readers and critics have collectively done much to map the contours of this 'space' in relation to the Gothic. For example, David Punter and Elizabeth MacAndrew have demonstrated that the Gothic was an

[8] Bakhtin, *Dialogic Imagination*, 261. Further references appear in the text.
[9] Patricia S. Yaeger, ' "Because a Fire was in my Head": Eudora Welty and the Dialogic Imagination', *PMLA* 99/5 (Oct. 1984), 956.
[10] Ian Reid, 'When is an Epitaph Not an Epitaph? A Monumental Generic Problem and a Jonsonian Instance', *Southern Review*, 22/3 (Nov. 1989), 209.

important bourgeois form, that it endured beyond its initial
flowering between 1796 and 1825, and that it was appropriated in different ways by a large number of later writers, many
of whom are often considered 'realist'. In describing the
Gothic's sources, development, and what they perceive to be
its salient features, these critics and others—such as J. M. S.
Tompkins, Edith Birkhead, Montague Summers, Maurice
Lévy, Coral Ann Howells, Ann B. Tracy, and Linda Bayer-
Berenbaum—have done much to stimulate interest in a genre
which has long been denigrated as 'popular' and excluded
from constructions of a canon of 'great' literature. Accordingly, it is to a consideration of the main strengths and problems of this body of criticism that I will first turn.

Critical Approaches to the Gothic

Since the publication in 1969 of Robert D. Hume's positive
revaluation of the Gothic novel, what he called its 'psychological interest' has been explored in a variety of ways. For
example, Elizabeth MacAndrew, in *The Gothic Tradition in
Fiction* (1979), evidently perceives the Gothic as a precursor
to the work of Freud in its appeal to a supposedly eternal facet
of the human psychic make-up. It is, she says, 'a literature of
nightmare' and evil; its conventions, often those of myth,
folklore, fairy-tale, and romance, 'have literary significance
and the properties of dream symbolism as well'.[11] Writers
chose the Gothic mode to convey the idea that evil was within
humans, 'as a distortion, warping [the] mind', and not as an
external malevolent force. However, whereas in the earliest
Gothic romances good and evil were conceived as moral abso-
lutes, in later works these categories were relativized once
writers began to interrogate the nature of evil itself and explore the structure of the self.

In charting these diachronic changes *vis-à-vis* the repeated
use of folkloric and mythic devices, however, MacAndrew
reads the supernatural phenomena of early Gothic texts, such

---

[11] Elizabeth MacAndrew, *The Gothic Tradition in Fiction* (New York:
Columbia University Press, 1979), 1. Further references appear in the text.

as the bleeding statue in Walpole's *Otranto*, as 'translatable' into allegorical aspects of character (MacAndrew, p. 13). She thus underplays the role of the fantastic and ignores the way in which, during the nineteenth century, 'magic images' became progressively secularized or, as Theodore Ziolowski puts it, 'disenchanted'.[12] Images in 'Enlightenment' Gothic carry only their 'sublime', ancient magical associations. As faith in the supernatural diminishes, these magical images are transformed, so that rational explanations for supernatural phenomena sit alongside the older 'magic'. Still later, what seems supernatural is rationalized almost entirely in terms of an internalized psychology. By positing Gothic fiction as a form which, from its inception, is about 'psychological evil', MacAndrew tends to over-simplify her case.

Moreover, while she touches on the function of the sublime (Burke's 'pleasurable astonishment' and terror) in Gothic fiction, she does not examine closely the workings of sublime imagery and its aestheticizing discourse in any one text. Rather, she argues in general terms that the sublime could 'erode didacticism' by evoking understanding for villainous or evil characters:

having imaginatively inhabited the tortured mind of the evil character, [readers] see the potential for such evil in all minds, and experiencing compassion for it through an understanding of its psychological causes, they can no longer look on good and evil as absolute or as forces outside the human psyche. (MacAndrew, p. 44)

Apart from the homogenization of the reading process here, there is no acknowledgement that in some texts the sublime might challenge moral and epistemological norms or 'everyday legality' in other ways.

Yet MacAndrew is right in seeing a close link between eighteenth-century aesthetic theory and Gothic fiction. Although *Otranto* was remarkably popular with the reading public, going through twenty-one editions before 1800,[13] it was not uniformly well received by the critics. They frowned upon the

[12] Theodore Ziolowski, *Disenchanted Images: A Literary Iconology* (Princeton, NJ: Princeton University Press, 1977), 17.
[13] Wilmarth Sheldon Lewis, *Horace Walpole* (London: Rupert Hart-Davis, 1961), 158.

inclusion of supernatural events as 'sublime' instigators of
terror, yet appeared not to mind portrayals of the past in terms
of Gothic gloom and mystery—the ancestral castle with its
massive Piranesi-like vaults, staircases, galleries, and wind-
swept subterranean passages, or the sheltered but labyrinthine
monasteries and convents. Many of these features of the environment and architecture corresponded with those which, in
his *Philosophical Enquiry into the Origin of Our Ideas of the
Sublime and Beautiful* (1757), Edmund Burke had declared to
be 'sublime'.

By this Burke meant that such objects were able to produce
'the strongest emotion which the mind is capable of . . .
astonishment—that state of the soul, in which all its motions
are suspended with some degree of horror'.[14] Although it is
often unclear whether he is referring to real objects or their
depiction in art or both, and he tends to slide between two
uses of 'sublime', blurring cause and effect, Burke's views had
popular currency and were debated and reworked throughout
the latter half of the eighteenth century. This favoured the
interests of architectural and literary Gothicists like Walpole.
Mario Praz argues that the architectural settings of Piranesi's
Carceri, for example, answered to Burkean notions of the
sublime effect of infinity, and that the *Carceri* in turn 'penetrated the spirit of Gothic tales'.[15] Certainly there was no
doubt that Ann Radcliffe, like many of her readers, believed in
the value of Burkean terror and awe. Making a distinction
between terror and horror unknown to Burke, she described
terror as 'expand[ing] the soul . . . awaken[ing] the faculties to
a high degree of life'.[16] However, in her novels *The Mysteries
of Udolpho* (1794) and *The Italian* (1797), Radcliffe, unlike
Walpole, carefully rationalized apparent manifestations of the

[14] Edmund Burke, *A Philosophical Enquiry into the Origin of Our Ideas of
the Sublime and Beautiful*, ed. J. T. Boulton (London: Routledge & Kegan
Paul, 1958), ii. 57.
[15] Mario Praz, 'Introductory essay' to Fairclough, *Three Gothic Novels*,
16–20.
[16] Alan Dugald McKillop, 'Mrs. Radcliffe on the Supernatural in Poetry',
Journal of English and Germanic Philology, 31 (1932), 357. Samuel Holt
Monk, *The Sublime: A Study of Critical Theories in XVIII-Century England*
(New York: Modern Language Association of America, 1935), 218, argues
that Radcliffe 'was working on a definite theory of sublimity'.

supernatural after the event. As J. M. S. Tompkins concludes in *The Popular Novel in England 1770–1800* (1932), 'the demand for colour and sublimity . . . invariably brought with it the demand for the marvellous, and the critical world, which approved the first two qualities in measure, looked askance at the third'.[17]

Tompkins's carefully researched study of late eighteenth-century fiction was the first attempt to describe the Gothic in terms of its development of narrative form. She comments on the intricacy of Gothic plots, which was 'based upon the interweaving of a multiplicity of agents and motives' and was 'a necessary consequence of the cult of suspense, mystery and surprise' (p. 346). Well-sustained Gothic plots contrasted favourably with the 'shapeless narratives' of Sentimental fiction and, from Tompkins's perspective, 'taught novelists to control a complicated story'.

While MacAndrew does not make such a clear-cut distinction between Sentimental and Gothic fiction in matters of structure, she does examine the uses of mediated narration. She points out that *Otranto* is a framed narrative like Clara Reeve's *The Old English Baron* and that both hese works make use of the device of the discovered manuscript as a means of authenticating their accounts, achieving a sense of distance or 'pastness' and preparing the reader to follow the story on its own terms. An important effect of mediated narration is to suggest a closed world corresponding to an inner state, especially when a letter-writer pens her missives from an isolated place and details her sufferings at the hands of a villain. Here the epistolary mode can be used to show the virtuous hero or heroine invaded and threatened by dark or evil forces.

More commonly in Gothic fiction, however, a variant on the epistolary mode, multiple narration, is used to the same effect. Thus a narrator who appears in the frame of a story can relay to another character a story of perhaps long-forgotten or enigmatic people and events, of a world invaded by disorder and evil. In later Gothic works—Mary Shelley's *Frankenstein*

---

[17] Joyce Marjorie Sanxter Tompkins, *The Popular Novel in England 1770–1800* (London: Constable, 1932), 209. Further references appear in the text.

(1818), Charles Maturin's *Melmoth the Wanderer* (1820), Emily Brontë's *Wuthering Heights* (1847), and Henry James's *The Turn of the Screw* (1898)—such systems of mediated narration are deployed with horrifying effect. Arguing along these lines, MacAndrew thus sees mediated narration as an 'enabling device' in Gothic fiction, establishing texts as fantasy and 'laying the groundwork for symbolic interpretation' (MacAndrew, p. 35).

Concomitantly, she stresses a point made elsewhere by Robert Kellogg: that when a narrator tells his or her listeners a story, this 'places the reader[s] in the same relation to the world described as the listeners of the tale' (MacAndrew, p. 110), those whom Gerald Prince has called the 'narratees'.[18] The fictive world of the novel then becomes 'a symbolic construct with the reader carefully positioned in relation to it. A sense is created of entering a strange and wonderful place, a closed world within the everyday world' (MacAndrew, p. 110). It is in this way, MacAndrew concludes, that Gothic and Sentimental novels go along the same path 'to lead us into the landscape of the mind' (p. 110). This is not to say that the closed worlds which they portray are entirely cut off; rather the effect usually depends on our sense of the narrators and characters moving in and out of the closed world to another. As Gothic settings move from the remote past somewhere in Europe (as in *Otranto*) to the reader's own time and country (as in *Melmoth the Wanderer*), mediated narration is used to maintain the strangeness which wild exotic regions had once presented, and induce readers to associate the mind and feelings depicted with their own individual psychic reality.

Tales within frameworks and tales within tales are, it seems, frequent phenomena in the fiction labelled 'Gothic', and works such as *Melmoth the Wanderer*, *Frankenstein*, and *Wuthering Heights* have often been discussed from this point of view by theorists of 'spatial form' and, more recently, by

---

[18] Robert Kellogg, 'Oral Narrative, Written Books', *Genre*, 10/4 (1977), 660, and Gerald Prince, 'Introduction to the Study of the Narratee', in Jane Tompkins, *Reader-Response Criticism* (Baltimore: Johns Hopkins University Press, 1980), 7–25.

George E. Haggerty in *Gothic Fiction/Gothic Form*.[19] However, MacAndrew's extended discussion of this feature of Gothic fiction is more usefully interactionist than most in its emphasis on the devices of mediated narration as clues to how such works are to be read, although she does not at any time problematize the notion of 'the reader', a construct which in recent years has taken various formulations.[20]

This aside, MacAndrew has pinpointed some of the most commonly observed features of Gothic fiction—the thematic emphasis on extreme states of mind and an attendant preoccupation with good and evil, a range of Gothic topoi, and those formal aspects of narrative structure which the Gothic has appropriated: mediated narration and story within story. She also moves towards an intertextual approach in seeking to 'show how the connections between one work and another add to meaning' and how the use of a convention cues the reader in particular ways (p. ix). Where she is less enlightening is in her lack of theoretical enquiry and failure to situate texts historically.

Exploring the Freudian parallel with greater subtlety and depth than MacAndrew, William Patrick Day argues that both the Gothic and Freud's system of thought are 'responses to the problems of selfhood and identity, sexuality and pleasure, fear and anxiety as they manifest themselves in the nineteenth and early twentieth centuries'.[21] Like MacAndrew, he addresses the interrelationship of Gothic conventions, focusing on 'the dream/nightmare narrative characteristic' in order to demonstrate how it compels readers to interpret Gothic texts

[19] See e.g. Joseph A. Kestner, *Spatiality in the Novel* (Detroit: Wayne University Press, 1978), 73–4, and Haggerty, *Gothic Fiction/Gothic Form*, 27–35.
[20] See Shlomith Rimmon-Kenan, *Narrative Fiction: Contemporary Poetics* (London and New York: Methuen, 1983), 118–29. MacAndrew does not make the now common distinctions among a 'narratee' (to whom a story or letter is supposedly addressed), an 'implied reader' (someone silently posited by the text as a whole who would interpret it all appropriately), and a 'historical reader' (a real-life recipient of a text who has made a specific but necessarily partial response).
[21] William Patrick Day, *In the Circles of Fear and Desire: A Study of Gothic Fantasy* (Chicago and London: University of Chicago Press, 1985), 181.

symbolically. Thus Day reads each of his chosen texts as an embodiment, with variations, of a monomyth about the descent of the protagonist—either passive heroine or Faustian villain—into the 'Gothic underworld', a world in which she or he is 'enthralled' to fear or desire. The problem with his account is that not all Gothic texts can be made to conform to this mythical pattern and ultimately such reiteration of symbolic meanings is of less interest than an approach which examines how different interpretations can be and are generated by readers.

Yet another group of critics situates the rise of Gothic fiction within a broad cultural movement of Gothic revival, with its own definable social and psychological causes. Like the word 'Gothic' itself, this revival is seen to be tied closely to architecture.

In his massive compendium, *The Gothic: Literary Sources and Interpretations through Eight Centuries*, Paul Frankl tells us that in the mid-fifteenth century in relation to architectural sculpture, 'Gothic' (*gotiche*) meant 'rustic', 'boorish', 'coarse'.[22] It carried connotations of inferiority, associated as it was with the Goths who in AD 410 had destroyed Rome. Used of buildings during the early Renaissance, it had come to suggest that the medieval architecture of the twelfth century, with its unprecedented pointed arches, soaring verticality, stained-glass windows, labyrinthine patterns and filigreed tracery, was inferior to classical Roman.

However, for the eighteenth-century revivalists of medieval architecture, among whom were numbered the aristocratic author of *Otranto* himself, 'Gothic' was far from being a pejorative term, even if its extension began to swell. With their inadequate historiography, these enthusiasts simply elided the conceptual implications of style changes through the centuries. Although the most common reference point was the flamboyant Gothic of the fifteenth and sixteenth centuries rather than the Gothic proper of the Abbey St-Denis of 1150, all things post-Roman to the middle of the seventeenth century were 'Gothic'. 'Gothic' meant 'ancestral', as Mark Madoff has

---

[22] Paul Frankl, *The Gothic: Literary Sources and Interpretations through Eight Centuries* (Princeton, NJ: Princeton University Press, 1960), 259–60.

observed,[23] and a positive value of the word was
be used in opposition to 'classical'. David Pur
Literature of Terror (1980), neatly summarizes
late eighteenth-century usage:

> Where the classical was well ordered, the Gothic was chaotic, ...
> simple and pure, Gothic was ornate and convoluted; where the
> classic offered a set of cultural models to be followed, Gothic
> represented excess and exaggeration, the product of the wild and
> uncivilized.[24]

Hence the term and all that it represented gained significance
as a corrective to discourses embodying Augustan ideals of
Reason and Order.[25]

This shift in cultural value, which, according to Punter, was
very marked by the 1780s but by no means universal, had
widespread ramifications not only in architecture but also in
art and music. Punter quotes from Bishop Hurd's *Letters on
Chivalry and Romance* (1762) to illustrate how past literature
began to be revalued under the aegis of a 'revival of Gothic'—
how Chaucer, Spenser, Shakespeare, Milton, Jacobean drama,
'folk-poetry', and ballads such as those published in Percy's
Reliques of Ancient Poetry (1765), were all read afresh. The
Gothic fiction which appeared in profusion between Walpole's
The Castle of Otranto and Mary Shelley's *Frankenstein* (1818)
is seen as part of this revaluation. Set in the distant exotic past,
Otranto, for instance, owed much to Shakespeare, as Walpole
later claimed. Though modelled on his own reconstruction of
Gothic architecture, Strawberry Hill, the castle which gives
the work its title is also reminiscent of that in *Hamlet*, while
Walpole's puppet-like tyrant, Manfred, is familiar to readers
of Shakespeare's histories in his frenzied attempts to ward off
the challenge of the good prince. In addition there are

---

[23] Mark Madoff, 'The Useful Myth of Gothic Ancestry', *Studies in Eighteenth Century Culture*, 8 (1979), 338. Further references appear in the text.
[24] David Punter, *The Literature of Terror: A History of Gothic Fictions from 1765 to the Present Day* (London: Longman, 1980), 5.
[25] See also Samuel Kliger, 'The "Goths" in England: An Introduction to the Gothic Vogue in Eighteenth-Century Aesthetic Discussion', *Modern Philology*, 43 (1945), 105–17, and Longueil, Alfred E., 'The Word "Gothic" in Eighteenth Century Criticism', *Modern Language Notes*, 38 (1923), 453–60.

providential signs of disorder drawn from folk- and fairy-tale—a magic helmet, animated picture, bleeding statue, *memento mori* skeleton, ghostly giant—while virtuous, long-suffering heroines are subjected to numerous terrors, and scenes of servant 'foolery' are interspersed with the deeds and deliberations of princes. In alluding to some of these similarities, Punter points out that Walpole stressed Shakespeare's example in order to give himself licence, particularly in the matter of the supernatural.

Maurice Lévy's *Le Roman gothique anglais, 1764–1824* (1968), and Linda Bayer-Berenbaum's *The Gothic Imagination* (1982), insist more closely on architecture as the essential symbolic and structural model for Gothic fiction. Like Devendra Varma's *The Gothic Flame* (1957) and G. R. Thompson's *The Gothic Imagination: Essays in Dark Romanticism* (1974), these studies suggest that, in an age of rationalism, the Gothic offered a religious or spiritual dimension, a way of approaching the sacred.

Linda Bayer-Berenbaum, for example, argues for a close relationship between Gothic architecture and literature in that both '[express] a coherent aesthetic and philosophic perspective'.[26] She perceives the restless energy of Gothic architecture, with its infinitude of repetition, its 'progressive divisibility into smaller and smaller parts', and the contrast of this with enormous height and boundless interior, as a form designed to challenge the percipient's imagination, heighten feeling, and induce a spiritually altered state.

One can, of course, think of several early nineteenth-century Romantic writers who also described elevations of feeling in this way. In *Die Wahlverwandtschaften* (1808), Goethe, for example, has Ottilie visit a Gothic church which is in the process of being restored; once there, she notes the coloured light shafting through the stained glass, the beauty of the vault, and 'it seemed to her that she was and was not'.[27] Ottilie's intensified state of mind and feeling do indeed take

[26] Linda Bayer-Berenbaum, *The Gothic Imagination* (London and Toronto: Associated University Press, 1987), 47. Further references appear in the text.
[27] Johann Wolfgang von Goethe, *Elective Affinities*, trans. R. J. Hollingdale (Oxford: Basil Blackwell, 1971), 142.

her 'beyond the confines of orderly or restrictive limitations' (Bayer-Berenbaum, p. 71). Coleridge, too, in his lectures of 1818, wrote of the power of Gothic architecture to expand one's sense of reality. Constrasting Gothic with classical Greek, he argued that only the Gothic was sublime: 'On entering a cathedral, I am filled with devotion and awe; I am lost to the actualities that surround me, and my whole being expands into the infinite; earth and air, nature and art, all swell up into eternity.'[28] Then extending his argument to poetry, Coleridge affirmed the value of 'the heroic songs of the Goths . . . the poetry of the middle ages'.

However, by the time Coleridge wrote his paean to Longinian aesthetics, mythmaking about the ancestral Goths had endured for over a century. It seems, as Mark Madoff claims, that it had endured because it was useful. As we shall see in relation to the Gothic romances written by Horace Walpole and Clara Reeve, since the Goths and their practices were located in such an extensive and vague historical time and place, they could be made to symbolize whatever their inventors needed—'racial pride, communal solidarity, political controversy, cultural disintegration (or revival) and internal revolution' (Madoff, p. 348).

Thus, if Bayer-Berenbaum often makes striking and convincing analogies between Gothicism in art and literature at the levels of structure, grotesquerie, and potential effects on percipients through the Gothic's suggestions of an intensified and expanded reality, she does not proceed to explore the social and ideological implications of this aesthetic for the different social and cultural formations in which it has in some form continued to survive. To be fair, in her introduction she does briefly speculate on the significance of the current 'Gothic revival' in modern America. And her observation, that 'Gothic literature continued to portray all states of mind that intensify normal thought or perception' (p. 25), certainly seems a valid and useful one. But, like many critics who attempt to isolate the essential characteristics of a category by

[28] Samuel Taylor Coleridge, 'General Character of Gothic Literature and Art', in id., *Miscellanies, Aesthetic and Literary*, ed. T. Ashe (London: George Bell, 1885), 92–3.

looking for what is common to a set of artefacts, she concentrates on the formal and thematic aspects of the Gothic to the neglect of their complex social relations within different cultural frames. After acknowledging briefly what she calls 'the anti-establishment tenor in Gothic literature' (p. 43), she goes on to discuss the similarities of formal aspects of structure and imagery in five works—*Melmoth the Wanderer, Frankenstein,* 'The Haunters and the Haunted', *Uncle Silas,* and *On the Night of the Seventh Moon*—but without considering their historical and social contexts, intertextual dimensions, or the reception, reproduction, and interpretation of these works by successive readers and critics.

David Punter's *The Literature of Terror* and R. Paulson's *Representations of Revolution, 1789–1820* both go some way to supplying such a perspective by situating the Gothic historically and focusing on its socio-political nature, an emphasis which can be justified by examination of late eighteenth-century reviews and other writing.

In 1788 a new edition of Hurd's *Letters on Chivalry and Romance* appeared. The additions and deletions make for interesting comparisons. Deleted were sentences and phrases such as the following:

Consider, withall, the surprizes, accidents, adventures which probably and naturally attend on the life of wandering knights; the occasion there must be for describing the wonders of different countries, and of presenting to view the manners and policies of different states . . .

. . . the horrors of he Gothic were . . .

The mummeries of the pagan priests were childish, but the Gothic Enchanters shook and alarmed all nature.[29]

Hurd's purpose would seem to have been to 'contain' the Gothic imagination by subtly rewriting the myth of the ancestral Goth. Was it just coincidence that he edited out these passages on the eve of the French Revolution? During the decade which followed that momentous upheaval, Gothic novels appeared in profusion and were extremely popular. Many were formulaic and crudely sensational in their depic-

---

[29] Richard Hurd, *Hurd's Letters on Chivalry and Romance,* ed. Edith J. Morley (London: Henry Trowde, 1911), 73.

tion of the past; and their surfeit of wildness a
predictably brought the genre into further critical
Reviewing *The Castle of St. Vallery* for the *Monthly*
November 1792, Thomas Holcroft complained th
romance writers were feeding 'that superstition which debilit-
ates the mind, that ignorance which propagates error, and that
dread of invisible agency which makes inquiry criminal'
(Tompkins, p. 217).

Against this background, the literary value of the romances
of Ann Radcliffe and Matthew Lewis stood out, but while the
former gained critical approbation, the latter evoked outrage.
A contemporary, the Marquis de Sade, made this comment
about their deployment of supernatural terror:

This genre was the inevitable product of the revolutionary shocks
with which the whole of Europe resounded. For those who were
acquainted with all the ills that are brought upon men by the wicked,
the romantic novel was becoming somewhat difficult to write, and
merely monotonous to read: there was nobody left who had not
experienced more misfortunes in four or five years than could be
depicted in a century by literature's most famous novelists: it was
necessary to call upon hell for aid in order to arouse interest, and to
find in the land of fantasies what was common knowledge from
historical observation of man in this iron age. But this way of writing
presented so many inconveniencies! The author of the *Moine* failed
to avoid them no less than did Mrs. Radcliffe; either of these two
alternatives was unavoidable; either to explain away all the magic
elements, and from then on to be interesting no longer, or never raise
the curtain, and there you are in the most horrible unreality.[30]

Here de Sade is suggesting that Gothic novels were registering
the disorder of Europe; they were an attempt to explore the
terrifying realities of their time. He does not claim that they
were an *incitement* to disorder. Yet they have often been read
as such—from Coleridge, who attacked *The Monk* as 'a
mormo for children, a poison for youth and a provocative for
the debauchee', through to modern-day critics who have argued that the Gothic novel encouraged 'large-scale social subversion'.[31] Recent feminist critics, too, have argued that

[30] Mario Praz, 'Introductory essay' to Fairclough, *Three Gothic Novels*, 14.
[31] Samuel Taylor Coleridge, *Coleridge's Miscellaneous Criticism*, ed. T. M.
Raysor (London: Constable, 1936), 374, and Kiely, *Romantic Novel in England*, 36.

Gothic fiction written by women was in its own way subversive of patriarchal norms and humanist notions of unified
subjectivity, claims which I will consider more fully in the next
chapter.

On the other hand, some critics, such as Rosemary Jackson
in her polemical *Fantasy: The Literature of Subversion* (1981),
written from a Marxist, post-structuralist perspective, and
Montague Summers in *The Gothic Quest* (1938), have claimed
that the Gothic is a conservative genre. Summers, for example,
takes Michael Sadleir to task for commenting that the Gothic
romance was 'as much an expression of a deep subversive
impulse as the French Revolution'.[32] Arguing that 'the great
Gothic novelists abhorred and denounced political revolution', Summers claims that the Gothic sprang from 'a genuine
spiritual impulse' (Summers, p. 399), while in his introduction
he explains the popularity of the Gothic in terms of its ability
to provide escape from 'the troubles and carking cares of
everyday life' (pp. 12–13). A connoisseur of the Gothic, Summers appears to have been most anxious to promote it as a
neglected but respectable genre, indeed to valorize it as 'an
aristocrat of literature'. But, as David Punter remarks, he too
often falls into 'the trap of special pleading' (Punter, p. 17). A
closer examination by the author of what he himself at one
point calls the Gothic's 'extravagances' would have been more
appropriate.

Although Rosemary Jackson argues from a different position that the Gothic is a conservative genre and I will also
examine her claims later, it is worth pointing out here that,
ultimately, it does not seem useful to treat Gothic novels as
relatively homogeneous in order to argue that they are conservative or subversive, as critics interested in the question have in
the main tended to do. If we consider *Otranto* and *The Old
English Baron* even briefly, we soon see that the eighteenth-
century myth of the ancestral Goth can be put to different uses
and that its potential for subversion is largely dependent on
the use made of the fantastic.

Walpole's readers were appreciative of his 'Gothic Story' as
is evident from comments of the day. One hostile reviewer

[32] Montague Summers, *The Gothic Quest* (New York: Russell & Russell,
1964), 398. Further references appear in the text.

allowed that, despite its 'monstrosities', the narrative 'was kept up with surprising spirit and propriety', another that it was the work of a 'genius evincing great dramatic powers'.[33] Even Macaulay, who disliked Walpole, later wrote that the excitement was 'constantly renewed', that the story 'never flags for a single moment'; and Lowndes the publisher described it to Fanny Burney as 'snug'.[34] Those qualities admired here, the suspense and pace of the narrative, as well as the condemned 'monstrosities', are inextricably tied to the novel's introduction of the fantastic.

Constructed in five chapters reminiscent of Shakespearian tragedy, *The Castle of Otranto* prepares readers for the climactic downfall of the House of Manfred by a succession of supernatural portents. Each augury can be read as working with the others towards the fulfilment of the ancient prophecy set down on the first page:

That the castle and lordship of Otranto should pass from the present family, whenever the real owner should be grown too large to inhabit it.[35]

On the next page, a giant helmet with sable plumes falls from heaven. It smashes down on Conrad, Manfred's son and heir, killing him on the day he is to be married to Isabella. Fantastic omens multiply when Manfred declares his intention to divorce his wife and marry Isabella. The sable plumes of the helmet wave back and forth 'in a tempestuous manner', and a portrait of Manfred's grandfather heaves a sigh before stepping from its frame. Isabella makes her escape as Manfred cries, 'Do I dream . . . or are the devils themselves in league against me?' (*Otranto*, p. 60). Readers may thus feel impelled from one crisis to the next until finally any potential for rational resolution which the story may have had is excluded. After Manfred has killed his own daughter, Matilda, by stabbing her in mistake for Isabella, a mighty clap of thunder

[33] Quoted from the *Critical Review* and *Monthly Review* respectively by Devendra P. Varma, *The Gothic Flame* (London: Arthur Baker, 1957), 63.
[34] Ibid. 64, for Macaulay's comments. For Lowndes's comment, see Dorothy Margaret Stuart, *Horace Walpole* (London: Macmillan, 1927), 167.
[35] Fairclough, *Three Gothic Novels*, 51. Further references appear in the text.

shakes the castle to the foundations and the gigantic form of Alphonso the Good rises from the ruins before the eyes of the assembled characters. They fall 'prostrate on their faces, acknowledging the divine will' (pp. 145–6), and subsequently the penitent Manfred abdicates to enter a convent (*sic*). The marvellous is present here unequivocally, acquiring its specific quality, as Gerhard Hoffmann points out, 'by its integration into the context of a pattern of justice and punishment'.[36] Although Walpole's 'Gothic Story' has appeared to challenge rationalism, the values of his class are still intact, with punishment duly inflicted on those who dare to usurp the inherited rights of the aristocracy.

More than one critic has pointed out that, despite its attempt at novelistic verisimilitude, examples of 'common life' or familiar eighteenth-century social and cultural conventions do not stand out in the descriptions of the Gothic past in *Otranto*.[37] The past is, in fact, inextricably connected with the supernatural. The novel constructs a time in which the forbidden, the wild, the impure—usurpation, incest, murder—dominate but ultimately lose out against transcendent virtue. 'Thou art no lawful prince' (*Otranto*, p. 130), Father Jerome tells Manfred. But the ethical norms which he, Hippolita, Matilda, Isabella, and Theodore collectively assert require an obtrusive Providential Will to restore order. Again and again Manfred the usurper is confronted with the marvellous, until finally a 'divine' retribution destroys not the man but the effect of his crimes— the castle. Affairs of state are settled when he abdicates in favour of Theodore, the rightful heir to Otranto. However, political order has been purchased at the price of Matilda's death, leaving all 'disconsolate' and Theodore grief-stricken; the latter will marry Isabella only because with her he may 'forever indulge the melancholy that had taken possession of

---

[36] Gerhard Hoffmann, 'The Fantastic in Fiction: Its "Reality" Status, its Historical Development and its Transformation in Postmodern Narration', in Herbert Grabes with Hans Jürgen Diller and Hans Bungert, eds., *Yearbook of Research in English and American Literature* (Berlin and New York: Walter de Gruyter, 1982), 294. I am much indebted to Hoffmann's theory of the fantastic. Further references in the text.

[37] See e.g. Punter, *Literature of Terror*, 50.

his soul' (*Otranto*, p. 148). Symbolically, the ancestral Goths remain associated with a haunting strangeness and error at the same time that they allow for renewal of order.

On the other hand, in Clara Reeve's widely read *Old English Baron*, written in imitation of Walpole's tale, the Gothic past is not so much a source of the fearfully strange as of the comfortingly familiar. True, the account grows increasingly sinister as Sir Philip Harclay returns from the wars to find his friend, Lord Lovel, dead and his estate in the hands of Lord Baron Fitz-Owen. But whereas Walpole has set his tale in what J. M. S. Tompkins calls 'vaguely mediaeval Italy', Reeve sets hers in the merry England of the reign of Henry VI where cottagers sup upon 'new-laid eggs and rashers of bacon with the highest relish', and industrious wives and daughters milk the cows and feed the poultry.[38] And, unlike Walpole's villain, Reeve's usurper, Sir Walter Lovel, does not dominate the action; he is encountered only briefly towards the end. Instead, the focus is on Edmund, who, like Theodore in *Otranto*, is not really a commoner but a young man of noble origins deprived of what is rightly his. In discovering the secret of his birth, re-establishing his family connections, and settling his claim, Edmund displays bourgeois virtues of modesty, courage, energy, generosity, compassion, loyalty, obedience, and nobility of sentiment (*Old English Baron*, p. 8). In fact, depiction of Gothic life is largely confined to models of exemplary conduct, suggesting that these eighteenth-century middle-class virtues are timeless and stem from England's Gothic past.

Thus, despite references at the end of the romance to the 'overruling hand of Providence' and 'the certainty of Retribution', the supernatural does not carry the weight we find in *Otranto*. Supernatural manifestations are mainly limited to the appearance to Edmund—in dream form and narrated by

[38] Clara Reeve, *The Old English Baron*, in *Limbird's edition of The British Novelist; forming A Choice Collection of the Best Novels in the English Language* (London: J. Limbird, 1831), i. 3–4. There are six novels, paged separately, in vol. i: Ann Radcliffe, *Mysteries of Udolpho* and *Romance of the Forest*; Clara Reeve, *Old English Baron*; Horace Walpole, *Castle of Otranto*; Ann Radcliffe, *Castles of Athlin and Dunbayne* and *Sicilian Romance*. Further references appear in the text.

him after the event—of the 'respectable' ghosts of his true
parents, Lord and Lady Lovel, a tameness of usage which was
to bring forth scorn from Walpole.[39] While Reeve's romance is
not quite as 'dull and insipid' as Walpole would have had
others believe—she does further techniques for presenting and
solving mystery, such as the haunted chamber and revelatory
dream—her rationalist, decorous approach to depicting the
supernatural does effectively defuse its potential for terror,
bringing it, as David Punter claims, 'within the field of bourgeois feelings and responses'.[40]

It is as if Reeve had set out to obey Fielding's caveat in *Tom
Jones* (1749):

I think it may very reasonably be required of every writer that he
keeps within the bounds of possibility . . . The only supernatural
agents which can in any manner be allowed to us moderns, are
ghosts, but of these I would advise an author to be extremely
sparing. These are indeed, like arsenic and other dangerous drugs in
physic, to be used with the utmost caution; nor would I advise the
introduction of them at all in those works, or by those authors, to
which, or to whom, a horse-laugh in the reader would be any great
prejudice or mortification.[41]

In the preface to *The Baron*, Reeve makes much of the need to
keep 'within the utmost *verge* of probability' and, like Fielding, even suggests that Walpole's 'violent' depictions of the
marvellous 'excite laughter' (*Old English Baron*, p. vi). Not
that supernatural narratives were no longer written or read at
this time. As Edith Birkhead in *The Tale of Terror* (1921)
reminds us, there was still a demand for stories which featured
devils, ghosts, witches, wraiths, apparitions, and so on. Although the supernatural was absent from the *novel* during the
first half of the eighteenth century, it was still present in the
translations of fairy- and folk-tales and in the chapbooks
published during that period.[42] Such tales appeared to nourish
curiosity and desire for excitement. It may have been decreed

[39] Walpole's comments are quoted in Varma, *Gothic Flame*, 78.
[40] Punter, *Literature of Terror*, 55.
[41] Henry Fielding, *Tom Jones* (London: Dent, 1962), pt. 1, 315–16.
[42] Edith Birkhead, *The Tale of Terror* (London: Constable, 1921), 12.

in 1736 that witchcraft was no longer a statutory offence, but belief in the devil's minions was alive and well in some quarters, and a fascination with them persisted generally. With *Otranto* this oral tradition of legend, folk-tale, and superstitious terror began to work its way back into literature. However, Reeve's matter-of-fact treatment of her ghosts brings her romance more into line with mainstream Sentimental fiction. In short, Reeve uses the lexicon of Gothic ancestry differently from Walpole. *The Baron* largely eschews passion, the supernatural, and the tabooed, and postulates an ideal society where, in Mark Madoff's words, 'courtship is by strict rule of negotiation and cash value'.[43]

The contrasts I have been making between *Otranto* and *The Old English Baron* focus attention on the different socio-political readings which can be made of Gothic narratives according to their differing mix of 'common life' and supernatural incidents. If the Gothic can be used to vindicate middle-class values, as in Reeve's romance, it can perhaps also be used to interrogate them, given an effective way of relativizing normative ways of perceiving and feeling. Such a violation of norms would require techniques for introducing and maintaining a fantastic discourse in ways more subtle and sophisticated than Walpole or Reeve could achieve with their direct approaches. This technical problem may be understood in Fredric Jameson's terms as 'that of slipping past the bougeois reality principle', or, in the words of George E. Haggerty, as 'develop[ing] a form that combines the haunting forces of an unreal world with an objective fictional world both palpable and real'.[44] The question of how this problem was met by later writers in the Gothic mode—the novelists, Ann Radcliffe, Matthew Lewis, Mary Shelley, for example, and later, nineteenth-century writers of short fiction—will become apparent in later chapters.

In summary, we have seen that critics and theorists such as MacAndrew, Day, Bayer-Berenbaum, Jackson, Madoff, Punter, and Tompkins attempt to define the Gothic thematically by

...ne significance of Gothic conventions. Their work
...a number of forms: theological, psychoanalytic,
...r structural, and historical/political. However, sev-
...se critics foreground the idea that the Gothic them-
.../phenomenon of fear and evil in extreme situations.
... or example, says that fear 'in a vast variety of forms,
crops up in all the relevant fiction . . . exploring Gothic is also
exploring fear and seeing the various ways in which terror
breaks through the surfaces of literature' (Punter, p. 21). For
him the Gothic depicts 'states of mind, in extreme and grotesque form' (p. 85.) It will be remembered that Bayer-Berenbaum also claims that Gothic literature portrays states of mind
that intensify and distort perception, thought, and hence 'reality' (Bayer-Berenbaum, pp. 25, 78). And for MacAndrew,
too, the Gothic focuses on extreme states of mind, giving
shape to concepts of good and evil and the nature of perception, while Day claims that the Gothic 'investigates the dy-
namics of that inner life, those phenomena we call states of
mind and modes of consciousness' (Day, pp. 180–1). Such
comments focus attention on the language of the fantastic in
Gothic fiction and the ways in which it can be used to relativize normative ways of perceiving and feeling.

But first, what precisely is 'the fantastic'? To this point it
may seem that I have used the term more or less indiscriminately to refer to a type of discourse which introduces supposedly supernatural, unnatural, or strange events, irrespective of
whether these are subsequently explained, as in Walpole's
Otranto, or given a status somewhere in between, being partly
accounted for and partly not, as in Reeve's much-maligned
Old English Baron. Can this usage be justified? The fantastic,
after all, like the Gothic itself, is a contested category and
there have been many recent attempts by theoreticians to
define it. Clarification of the concept is necessary before
we can posit a way in which, using the theories of Bakhtin, we
might read Gothic fiction.

The Fantastic and its Role in Gothic Fiction

In his *Introduction à la litterature fantastique*, Tzvetan Todorov, one of the best-known theoretical exponents of the fant-

astic, subjects the notion to a rigorous structural analysis, conceiving it both as a genre and as an aesthetic category.[45] From my perspective, however, there are significant problems in treating it as a genre. The first is Eric Rabkin's point, that the wide range of works which we may want to call in some way 'fantastic' is much too large to constitute a single genre, as it includes 'whole conventional genres such as fairy tale, detective story, and Fantasy'.[46] And, we might add, Gothic romance. A second problem is made clear by Christine Brooke-Rose in *Rhetoric of the Unreal*: Todorov's definition of the fantastic is so narrow that, as a *historical* genre, it turns out to have existed only during a very short period more or less coextensive with the first flowering of the Gothic novel and its 'brief aftermath'.[47] Indeed, if we exclude Poe's 'The Black Cat', about which he has some doubts, then for Todorov the fantastic manifests itself in a 'pure' form in but two works: Henry James's *The Turn of the Screw* (1898) and Prosper Mérimée's *La Venus d'Ille* (1841)—and even the latter is not a clear-cut case (Todorov, pp. 43, 84; Brooke-Rose, p. 64). Thus, on his own account, the fantastic seems 'an evanescent *element*' rather than 'an evanescent *genre*' (Brooke-Rose, p. 65). For these reasons, I shall limit my remarks to consideration of Todorov's account of the fantastic as an aesthetic category.

For him the fantastic is 'that hesitation experienced by a person who knows only the laws of nature, confronting an apparently supernatural event'; it is, therefore, 'to be defined in relation to . . . the real and the imaginary' (Todorov, p. 25). More fully, apparently supernatural phenomena can be explained by 'the reader implicit in the text' (p. 31) in two ways: rationally, by natural causes, and irrationally, by supernatural ones. In the first case we are dealing not with the fantastic but 'the uncanny' (*l'étrange*, Freud's *das Unheimliche*); and in the second, we have entered the realm of 'the marvellous' (*le*

---

[45] Tzvetan Todorov, *Introduction à la litterature fantastique*, trans. *The Fantastic* by Richard Howard (Cleveland and London: Case Western Reserve University Press, 1973). Further references appear in the text.
[46] Eric S. Rabkin, *The Fantastic in Literature* (Princeton, NJ: Princeton University Press, 1976), 117–18.
[47] Christine Brooke-Rose, *A Rhetoric of the Unreal* (Cambridge: Cambridge University Press, 1981), 62. Further references appear in the text.

merveilleux). The fantastic effect is created only for as long as we hesitate between these alternatives, and in most works this hesitation will be represented by at least one of the protagonists with whom the reader identifies. As a result, the fantastic, as such, becomes 'the dividing line between the uncanny and the marvellous' (Todorov, p. 27). A further requirement of the reader is that s/he must not interpret in a poetic or allegorical way any supernatural events described (as, for example, Mac-Andrew does in her reading of *Otranto*), because the *reaction* of the subject experiencing the seemingly supernatural is all-important.

Situating the fantastic exclusively on the border of the supernatural in this way has its problems, however, in that it becomes dependent on the appearance of certain supernatural motifs and topics which can be used to produce doubt. As Gerhard Hoffmann points out, this rules out other imaginative constructs, such as Gregor Samsa's horrifying, 'surreal' awakening and subsequent existence as a giant cockroach in Kafka's *Metamorphosis*, a narrative which we may well want to call 'fantastic' (Hoffmann, p. 273). Because there is no hesitation on the part of the characters in this tale, but rather a chilling and complete *absence* of surprise, 'an increasing natural atmosphere as the story progresses' (Todorov, p. 171) the reader does not experience hesitation; so, on Todorov's definition, *Metamorphosis* is not fantastic. At this point the narrowness of Todorov's definition may cause us to regard it as a liability rather than a useful heuristic tool. For by reducing the fantastic to the psychological phenomenon of hesitation, Todorov must restrict its presence to certain nineteenth-century texts, when obviously it is in evidence in others in various forms, including twentieth-century ones.

Yet his definition can perhaps be satisfactorily modified, as he has accepted the argument of previous theoreticians, such as Roger Callois, that the fantastic can be defined only in contrast to the 'real': 'The fantastic is always a break in the acknowledged order, an irruption of the inadmissible within the changeless everyday legality.'[48] This 'changeless everyday

---

[48] Roger Caillois, *Au cœur du fantastique* (Paris, Gallimard, 1958), quoted in Todorov, *Fantastic*, 26, and in Hoffmann, 'Fantastic in Fiction', 272.

legality', as a category, can be understood in different ways: as intratextual, fictional reality, and/or as the reality experienced by the (actual) reader in his/her everyday life. Accordingly, with Hoffmann, we can argue that the fantastic is 'constituted not only by the shock experienced by a figure in the text, but also (as in Kafka) by the contrast between the reader's expectations of what is and should be "real" and the "surreal" fictional representation of "reality" in the text' (Hoffmann, p. 273).

On this account, the specificity of the fantastic lies in its departure from the 'real', a departure which can be moderate (as in Reeve's *Old English Baron*) or more radical (as in Walpole's *Otranto*). Thus we can distinguish between works according to 'the *tension* that is built up and maintained in the work between the "real" and the seemingly "irreal"' (Hoffmann, p. 275). This allows that the fantastic may be 'merely an imaginative and unproblematical extension of the real, or it can challenge the norms of the supposedly real and thus conflict with it' (p. 283). In sum, Hoffmann's model is marked by a flexibility and elegance which makes it useful in reconstructing the intertextual relations of Gothic texts and assessing their potential for subversion of dominant discourses and their associated moral and cultural values.

Another theorist of the fantastic, Rosemary Jackson, in *Fantasy: The Literature of Subversion*, has also amended Todorov's definition of the fantastic. However, she dismisses the idea that there is any potential for subversion in the thematic transgressions of Gothic fiction, arguing that, on the contrary, it 'tended to buttress a dominant, bourgeois ideology, by vicarious wish fulfilment through fantasies of incest, rape, murder, parricide, social disorder'.[49] As indicated earlier, such an argument over-simplifies the effects of a fantastic discourse in Gothic fiction by treating the texts homogeneously and conceiving them one-dimensionally as a compensation for an overly rational mode of existence. However, because Jackson's work represents one of the few post-structuralist treatments of Fantasy literature, it is worth considering her arguments

---

[49] Rosemary Jackson, *Fantasy: The Literature of Subversion* (London and New York: Methuen, 1981), 175.

concerning the function of the fantastic in Gothic fiction in more detail.

Jackson is aware of the historical dimensions of the fantastic and its use in Gothic fiction, accounting for the gradual transition from the marvellous to the uncanny, as Ziolowski does, by allusion to the slow displacement of theology and belief in the supernatural by various positivist notions: 'the history of the survival of Gothic horror is one of the progressive internalization and cognition of fears as generated by the self' (Jackson, p. 24). She adduces support for this in Todorov's diagrammatic representation of the history of fantastic narratives:–

MARVELLOUS ———→ FANTASY ———→ UNCANNY
Supernatural   Unnatural   Natural

and concludes that during the nineteenth century the fantastic began to 'hollow out the "real" world', making it inexplicably unfamiliar or alien. By 'the real' here, she appears to mean the world of the text, for, extending an earlier analogy with optical paraxis, and drawing on Bakhtin, she writes: 'The fantastic exists as the inside, or underside of realism, opposing the novel's closed, monological forms with open, dialogical structures, as if the novel had given rise to its own opposite, its unrecognizable reflection' (Jackson, p. 25). Thus, as in Hoffmann's account of the fantastic, Jackson postulates a tension, an interaction between 'the real' and the apparently 'irreal', with, it seems, a fantastic discourse introducing those elements into the narrative which the dominant, positivist realism of an enlightened age cannot countenance.

Unlike Hoffmann, though, Jackson wishes to maintain the fantastic as a literary mode which is *discrete* from that of the marvellous. For this reason, she modifies Todorov's scheme, rejecting the uncanny because it is a psychoanalytic rather than literary category (Jackson, pp. 32, 68) and placing the fantastic between the opposite literary modes of the mimetic and the marvellous in order to claim that it 'confounds' elements of both. Thus her exposition ultimately suggests that the fantastic is an imperfectly integrated discourse which utilizes two ultimately incompatible discourses. But, if this is so, how can the fantastic 'enter a dialogue with the "real" ', when, on her own account, it is itself constituted through the interplay of the mimetic and the marvellous? Even if the 'real' here refers to extra-textual reality as perceived by the reader, how does the fantastic as 'a mode of writing' enter and incorporate a dialogue with this 'real' as part of *its* (i.e. the fantastic's) essential structure?[50] This illogically arises, I would suggest, from Jackson's desire to define 'the fantastic' too narrowly, making the term synonymous with 'subversive', instead of allowing that the fantastic is a mode of discourse which includes different ways of extending and negating 'everyday reality'—the marvellous, the uncanny (as epistemological categories)—and that it may or may not have a subversive function.

After all, whether a Gothic narrative can be described as subversive will depend not only on the nature of the fantastic discourse utilized in the text, but also on how it is perceived by the reader, who takes his or her own expectations and contextual frames to any narrative. It has already been mentioned that the prevailing philosophical climate of the late eighteenth century was such that it denied reality to ghosts and evil spirits. But not everyone's world view was structured by that rationalism. And even among those for whom Enlightenment values were dominant, the limits of what was considered scientifically or empirically possible would have varied. Today, the depiction of a cloned human being in a narrative would not be seen as a radical departure from the reader's everyday world because cellular fusion and the cloning of genes are actualities. 'We live in Gothic times', as Angela Carter has remarked.[51] But in, say, 1800, such an event depicted in a tale would have seemed to many a representation of the empirically impossible, an instance of the marvellous, perhaps of sorcery.

Reading from her Marxist perspective, Jackson denigrates fantasies which move towards the realm of the marvellous

---

[50] This point is made also in Eric Rabkin, 'Review of *Fantasy: The Literature of Subversion* by Rosemary Jackson', *Genre*, 14/4 (Winter 1981), 524.
[51] Angela Carter, *Fireworks* (London: Quartet Books, 1974), 122.

because 'they serve to stabilize social order' (Jackson, pp.
173–4); but, in so doing, she overlooks the possible tension
between hegemonic and counter-hegemonic philosophic assumptions which the presence of the marvellous can produce,
depending on the position from which such stories are read. At
least one late eighteenth-century Gothic tale in which the
marvellous was deployed to resolve the exigencies of plot
provoked considerable unease—and throughout two centuries
M. G. Lewis's *The Monk* has rarely been thought to be socially
conservative at all.

The paradigmatic subversive Gothic text for Jackson is Bram
Stoker's *Dracula* (1897). This is because it lends itself to a
'structuralist' rather than 'merely thematic' reading, one in
which the fantastic can be shown being used to 'threaten to
disrupt or eat away at the "syntax" or *structure* by which
order is made' (Jackson, p. 72), to make, in effect, a 'violent
attack upon the symbolic order' (p. 103). Such 'syntactic'
transgression is truly subversive, as it attempts to 'depict a
reversal of the subject's cultural formation' (p. 177). However,
in my view, this brand of 'subversion' should not be confused
with a political activism which seeks to transform society in
the interests of a particular class, ethnic, or gender group.
In support of her claim for the presence of an 'erosive activity'
in the literary fantastic, Jackson draws on the psychoanalytic
theories of Freud, Lacan, and Kristeva to demonstrate the
workings of repressed desires in certain narratives. But these
theories and their application are not unproblematic in themselves, as Jackson at one point admits, while continuing to
claim that they are 'indispensable' (Jackson, p. 88). In ap-
plying them to Gothic texts she again ignores specifically
socio-political, literary, and intertextual dimensions as well as
the differential nature of reader response. As Marie MacLean,
in her review of Jackson's book, concludes: 'The theories in
themselves are fascinating, but when they in turn are used as
ideologies and lead to value judgements, then some manipulation of the evidence to fit the theory becomes inevitable.'[52]

[52] Marie MacLean, 'Recent Approaches to Speculative Fiction', *AUMLA* 59
(May 1983), 118–25.

Finally, even if one allows coherence and consistency to Jackson's Lacanian interpretations, it is not clear that 'syntactic' transgression in a text constitutes 'a subtle invitation to transgression' on the reader's part (Jackson, p. 180) while 'thematic' transgression does not. For if fantastic texts do attempt 'to depict a *reversal* of the subject's cultural formation' (p. 177), an entropic pull or return to undifferentiation, such a 'correction' of the cultural order via the fantastic can, in the words of Hoffmann, 'take place only against the background of a schema of order and thus dialectically creates the idea of order out of that "disorder" ' (Hoffmann, p. 278). Thus we return to the position that the 'subversiveness' or otherwise of forms of transgression ('thematic' *or* 'syntactic') in fantastic narratives, including the Gothic, will depend on the positions from which they are read, as well as the type and degree and maintenance of tensions between order and disorder, 'real' and 'irreal', depicted.

In summary, from Jackson and Hoffmann we can take the notion that we find in the Gothic an irruption into the 'real', as schematized by the text, of the unusual, the unnatural, the tabooed. In more concrete terms, Gothic writers draw on folklore, fairy-tale, myth, legend, superstition, and theories of the sublime to introduce the unnatural and preternatural into their fiction, and this fantastic discourse may operate as a corrective to depictions of 'everyday legality'. Such relativization of a normative epistemological and ethical schema presupposes the presence of the schema, i.e. a discourse of realism, in which are inscribed commonly accepted cultural conventions and values. As Hoffmann explains,

there is always a background–foreground relationship between the fantastic, which violates the schema, and the real, which establishes it. This relationship is variable, in the sense that what is background can become foreground, and vice versa. This process may repeat itself, reversing, contradicting, complicating the picture of the world . . . In this process the fantastic marks the deficiencies of the schema, its weak points, and can contribute, in Freud's words, to a 'cognizance of what has been displaced'. (p. 276)

In short, the individual Gothic text, through its incorporation of the fantastic, may have the potential to subvert normative ways of perceiving the world.

*Bakhtin's Concept of Heteroglossia and the Plural
Dimensions of Reading Gothic Fiction*

According to Coral Ann Howells, 'the Jamesian dictum "Try
to be a reader on whom nothing is lost" is certainly not
appropriate when reading a Gothic novel'. Because it keeps
the reader in a state of suspense, the Gothic is meant to be read
quickly; there is a 'need for us . . . to discriminate and to vary
the kind of attention we give to different parts'.[53] For Howells,
this means concentrating on depictions of the life of feelings
in the novels. A preoccupation with fear, terror, and other
intense emotions is preserved from one novel to another, reflecting the anxieties of the novelists who, like their characters, manifest the effects of 'the extreme development of the
eighteenth-century cult of Sensibility' (p. 8).

While I agree with Howells and other critics that the Gothic
invariably depicts extreme states of mind, I wish to abjure
readings which 'acknowledge only one single language and a
single authorial individuality expressing itself directly in that
language' (Bakhtin, p. 265).

The pertinent theory here is again from 'Discourse in the
Novel' in *The Dialogic Imagination*. Here Bakhtin suggests
that we should read novels with close attention to their heterogeneity. By this is meant the various discourses, styles, speech
patterns, ideologies, which may merge with or confront one
another, interacting dynamically, in what becomes a multi-
voiced and multi-styled discourse or 'heteroglossia'. Thus we
need to study closely each dialogue of discourses in its historical context:

A stylistic analysis of the novel cannot be productive outside a
profound understanding of heteroglossia, an understanding of the
dialogue of languages as it exists in a given era. But in order to
understand such a dialogue, or even to become aware that a dialogue
is going on at all, mere knowledge of the linguistic and stylistic
profile of the languages will be insufficient: what is needed is
a profound understanding of each language's socio-ideological
meaning and an exact knowledge of the social distribution and

[53] Coral Ann Howells, *Love, Mystery and Misery: Feeling in Gothic Fiction*
(London: Athlone Press, 1978), 2–3.

ordering of all the other ideological voices of the era. (Bakhtin, p. 417)

It is apparent from this that Bakhtin does not subscribe to a mimetic theory of the novel. If, as John Frow puts it, literature is to 'be understood as a discourse which transforms other structures of discourse', then 'its raw material, its "content", would not be of a different order from itself'.[54] Or, in the words of Maria Shevtsova,

Social reality, which, Bakhtin insists, is not only heterogeneous but contradictory, is everpresent within the novel because its languages are the only languages available to the novel. Which languages are borrowed and reworked identifies the type of culture with which the novel engages (for instance, popular, learned, criminal, *salon* cultures).[55]

Because Gothic novels and tales are in this sense metadiscourses working on prior discourses which embed values and positions of enunciation of those values, the effects produced in the dialogic exchange or 'intertextual operation of one discourse upon another'[56] will constitute the novel's reality, permeating it at the level of space, time, plot, character, and narrator.

Obviously, then, if we wish to assess a text's potential for meaning—including subversion of 'official' or hegemonic values embodied in the text—we need to be aware of the various concerns which, singly or otherwise, can be produced by different audiences as its organizing principle(s). More particularly, we need to be aware of 'social speech types' on which the Gothic might be said to draw: 'social dialects, characteristic group behavior, professional jargons, generic languages, languages of generations and age groups, tendentious languages, languages of the authorities, of various circles and passing fashions, languages that serve the specific sociopolitical purposes of the day' (Bakhtin, pp. 262–3). Some reference to these forms in relation to the Gothic has already been made—the importance for early Gothic texts of discourses of the sublime,

---

[54] John Frow, 'Voice and Register in *Little Dorrit*', *Comparative Literature*, 33/3 (Summer 1981), 260.
[55] Shevtsova, 'Dialogism in the Novel', 754.
[56] Frow, 'Voice and Register', 260.

of Sentimentalism, realism, superstition, myth, legend, folk-
and fairy-tale. For example, the castle as literary reminder of
an ancestral or Gothic past of 'dynastic primacy and transfer
of hereditary rights' (prominent in Walpole's *Otranto*, Reeve's
Old English Baron, and Radcliffe's *The Mysteries of Udolpho*)
is overlaid or criss-crossed with meanings from legend, fairy-
tale, history, architecture, and an eighteenth-century aestheticizing discourse of the sublime.[57]

More, if what we have in the Gothic is 'an artistic system of
languages', our task in reading is to examine both the intra-
textual 'dialogic' relations of our selected texts and how they
construct themselves in relation to prior discourses. In Bakhtin's terms,

the real task of stylistic analysis consists in uncovering all the
available orchestrating languages in the composition of the novel,
grasping the precise degree of distancing that separates each language from its most immediate semantic instantiation in the work as
a whole, and the varying angles of refraction of intentions within it,
understanding their dialogic interrelationships and—finally—if
there *is* direct authorial discourse, determining the heteroglot background outside the work that dialogizes it . . . (Bakhtin, p. 416)

For Bakhtin, the system of languages which constitutes the
novel is 'never unitary' because it is part of that 'uninterrupted
process of historical becoming that is characteristic of all
living language' (p. 288). Despite being reinterpreted and arranged into an apparent stylistic unity by an author, the strati-
fied languages of the novel continue to speak with the socio-
cultural intentions of their previous contexts:

Language is not a neutral medium that passes freely and easily into
the private property of the speaker's intentions; it is populated—
overpopulated—with the intentions of others. Expropriating it, for-
cing it to submit to one's own intentions and accents, is a difficult
and complicated process. (Bakhtin, p. 294)

This process of expropriation by speaker or writer involves
an orientation of the utterance towards both object or theme

---

[57] 'Each word tastes of the context and contexts in which it has lived its
socially charged life; all words and forms are populated by intentions' (Bakhtin, *Dialogic Imagination*, 293). Bakhtin alludes to the symbolic richness of
the castle in Gothic fiction in 'Forms of Time and Chronotope in the Novel',
in *Dialogic Imagination*, 245–6.

THEORIES OF THE GOTHIC   47

and addressee. The word enters a hostile linguistic environment 'of alien words, value judgements and accents', that is, a
specific conceptual horizon which can shape the entire discourse as 'the speaker strives to get a reading on his own word'
(p. 282). Allon White sees this as 'a kind of reader-oriented
self-consciousness', with each utterance being nuanced in such
a way as to gain power for itself.[58]

However, while certain discourses may strive for and achieve
dominance, no discourse can become totalizing: 'Alongside
the centripetal forces, the centrifugal forces of language carry
on their uninterrupted work; alongside verbal-ideological centralization and unification, the uninterrupted processes of decentralization and disunification go forward' (Bakhtin, p. 272).
To the extent that the novel keeps open and unresolved the
conflicts of voices and languages which constitute it, it remains 'dialogic'. Its discourse 'is structured on an uninterrupted mutual interaction with the discourse of life' (Bakhtin,
p. 383). Indeed, as a prose art form, it presupposes 'a deliberate feeling for the historical and social concreteness of living
discourse, as well as its relativity, a feeling for its participation
in historical becoming and in social struggle' (Bakhtin, p. 331).

Utilizing Bakhtin's conceptual framework, we can examine
ways in which selected Gothic novels and tales incorporate—
by repetition or transformation—both artistic and extra-artistic
genres: folk-tales, myths, songs, letters, poems, dramatic
scenes, the everyday discourses of different class, occupational, and interest groups, scholarly, philosophical, aesthetic,
ethical, religious, and medical treatises, and so on. By focusing
on these intertextual aspects of the novels, we may be able to
locate tensions within and between the discursively constructed perspectives not only of different socio-cultural and
class groups, but also (and Bakhtin does not say this) of men
and women. For an author's dialogue with the 'already
formed', discontinuous languages which she appropriates, re-
accentuates, and reorganizes into 'an intentional hybrid' will
reveal something of the 'alien' ideologies which she desires to

---

[58] Allon White, 'Bakhtin, Sociolinguistics and Deconstruction', in Frank
Gloversmith, ed., *The Theory of Reading* (Brighton: Harvester Press, 1984),
128.

mute, disrupt, or dislodge in order to gain a position from which to tell her story. According to Bakhtin, some words resist being assimilated into new contexts, being limited by prior semantic and semiotic patterning to a degree which makes them 'sound foreign in the mouth of the one who now speaks them'.[59] These words instead continue to carry the point of view, intentions, or accents of the varied social forces ('a profession, a genre, a particular tendency, an individual personality') which have become the dominant ones (Bakhtin, p. 293). Other words are simply appropriated without any relativization occuring, while at yet other times there occurs a 'stylization' of alien texts, whereby a distance is established between the incorporated text and its prior meaning(s)—'there takes place an ideological translation of another's language and an overcoming of its otherness' (Bakhtin, p. 282). By such stylistic interventions and reaccentuations are traditions within texts and history opened up to rupture and ambiguity, as spaces are made for dominant cultural myths to be tested or 'decentred' and new points of view to emerge. An example given by Bakhtin is Dickens's reaccentuation of the comic figure and language of the miser: 'the traditionally comic image of the miser helps to establish hegemony for the new image of the capitalist, which is then raised to the tragic image of Dombey' (p. 421).

At this point it might be objected that there remains an interest in authorial intentionality here, and that this is inappropriate in a study which purports to be a reader-oriented reconstruction of each Gothic text's intertextual relations with prior discourses. After all, does not talk of reaccentuating and expropriation again point back to an essential self and the sort of author-oriented approach to reading espoused by Elizabeth Napier's *Failure of the Gothic*? And is not such a residual humanism at odds with a post-structuralism which posits an authorial subjectivity constantly in process, being reconstituted in discourse each time the author speaks?

While it is true that Bakhtin frequently does use a conceptual language derived from the German idealist tradition, speaking

[59] Yaeger, 'Because a Fire was in my Head', 956.

of 'an individual consciousness' (p. 293) and the 'refracting of authorial intentions' (p. 315), he actually rejects the notion of the transcendental subject—an autonomous, unified self which formulates thought and then encodes it, using language and genre. For him, the act of constructing the self involves assimilating the words and discourses of others in a process of interiorization which always leaves us split as subjects: 'In the everyday rounds of our consciousness, the internally persuasive word is half-ours and half-someone else's' (Bakhtin, p. 345). Thus he stresses the material, linguistic, and social nature of human consciousness. Ideological development occurs only with an intense struggle within us for hegemony between competing discursive practices. At any particular historical moment there are a finite number of discourses in circulation and we take up coexistent subject positions in relation to them:

Every concrete utterance of a speaking subject serves as a point where centrifugal as well as centripetal forces are brought to bear. The processes of centralization and decentralization, of unification and disunification, intersect the utterance; the utterance not only answers the requirements of its own language as an individualized embodiment of a speech act, but it answers the requirements of heteroglossia as well; it is in fact an active participant in such speech diversity. (Bakhtin, p. 272)

Ken Hirschkop puts it this way:

In this 'dialogical' conception of language the structure of a style is not determined by a pre-existing logic of content or intention, but by the requirements for asserting a certain *position* in relation to one's conditions. Such a 'position of a personality' is social insofar as its stylistic shape and its content are enforced upon it by its competition with other representations in the multi-styled discursive world. Speech is thus internally divided: the meaning of an utterance is not a 'present' signified because it exists in the form of a relation to those other utterances which, for a variety of reasons, are deemed to constitute its context.[60]

So for Bakhtin the human subject is not unified, autonomous, and free, but neither is it, as in Saussurean linguistics,

[60] Ken Hirschkop, 'The Social and the Subject in Bakhtin', *Poetics Today*, 6/4 (1985), 771.

simply a passive recipient of a pre-given society. The self can only be constructed through relationship to others by means of sign production; and the same is true for meaning. In Allon White's words, 'meaning is only constructed *between* people, intersubjectively as address and response, as active dialogic utterance *intervening* across an already constituted cultural field'.[61] Bakhtin expressly argues against a psychologistic 'struggle of wills' (Bakhtin, p. 273), but his model connects us with history, allowing for agency, process, and change.

If this is humanistic, so be it. As Allon White indicates, the 'crude binaryism' of the opposition 'classic humanism/post-structuralism' in much post-structuralist discourse is ripe for exposure as an instance of 'perfunctory and impoverished' underpinning of post-structuralism's own concerns.[62] In any case, Bakhtin's humanism is a far cry from Napier's expressivist model of humanism in which the failure of authors to appreciate their own novels' potential meanings, including ambiguities and contradictions, can result only from their own ineptitude. Bakhtin's talk of the novel as 'an intentional and conscious hybrid' (p. 366) with 'intentional potential' makes it clear that, for him at least, works always carry a 'surplus' of meaning:

Every age re-accentuates in its own way the works of its most immediate past. The historical life of classic works is in fact the uninterrupted process of their social and ideological re-accentuation. Thanks to the intentional potential embedded in them, such works have proved capable of uncovering in each era and against ever new dialogizing backgrounds ever newer aspects of meaning; their semantic content literally continues to grow, to further create out of itself. (Bakhtin, p. 421)

Reaccentuation is able to occur because, as we have seen, writers cannot control or 'own' in any ultimate sense the meanings and use of their words. Indeed, according to Bakhtin, a novelist 'welcomes the heteroglossia and language diversity of the literary and extraliterary language into his [sic] own work not only not weakening them but even intensifying them' (p. 298). She or he implicitly understands that this is how works become rich in meaning over time—in Bakhtin's sense, semiotically rich and subject to 'unfinalizability'. For example, against a new and different background, a parody may be 'lost to perception' entirely, or a 'parodied discourse' may suddenly 'offer internal dialogic resistance to the parodying intentions' (Bakhtin, p. 419), a phenomenon we will return to in Chapter 4 in our discussion of Eaton Stannard Barrett's *The Heroine* and Jane Austen's *Northanger Abbey*.

We need also to note, however, that discursive tension or ambiguity in fiction is not *inherently* 'subversive', as some users of the Bakhtinian model have assumed. As David Shepherd again points out in 'Bakhtin and the Reader',

the meaning of a text will change as it is read in new contexts by always historically and socially situated readers who will always bring to it (shared) presuppositions about, among other things, the nature of literature, literary meaning, aesthetic value and so on, and may in turn find these presuppositions being modified in the process of their dialogic encounter with the text.... the dialogic act of reading is disruptive of the seemingly fixed positions of text and reader; these positions cannot come through the dialogic encounter unchanged because they do not pre-exist it. Difficult though it may be, it is important not to lapse into what John Frow calls an 'assumption of entities fully constituted prior to the textual process'.[63]

Thus it is always the specific conjunctural status of particular discourses, rather than any immanent or inherent qualities, which gives those discourses a particular political force.[64]

For this reason, before embarking on dialogic readings of several works of Gothic fiction, I wish to dispute in the next chapter some further recent generalizations about the 'subversive' nature of the Gothic. Feminist discussions of the Gothic have often attempted to claim it as a 'female' genre, either directly on grounds of its authorship and audience, or in terms of its thematization of female anxieties. In examining

[63] David Shepherd, 'Bakhtin and the Reader', in Hirschkop and Shepherd, eds., *Bakhtin and Cultural Theory*, 99.
[64] I am indebted to John Frow for this succinct statement of the Bakhtinian position I wish to adopt.

these claims, my intention is to discuss the status of female authorship in relation to concrete eighteenth- and nineteenth-century institutions and ideologies rather than to deterministic, post-Saussurean models of female language and culture. I will also view questions of gender as intricate political constructs which are given a variety of accentuations in Gothic novels, but which cannot be seen to exhaust those novels' possibilities of meaning and reception.

2

Women and the Gothic

Feminist Appropriations of the Gothic

Since the mid-1970s, critics and theorists both male and female have attempted to link the supposed subversiveness of the Gothic to its perceived existence as the gendered use of a particular literary form. 'It is no accident', writes David Punter, 'that many of the most important Gothic writers of the last two centuries—Radcliffe, Mary Shelley, Dinesen, Carter—have been women.'[1] 'It is no accident', writes Rosemary Jackson also, 'that so many writers of a Gothic tradition are women: Charlotte and Emily Brontë, Elizabeth Gaskell, Christina Rossetti, Isak Dinesen, Carson McCullers, Sylvia Plath, Angela Carter, all of whom have all [sic] employed the fantastic to subvert patriarchal society' (Jackson, pp. 103-4).

But the question of gendered writing is a particularly vexed one. One may believe that all writing or forms of writing are 'marked' by gender; demonstrating this has proved extremely difficult. And before we can reconstruct the intertextual relations and reception of Gothic texts which were written by men and women in the 'revolutionary' decade of the eighteenth century and later, we need to be clear about the sorts of heuristic devices or strategies which have been used in making claims about the Gothic as 'women's fiction'.

One important strategy found in the work of French feminists and their followers during the 1980s has been built on post-Saussurean linguistics and Lacanian psychoanalysis as it is used to explain women's oppression. In Lacan's theory, language itself is held to oppress women. Because women's subjectivities are constructed in and by an institutionalized and inherently phallogocentric system of signs (the symbolic

[1] Punter, *Literature of Terror*, 411.

Binary oppositions — Inferior
women
in life in
literature

order), so the argument goes, women's relation to language is always a negative one. According to Lacan, women are 'excluded by the nature of things, which is the nature of words'.[2] Women are placed in an inferior position in the binary opposition: Man/Woman. The woman is viewed as the man's other and not in her own right as different or other. Speaking from the place of the Other, women thus have the choices only of silence, of adopting the language and logic of men, or of producing something 'other' itself, such as discourses not controlled by the symbolic order, that is, discourses which do not conform to male rules of rationality or logic, clarity, conciseness, and consistency. Such discourses could arise only from a pre-Oedipal, pre-linguistic, mother–infant form of communication.

Intro

In line with such theory, some feminist critics claim that women's writing can show linguistic traces of the exclusion which, in Western theoretical discourse, has defined their condition as women. Language must always fail women, leaving them split between their experiences and the difficulties of articulating them. And in this position, one analogous to mutedness, silence, absence, and madness, woman's writing can be marked by some form of textual disruption or subversion.

From within such a post-Saussurean, Lacanian framework, Rosemary Jackson, for example, claims that Mary Shelley's writings 'open an alternative "tradition" of "female Gothic" ' as they 'fantasize a violent attack upon the symbolic order'.[3] Other theorists, such as Xavière Gauthier, Chantal Chawaf, Marguerite Duras, Hélène Cixous, and Luce Irigaray, who see women only as silenced or speaking and writing as men do, call for the creation of an *écriture féminine* which will enable women in the future to transcend patriarchal language by 'writing the body'—female sexuality—into existence.[4]

[2] Jacques Lacan, *Le Seminaire XX: Encore* (Paris: Editions du Seuil, 1975), 68, quoted in Deborah Cameron, *Feminism and Linguistic Theory* (London: Macmillan Press, 1985), 125.

[3] Jackson, *Fantasy*, 103.

[4] Various statements by these authors can be found in Elaine Marks and Isabelle de Courtivron, eds., *New French Feminisms: An Anthology* (Amherst: University of Massachusetts Press, 1980), 163, 170–8, 251–2.

Apart from confusions arising from the meaning of the term *écriture féminine*, which can mean both 'female' and 'feminine' writing, there are serious problems with the attempts of French feminists to find a way through the depressing, all-encompassing patriarchy posited by Lacanian psychoanalysis. As Deborah Cameron has shown, a significant problem with their explanations of women's oppression is their linguistic determinism, the assumption that language *per se* is male and oppresses women. In her words,

[Lacan's] theory of language and sexual identity offers no explanation *why* the symbolic order is patriarchal. It can deal with matters of sexual differentiation, but it cannot deal directly with sexual power.

In fact it seems to me that despite all their disclaimers, despite their awareness of the contextuality of meaning, Lacan and the Lacanians do indulge in a covert Saussurean determinism which allows meanings to be fixed (though liable to 'slippage') by the linguistic system. For the important concept in Lacanian accounts of language acquisition is the idea of *inserting oneself in a pre-existing order*: and it is difficult to see how anyone could do this unless the order, and the meanings it made available, were fixed and stable, produced outside the individual and enjoined on her as the price of entry into human society.[5]

Moreover, although there are significant differences between French feminists, a common feature of their statements is that *écriture féminine* is often troped as music. It is thereby constituted as contiguous with modern aesthetics, the 'musicalization of art', and would thus seem to be indistinguishable from avant-garde writings by men, such as James Joyce's *Ulysses* and *Finnegans Wake*. In short, this type of theorizing about women's writing has significant drawbacks, particularly as it presents a negative and pessimistic view of women's linguistic powers and hence of the different types of literature, the Gothic novel included, which women have actually produced.

Another, more useful, feminist strategy has been to claim that writings by women constitute a separate category because they register the conditions of disadvantage under which

---

[5] Cameron, *Feminism and Linguistic Theory*, 124.

female, as opposed to male, authors have laboured. Mary Jacobus, for example, has argued that

> We need the term 'women's writing' if only to remind us of the social conditions under which women wrote and still write—to remind us that the conditions of their (re)production are the economic and educational disadvantages, the sexual and material organizations of society, which, rather than biology, form the crucial determinants of women's writing.[6]

A further point in favour of the term 'women's writing' is that the problems of literary value so often raised in traditional criticism of 'women's literature' can be avoided in order to facilitate a more comprehensive representation and examination of what women have actually written. When, during the Second World War, B. G. MacCarthy set out to chronicle the work done by British women writers in the novel, she felt constrained to 'judge them not in relation to their opportunities but by the standard which men, with every advantage on their side established'.[7] For as long as such androcentric assumptions of value are maintained, it is impossible to say much about works by women beyond damning their faults and praising their virtues; certainly there is no justification for giving women's diaries, letters, small-scale magical stories, or Gothic fiction a more conspicuous place in literary history.

However, as we shall see in the next section, because it again tends to suggest that women's writing is homogeneous and to universalize women as victims, the socio-cultural approach to women's writing is also too often negative. I agree with Deborah Cameron that we need to look for the historical moment and circumstances in which particular discursive practices used by women arise, the specific cultural group which initiates it and/or whose authority and interests maintain it.[8] When such analysis is actually made, it is often found that the relation of women to various discourses in fact varies over time.

[6] Mary Jacobus, 'The Question of Language: Men of Maxims and *The Mill on the Floss*', *Critical Inquiry*, 8/2 (Winter 1981), 209.
[7] Bridget G. MacCarthy, *The Later Women Novelists, 1744–1818* (Oxford: Cork University Press, 1947), 280.
[8] Cameron, *Feminism and Linguistic Theory*, 153.

While the term 'women's writing' has obvious advantages, application of the epithets 'male' and 'female' to writing is more problematic. It is, as Ken Ruthven suggests, 'clearly preferable to have the female Gothic isolated as a separate category than to have the texts which comprise it treated as inferior or decadent manifestations of a type of fiction for which the normative criteria are novels written by men'.[9] But the term which he accepts also suggests all too readily an *a priori*, biologically based dichotomy and symmetry. For example, male Gothic/female Gothic may be seen as distinct types which can be made to correspond to those categories of 'horror Gothic' and 'terror Gothic' (supposedly epitomized by the work of Matthew Lewis and Ann Radcliffe respectively) that have been so frequently utilized since Robert D. Hume drew attention to them in 1969.[10] Such connotations blur or mask the issues which Jacobus and socio-cultural critics highlight. While the fact of certain biological distinctions between the sexes is indisputable, that these have any necessary psychological and cultural consequences is not clear.[11] Thus, in an effort to avoid essentialist conceptions of 'woman' being associated with 'women's writing', the term 'female Gothic' would seem to have been best avoided in investigations of whether, and if so how, writing is inflected by gender.[12] The fact is,

---

[9] Ken Ruthven, *Feminist Literary Studies: An Introduction* (Cambridge: Cambridge University Press, 1984), 119.

[10] Robert D. Hume, 'Gothic versus Romantic: A Revaluation of the Gothic Novel', *PMLA* 84/2 (Mar. 1969), 284–5, and James Ralph Foster, *The History of the Pre-Romantic Novel in England* (New York: Modern Language Association, 1949, and London: Oxford University Press, 1949), 189.

[11] Robert William Connell, *Gender and Power: Society, the Person and Sexual Politics* (Sydney: Allen & Unwin, 1987), ch. 4. For a discussion of the current use of the concept of gender as a category of analysis, see Hester Eisenstein, *Gender Shock: Practising Feminism on Two Continents* (Sydney: Allen & Unwin, 1991), ch. 9.

[12] Sally McConnell-Ginet with Ruth Borker and Nelly Furman, eds., *Women and Language in Literature and Society* (New York: Praeger, 1980), 16, define gender as 'the cultural meaning attached to sexual identity'. Hester Eisenstein, in *Contemporary Feminist Thought* (London and Sydney: Unwin, 1984), 7, defines 'gender' as 'the culturally and socially shaped cluster of expectations and behaviour assigned to that category of human being [male, female] by the society into which the child was born'.

however, that the use of 'female Gothic' is well established in studies of 'gender and genre', and another way into our topic is to consider how the widespread use of this labelling has come about.

The Invention of Female Gothic

'From its beginnings', wrote Leonard Wolf in the *New York Times Book Review* in 1973, the Gothic novel was 'genteel and demonic'. But, he went on, it was also something else:

Despite the triumphs of Lewis and Maturin, the Gothic novel was something of a cottage industry of middle class women—as if women, oppressed by needlepoint, whalebone stays, psychic frustrations, shame and babies, found in the making and consuming of these fictions a way to signal to each other (and perhaps the world of men) the shadowy out-lines of their own pain.[13]

Wolf was reviewing a set of ten 'second- to fifth-rank' eighteenth-century Gothic novels reissued by Arno Press, and, while generally impressed with the volumes, he wished to point out the failure in general of their introductory material to explore the relationship between eighteenth-century women and the popularity of the Gothic mode in fiction.[14] 'Gothic fiction', he added, 'ought to be of special interest to critics and historians in the context of the contemporary resurgence of the women's movement.'[15]

As if in reply, the following year Ellen Moers published two articles in the *New York Review of Books* on what she called 'Female Gothic'—'the work that women writers have done in the literary mode that, since the eighteenth century, we have

---

[13] Leonard Wolf, 'Gothic Novels', *New York Times Book Review* (14 Jan. 1973), 2.

[14] Wolf does acknowledge the contribution made by Coral Ann Howells in her introduction to Mary Anne Radcliffe, *Manfroné: Or the One Handed Monk* (New York: Arno Press, 1972). Howells went on to publish *Love, Mystery and Misery: Feeling in Gothic Fiction* in 1978, but it was eclipsed by the publication in the previous year of Ellen Moers, *Literary Women* (London: W. H. Allen, 1977), which contained a chapter on 'Female Gothic'.

[15] Wolf, 'Gothic Novels', 2.

called the Gothic'.[16] But to the Gothic of the 1790s Moers gave
little attention, preferring to focus on Mary Shelley's *Frankenstein* (1818), which, she claimed, 'brought a new sophistication to literary terror'. Ann Radcliffe's use of the Gothic she
saw as merely compensatory to women: 'a feminine substitute
for the picaresque, where heroines could enjoy all the adventures and alarms that masculine heroes had long experienced,
far from home, in fiction'.[17] The Gothic in the Radcliffean
style became 'a make-believe puberty rite for young women',
one in which the good daughter must suffer 'paternal trials
and tortures' before finding happiness with a 'palely satisfac-
tory' father-substitute. *Frankenstein* on the other hand, although 'without a heroine' or 'even an important victim', was
a more important transformation of Gothic conventions. For
Shelley's novel was no less than 'a birth myth', one which had
been 'lodged in the novelist's imagination . . . by the fact that
she herself was a mother'. In its 'motif of revulsion against
newborn life, and the drama of guilt, dread, and flight surrounding birth and its consequences', her novel was in fact
'most interesting, most powerful and most feminine'.[18]

   With this psychological orientation (and privileging of Shelley's text as prototypical), Moers ultimately moves beyond the
discussion of Gothic texts as belonging to distinct historical
moments. Instead she constructs an overarching framework in
which 'Female Gothic'—whether by Shelley, Emily Brontë,
Christina Rossetti, or Carson McCullers—can be read as
psycho-biographical expressions of women's sexual feelings,
particularly fear, guilt, depression, and anxiety. In this she is
supported to some extent by the work of Coral Ann Howells,
who, in *Love, Mystery and Misery* (1978), seems independently to have reached a similar conclusion. Howells sees
'the dread of sex' at the core of Gothic fiction; '[it] is basic',
she says, 'to many of its conventions of anxiety and terror'.[19]

---

[16] Ellen Moers, 'Female Gothic: The Monster's Mother', *New York Review
of Books*, 21/4 (21 Mar. 1974), 24–8, and ead., 'Female Gothic: Monsters,
Goblins, Freaks', *New York Review of Books*, 21/5 (Apr. 1974), 35–9. These
articles were reprinted substantially unchanged in her *Literary Women*.
[17] Moers, 'Female Gothic: The Monster's Mother', 24.
[18] Ibid. 25.   [19] Howells, *Love, Mystery and Misery*, 13.

It should be noted, however, that Wolf and Moers were by no means the first to reflect on the popularity of Gothic fiction with women writers and readers; nor were they the first to suggest ways in which this phenomenon might be explained. Discussing 'lesser women novelists' in *Frail Vessels* in 1969, Hazel Mews had commented that the story of the rise of the Gothic had often been recounted and that she need only mention 'the seemingly surprising fact' that it 'should be a genre in which the gentle sex was so successful'. For her there seemed little doubt that 'adventures and horrors viewed from a safe distance in the pages of the novel may have contained an element of compensation for lives lived in circumstances too sheltered and confined'.[20] Gothic fiction is thus represented by Mews as both escapist and conservative.

In this she follows another critic unmentioned by Moers and Wolf—J. M. S. Tompkins, who in 1932 devoted a lengthy chapter to 'The Female Novelists', as well as one to 'The Gothic Romance', in her *Popular Novel in England 1770–1800*. Tompkins argues that women writers of the late eighteenth century were 'moralists, satirists, dreamers': 'In their hands the novel was not so much a reflection of life as a counterpoise to it, within the covers of which they looked for compensation, for ideal pleasures and ideal revenge' (p. 129). Commenting on the extensive audience for the Gothic, she also posits a predominantly female reading community: 'Women . . . liked to read what women had written, to meet in books with a reflection of their own interests and point of view' (p. 120). Such a conclusion is disputed by Elizabeth MacAndrew in *The Gothic Tradition in Fiction*. Conscious that the Gothic is often tagged and denigrated as a 'literature "for women by women" ', MacAndrew claims, with some justification, that this reputation in respect to the early Gothic text is unfounded:

The Gothic authors were not women striving to satisfy the longing for excitement in their home-bound sisters of little education. They were of both sexes and had interests parallel to those of their contemporaries, who were busy learnedly unearthing the old ballads, the Nordic myths, and other phenomena of the 'Dark Ages', or

[20] Hazel Mews, *Frail Vessels* (London: Athlone Press, 1969), 25.

those who invented their own versions, as Macpherson and Chatterton did. In search of symbolic constructs for their fictional worlds of the mind these authors exhibited the same affinities as their archaizing contemporaries. (MacAndrew, p. 37)

Moreover, she reminds us, educated women such as Ann Radcliffe and Clara Reeve wrote about the literary theory on which their novels were based, and their works were appreciated by a wide-ranging audience, one which included eminent male writers, and which went far beyond 'the frequenters of circulating libraries'. For all that, Tompkins's evidence—both of a sexist standard which designated types of writing appropriate to men and women, and of the conditions under which women wrote—should give us pause. Though broad in scope, her work constitutes a very valuable initial resource for any study of the Gothic as it was written by women.

Some earlier critics went further than Tompkins by suggesting that women, by nature as well as situation, had an especial aptitude for fiction, a notion later perpetuated by Ian Watt in his *Rise of the Novel*.[21] One such critic, Joyce M. Horner, in the last part of *The English Women Novelists and their Connection with the Feminist Movement 1668–1797* (1930), began to explore the problem of the terms in which the relationship of women to the novel might be described. 'We have to discover whether women have any special qualifications that fit them for this kind of writing', she says, 'and whether there is anything in their contribution to the novel which only women could have given.'[22] Having examined stylistic features of eighteenth-century works by both men and women, Horner affirms her belief in 'a different psychology underlying' the writing of each sex. A woman is in closer contact with her feelings and this enables her 'to test the feelings of others' fictionally—something which constitutes both her strength as a novelist and her weakness: 'It argues a great power of self-knowledge in the writer and a firmer hold on reality. On

[21] Ian Watt, *The Rise of the Novel* (Harmondsworth: Penguin Books, 1963), 310.
[22] Joyce M. Horner, *The English Women Novelists and their Connection with the Feminist Movement 1668–1797* (Northampton: Folcroft Library Editions, 1973), 80.

the other hand, it argues an inferior power of escaping from
self and a weaker sense of ideality . . .'.[23] Whether it is univers-
ally true that the female psyche is 'different in kind' from that
of the male, however, or whether the qualities of writing which
seem to indicate a female mind 'really point only to a mind
governed by a feminine tradition', is a question which, not
surprisingly, Horner says she cannot resolve. Eighteenth-
century methods of education assumed as fact that women had
one type of mind and men another. Thus, 'whatever happens
in the future', as the sexes 'participate more and more in the
same experiences . . . the women's novels of the past would
seem to belong to the Mental Females'.[24]

Despite the greatly increased sophistication of more recent
semiotic and psychoanalytic approaches, the problem so simply foregrounded by Horner—of the extent to which we can
differentiate between the biological and the social—has continued to dog discussion of women and their writing.[25] Within
the context of renewed discussions of feminism, 'excavations'
of women's writing and explorations of relationships between
genres and gender have continued apace. Following Moers,
feminist critics have been able to produce a variety of interpretations which suggest that women use Gothic conventions
to subvert existing patriarchal notions about the nature of
women and their place in culture and society. However, much
of this criticism has continued to rely on what is basically an
'expressive-realist' theory of the literary text,[26] an approach
discussed in the last chapter in respect to Napier's *Failure of
the Gothic*. Such theory often assumes that the woman writer
must have experienced the feelings and convictions about
which she writes. It is thus open to the criticism made by
Margaret Atwood in 1979 that such a view is both noxious

---

[23] Ibid. 142.   [24] Ibid. 145.
[25] See Terry Lovell, 'Writing Like a Woman: A Question of Politics', in
Francis Barker *et al.*, eds., *The Politics of Theory* (Proceedings of the Essex
conference on the Sociology of Literature, July 1982, Colchester: University
of Essex, 1983), 21–2.
[26] The phrase used by Catherine Belsey, in *Critical Practice* (London:
Methuen, 1980), 7–20, of those theories which view the literary text as an
expression of the anterior convictions of the author or his/her experience of
the society in which s/he lives.

and false in its implicit assumption that women are not capable of invention.[27]

Speaking of the Gothic in *The Madwoman in the Attic*, for example, Sandra Gilbert and Susan Gubar comment on the pervasive use of spatial imagery by nineteenth-century women writers. They suggest that 'imagery of enclosure reflects the woman writer's own discomfort, her sense of powerlessness, her fear that she inhabits alien and incomprehensible places. Indeed, it reflects her growing suspicion that what the nineteenth century called "women's place" is itself irrational and strange.'[28] In addition to the gloomy castle or mysterious house, they see 'ladylike veils and costumes, mirrors, paintings, statues, locked drawers, trunks, strongboxes' and so on as 'paraphernalia of "women's place" ' used by women writers to enact a 'symbolic drama of enclosure and escape'.[29] Faced with the problem that male writers in the Gothic mode, such as Dickens and Poe, also employ imagery of enclosure and escape, they insist on a functional difference:

Women authors, however, reflect the literal reality of their confinement in the constraints they depict, and so all at least begin with the same unconscious or conscious purpose in employing such spatial imagery. Recording their own distinctively female experience, they are secretly working through and within the conventions of literary texts to define their own lives.[30]

Because male authors are 'so much more comfortable' with their literary role, they can be more 'objective', their images of confinement being 'metaphysical and metaphorical' rather than 'social and actual'. The examples given by Gilbert and Gubar are far from convincing, and, interesting as their hypothesis is, it is difficult to see how it could be proved. Moreover, the situation which women's use of the Gothic supposedly 'reflects' is for them always essentially psychological and negative, because it is one constructed out of personal relationships riven by a continuing female anxiety.

[27] Margaret Atwood, 'You Can't Be Exclusively Feminist', *Spare Rib*, 83 (1979), 35.
[28] Sandra M. Gilbert and Susan Gubar, *The Madwoman in the Attic* (New Haven, Conn. and London: Yale University Press, 1979), 84.
[29] Ibid. 85.   [30] Ibid. 87.

Certainly, as already indicated, there is evidence to suggest that, at certain historical moments, the social conditions under which men and women authored the Gothic differed considerably, an issue that will be taken up in the next section. But there are problems with the methodology of *The Madwoman in theáAttic*, both as feminist and literary-critical discourse. In analysing the nineteenth-century 'female imagination', Gilbert and Gubar virtually postulate an essential self and culture which transcends the history of particular works. Adapting Harold Bloom's 'Oedipal' theory of literature, they read *Frankenstein*, along with later works, in terms of the female author's ' "anxiety of authorship"—a radical fear that woman cannot create and that, because she can never become a "precursor", the act of writing will isolate or destroy her'.[31] Yet this universalistic assumption, which is at least in part determined by the Bloomian framework, is surely something which feminists should be concerned to interrogate, since any real changes in the past situation of women in society appear thereby to be excluded. As Julia Prewitt Brown has succinctly put it, *The Madwoman in the Attic* 'insists on the alienation it deplores by denying women's relation to the larger cultural situation'.[32] The appropriation by Gilbert and Gubar of the texts they select and read—whether they be *Northanger Abbey, Frankenstein, Jane Eyre, Wuthering Heights, Middlemarch,* or Emily Dickinson's poetry—is made for the present, the 'now' of need for a gender-determined framework in which to insert these commonly taught Victorian texts and find new feminist significance. However, their particular appropriation ensures that women and their writing remain trapped in the personal, the private, the subjective, body and nature as against the political, the public, the objective, mind and culture. The larger tension-filled discursive environments in which Gothic and other texts emerge and are later reproduced are largely ignored, as are the ways in which these texts are differentially received at particular historical moments.

[31] Ibid. 49.
[32] Julia Prewitt Brown, 'Review of *The Madwoman in the Attic* by Sandra M. Gilbert and Susan Gubar', *Studies in Romanticism*, 20 (Spring 1981), 132.

This last criticism can equally be made of an anthology of essays entitled *The Female Gothic*, edited by Juliann Fleenor. The volume announces itself as an extension of Ellen Moers's attempt 'to place women's literature in relation to itself' as 'a cohesive body of work with its own images and interrelationships'.[33] Amplifying this in her introductory essay, Fleenor defines the female Gothic as follows:

It is essentially formless, except as a quest; it uses the traditional spatial symbolism of the ruined castle or an enclosed room to symbolize both the culture and the heroine; as a psychological form it provokes various feelings of terror, anger, awe, and sometimes self-fear and self-disgust directed towards the female role, female sexuality, female physiology and procreation; and it frequently uses a narrative form which questions the validity of the narration itself. It reflects a patriarchal paradigm that women are motherless yet fathered and that women are defective because they are not males.[34]

Here we find traces of MacAndrew's observation—noted in Chapter 1—about the frequent presence in the Gothic of mediated narration, of narrative within narrative. There are also Moers's suggestions about psychological imagery relating to childbirth. And, like Gilbert and Gubar, while allowing that most of the characteristics which she describes 'can apply in differing degrees to the Gothic as written by men', Fleenor argues that 'the use of spatial imagery is different especially with the feelings of self-fear and self-disgust'. So, once again, understanding the Gothic as written by women is to explain it in terms of the author's continuing psychological dis-ease within an androcentric culture—a condition of identity which, consciously or unconsciously, controls the constitutive features of the form:

The writer's feelings are frequently illustrated by the image of enclosed space, an image which conveys repression and frustration as well. Spatial imagery, images of enclosed rooms or houses, suggests either the repressive society in which the heroine lives or the heroine herself, and sometimes, confusingly, both.[35]

[33] Juliann Fleenor, ed., *The Female Gothic* (Montreal and London: Eden Press, 1987), 7.
[34] Ibid. 15.   [35] Ibid. 12.

A more sophisticated feminist interpretation of spatial conventions, which owes much to this work, as well as to Eve Kosofsky Sedgewick's *The Coherence of Gothic Conventions*, is found in Eugenia C. DeLamotte's *Perils of the Night* (1990). DeLamotte sets out to argue 'against a tendency . . . to masculinize the Gothic canon'. Quoting Fredric Jameson's dictum that 'genres are essentially contracts between a writer and his [*sic*] readers' and are 'literary institutions', she postulates that Ann Radcliffe 'first codified the original provisions of the "contract" on which [the Gothic] institution was based'. For her, the original Gothics, women's tales for women readers, generate a terror which 'has its primary source in an anxiety about boundaries', physical or metaphorical. In the Gothic are to be found boundaries 'that shut the protagonist off from the world, those that shut the protagonist in, and those that separate the individual self from something Other'. Part II of her book, devoted specifically in its readings to the issue of the Gothic as a women's genre, emphasizes conventions which stand for 'the vulnerability of women to intrusions from an outside world to which, in another sense, they have frustratingly little access'.[36] Again the condition of women as victims is universalized.

Against such readings it must be reiterated that women writers and their readers also belong to a particular ethnic or socio-cultural group, a class, a nation, a particular historical and social formation. To read the Gothic only as 'proof simple of patriarchal squalors'[37] is to forget or ignore that such a model suppresses much else of the differential enmeshment of texts in circumstance, time, place, and society. It limits a text's amplitude of potential meanings and can set up feminist criticism as yet another authoritarian discourse. If we wish to assess a Gothic text's potential for subversion we need to look for more than sexism in its conventions, conditions of production, circulation, and reception, although this aspect *is*

[36] Eugenia C. DeLamotte, *The Perils of the Night: A Feminist Study of Nineteenth-Century Gothic* (Oxford: Oxford University Press, 1990), 1, 11, 19, 26.
[37] Catherine R. Stimpson, 'Feminism and Feminist Criticism', *Massachusetts Review*, 24/2 (Summer 1983), 282.

obviously of importance. Nor should we lose sight of the fact that the obsessive anxiety and terror apparent in so much Gothic fiction is supplied by the threat of one being (or institution) exerting total power over another—a terror which, as David Seed points out, can supply 'a broader theme than specifically sexual fear or domination'.[38]

What I am suggesting, then, is that a theoretical negativity is retarding rather than advancing the feminist project. I share with Myriam Diaz-Diocaretz the conviction that

the self-proclaimed authoritative word of patriarchy excluding women at different levels is not conclusive, is not and can never be the last word. If women in specific collective or individual situations have been muted, this cannot be a permanent situation, nor is it a universal, all-encompassing, or abstract condition.[39]

Her argument is based on 'the very existence of feminist discourse as a strategy to disclose the hegemony of patriarchal discursive structures'. As Bakhtin made clear, discourse is always unfinalized. Indeed, the power of his idea of unfinalizability and its importance for women can be seen again when we examine the historical circumstances in which the novel itself arose. Bakhtin's theory of dialogism allows us to offer a new account of women's role in this rise, one which counters the negativity of much feminist literary-critical praxis.

Eighteenth-Century Women Writers and the Discourses of Sensibility and Genius

As we have seen, for Gilbert and Gubar, in their construction of a 'great tradition' beginning with the works of Jane Austen, the woman writer's 'anxiety of authorship' is all-pervasive. It is posited as the major hurdle facing women who aimed to achieve authority in 'telling their own stories', that is, in telling stories which dealt with experiences central to women and which employed female personae. But if, as they argue,

---

[38] David Seed, 'Gothic Definitions', *Novel*, 14/3 (Spring 1981), 271.

[39] Myriam Diaz-Diocaretz, 'Bakhtin, Discourse and Feminist Theories', *Critical Studies*, 1/2 (1989) 131.

the female author was always a cultural anomaly[40] because
'denied the economic, social, and psychological status ordinar-
ily essential to creativity',[41] we are left with the problem of
explaining just how women writers so rapidly appropriated
the novel during the eighteenth century.[42]

As the *Monthly Review* commented in 1773, 'this branch of
the literary trade' was 'almost entirely engrossed by the
Ladies'.[43] Furthermore, we cannot simply dismiss the phenomenon, *pace* Ian Watt, as 'a purely quantitative assertion of
dominance'.[44] Nor can we award these writers the 'parsley
wreath' of a gratuitous popularity only with readers of their
own sex, of anachronistically referring to their products as
'Silly Novels by Lady Novelists'.[45] For female authority in the
genre, at least in some quarters, *was* being acknowledged. 'Of
the various species of composition which come before us',
claimed the *Monthly Review* again in December 1790, 'there
are none in which our writers of the male sex have less
excelled, since the days of Richardson and Fielding, than in the
arrangement of the novel.' Indeed, the reviewer went on to
complain, 'Ladies seem to appropriate to themselves an exclusive privilege in this kind of writing.'[46] Richard Polwhele, too,
in the preface to his satire on women *The Unsex'd Females*
(1789), complained that it was 'a sign of the corruption of the
age that works by women should be judged on their merits,
with the same impartiality as it seems right to exercise towards

[40] Vineta Colby prefaces *The Singular Anomaly* (New York and London:
New York University Press and London University Press, 1970) with W. S.
Gilbert's lines for Ko-Ko's 'Little List' in *The Mikado*: 'And that singular
anomaly, the lady novelist | I don't think she'd be missed—I'm sure she'd not
be missed.'
[41] Gilbert and Gubar, *Madwoman in the Attic*, 71.
[42] This question is also the subject in Nancy Armstrong, 'The Rise of
Feminine Authority in the Novel', *Novel*, 15/2 (Winter 1982), 127–45. Armstrong agrees that Gilbert and Gubar do not account for what appear to be
the facts of women's appropriation of the novel, but her account focuses on
19th- rather than 18th-cent. authors.
[43] Cited in Tompkins, *Popular Novel in England*, 120.
[44] Watt, *Rise of the Novel*, 310.
[45] The title of an essay by George Eliot, cited by Gilbert and Gubar,
Madwoman in the Attic, 72.
[46] Cited in Tompkins, *Popular Novel in England*, 120–1, n. 3.

men'.[47] The rise in the authority of novels penned by women continued throughout the 1780s and 1790s, despite the conspicuous and frequent condescension of male critics. This is instanced by the fact that anonymous publication by women 'decreased somewhat',[48] and, with the enormous popularity of Ann Radcliffe's Gothic romances, recognition of 'true' literary merit was more in evidence, as will be seen when, in Chapter 3, we come to examine the reception of her work.

How, then, are we to account for the rising fortunes of women on the literary scene?

The commonly proffered (but also recently contested) explanation is that women of the middle class, more leisured than previously, used their spare time at home in reading and literary pursuits.[49] Another consideration is the growth of book publishing and marketing as entrepreneurial enterprises; women, like men, no longer needed to be dependent on patrons.[50] But these points do little to explain the surmounting by women of difficulties in making public their work. It was, after all, a time when women's labour had been devalued by the growth of a market-place economy,[51] when marriage, virtually the only respectable path for women, immediately suspended or 'covered' their legal and social status,[52] when education for girls and young women was haphazard in the extreme,[53] and when the maintenance of reputation or propriety was very important.[54] How was it that women could

[47] Quoted in Margaret Kirkham, *Jane Austen, Feminism and Fiction* (Brighton: Harvester, 1983), p. xvi.

[48] Mary Poovey, *The Proper Lady and the Woman Writer* (Chicago and London: University of Chicago Press, 1984), 36.

[49] Richard D. Altick, *The English Common Reader* (Chicago: University of Chicago Press, 1957), 45; Armstrong, 'Rise of Feminine Authority in the Novel', 128 n. 5.

[50] Poovey, *Proper Lady and the Woman Writer*, 36–7.

[51] Viola Klein, *The Feminine Character: History of an Ideology* (London: Kegan Paul, French, Trubner, 1946), 14–15.

[52] Irene Taylor and Gina Luria, 'Gender and Genre: Women in British Romantic Literature', in Marlene Springer, ed., *What Manner of Woman: Essays on English and American Literature* (New York: New York University Press, 1977), 98–9.

[53] Ibid. 100–1; Josephine Kamm, *Hope Deferred: Girls' Education in English History* (London: Methuen, 1965), chs. 6–10.

[54] Poovey, *Proper Lady and the Woman Writer*, ch. 1.

write with confidence about courtship, marriage, education, authority, domestic issues, and women's feelings and status, whether in the Sentimental or Gothic mode? And, more particularly, why were they able to give freer reign than previously to the imagination, thereby emancipating the novel from the injunctions of Fielding and Clara Reeve about use of the supernatural and those of Dr Johnson about didacticism as the exclusive purpose of the novel?[55] Was it, perhaps, that women at this time believed that they had something special to offer in writing romances and novels?

Katharine M. Rogers, in *Feminism in Eighteenth-Century England*, stresses the positive aspect of Sentimentalism as a literary cult which, though it can be viewed 'as undermining the cause of women's rights by glorifying female martyrdom and exaggerating female helplessness', yet asserted the worth of 'feminine perceptions and values', so giving women 'confidence to express themselves and to claim emotional fulfilment'.[56] A similar argument is put forward by Mary Poovey, who claims that 'the novel of sensibility, developing along the patterns established by Richardson, provided women with a genre apparently tailor-made for their experience, confined as it was to domestic concerns and affairs of the heart'.[57] In support she quotes from Hannah More's *Strictures on the Modern System of Female Education* (1799). Although More's work, like the novels of Ann Radcliffe and Jane Austen, is often critical of excessive sentimentalism, it affirms women's 'natural' suitability for this mode of composition:

In almost all that comes under the description of polite letters, in all that captivates by imagery or warms by just and affecting sentiment, women are excellent . . . They are acute observers, and accurate judges of life and manners, as far as their own sphere of observation extends; but they describe a smaller circle.

Poovey's comment on this statement is that the qualities of observation and judgement which women displayed, as well as

[55] Dr Johnson's prescriptions of 1780 are discussed by Birkhead, *Tale of Terror*, 7.
[56] Katharine Rogers, *Feminism in Eighteenth-Century England* (Urbana, Chicago, and London: University of Illinois Press, 1982), 143.
[57] Poovey, *Proper Lady and the Woman Writer*, 37–8.

their novelistic strategies, were 'characteristically feminine', but not in More's sense of being 'natural to women'. Rather, it was that their novelistic abilities 'characterized women's learned or internalized responses to the objective female social situation, which was founded on the prerogatives of bourgeois society and imposed by propriety'.[58]

It could equally be adduced, however, that this naturalization and privileging of sensibility in women, to which More's *Strictures* and other conduct books subscribed, was as much a function of 'medical' discourse as of representations of femininity in Richardson and later Sentimental or Gothic novels. John Mullan, for example, has recently demonstrated that the often popularized writings of eighteenth-century physicians—on melancholy, hypochondria, hysteria, and other nervous disorders—share with Sentimental novels 'the ambivalence of a sensibility which can stand for either privilege or affliction'.[59] In both forms of writing sensibility is established as fashionable, and, especially when it is not excessive and hence severely afflictive or improper, it is celebrated as a desirable and enviable asset to which women may lay particular claim, even if they are thereby also inherently 'more subject to nervous complaints and have them in a higher degree'.[60]

According to the medical forms of the myth, 'only men of a particular merit or refinement tend to suffer from what is called hypochondria': scholars, writers, those who remove themselves from the mercantile world and lead a sedentary life.[61] In this way the domain of sensibility is constituted in opposition to the world of economic and political power. William Stukely's explanatory model of nervous disorder of 1723, for instance, goes as follows: 'We know 'tis a common observation in our practice, that the modish disease call'd the

---

[58] Ibid. 43. See also Hannah More, *Strictures on the Modern System of Female Education*, 2nd edn. (London: T. Cadell, Jr. and W. Davies, 1799), ii. 26.

[59] John Mullan, 'Hypochondria and Hysteria: Sensibility and the Physicians', *Eighteenth Century: Theory and Interpretation*, 25/2 (Spring 1984), 142. A later version of this appears as the final chapter of his *Sentiment and Sociability: The Language of Feeling in the Eighteenth Century* (Oxford: Clarendon Press, 1988), 201–40.

[60] Ibid. 147, 151.   [61] Ibid. 146.

vapours, and from its suppos'd seat, the SPLEEN, does frequently attack scholars *and persons of the soft sex most eminent for
wit and good sense.*'[62] This reasoning is virtually repeated
forty-five years later in William Smith's *Dissertation upon the
Nerves*: 'People of weak nerves are generally quick thinkers
from the delicacy of their sensitive organs.'[63] So, although in
such writing a distinction is often made between hypochondria (here meaning 'fatigue of mind', 'morbid melancholy',
'gloom and despair') and hysteria as (asymmetrical) afflictions
of men and women respectively, the association of a 'Disease'
(heightened sensibility which can pass into infirmity or 'Lun-
acy'), with specialized faculties or abilities, is the same for
both sexes. Robert Whytt's *Observations on the Nature and
Cures of those Disorders which have commonly been called
Nervous, Hypochondriac or Hysteria* (1765) puts it this way:

It is true that in women, hysteric symptoms occur more frequently,
and are often much more sudden and violent, than the hypochondriac in men; but this circumstance, which is only a consequence of
the more delicate frame, sedentary life, and particular condition of
the womb in women, by no means shews the two diseases to be,
strictly speaking, different.'[64]

Despite the reworking by Whytt and other physicians of the
old formulas about the womb, and the attendant emphasis on
the entire female body as 'an ever visible corpus of signs given
over to their practice of interpretation',[65] their often contradictory articulations of the myth of sensibility—'the ambiguous susceptibility'—open up a visible crack for aspiring
women writers. My conjecture is that it was one whereby
middle-class women could get a firmer foot in the door of
literature and other 'sedentary' intellectual pursuits and begin
to challenge the dominance of men.

[62] William Stukely, *Of the Spleen* (London, 1723), 25, quoted in Mullan,
'Hypochondria and Hysteria', 147 (my italics).
[63] William Smith, *A Dissertation upon the Nerves* (London: W. Owen,
1768), 191, quoted in Mullan, 'Hypochondria and Hysteria', 147.
[64] Robert Whytt, *Observations on the Nature, Causes and Cures of those
Disorders which have been commonly called Nervous, Hypochondriac, or
Hysteria* (Edinburgh: J. Balfour, 1765), 105, quoted in Mullan, 'Hypochondria and Hysteria', 153.
[65] Mullan, 'Hypochondria and Hysteria', 157.

Josephine Donovan, on the other hand, deflecting interest in the cult of sensibility, argues in 'The Silence is Broken' that 'it was lack of education rather than any particular affinity with sentiment that led women to dwell upon feeling in their fiction'.[66] That is, in default of an intellectual education, women could only fall back—with a sense of inferiority—on their own experience, confined as it was to matters of love, marriage, family, and this was what attracted them to writing in the medium of the novel during the course of the eighteenth century. This view appears to be supported by the comments of Mrs Eliza Haywood in the Dedication to her Sentimental novel, *The Fatal Secret* (1724):

But as I am a Woman, and consequently depriv'd of those Advantages of Education which the other Sex enjoy, I cannot . . . imagine it in my Power to soar to any subject higher than that which Nature is not negligent to teach us. Love is a topick which I believe few are ignorant of; there requires no aids of learning . . .[67]

However, Donovan fails to comment here on the tone of reproof, bordering on sarcasm, which is suggested by the choice of 'depriv'd' and 'negligent': Nature, unlike (male) Culture is 'not negligent'. Mrs Haywood can also be read as calling for 'a return to Nature', a privileging of Nature over Culture; beneath her disavowals of (male) learning lies a belief and confidence in the worth of Nature's lessons and her own ability to write about them. One suspects that she would have endorsed the sentiments of Mary Astell's Preface to *Travels of an English Lady in Europe, Asia and Africa* (1724):

Let the Male-Authors with an envious eye
Praise coldly, that they the more decry:
Women (at least I speak the Sense of some)
This little Spirit of Rivalship o'ercome.
I read with transport, and with Joy I greet
A Genius so sublime and so Complete,
And gladly lay my Laurels at her Feet.[68]

[66] Josephine Donovan, 'The Silence is Broken', in McConnell-Ginet, ed., *Women and Language in Literature and Society*, 209.
[67] Ibid. 208–9. Also cited in Robert Adams Day, *Told in Letters: Epistolary Fiction Before Richardson* (Ann Arbor: University of Michigan, 1966), 81.
[68] Cited in Kirkham, *Jane Austen, Feminism and Fiction*, 7.

The Travels of Lady Mary Wortley Montagu, according to Astell, are written with a freshness and originality not found in the writings of men.

A further but related reason put forward by Donovan for the gravitation of women towards the novel concerns the way in which the new genre broke with established literary conventions. Because there were no acceptable classical models for the novel and it dealt with everyday life in the 'plain style' it was excluded from consideration as 'high' or serious literature, an attitude which prevented male writers of the educated élite from appropriating it while allowing women and 'other cultural outsiders (less educated men)' the freedom to use and develop it.[69] Women, already well practised in the writing of letters, diaries, and journals, were able to benefit from the ease with which they could employ these often anecdotal and narrative forms.

Now, the notion of the novel's break with classical convention is a valid and important point to make. However, this argument also leads her in a negative direction. By her reference to 'less educated men' as 'other cultural outsiders', Donovan appears to be gesturing in the direction of Richardson, who we know, on his own account, had 'only common School-Learning'.[70] Richardson's use of what Ian Watt calls 'an essentially feminine, and from a literary point of view, amateur, tradition of letter-writing' did expose him to spoof, parody, and adverse criticism by those who considered him something of a literary upstart.[71] On the other hand, his *Pamela* (1740–1), *Clarissa* (1747–8), and *Sir Charles Grandison* (1753–4) were also extremely popular, more often than not praised, and the issues they raised seriously debated by many eminent and learned people. There was, it seems, a sense of the novel's potential as the modern form just as there was a similar excitement about the future of film for a mass audience early in this century. So much so that Terry Eagleton, in a recent work, conceives of Richardson as a Gramscian 'organic

---

[69] Donovan, 'Silence is Broken', 209–10.
[70] T. C. Duncan Eaves and Ben D. Kimpel, *Samuel Richardson: A Biography* (Oxford: Clarendon Press, 1971), 10.
[71] Watt, *Rise of the Novel*, 201; Eaves and Kimpel, *Samuel Richardson*, 140–1, 200, 511.

intellectual' and the chief protagonists of his novels as 'public property subject to strategic uses, lynchpins of an entire ideological formation'.[72] Richardson's printing firm, too, is seen as a 'thriving capitalist enterprise . . . the centre of a vast ideological network, the nub of a whole discursive formation'.[73] Fashionable rhetoric aside, Eagleton's point that Richardson's novels made a strong challenge to aristocratic values, including what Ian Watt calls 'traditional decorums of prose', and helped establish 'the 'feminization' of language and values . . . which is closely allied with the emergence of the bourgeoisie',[74] is borne out by Eaves and Kimpel's monumental *Biography*. There, in the descriptions of Richardson's life and reception of his works, we see the justice of Eagleton's Foucauldian claim that Richardson's texts 'entwine with commerce, religion, theatre, ethical debate, the visual arts, public entertainment'—that they become 'organizing forces of . . . the bourgeois "public sphere" '.[75] Richardson is not to be regarded simply as participating in this sphere, but as *helping to construct it*. And, for this reason, Donovan's description of Richardson as a 'cultural outsider' won't do.

Indeed, she herself reproduces Ian Watt's surmise that Richardson was consciously attempting to overturn the neoclassical tradition:

There is at least a strong suggestion in *Clarissa* that he regarded his own literary style as infinitely superior to those of the classically educated . . . Anna Howe [a character in *Clarissa*] tells us that '*mere* scholars' too often 'spangle over their productions with metaphors; they rumble into *bombast*: the *sublime* with them, lying in *words* and not in sentiment'; while others 'sinking into the classical pits, there poke and scramble about never seeking to show genius of their own'.[76]

---

[72] Terry Eagleton, *The Rape of Clarissa* (Oxford: Clarendon Press, 1982), 5.
[73] Ibid. 7.
[74] In speaking of the 'feminization of language and values', Eagleton, *Rape of Clarissa*, 14, pins the gender of literary language not to the sex of the writer, but to the conventions of a genre (the novel) and the changing values of a reading formation.
[75] Ibid. 6.
[76] Donovan, 'Silence is Broken', 210; Watt, *Rise of the Novel*, 194. For other, similar passages in Richardson's writing, see Eaves and Kimpel, *Samuel Richardson*, 89, 568, 587.

Here and elsewhere Richardson's texts repudiate classical conventions in favour of something (to which I shall return later) called 'genius of [one's] own'. Yet Donovan goes on to stage the emergence of women novelists (to whom 'other cultural outsiders' such as Richardson are assimilated) as a phenomenon dependent almost entirely on women's lack of classical education, their isolation from the larger culture, and 'the breakdown of classical control over literature and the emergence of a non-traditional genre like the novel'. My contention is that all of these factors are either negative attributes or *faits accomplis* which betoken little space-clearing, leverage, or struggle on the part of women themselves. True, she does discuss in detail the tradition established by women in the early seventeenth century, of semi-private letter-writing and autobiography or memoir in the vernacular, a practice which frequently involved their championing of 'the plain style'; but women's capitalization on this asset is always seen as awaiting other developments in which they seem to play no part.[77]

That women, like men, were intimately involved in the struggle to redefine 'literature', were *themselves* instrumental in helping to shape a new, predominantly bourgeois, practice of writing is evident from the activities of those critically astute literary women—most often ladies of the 'bluestocking' salons—who surrounded Richardson and with whom he established solidarity. Again, Eagleton sums up neatly the detailed descriptions of Richardson's activities which we have from Eaves and Kimpel: 'he is preoccupied with the material practice of writing, the potentially endless process of wrangles and revisions, the complex business of circulating drafts, conflating criticisms, initiating dialogues and establishing friendships.'[78] Despite his doctor's diagnosis of 'Scurbutico Nervoso from a secondary studious life',[79] Richardson did not shrink from contact with others and did not neglect his business interests. Nor must it be thought that the women who, like his male friends, read his manuscripts, debated their nuances,

[77] It is of interest that, in two recent essays, Donovan has moved some way from this position to make use of a Bakhtinian approach. I will examine these essays in the final section of this chapter.

[78] Eagleton, *Rape of Clarissa*, 11–12.

[79] Mullan, 'Hypochondria and Hysteria', 145.

wrote him letters, and helped sustain 'a constant circulation of discourse', did so in any merely sycophantic way. As Eagleton says, 'fervent discussions around the gradually evolving Clarissa or Grandison, anguished contentions over their desirable destinies, became modes of ever finer ideological formulation, scrupulous probings of precise meanings'.[80]

Margaret Kirkham, in *Jane Austen, Feminism and Fiction*, also stresses the opening up of dialogue and the questioning of moral and social values which were precipitated by the writing of Richardson's novels.[81] The family, the relations between the sexes, the proper conduct of men and women, the portrayal in novels of 'mixed characters'—positions were defined, formulations challenged, in letters running to sets or series of hundreds of pages.[82] Hester Mulso and Elizabeth Carter, for example, maintained that Clarissa was 'too fearful of the curse of an unjust father'. Frances Grainger and Sarah Chapone also questioned the complete submission of daughters to parental authority. The latter particularly disputed Clarissa's meekness in allowing her father to keep the estate willed to her by her grandfather. Richardson appeared to her 'to have promulgated the harsh idea that women should never be independent and thus to have denied that they are members of society and free agents'.[83]

These women were also alert to what John Duncombe called Richardson's 'weak strains', that is, his sometimes ambivalent support of the parity of male and female genius, and long disputations regarding the cultivation of the female mind were common.[84] Richardson might write to Lady Bradshaigh (who did not approve of learning in women) that if a woman had genius, it should be allowed to take its course, 'as well as in men', but this apparent 'feminism' was misleading as it was usually qualified by a concern for the priority of domestic duties. Of this Eaves and Kimpel give ample evidence, concluding that 'whenever Richardson appears as a favourer of women's genius, which ... should not be suppressed, he

---

[80] Eagleton, *Rape of Clarissa*, 12.
[81] Kirkham, *Jane Austen, Feminism and Fiction*, 16–29.
[82] Eaves and Kimpel, *Samuel Richardson*, 345.
[83] Ibid. 200, 288, 353.   [84] Ibid. 200, 345, 563.

quickly adds that a woman who neglects her domestic duties is good for nothing'.[85] Such ambivalence was, however, always a catalyst to further discussion and, overall, it can be said that Richardson was not backward in recognizing—at least in letters to male friends—'Women of real Genius', such as Miss Highmore, Miss Mulso, and Mrs Carter.[86] His support could hardly have failed to contribute to the growing confidence of women in pursuing questions related to morals, education, and literature, whether in discussion or writing. Furthermore, such women of the Richardson coterie and other bluestocking circles—women who gained reputations as readers and conversationalists, or as writers—must *themselves* have given authority to the viewpoint of women in writing.

Certainly Mary Poovey is of this opinion:

the informal society of the Bluestockings provided a model for the literary women . . . Elizabeth Carter for example, read Latin, Greek, Hebrew, French, Italian, Spanish, German, Portuguese and Arabic, published her first poem at seventeen, made 1,000 pounds by the subscription publication of her translation of Epictetus, and saw her collected poems go into three editions. Such 'Blues' as Elizabeth Montagu, Emily Boscawen, Hester Chapone, and Hannah More were significant because they preserved their unimpeachable reputations *and* published for profit and public esteem. Thus they helped elevate what had been genteel amateurism into an acceptable professional career.[87]

In this she confirms the findings of Robert Halsband who makes the further point that the English Bluestocking assemblies were more attractive than the French salons in that they were 'not intended to be pretentiously learned'.[88] From their letters to one another, it can be seen that these women valued the power of imagination and laid claim to a heightened, artistic sensibility in their often melancholy appreciation of the sublime in nature. They wrote frequently of their reading

---

[85] Ibid. 564.   [86] Ibid. 565.
[87] Poovey, *Proper Lady and the Woman Writer*, 37.
[88] Robert Halsband, 'Lady of Letters in the Eighteenth Century', in Irvin Ehrenpreis and Robert Halsband, eds., *The Lady of Letters in the Eighteenth Century* (William Andrews Clark Memorial Library, Seminar Paper 29, Los Angeles: University of California Press, 1969), 46.

and, as they travelled, of their responses to natural scenery and architecture. Rejecting the Greek and Roman classics which formed the basis of the education system for men, they favoured 'the productions of the Gothic Muse'.[89]

At this time, then, writing gained in respectability as a professional pursuit for women and their texts influenced later works by both sexes. For example, it is clear that Ann Radcliffe supplemented handsomely whatever resources she and her husband possessed by receiving £500 for *The Mysteries of Udolpho* and £800 for *The Italian*. Though little is known of her life, according to the *Annual Biography and Obituary for 1824*, as a child she met Mrs Piozzi and Mrs Montagu and so knew of their activities even if she chose not to enter literary circles in adult life—a choice for which her recurrent attacks of asthma may have accounted more than a little. An opportunity to meet Elizabeth Carter was lost on account of the ill health of her journalist husband, William, proprietor and editor of the *English Chronicle*.[90] Nevertheless, it seems certain that Radcliffe both knew and drew on the work of the 'Blues'. Thomas Green comments in his *Diary of a Lover of Literature* (1800) on her use, in *The Mysteries of Udolpho*, of Mrs Piozzi's *Observations and Reflections made in the Course of a Journey through France, Italy and Germany*, and further comparisons made by Clara Frances McIntyre have suggested the extent of this debt.[91] Radcliffe's heroines also share Elizabeth Carter's Burkean view that ' "sublime views of wild uncultivated nature", whether in nature or in Salvator, caused "the soul to expand itself and feel at once both the greatness of its capacities and the littleness of its pursuits" '.[92] Her works, in short, like those of her contemporary Matthew Lewis, mesh into intertextual relationships with the writings of women as well as of men.

[89] Elizabeth Carter, *Letters to Mrs. Montague between the Years 1755 and 1800*, ed. Revd Montague Pennington (London: F. C. & J. Rivington, 1817), ii. 311, 312.
[90] Clara Frances McIntyre, *Ann Radcliffe in Relation to Her Time* (New Haven, Conn. and London: Yale University Press, 1920), 23.
[91] Ibid. 58–61.
[92] Eugene Bernard Murray, *Ann Radcliffe* (New York: Twayne Publishers, 1972), 58.

It is also possible to view women's investment at this time in
the Sentimental mode and later, in the Gothic mode, more
positively than critics like Donovan have done. The increasing
subscription to notions of 'sensibility' and 'genius' were closely connected; the former, among other things, included the
ability to arrive at a truth instinctively. Continued demonstration and representation of possession of both attributes by
women could perhaps be thought to make them paradigmatic
examples of 'the author', even if those same attributes also
required them to be sensitive and reticent about declaring their
authorship openly in the market-place. It may have been true
that 'in the minor fiction of the eighteenth century anonymity
was the rule' and that 'women writers in particular . . . affected this concealment',[93] but such delicacy often did not
prevent them from circulating their work amongst their peers,
à la Richardson, before publication, or from writing prefaces
to their work which gave clues to who the author might be. In
many cases these prefaces were even signed.[94] Those who did
publish under their own names almost always gave some
justification for doing so which would cancel out the negative
impression of publishing for fame or profit. Sarah Fielding,
Charlotte Smith, and Eliza Parsons, for example, wrote out
of real financial necessity, Clara Reeve and Ann Radcliffe
avowedly to instruct or provide temporary escape for the
reader from cares and grief.[95] Richardson had published his
first novel, *Pamela, or Virtue Rewarded*, anonymously, Walpole his *Otranto* pseudonymously, and once the fears induced
by their risk-taking had been alleviated by the approbation
their works received, they declared their authorship openly.
The code operating here in their favour seems to have been
that sensibility is modest but 'genius will out'. It is alluded to

[93] Dorothy Blakey, *The Minerva Press 1790–1820* (London: Oxford
University Press, 1939), 48.
[94] Tompkins, *Popular Novel in England*, 117; Ehrenpreis, *Lady of Letters
in the Eighteenth Century*, 39.
[95] Tompkins, *Popular Novel in England*, 117, comments on financial
necessity, as does Bette B. Roberts, *The Gothic Romance: Its Appeal to
Women Readers and Writers in Late Eighteenth-Century England* (New York:
Arno Press, 1980), 18–19; Clara Reeve, *Old English Baron*, Preface; Ann
Radcliffe, *The Mysteries of Udolpho* (Oxford: Oxford University Press,
1980), 672.

by John Aikin when he writes of the 'pursuit of excellence' in the artist of genius: 'It is, indeed, a disposition so ready to burst forth into display, that it scarcely admits of concealment, and as Dryden beautifully says of Mrs. Killegrew, whom he represents as fired with passion for universal excellence, the "bright soul breaks out on every side".'[96] This code is utilized by Mrs Brooke in *The Excursion* (1771) when the poet-heroine, Maria, having kept her writing activities secret, decides to publish—but not before she has decided to submit her work to a distinguished critic for advice. The authorial comment on Maria's reaction as she rereads her poem is as follows: 'Diffident as she was by nature, that enthusiasm inseparable from true genius broke through the veil which modesty would have thrown over the merits of this piece.'[97] Maria's opinion is subsequently confirmed, and the incident would seem to offer a model of authorial behaviour for women, including Mrs Brooke herself.

So many novels were published and circulated via circulating libraries during the final decades of the century, however, that the monetary aspect of publishing was acutely visible, a foregrounding that was exacerbated by unscrupulous practices in the publishing trade.[98] Among other reasons, this, ironically, may have been a factor in encouraging more authors, including women, to sign their work at this time.[99] Dorothy Blakey, in *The Minerva Press*, cites the case of a woman who published a signed Advertisement in her novel to prevent misappropriation of her name and/or work.[100]

Nowadays the earlier reticence and retirement of women authors is often viewed as a sign of their impotence, passivity, and subordination, the deliberate relegation of women in general to the private sphere, their 'proper sphere' as it was called by moralists of the time. Women, it was said, should be 'contributing daily and hourly to the comfort of husbands, of

---

[96] John Aikin, 'Thoughts on the Formation of Character', in *Memoir of John Aikin, M.D. with a Selection of his Miscellaneous Pieces, Biographical, Moral and Critical* (London: Baldwin, Cradock, and Joy, 1823), 387.

[97] Quoted in Tompkins, *Popular Novel in England*, 118.

[98] Blakey, *Minerva Press*, 29–30.

[99] Tompkins, *Popular Novel in England*, 20.

[100] Blakey, *Minerva Press*, 49–50.

parents, of brothers and sisters . . . in the intercourse of domestic life'.[101] And while it is true that freedoms and opportunities for women were limited by the operation of powerful
patriarchal norms, it should be noted that, from a late eighteenth-century perspective, the failure of a woman to 'own' her
work was not necessarily a function of a specifically 'female'
anxiety or sense of inferiority. Likewise, to have a father,
brother, or husband negotiate with a publisher (as was the case
with Fanny Burney, Jane Austen, Mary Shelley, and probably
Ann Radcliffe) was not necessarily experienced as a great
incapacity. If a dominant cultural code was that 'sentiment
and sensibility are displayed only through movements of retreat and specialization, only as they are opposed and excited
by the world',[102] then authorial reticence was 'natural', a
modesty predicated on one's sensibility, rather than simply on
the fact of being female. Sensibility may have been constituted
'in various ways, out of an opposition to a "world" of masculine desire, commercial endeavour and material ambition',
but this privileged 'feminine' model of behaviour—either of
virtue or affliction—was not confined to women or to novelists. At least one commentator, John Aikin, complained about
the 'cant of authorship' attendant on professions of sensibility
with which poets prefaced their anthologies.[103] Nor was sensibility always deemed available to 'the common people', male
or female.[104] As we shall see in the following chapter, the
sensibility and benevolence of the semi-aristocratic Monsieur
St Aubert in Ann Radcliffe's *The Mysteries of Udolpho* are
coextensive with his desire for retirement from 'the busy
scenes of the world', for a return to nature: 'he retired from
the multitude "more in *pity* than in anger", to scenes of simple
nature, to the pure delights of literature, and to the exercise of
domestic virtues.'[105]

[101] Thomas Gisborne, *Enquiries into the Duties of the Female Sex* (London: Cadell and Davies, 1797), 12. Mary Poovey, in *Proper Lady and the Woman Writer*, ch. 1, also cites various moralistic tracts by clergymen and Evangelical reformers who wished to confine women to domestic interests and activities.
[102] Mullan, 'Hypochondria and Hysteria', 146.
[103] Aikin, *Miscellaneous Pieces*, 452.
[104] Mullan, 'Hypochondria and Hysteria', 149–50, 173.
[105] Radcliffe, *Udolpho*, 1. Further references appear in the text.

Similarly, it is in such retirement that Emily St Aubert's own 'native genius', 'uncommon delicacy of mind . . . and ready benevolence' are nourished (*Udolpho*, pp. 3, 5). It is not without significance that Emily is established in the first chapter of the novel as a budding poet, one who has been given 'an exact acquaintance with every part of elegant literature', and who has 'discovered in her early years a taste for works of genius' (*Udolpho*, p. 6). In this novel, men and women outside the world of mercantile and political life—that is, of commercial enterprise and material ambition—are susceptible to hypochondria, melancholy, nervous disorder, and, by this very 'excess', to the possibility of evil in the form of greed, lust, or madness. But those who strive for virtuous balance are also endowed with 'exquisite sensibility', imagination, and delicacy—and the capacity for art or writing which comes out of them.

Pope alluded to the dual aspect of the 'nervous disease' as early as 1712, in that section of *The Rape of the Lock* where the gnome is made to address the wayward Queen who rules women:

> Parent of Vapours and of Female Wit,
> Who give th' *Hysteric* or *Poetic* Fit,
> On various Tempers act by various ways,
> Make some take Physick, others scribble Plays.'[106]

According to Robert Halsband, here women dramatists are ridiculed 'not so much because they are women writers as because they inhabit Grub Street'.[107] They possess what John Duncombe, that champion of female genius, in 1754 termed a 'bold, unblushing mien'.[108] Pope's allusion is to the sexual indiscretions and frank commercialism of the hack dramatist, as represented by the successful women dramatists of the late Restoration period. Such was their reputation that later

---

[106] Alexander Pope, 'The Rape of the Lock', in *The Poems of Alexander Pope*, ed. John Butt (London: Methuen, 1963), 234.

[107] Robert Halsband, 'Women and Literature in 18th Century England', in Paul Fritz and Richard Norton, eds., *Women in the 18th Century and Other Essays* (Toronto and Sarasota: Samuel Stevens Hakkert, 1976), 61.

[108] John Duncombe, 'The Feminiad, or Female Genius', in Dominic Bevan Wyndham Lewis and Charles Lee, eds., *The Stuffed Owl: An Anthology of Bad Verse* (London and Melbourne: Dent, 1984), 102.

women writers shrank from writing for the public stage.[109] During the latter half of the eighteenth century, however, the novel was the conspicuous genre, and much greater critical praise and authority began to be given to women writers and to the individual's nurturing of artistic talent in general. The question of how these developments arose has been addressed in part by consideration of the impact of Richardson's texts, the 'feminization' of the novel, the cult of sensibility, and the Bluestocking circles. But there is a further dimension to this story, one which involves explication of the changing nature of the concepts of 'genius' and what it meant to be an author.

Eighteenth-Century Women Writers and 'Original Genius'

Taking up a challenge made by Michel Foucault in 'What is an Author?' Martha Woodmansee sets out to explore the genesis of the modern (pre-structuralist) concept of the author, which she defines as 'an individual who is solely responsible—and therefore exclusively deserving of credit—for the production of a unique work'.[110] In the main her argument is made with reference to the emergence of copyright and the professional writer in Germany, but what she says about the ways in which some eighteenth-century theorists and writers set about redefining the nature of writing is, I believe, relevant to the emergence of the woman novelist in England and invites further exploration.

According to Woodmansee, from the time of the Renaissance until about the middle of the eighteenth century, the 'author' was an unstable marriage of two distinct concepts. Primarily he was constituted as a craftsman: 'master of a body of rules, preserved and handed down to him in rhetoric and poetics, for manipulating traditional materials in order to achieve the effects prescribed by the cultivated audience of the court to which he owed both his livelihood and social

---

[109] F. P. Lock, 'Astrae's "Vacant Throne": The Successors of Aphra Behn', in Fritz and Norton, eds., *Women in the 18th Century and Other Essays*, 27.

[110] Martha Woodmansee, 'The Genius and the Copyright: Economic and Legal Conditions for the Emergence of the "Author" ', *Eighteenth Century Studies*, 17/4 (Summer 1984), 425–48.

status'.[111] As this concept did not always seem sufficient to account for a writer's achievement of really outstanding work, however, an adjunct or supplement was invoked—that of an inspirational Muse, or of God himself. Despite an apparent incompatibility between these notions, they continued to exist side by side 'until well into the eighteenth century'. Neither of these models, Woodmansee notes, ascribe personal responsibility to the writer for his creation; rather, the mind of the creative subject is always governed by independent forces even when he is considered to be inspired: 'the inspired moments of his work—that which is novel and most excellent in it—are not any more the writer's sole doing than are its more routine aspects, but are instead attributable to a higher, external agency—if not a muse then to divine dictation.'[112]

During the course of the eighteenth century, theorists moved away from this explanatory framework both by minimalizing (and sometimes discarding) the element of craftsmanship and by foregrounding the inspirational aspect. But the latter now was internalized, that is, it 'came to be regarded as emanating not from outside or above, but from within the writer himself'. The distinction is an important one; for once 'inspiration' came to be conceptualized in terms of what was called 'original genius', the 'inspired work was made peculiarly and distinctively the product—the property—of the writer'. The writer, in short, became both an author, replete with its Latinate sense of *auctor* (originator, founder, creator), and an owner.

Woodmansee's illustration of this shift in the cultural meanings attaching to writerly identity is convincing but brief, made by reference to statements from writers at either side of the new development. Her primary interest, as already indicated, is in the impact of the new meanings on the German cultural scene, particularly the use made by German writers of the idea of literary ownership to justify, in the form of a copyright law, legal recognition of that ownership. To this end she quotes from Edward Young's *Conjectures on Original Composition* (1759) which 'preached originality in place of

---

[111] Ibid. 426.   [112] Ibid. 427.

the reigning emphasis on the mastery of rules extrapolated from classical literature and . . . located the source of this essential quality in the poet's own genius'.[113] This work, she claims, had a profound effect in Germany, where it appeared by 1761 in two separate translations and was taken up and developed by writers of the calibre of Goethe, who produced theories of the arts which placed the author-genius, as creator of something original, at their centre. The influence of the *Conjectures* on English writers, on the other hand, falls outside the scope of Woodmansee's essay; it is not considered beyond the assertion that the work 'attracted relatively little attention in England'.

Yet its impact on the English scene was not as insignificant as Woodmansee suggests. For although it is true that Pope had already gained fame and fortune through his writing by 1730, women at that time were only just in the process of becoming professional writers and journalists—that is, for the first time becoming able to earn a living through the sale of their writing. Aphra Behn (1640–89) is believed to have been the first woman to earn her living in this way. And she was followed by three other 'remarkable poetesses and scribblers'—Susannah Centlivre, Mary Delarivière Manley, and the novelist Eliza Haywood, the only one still alive at the time when Richardson's novels were gaining reputation and renown. Less well known were the poets Mary Barber, Mary Chandler, Mary Masters, and Elizabeth Rowe, playwrights Mary Pix and Catherine Trotter, and about ten writers of fiction, including Sarah Fielding.[114] Such women were usually considered beyond the pale of respectability—'in general the low repute of fiction and the low repute of women who wrote it reinforced each other'—and they often became the butt of satire.[115] But by the mid-century women writers were increasing in number and output rapidly, as Dr Johnson noted:

In former times, the pen, like the sword, was consigned by nature to the hands of men . . . a female writer, like a female warrior, was considered a kind of eccentric being that deviated, however illustri-

---

[113] Ibid. 430.
[114] Ehrenpreis, *Lady of Letters in the Eighteenth Century*, 32–3.
[115] Ibid. 57.

ously, from her due sphere of motion, and was, therefore, rather to be gazed at with wonder, than countenanced by imitation . . . the revolution of years has now produced a generation of Amazons of the pen, who with the spirit of their predecessors have set masculine tyranny at defiance, asserted their claim to the regions of science, and seem resolved to contest the usurpation of virility . . . To what cause this universal eagerness of writing can be properly ascribed, I have not yet been able to discover.[116]

Ian Watt estimates that about 2,000 novels had been published by 1800, the majority of them written by women.[117]

As a document which asserts the equality of all 'human souls' and entertains the possibility of there having lived 'many a genius . . . which could neither write nor read',[118] the *Conjectures* would seem to have been a potentially enabling document for aspiring writers who had been excluded from the benefits of a classical education or, like Mary Astell (1666–1731), disputed the absolute necessity of classical authority to literary production.[119] Certainly the distillation of ideas which Young brought together appears to have encouraged working-class writers. The *Monthly Review* of 1778 might deem it presumptuous of any tailor, cobbler, or weaver to compose and seek to publish verse, but plebeian poets such as John Lucas and Ann Yearsley were most eloquent in their response to criticisms of the poetic imagination of working-class people. Ann Yearsley, whose 'primitive genius' was discovered and patronized by Hannah More, also produced a historical drama and a four-volume Gothic novel. Denying the value of traditional rules of composition, Yearsley, in her poem 'On Genius Unimproved', 'recommends to an "unlettered Poet" that he should ignore all these rules and regulations and give free vent to his inspiration and creative urge, which she holds to be present in greatest abundance in "untaught Minds". Her

---

[116] Samuel Johnson, *Johnson: Prose and Poetry* (London: Rupert Hart-Davis, 1963), 284.

[117] Watt, *Rise of the Novel*, 302, 310. Approximately 600 titles have been listed by Dale Spender, *Mothers of the Novel* (London and New York: Pandora Press, 1986), 119–37.

[118] Edward Young, *Edward Young's Conjectures on Original Composition*, ed. Edith J. Morley (Manchester: Longmans, Green, 1918), 17.

[119] Lock, 'Astrae's "Vacant Throne" ', 27.

own artistic sensibility she described in a similar way . . .'.[120]
Likewise the *Conjectures* urges the writer to place a greater
reliance on his own 'innate' wisdom, to tease out his own
'dormant, unsuspected abilities':

> let not great examples, or authorities browbeat thy reason into too
> great a diffidence of thyself: Thyself so reverence as to prefer the
> native growth of thy own mind to the richest import from abroad;
> such borrowed riches make us poor. The man who thus reverences
> himself, will soon find the world's reverence to follow his own. His
> works will stand distinguished; his the sole property of them; which
> property alone can confer the title of an author; that is, of one who
> (to speak accurately) thinks, and composes; while other invaders of
> the press, how voluminous, and learned soever, (with due respect be
> it spoken) only read and write.[121]

Such a 'democratic' view of the literary enterprise surely ought
to have had particular reverberations amongst women of all
classes.[122] What sort of circulation and reception in England,
then, did Young's text have?

According to Edith J. Morley, the first edition of 1,000
copies sold very rapidly and was followed by a second edition
in the same year.[123] Thereafter, however, the work was not
again separately printed, but appeared in volumes of Young's
works in 1770, 1774, 1778, 1798, and 1854. It would thus
appear that, although the *Conjectures* was neglected in the
nineteenth century, it was readily available during the latter
half of the eighteenth. As Morley demonstrates, discourse
about 'original' as opposed to 'imitative' genius had in fact
been in circulation since the beginning of the century, but it
had taken Young 'to sum up and emphasize their scattered
remarks in an essay, brief, brilliantly pointed, enthusiastic and

---

[120] H. Gustav Klaus, *The Literature of Labour: Two Hundred Years of Working-Class Writing* (Brighton: Harvester Press, 1985), 16–21.

[121] Young, *Conjectures*, 24.

[122] It might be objected that the discourse of the *Conjectures* is 'already sexed' because words such as 'man' and 'his' are employed. However, as Carol Steedman, *The Tidy House: Little Girls Writing* (London: Virago, 1982), 140–1, points out, women, on hearing (at times, supposedly sex-neutral) pronouns, have long refused to think of a man. Rather, they have thought of a genderless 'human being' or 'person'.

[123] Young, *Conjectures*, 50.

readable'.[124] Young's treatise was a 'sort of lit
Rights and Declaration of Independence', and,
that in literary circles the essay was received wit
able interest' and was 'eagerly discussed', Morley
Bibliography references from the *Gentleman's*
Scots Magazine, *Monthly Review*, *Critical Review*, and the
letters and journals of well-known figures: Horace Walpole,
Warburton, Richardson, Shenstone, Johnson, Boswell, Blair,
Mrs Hester Thrale Piozzi, Mrs Montagu, and Mrs Delany.
This reception suggests that Young's radical romanticism was
indeed influential in England and appropriated by women
writers as well as men.

Mrs Piozzi, for example, wrote that the *Conjectures* was 'the
wittiest piece of prose our whole language has to boast'.[125]
Mrs Delany recommended it to her sister with the comment
that it was 'written with the spirit of twenty-five rather than
fourscore years of age'.[126] And Mrs Montagu, writing of it in
a similar vein to Mrs Carter, compared genius to a needle
which finds itself lost in a haystack of learning, to which she
added humorously that Dr Young had been so categorical in
his affirmations, that she was sent in search of her own genius;
as she had stored only a little hay, she was counting on finding
it under that small portion but to date she had not made much
progress in her search.[127]

That Young's piece should have prompted such self-cultiva-
tion and tropes from middle- and upper-class women is not
surprising. We are ignorant not only of 'the dimensions of the
human mind in general, but even of our own', he wrote, and
therefore, when writers stumble on their 'yet unsuspected
genius', their surprise is great, as if they had seen a 'lucid
meteor in the night'. In fact, such is the specularity of the
writer's experience that

[124] Ibid., p. xiii.
[125] Hester Lynch (Salusbury) Thrale Piozzi, *Thraliana: The Diary of Mrs.
Hester Lynch Thrale 1776–1809*, ed. Katherine C. Balderstone (Oxford:
Clarendon Press, 1942), i. 354.
[126] Mary Delany, *The Autobiography and Correspondence of Mary Granville, Mrs. Delany*, ed. Lady Llanover (London: Richard Bentley, 1861), 559.
[127] Walter Thomas, *Le Poète Edward Young, étude sur sa vie et ses œuvres*
(Paris: Hachette, 1901), 476.

. . . 'it may be said to him, as to Eve at the lake,
What there thou seest, fair creature is thyself.'
Milt.
Genius, in this view, is like a dear friend in disguise; who, while we
are lamenting his absence drops his mask . . .'[128]

At no time had the descriptions of geniuses and women of sensibility been so close.

In addition to the serious attention given by the educated public to the doctrine of 'original genius'—which, interestingly for our study of the Gothic, also carried connotations of 'as in the origins of the world'—Young's spirited work was important for another reason. The association with Richardson which it invoked made it significant as a legitimation of the novel (Latin, *novellum*, new) as an 'original' and respectable literary form.

The essay's full title is *Conjectures on Original Composition in a Letter to the Author of Sir Charles Grandison*, and, as Alan D. McKillop showed long ago, Richardson was not merely 'the passive recipient of a dedication'. On the contrary, via a series of epistolary exchanges with Young, he had 'often played the part of a pietistic critic', encouraging his friend to mesh the theme of original with moral genius.[129] Within this context, we can read the following passage from the *Conjectures* as an allusion to Richardson and his novels:

A friend of mind has obeyed that injunction [to use one's talents for pietistic ends]; he has relied on himself, and with a genius, as well as moral, as original . . . has cast out evil spirits; has made a convert to virtue of a species of composition, once most its foe.[130]

This bid for a new Christian dispensation for the novel inspired both further experiment in the form and a more confident defence of its moral and cultural value.

Walpole's *Otranto*, written within five years of the *Conjectures*, can be taken as a case in point. Young had spoken of how 'an Original, by being . . . new, adds admiration to sur-

---

[128] Young, *Conjectures*, 23.
[129] Alan Dugald McKillop, 'Richardson, Young and the Conjectures', *Modern Philology*, 22 (May 1925), 404.
[130] Young, *Conjectures*, 34.

prize', and brings us under the writer's power: 'on the strong wind of his imagination, we are snatched from Britain to Italy . . . we have no home, no thought of our own; till the magician drops his pen . . .'.[131] *Otranto*, of course, is set in Italy, but more striking is the way in which Walpole obliquely makes a claim for the combined originality and piety of his Gothic tale.

In the Preface to the first edition, for example, adopting the persona of translator, he discourses on the beauty and simplicity of the 'original Italian' and the way in which the reader's attention is never relaxed. He then praises the tale's worth on moral grounds: 'The piety that reigns throughout, the lessons of virtue that are inculcated, and the rigid purity of the sentiments, exempt this work from the censure to which romances are but too liable.'[132] Even more pointed are his comments in the Preface to the second edition where he reveals 'the grounds on which he composed' *Otranto* and seeks pardon for his earlier deception. His work is now promoted as an attempt at something new—the blending of 'two kinds of romance'. His 'rule was nature' but in at least one aspect of his work he believed himself an imitator, his model being Shakespeare (lauded by Young as 'a star of first magnitude among the moderns'). Where, then, did that leave him as an author? In his final paragraph, Walpole sums up as follows:

The result of all I have said, is to shelter my own daring under the cannon of the brightest genius this country, at least, has produced. I might have pleaded, that having created a new species of romance, I was at liberty to lay down what rules I thought fit for the conduct of it: but I should be more proud of having imitated, however faintly, weakly, and at a distance, so masterly a pattern, than to enjoy the entire merit of invention, unless I could have marked my work with genius as well as with originality.[133]

With such profession of modesty is the attempt made to have it all ways; but Walpole obviously wants his readers to remember his work as an 'original composition' and himself, in an important respect, as the author-owner of his creation in Young's sense.

---

[131] Ibid.　　[132] Walpole, *Castle of Otranto*, 41.　　[133] Ibid. 48.

find Clara Reeve calling her first book *Original*
eral Occasions (1769). Her second, *The Cham-*
(later renamed *The Old English Baron*), is
the Preface as 'of a species, which though not
the common track'. Here Reeve makes it clear
that she is more than just an imitator. Critical of *Otranto*, she
composes upon Walpole's plan in order to deviate from it and
remedy the 'defects' of that 'singular book'.[134] Of the value of
such Gothic stories when given to serious moral purpose she
has no doubt: 'The business of Romance is, first, to excite the
attention; and, secondly, to direct it to some useful, or at least
innocent end. Happy the writer who attains both these points,
like Richardson!'[135] While it is true that Reeve withheld her
full signature from her work until 1788, the clarity and confidence with which she states the purpose of the form is
significant. No longer, it seems, need the novel or romance be
considered as necessarily lacking in respectability.

As we shall see in succeeding chapters, following Richardson
and Young, novels from *Otranto* to *Frankenstein* alluded in
some way to unmediated invention as the *sine qua non* of
authorship. Popular theory, too, continued to propound the
independent, primitive, or underived nature of 'original composition'. William Duff's *Essay on Original Genius* (1767), for
example, maintained that 'a Poet of original Genius has very
little occasion for the weak aid of literature: he is self-taught
... Nature supplies the materials of his composition; his senses are the underworkmen, while Imagination, like a masterly
Architect, superintends and directs the whole.'[136] It was, no
doubt, of such articles of faith that Mrs Piozzi was thinking
when in 1789 she commented that the current fashion made
well for women, as learning no longer figured prominently in
composition. 'Ladies', she continued, 'have therefore as good
a chance as People regularly bred to science in Times when
fire-eyed fancy is said to be the only requisite of a popular
poet.'[137] Duff at this time, moreover, sanctioned 'the invention

---

[134] Reeve, *Old English Baron*, p. vi.   [135] Ibid., p. v.
[136] William Duff, *An Essay on Original Genius* (London: E. and C. Dilly,
1767; reprint edn. New York: Garland, 1970), 281.
[137] Piozzi, *Thraliana*, 730, inc. n. 5.

of supernatural characters . . . and the exhibition of them, with their proper attitudes and offices' as 'the highest efforts and the most pregnant proofs of truly ORIGINAL GENIUS'.[138] Adumbrating the Gothic romances of Mrs Radcliffe, he writes of the 'shadowy substances and unreal objects' which the author calls into existence; such apparitions 'glide, like spectres, in silent, sullen majesty'. In reading about them, 'the blood runs chill in our veins, and our hair stiffens with horror'.[139]

Nor is this all. 'True Genius', according to this theorist, 'is removed from the din and tumult of business and care'; it blossoms best 'in the peaceful vale of rural tranquillity'.[140] Here we find artistic sensibility once more aligned with that split in the social world between public and private life—the detachment of the 'feminine' sphere which was to be mythicized in Radcliffe's *Udolpho* as an ancestral cultural ideal frighteningly threatened by an aggressive, individualistic energy. Finally, for Duff, Genius is indicated by such 'properties' as 'vivid and picturesque description', 'sublimity', 'irregular greatness', 'wildness of Imagination', and 'Enthusiasm'—all of which, as we shall see, are again deemed by her late eighteenth-century critics to be prominent features of Radcliffe's romances.

The last of these properties requires some explanation. Duff distinguishes between a good and a bad form of Enthusiasm: the latter proceeds 'from an overheated and distempered imagination' and is 'supposed to imply weakness, superstition and madness', while the former implies 'an ardor of Fancy wrought up to transport'.[141] This distinction approximates that popularly explored and naturalized by eminent physicians at this time in their pre-psychiatric discussions of nervous disorder, melancholia, hypochondria, and hysteria. That is, the ambivalent status of sensibility is reproduced in the 'artistic-theoretical' categories of Enthusiasm and Imagination, which, like sensibility, are further scrutinized, manipulated, and exploited in the writings of the novelists. Certainly Mrs

---

[138] Duff, *Essay on Original Genius*, 143.   [139] Ibid. 177.
[140] Ibid. 294.   [141] Ibid. 170–1.

Radcliffe's heroine, Emily, in her resolute bid for self-command, swings precariously on the pendulum of sensibility between sublime rapture and 'the illusions of a distempered imagination'.[142] Moreover, Radcliffe finally explains away the earlier fearful visions to which Emily has been subject and for which she has found no immediate rational explanation. Had the novel done otherwise, it might perhaps have been read by her contemporaries as symptomatic of the author's own afflictive, rather than virtuous, sensibility. As it was, when Radcliffe left off writing in favour of travel, after the publication in 1796 of *The Italian*, wild rumours circulated about the state of her health. One story even had it that 'excessive use of her imagination in representing extravagant and violent scenes had driven her insane, and that she was ending her days in an asylum'.[143] However, lest it be thought that only women writers were singled out for such ascriptions of madness, it is as well to remember that many of the early Romantic poets went mad, including Collins and Cowper, and there was a reported marked increase in 'nervous diseases' among the English generally by the end of the century.[144] Thus, over a range of practices, did the discourses of sensibility and genius construct and call forth the objects of their description.

In sum, it can be said that there is considerable point in the passing claim made by Irene Tayler and Gina Luria that 'romantic theory greatly influenced women as novelists'.[145] The ranking of sensibility over and against the competitive values of the 'world' which we find in Sentimental novels and medical discourse privileged a particular type of femininity. As participants in the writing and criticism of Richardson's novels, women contributed to a 'feminization' of values, language, and literature that empowered them over succeeding decades and favoured their development as authors. With the concomitant shift in the notions of 'genius' and 'author', they actively promulgated and legitimized their lore, tastes,

---

[142] Radcliffe, *Udolpho*, 48, 95.
[143] McIntyre, *Ann Radcliffe in Relation to Her Time*, 19.
[144] Michel Foucault, *Madness and Civilization: A History of Insanity in the Age of Reason*, trans. Richard Howard (London: Tavistock, 1967), 212–14.
[145] Taylor, 'Gender and Genre', 105.

judgements, and feelings as the fit subject-matter of literature. After the publication of the *Conjectures*, for a time, women of sensibility could more popularly be construed as having both moral authority and the potential for genius. They quickly attempted to give witness in writing to these capacities, particularly in their development of the new novelistic genres and discussions of the theories on which these works were based.

The Prefaces of Clara Reeve have already been discussed in this respect; also relevant is the work of Anna Laetitia Aikin (Mrs Barbauld), successful poet, editor, and author of popular works for children, as well as of tracts on politics and religion. Commenting in one of her *Miscellaneous Pieces* (1773) on 'the greediness with which tales of ghosts and goblins . . . are devoured by every ear', she takes a different tack from Reeve *vis-à-vis* the supernatural. For Aikin, the pleasure received in exploring the mysterious and the supernatural in fiction is both explicable and justifiable by reference to the operations of the Burkean sublime:

A strange and unexpected event awakens the mind, and keeps it on the stretch; and where the agency of invisible beings is introduced, of 'forms unseen and mightier far than we', our imagination, darting forth, explores with rapture the new world which is laid open to its view, and rejoices in the expansion of its powers. Passion and fancy co-operating elevate the soul to its highest pitch; and pain of terror is lost in amazement. Hence the more wild, fanciful and extraordinary are the circumstances of a scene of horror, the more pleasure we receive from it.[146]

Folk and fairy lore, traditionally preserved by women, is thus invested by her with the new literary importance also assigned to it by enthusiasts for the Gothic, such as Bishop Hurd. Given such contributions by women to literary debates and trends in the latter half of the eighteenth century, we can conclude that women were actively engaged in the development of the novel.

By the same token, however, the cult of moral and aesthetic sensibility naturalized the removal of women from the domain of political and commercial action; by the end of the century, their domestic seclusion or confinement to sedentary

[146] Anna Laetitia (Aikin) Barbauld and John Aikin, *Miscellaneous Pieces*, 3rd edn. (London: J. Johnson, 1792), 125–6.

'feminine' pursuits was predicated on an unalterable disposition by those who wished to effect a reformation in manners
in all ranks of society. Many Evangelical moralists, for example,
saw in 'the proper lady' the very model of virtue and good
conduct. Paradoxically, this did not prevent writers of conduct
books from addressing women—often and at length—on specific ways in which their supposedly innate 'feminine' virtues
were to be inculcated. As Terry Eagleton comments in *The
Rape of Clarissa*, 'the "exaltation" of women, while undoubtedly a partial advance in itself, also serve[d] to shore up
the very system which oppresse[d] them'.[147] This contradiction
was exposed by Mary Wollstonecraft in *A Vindication of the
Rights of Woman* (1792)—a proto-feminist and anti-Romantic
work which attempted 'to persuade women to endeavour to
acquire strength, both of mind and body, and to convince
them that the soft phrases, susceptibility of heart, delicacy of
sentiment and refinement of taste, [were] almost synonymous
with epithets of weakness', epithets which would soon constitute them as objects of contempt.[148] Indeed, in 1807 in his
Letters on the Intellectual and Moral Character of Women,
William Duff now attacked Wollstonecraft's own 'energy', as
unnatural or inappropriate to her sex:

I am confident, that those of her own sex, who are most distinguished by a delicacy of sentiment, by true feminine sensibility, and
by a just sense of the genuine rights of women, will not think
themselves much obliged to the contumacious spirit of a combatant,
who hath stretched those rights beyond their natural and proper
bounds.[149]

His work is a testimony to the strong impact of the writing of
not only Wollstonecraft, but female authors in general. In an
emphatic delimiting of his earlier democratic study of original
genius, he downgraded the quality of imagination in women
to being 'more gay and sprightly than in men', but 'less vigor-

[147] Eagleton, *Rape of Clarissa*, 15.
[148] Mary Wollstonecraft, *A Vindication of the Rights of Woman: With
Strictures on Political and Moral Subjects* (London: Source Book Press, 1972),
17–18.
[149] William Duff, *Letters on the Intellectual and Moral Character of
Women* (Aberdeen: J. Chalmers, 1807; reprint edn. New York and London:
Garland, 1974), 101.

ous and extensive'. Moreover, he was now careful to tell women that they had no prior claim to that 'power of deep musing thought, and that sublime melancholy which is the inseparable concomitant of genius'. For, 'Of that creative power and energy of imagination, which is exerted in calling into existence things that are not, and, in bestowing on shadowy forms all the colours of life and reality . . . I do not remember to have met with any remarkable examples in your sex.'[150] Women such as Mrs Carter, Miss More, and Miss Seward are credited with ability in writing 'the tender, elegiac and descriptive kinds of poetry'; likewise women, from 'readiness of invention' and 'vivacity of fancy, which they inherit from nature' have considerable power in composing 'Memoirs, Romances, and Novels'; but letters are their real forte, he concludes. With such firm positioning of the capacities of 'female genius', it is no accident that by 1818, the year of publication of Mary Shelley's *Frankenstein*, genius had come to be closely associated with the male Romantic poet, who took upon himself a God-like role—as 'legislator' for mankind.

Reading Late Eighteenth- and Early Nineteenth-Century Gothic Fiction Dialogically

We have seen how women in specific collective or individual situations are not necessarily silenced or muted, but can expropriate language to counter existing and prevailing discourses, and open or generate new practices in writing. We need now to develop a reading practice which will remain sensitive to the discourses constituting gender and the meaning of women's lives at the time of writing, but which will avoid focusing on gender in isolation from other aspects of identity.

For example, it is tempting to read many of the novels written by women towards the end of the eighteenth century as incipiently 'feminist'. For Katharine M. Rogers, their claim to this label lies in their departures from stereotypical

---

[150] Ibid. 29.

eighteenth-century representations of passive or insipid femininity and their concern with problems of money and inheritance.
Presented from the point of view of an exemplary heroine,
novels such as Charlotte Smith's *Emmeline* (1788), *Ethelinde*
(1789), *The Banished Man* (1794), and *Marchmont* (1796),
Charlotte Lennox's *Euphemia* (1790), Ann Radcliffe's *Udolpho* (1794), and Fanny Burney's *Camilla* (1796) affirm the
active 'thinking powers' of women as well as female sensitivity
and delicacy.[151] On the other hand, male characters are often
satirized for their lack of moral and rational control, their
mismanagement of resources, their insensitivity, arrogant assumptions, and attempted manipulations of women. If, because of their own limitations, men fail to recognize trivial
minds and narrow sympathies in those women who pride
themselves on conventional female accomplishments and behaviour, so much the worse for them. Pompous displays of
learning by men also come off badly when compared with
exemplary 'female understanding' or intelligence. To many
modern readers, of course, the female protagonists of these
novels will still appear submissive and complicit with the gross
inequalities which hold them in thrall. Chastity as the *sine qua
non* of female virtue, indifference to female sexual desire and
fulfilment in marital relationships, and the dependence con-
sequent on an inability of women to work for a living, hardly
square with present-day notions of female liberation. But when
framed by what we know of those eighteenth-century discourses which represent women as models of docile behaviour,
the endowment of heroines 'with presence of mind and strength
to withhold compliance or control their own impulses' can
appear as an inscription in fiction of female assertiveness.[152]
Commenting on the way in which emphasis on 'a separate
woman's world' of delicacy, trial, and difficulty could continue
to reinforce that concept, Rogers nevertheless concludes that

The delicate distresses of this fiction are less significant than its
presentation of women's feelings about their acquaintances, from
suitors to neighbours, and its consideration of women's problems,
from social boredom to finding the right mate, to dealing with an

[151] Rogers, *Feminism in Eighteenth-Century England*, 149–79.
[152] Ibid. 152.

unsatisfactory husband, to supporting themselves. The persistent
charge that they were inflammatory—hard to understand in terms of
the actual works—may reflect the justified suspicion that they were,
however covertly, a form of female assertion. In any case, by formul-
ating women's wishes and complaints, they helped to develop
feminine awareness if not feminism.[153]

This again raises the question of reading Gothic texts representative of the 1790s, such as Radcliffe's *Udolpho* and *The
Italian*, Lewis's *The Monk*, and Austen's parodic *Northanger
Abbey*. For if, following Rogers, we place the texts by Radcliffe and Austen exclusively in a frame of eighteenth-century
'feminism' where this term refers to an assertive awareness of
women's problems, trials, or oppression by men, then the
intertextual relationships of these works with Sentimental
novels stretching back to Richardson's *Clarissa*, will be em-
phasized at the expense of the use in the Gothic of remote
settings and the fantastic—important relativizing features
which, as we surmised in Chapter 1, allow an exploration and
interrogation of the ethical and epistemological schema constituted by the text as normative. And so we may, like Louis I.
Bredvold and Coral Ann Howells, become convinced that 'the
novel of terror was only a variant of the novel of sensibility,
exploiting a fresh excitement, trying to push suspense and
apprehension to the utmost'.[154] Once this evaluative note
creeps into the discussion, much of the shifting ambiguity and
many-sidedness of the Gothic goes unheeded.

In contrast, the Bakhtinian mode of reading which I outlined
near the end of Chapter 1 should remain sensitive to the
diversity of social and cultural discursive practices prominently in existence when Gothic fiction was first produced in large
quantities. It should not presume the centrality of feminist
concerns; nor should it posit a 'static dichotomy between
non-dominant (the social realm of women) and *dominant*
(patriarchy) material forces, but . . . a fully dynamic field in
which *all situations of the word* become equally contested and
challenged'.[155]

[153] Ibid. 171.
[154] Louis Bredvold, *The Natural History of Sensibility* (Detroit: Wayne
State University Press, 1962), 88-9.
[155] Diaz-Diocaretz, 'Bakhtin, Discourse and Feminist Theories', 135.

Unfortunately, some feminist appropriations of Bakhtin have continued to operate with 'the gender deterministic notion of woman as the other'.[156] For example, in her most recent work, 'Women and the Rise of the Novel: A Feminist-Marxist Theory', Josephine Donovan argues that 'women's critical irony', which was 'rooted' in a 'marginal, feminine world' and 'economically based in use-value production', 'fractured the authoritative, monologic modes of earlier patriarchal forms, such as the epic and the romance, and established the dialogic, ironic mode characteristic of the novel'.[157] Again, in 'Style and Power', Donovan argues as follows:

The stylistic devices women employed in the early novel (as well as, in some cases, before and after) reflect their oppressed political position. Located on the margins, in unofficial zones, women used forms derived from their everyday familiar world, forms that expressed a paratactic nonsubordinating sensitivity, and which, finally, registered a resistance to the hierarchical subordinations of official modes, the 'word of the fathers'. In this way women contributed enormously to the creation of the dialogic counterhegemonic consciousness that Bakhtin saw embodied in the novel.[158]

Although both articles draw on Marxist and Bakhtinian theory to offer more positive accounts of women's role in the rise of the novel, I think that they err in assuming that the everyday forms utilized by women automatically made their novels subversive or 'counterhegemonic'. As Myriam Diaz-Diocaretz points out in 'Bakhtin, Discourse and Feminist Theories', 'To proceed from the hypothesis that the relationship between a particular group of women as writing subjects in a given society has been dominated by patriarchal structures, we have to assess *which areas of social discourse* function from a masculinist view and *in which contexts*.'[159] First of all, Dono-

---

[156] The phrase is that of Diaz-Diocaretz, ibid. 136. For an overview of feminist appropriations of Bakhtin, see Clive Thompson, 'Mikhail Bakhtin and Contemporary Anglo-American Feminist Theory', *Critical Studies*, 1/2 (1989), 141–61.

[157] Josephine Donovan, 'Women and the Rise of the Novel: A Feminist-Marxist Theory', *Signs*, 16/3 (Spring 1991), 462.

[158] Josephine Donovan, 'Style and Power', in Bauer and McKinstrey, eds., *Feminism, Bakhtin, and the Dialogic*, 90.

[159] Diaz-Diocaretz, 'Bakhtin, Discourse and Feminist Theories', 134.

van too uncritically equates patriarchy with Bakhtin's term, 'the word of the fathers', which he uses as a metaphor for 'the authoritative word . . . located in a distanced zone, organically connected with a past that is felt to be hierarchically higher'.[160] And, secondly, she slides too easily into a static dichotomy between 'the word of the fathers' and 'a feminist critical irony'. As stated earlier, the gendered perspective cannot be privileged to exclude all other variables, as the dialogic for Bakhtin entails a heterogeneous multiplicity of orientations working within the text. Furthermore, Bakhtin did not argue that irony was 'the defining ingredient' in the novel's constitution, as Donovan seems to think. For our purposes, in relation to eighteenth- and early nineteenth-century Gothic, although women's texts do often make use of stylization of prior discourses, giving them a new semantic orientation which resounds alongside earlier meanings, this is not the same technique as irony. As will be clear in Chapter 4, Bakhtin distinguishes between different forms of dialogic utterance, parody and stylization in particular, and further distinctions and clarifications are still needed in this area. Moreover, although Donovan's accounts deal with the use made by women of the 'dashaway' epistolary mode and paratactic syntax, in early writings by Margaret Cavendish, Jane Barker, and Delarivière Manley, she does not consider women's expropriation of folk- and fairy-tales and discourses of the sublime and sensibility, as well as other discourses, in later eighteenth-century fiction. It was in developing forms of the fantastic in fiction, as well as satiric and parodic irony, that women such as Ann Radcliffe and Jane Austen made of the novel a powerful genre which captured the popular imagination.

In our reading of such novels, however, we need to remember that *all* contemporary issues, along with the debates about sensibility and genius, the social and intellectual status of women, their sexuality and education, provided contexts for reading the early Gothic.

In the previous chapter, I mentioned how the eighteenth-century literary use of the castle carried strong connotations of the ancestral past, the dynastic transfer of property, but was

[160] Bakhtin, *Dialogic Imagination*, 342.

also encrusted with meanings from fairy-tales, superstitions, and legends as well as from the aesthetic discourse of the sublime. It can be added that a fascination with 'sublime' ruins, castles, dungeons, and prisons was also being fashionably encoded in a range of other cultural practices, such as architecture—the forbidding exterior of Newgate Prison, designed in 1769, being but one example. John Howard's *State of the Prisons in England and Wales* (1777) testifies to the horror which this 'tomb for the living' evoked, even in the most hardened criminals.[161] Thus it is possible that contemporary readers of the Gothic could have brought this contextual frame to the novels also.

Then again, we should remember that, in various governmental, religious, and journalistic quarters, life in Britain was being described not only as materialistic and corrupt, but also as threatened by the growth of liberal, 'Jacobin' ideologies and the material consequences of revolution across the Channel against an *ancien régime*. Here we can find complexities of allegiance and disparity between different sections of the community. For example, we can find points of agreement between 'Jacobin' feminists, such as Wollstonecraft, and conservative moralists, including anti-feminists, in relation to the excesses of sensibility and court culture. Yet Wollstonecraft perceived the domestication of women as another form of the female subjection found in court culture, while social conservatives, such as Hannah More, cautioned against wider freedoms and social roles for women as another version of courtly libertinism.

Nervous disorders, too, seemed to have taken on epidemic proportions and, given the close proximity of sensibility and madness in medical and other theoretical discourses of the day, 'the English malady' was being constituted as another threat to life and liberty. Those with 'delicate nerves', for whom sudden acute passions—whether of anger or joy— might be deleterious, were constant objects of concern. Persons deemed insane still continued to be incarcerated indiscriminately in institutions. Moreover, after 1770, Bethlehem

[161] Lorenz Eitner, 'Cages, Prisons and Captives in Eighteenth Century Art', in Karl Kroeber and William Walling, eds., *Images of Romanticism* (New Haven, Conn. and London: Yale University Press, 1978), 28.

Hospital (Bedlam) was no longer open to the sightseeing public; and perhaps this final step in sealing off the insane as the
unseen also added to the already emotive meanings conferred
on the confined and on places of confinement, such as dungeons and castles. Then, too, the responses of a legal system
unconcerned with the motivations for crime, or the rehabilita-
tion of the criminal, remained brutal and inflexible.[162] Such
was the popular hatred of prisons as bastions of authority
that, during the Gordon riots in London of 1780, violent mobs
broke into most of the gaols and set fire to the recently
completed Newgate Prison. Like the storming and demolition
of the Bastille nine years later, such acts were replete with
symbolic significance.

Any 'historical' readings we choose to make will, of course,
be subject to the practical difficulties of dealing with works
distant in time. They will also inescapably still be made from
and for the present. And that goes for *readings* of specific past
readings, as well as of the novels themselves. However, I
maintain that we can exclude much of our twentieth-century
world by delimiting fields of discourse which we consider to
describe a past version of the text and its readings in their past
contexts. Against the erosions of a hermeneutic scepticism it
can be argued that historical reconstructions need not be
severely compromised. The degree of anachronism could be
quite minor.[163] In delimiting certain fields of discourse, we are
conscious that we are reconstructing earlier modes of subjectivity, earlier social, economic, and cultural practices, and the
degree to which this perception can in fact be constituted by
the discourses with which we constitute our present-day realities is limited. As David Shepherd explains in 'Bakhtin and the
Reader',

a text continues to bear the marks of its past historical engagements
which, as well as being open to recontextualisation, must also place
some limit on the nature and degree of that recontextualisation.
Determinate meaning exists to the extent that the production of
meaning is contextual, and contexts are not freely interchangeable

---

[162] Ibid. 32.
[163] A similar point is made by Eric Donald Hirsch, Jr., in *The Aims of Interpretation* (Chicago and London: University of Chicago Press, 1976), 82.

or, *pace* Fish, wholly encompassed by the historical moment of a given interpretive community. If the activity of reading is based on dialogic relations between reader and text, and text and context, then these are relations which have a past as well as a present.[164]

Certainly, we can attempt to avoid privileging particular a-historical, theoretical, and critical discourses such as that of psychoanalysis, which did not exist in the eighteenth century. As was pointed out earlier in the case of the 'strong' readings made by Gilbert and Gubar in *The Madwoman in the Attic*, such discourses tend to reproduce earlier texts as continuously preoccupied with the same problems, so that any real sense of the differences between one historical moment and another is lost. Not only does this loss put into question the validity of the approach used by Gilbert and Gubar; it also restricts their method's usefulness as a political strategy. As Catherine Belsey has reminded us: 'It is the difference of the past which vindic-ates the possibility of thinking differently, and thinking differ-ently is a necessary though not a sufficient condition of living differently.'[165]

In Chapter 1 it was postulated that, in the Gothic, styliza-tions of folk- and fairy-tale, superstition, myth, and legend and a discourse of the sublime introduce the unnatural, the un-canny, and the preternatural (the fantastic) and that this rela-tivizes the 'everyday legality' constructed by other languages in the text. Often used with structures of recursion—repeti-tions and transformations of imagery, mediated narration, and story within story—the fantastic allows psychological states of oppression, anxiety, or obsession to be presented with a sub-jectively felt intensity not previously achieved in fiction. Blur-ring the boundaries between 'the real' and the feelings and perceptions produced by what is, perhaps, only partially known or perceived, the Gothic novel may put in doubt not only the 'real' itself, but also the stability of the sensitive and virtuous (Sentimental) hero or heroine, whose particular ac-cruals of good sense, ways of knowing, imaginative capacity, benevolence, and noble integrity can be explored and tested.

---

[164] David Shepherd, 'Bakhtin and the Reader', 98.
[165] Catherine Belsey, 'The Plurality of History', *Southern Review*, 17/2 (July 1984), 141.

In the chapters which follow I shall attempt some detailed readings of Gothic texts by considering the dialogic relations within and between the 'already formed' discourses which Ann Radcliffe appropriates for *The Mysteries of Udolpho* and *The Italian*, Matthew Lewis for *The Monk*, Jane Austen for *Northanger Abbey*, Eaton Stannard Barrett for *The Heroine*, and Mary Shelley for *Frankenstein*. Although each of these authors is English, it should not be thought that I consider the Gothic to be specifically an English genre. Texts by Wieland, Brockden Brown, Poe, and others are also central to its development. Indeed, an exemplar of the genre's structure can be found in a twentieth-century work, Isak Dinesen's anachronistic *Seven Gothic Tales*. However, limiting my study to one particular period and society serves its historical purposes. The ultimate aims, as stated in Chapter 1, will be, first, to discover the attitudinal positions which the chosen novels might be said to have offered readers at the time of their production; and, secondly, to assess the strength of any possible assaults on the readers' assumptions and values which those reading positions might have made. Because such 'historical' readings will allow comparisons not only with responses or readings (including parodic fictions) of their time, but also with later readings of the 'same' texts, this approach will provide a practicable way of noting differences in how each work has been appropriated at distinct historical moments. And from there we may be able to evaluate the Gothic mode's relative effectiveness in 'provoking unease'[166]—that is, its potential to challenge or subvert (patriarchal) authority across a range of social, economic, and cultural practices.

[166] Carter, *Fireworks*, 122.

3
Gothic Sublimity: Ann Radcliffe's
The Mysteries of Udolpho

Gothic Novels of the 1790s and Mythmaking about
Putative Gothic Ancestors

During the turbulent 1790s, allusions to the ancestral Goths as possessors of a dark, individualistic energy were made frequently and from a variety of discursive positions. Those of conservative temper, such as the editor of the *Gentleman's Magazine*, were liable to use the Goths as a trope for the French revolutionaries and their radical sympathizers in England:

Europe since the period when it was overrun by the Goths and the Vandals, has never experienced more alarm and danger than at the present moment—Religion, Manners, Literature, and the Arts, are all equally menaced by a foe, whose characteristic is a compound of impetuosity, ignorance and crime. To resist and counteract these machinations, has been the honest and unremitting endeavour of the *Gentleman's Magazine* and ever will be so, as long as our Political and Religious Constitution shall require our indefatigable support.[1]

On the other hand, in popular Whig writing, the Goths were associated with tyranny and turmoil in more ambivalent ways. For example, in her *Letters on Education* (1790), the radical historian Catharine Macaulay made reference to 'the beauties and advantages' of Gothic customs and attitudes, such as the dispensing 'with an equal hand the advantages of a classical

[1] *Gentleman's Magazine*, 43 (Jan. 1793), quoted in Poovey, *Proper Lady and the Woman Writer*, 16. See also Anna Seward in a letter to Edward Jerningham, dated 17 Feb. 1796, reprinted in Mary R. Mahl and Helene Koon, eds., *The Female Spectator* (Bloomington and London: Indiana University Press, 1977), 306.

education to all their offspring'.[2] But she also discoursed on
the Roman 'enormities' and 'vices' which the Barbarians
adopted and 'engrafted in the Gothic constitutions' after they
'had rendered themselves masters of the Roman Empire'. Subsequent abuses of power throughout the centuries could be
traced to this corrupting legacy (Macaulay, p. 267).

In appealing to the Gothic moment as sanction for the
transformation of society, Macaulay focused on the excesses
and inattention to familial 'order and harmony' of latter-day
descendants of the Gothic tyrant, their failings being the
source of contemporary discontent among the poor and of
licentiousness and extravagance in the young and rich. Traditions from the Gothic past, in this respect, had outlived their
usefulness and were oppressing the present. Whereas the unrest and 'subdivision of power' in Europe had once 'rendered
extensive buildings necessary for the security of each petty
tyrant', now there was no need for moated castles, huge halls,
or hospitable mansions to accommodate the dowagers and
younger branches of great families. Indeed,

it might be agreeable to true taste, and good policy, to prescribe a
lesser scale of magnificence in the buildings of individuals. . . . as
envy and covetousness are two passions which act powerfully on the
peace and harmony of the mind, the virtue of citizens will be in a
greater security where the wholesome restraint of sumptuary laws or
taxes properly imposed, banish those objects from society which are
adapted to inflame cupidity and excite vicious emulation. (Macaulay, pp. 306–7)

Macaulay's reference is to the vogue among the upper classes
in England for country house (mansion) building and estate
improvement which had gained momentum between the late
1740s and 1780s. These decades had seen an increasing con-
centration of land in large properties, the establishment of
architecture as a profession on its modern scale, the investiture
of scores of new peers and the spread of extravagant entertain-

  [2] Catharine Macaulay, *Letters on Education, with Observations on Religious and Metaphysical Subjects* (London: C. Dilly, 1790; reprint edn. New
York and London: Garland, 1974), 49. Further references to this work appear
in the text.

ments, masquerades, and *fêtes-champêtres*.[3] G. E. Mingay
estimates that 'by 1790 three-quarters of the land was occupied by tenants rather than owners'; he cites as factors pro-
moting this change in property ownership the access of
landlords to mercantile wealth (often through marriage), the
sale by small squires and freeholders of their properties, and
the enclosure of commons.[4] It is significant that, in her condemnation of displays of magnificence, the keeping of 'large
trains of useless servants', 'the waste of private fortune', and
the 'licentiousness' of great families, Macaulay makes no allusion to the myth of patronage—the sentimental morality of the
lord, squire, or gentleman of the manor, such as we find in
Clara Reeve's *The Old English Baron*—as a regulating force in
society. In fact, while discussing conduct literature for children
(and perhaps thinking of the wealth of stories influenced by
Richardson's *Pamela*),[5] she condemns 'the practice and cultivation of benign affections . . . from some carnal advantage with
which its votaries are to be constantly rewarded' (Macaulay,
p. 53). She also foregrounds powerful states of mind—envy,
covetousness, selfish will—as the mark of the individual in an
unequal society.

Such threatening states of mind are also characteristic of the
Gothic villains—Montoni, Schedoni, Ambrosio—who loom
large, with a fairy-tale intensity, in the ancestral worlds created by Ann Radcliffe and Matthew Lewis. Parental tyranny
as a romance or novelistic convention was of course not new,
but these figures differ from their prototypes in the works

³ Gordon Edward Mingay, *English Landed Society in the Eighteenth Century* (London: Routledge & Kegan Paul, 1963), 6, 24, 150–62, 167; Anthony
James Little, *Deceleration in the Eighteenth-Century British Economy* (London: Croom Helm, 1976), 90–2; Aileen Ribeiro, *The Dress Worn at Masquerades in England, 1730 to 1790, and its Relation to Fancy Dress in Portraiture*
(New York and London: Garland, 1984), 1–43.

⁴ Mingay, *English Landed Society in the Eighteenth Century*, 15, 76–8,
96–7, 179–82, 189–201. Mingay cites government office and overseas adven-
turing as of secondary importance in enabling existing great landlords 'to
expand their estates and rise to new levels of splendour and luxury'. Also the
exploitation by landowners of their land for industrial and mining purposes
was not really significant until late in the century (78–9).

⁵ Samuel Pickering, Jr., 'The "Ambiguous Circumstances of a Pamela"':
Early Children's Books and the Attitude towards Pamela', *Journal of Narrative Technique*, 14/3 (Fall 1984), 153–71.

of Walpole and Reeve in a significant respect. Unrestrained, either by rational sensibility or by external controls, and endowed with 'a perverse kind of strength and intellectual energy', they hold firmly to values radically different from the norm, 'defending their conduct by their own peculiar logic'.[6] This enables them to remain absolute and inscrutable in their offences against individuals and society, so that they are, as Sir Walter Scott noted, 'in some sort as fabulous as fairies or ogres'.[7] Montoni's face, for example, with its 'fire and keenness of . . . eye, its bold fierceness, its sudden watchfulness', is said to betray 'the spirit and vigour of his soul'. As chieftain of a band of 'Condottieri', Montoni seems unable to feel, unlike Walpole's Manfred who alternately lusts and repents. Montoni is 'a stranger to pity and fear'; 'delighting in the tumult and struggles of life', he possesses 'a sort of animal ferocity'.[8]

Among those oppressed by this villainous energy, no one, it seems, suffers more keenly than the young, single, upper-class woman, that 'very interesting object' (*Udolpho*, p. 121), able to be virtually bought and sold in marriage for the purpose of maintaining or building up the wealth of an often declining family estate. And the old Sentimental virtues, while still ultimately affirmed, no longer appear to provide quite the same unequivocal guarantees of support, benign intervention, and safe passage. Once the benevolent guardians and protective enclosures of the home environment are removed, the sensitive sons and daughters who uphold these virtues are sorely tried, as the detailed descriptions of their often intense doubts, fears, anxieties, and frustrations testify. Most importantly, sensibility itself as a source of virtue, creativity, and power is held up to close scrutiny, its contradictions, assets, and liabilities—particularly for women—being laid bare.

Given the polarization of public opinion over the events in France and, once England had declared war, the ease with

---

[6] E. W. Pitcher, 'Changes in Short Fiction in Britain 1785–1810: Philosophic Tales, Gothic Tales, and Fragments and Visions', *Studies in Short Fiction*, 13/3 (Summer 1976), 335.

[7] Walter Scott, *Sir Walter Scott on Novelists and Fiction*, ed. Ioan Williams (London: Routledge & Kegan Paul, 1968), 111.

[8] Radcliffe, *Udolpho*, 122, 157, 270, 277, 358. Further references appear in the text.

which radical opinions could be represented as disloyalty,[9] it must have been difficult for readers and writers of the 1790s to engage with literature independently of an awareness of contemporary, possibly subversive, ideologies. This very difficulty was itself alluded to in novels. Charlotte Smith's epistolary *Desmond* (1792), for example, self-consciously rehearsed and intervened in the debates about the French Revolution and the need for reform of constitutional and penal law in England.[10] *The Mysteries of Udolpho, The Monk*, and *The Italian* were not so explicit about political matters; but they were set in southern France and Italy where, in Sir Walter Scott's words of 1824, 'feudal tyranny and Catholic superstition still continue to exercise their sway over the slave and bigot, and to indulge the haughty lord, or more haughty priest, that sort of despotic power, the exercise of which seldom fails to deprave the heart and disorder the judgement'.[11] More significantly, perhaps, the social values, manners, and practices represented often did not correspond with the period designated by the author. So, while this dubious historicity and the fairy-tale stylization of characters did function at one level as distancing, 'fantasy' devices, readers could still recognize, in the characters and situations portrayed, elements which they might use in conceiving of themselves and their own social relations.

Coleridge, for instance, wrote of *Udolpho* that 'the style of accomplishments given to the heroine, a country young lady, brought up on the banks of the Garonne; the mention of botany; of little circles of infidelity, &c. give so much the air of modern manners, as is not counterbalanced by Gothic arches and antique furniture'.[12] No doubt, this was the view of many readers. Radcliffe had effected an illusion of past reality by articulating current discourses of sensibility and taste, as used by identifiable social groups in England, with a remote time and place—Gascony, in the year 1584.

[9] Gary Kelly, *The English Jacobin Novel* (Oxford: Oxford University Press, 1976), 10–11.
[10] Charlotte Smith, *Desmond* (London: G. G. J. and J. Robinson, 1792; reprint edn. New York and London: Garland, 1974), ii. 52–5, 60–8, 116–38, 146–8.
[11] Scott, *Sir Walter Scott on Novelists and Fiction*, 114.
[12] Coleridge, *Miscellaneous Criticism*, 357.

Appropriation of Discourses of Sensibility and Taste in
The Mysteries of Udolpho

Udolpho's narrative 'realism' relies a great deal on its pro-
jected middle- and upper-class audiences' taste for landscape,
that is, on pictures of nature rendered in painterly detail. As
Frank J. Messmann points out in his discussion of the aesthetics of eighteenth-century English gardening, 'The picturesque
habit of viewing nature meant that it was seen . . . as a series
of well-composed subjects such as had appeared in the landscape paintings of Salvator Rosa, Claude Lorraine, and Gas-
par Poussin.'[13] 'The scenery exquisitely painted' of Radcliffe's
previous novels, *A Sicilian Romance* (1791) and *The Romance
of the Forest* (1792), had been the focus of much praise,[14] and
in this respect *Udolpho* did not disappoint, even if some, like
Coleridge, felt that in the 'elegant description and picturesque
scenery' there was 'too much of sameness'.[15] Frequent 'set
pieces', sometimes with specific allusions to painters such as
Salvator Rosa,[16] were used in the novel not only for descriptions of nature and architecture, but also at times for accounts
of events. In the description of the funeral at Udolpho of
Madame Montoni, for example, the action is frozen in a
tableau after the manner of the seventeenth-century painter,
Domenichino.[17] Such 'picturesque' presentation was to continue to earn Radcliffe many tributes. In 1797 Thomas James
Mathias, who was highly critical of other women novelists,
hailed her as 'a poetess whom Ariosto would have acknowledged, as "La nudrita Damigella Trivulzia al sacro speco" ';
the physician, Nathan Drake, alluding to her in his *Literary
Hours* of 1800 as 'the Shakespeare of Romance Writers',

[13] Frank J. Messman, *Richard Payne Knight: The Twilight of Virtuosity*
(The Hague and Paris: Mouton, 1974), 62.

[14] Mrs Elizabeth Carter, in her Letters to Mrs Montagu, quoted in Clara
Frances McIntyre, *Ann Radcliffe in Relation to Her Time*, 36; *Monthly
Review*, 2nd ser. 3 (Sept. 1790), 91; *English Review*, 20 (Nov. 1792), 352–3.

[15] *Critical Review*, 2nd ser. 11 (Aug. 1794), 361–72; *British Critic*, 4 (Aug.
1794), 120; *Analytical Review*, 19 (1794), 144; *Gentleman's Magazine*, 64
(1794), 834.

[16] See e.g. Radcliffe, *Udolpho*, 30.

[17] For a useful discussion of this, see Howells, *Love, Mystery and Misery*,
140–2.

praised the beauty and terror of her scenic descriptions; and in 1824 Sir Walter Scott called her 'the first poetess of romantic fiction'.[18]

Radcliffe's technique of embellishment is utilized in *Udolpho* from the outset. Monsieur Aubert's château is described as having a view to the south, of

the majestic Pyrenées, whose summits, veiled in clouds, or exhibiting awful forms, seen, and lost again, as the partial vapours rolled along, were sometimes barren, and gleamed through the blue tinge of air, and sometimes frowned with forests of gloomy pine, that swept downward to their base. These tremendous precipices were contrasted by the soft green of the pastures and woods that hung upon their skirts; among whose flocks, and herds, and simple cottages, the eye, after having scaled the cliffs above, delighted to repose. (*Udolpho*, p. 1)

This type of sweeping physical detail may seem, as George E. Haggerty argues, 'structured only to suggest concrete specificity', the nouns and adjectives being actually 'selected to establish mood rather than describe in any specific way'.[19] Yet, once combined with descriptions of the modest improvements which, in the course of providing for his family, the sensitive St Aubert has made to his estate, such passages do more than evoke mood. As was pointed out in the previous chapter, the responsiveness to nature of St Aubert and Emily, and their voluntary retirement to and enjoyment of the domestic environment, both 'place' them socially and constitute them as characters of virtue and creativity—a creativity located in Duff's 'ENTHUSIASM of Imagination, which as it were hurries the mind out of itself'.[20] Other characters, such as Quesnel, Montoni, Madame Cheron, and the Countess De Villefort are positioned by their degree of lack of this definitive 'taste' and 'enthusiasm'.

---

[18] Thomas James Mathias, *The Pursuits of Literature: A Satirical Poem in Dialogue, With Notes* (London: T. Becket, 1801), 56; Nathan Drake, *Literary Hours or Sketches Critical and Narrative* (London: T. Cadell, Jr. and W. Davies, 1800; reprint edn. New York: Garland, 1970), i. 359; Scott, *Sir Walter Scott on Novelists and Fiction*, 103.

[19] George E. Haggerty, 'Fact and Fancy in the Gothic Novel', *Nineteenth Century Fiction*, 39/4 (Mar. 1985), 383–4.

[20] Duff, *Essay on Original Genius*, 171.

In establishing these norms of the supposedly real/ideal, Radcliffe's text intervenes in a discreet and genteel way in contemporary disputes about the aesthetic principles of siting and building country houses and landscaping the grounds— disputes which, in their day, were deemed not merely 'aesthetic' but were often aligned, in bursts of polemic, with certain political and social ideologies.

For example, Humphry Repton, a professional landscapist, claimed that he could not 'help seeing great affinity betwixt deducing gardening from the painter's studies of wild nature, and deducing government from the uncontrouled opinions of man in a savage state'.[21] Just as 'the neatness, simplicity and elegance of English gardening' had gained acceptance as 'the happy medium' between 'the wildness of nature and the stiffness of art', so the English constitution had steered a middle path between 'the liberty of savages and the restraint of despotic government'. For that reason, he concluded, 'experiments of untried theoretical improvement' should be 'tried in some other country'. Here Repton aligns efforts to reproduce or maintain (wild) Nature with radical politics in a stance which is deliberately provocative; for in 1794, the year of *Udolpho*'s publication, Richard Payne Knight and Sir Uvedale Price had initiated a public and at times acrimonious debate over his stress on utility and convenience at the expense of picturesqueness in landscaping. The terms of this debate constitute one context in which the early and late parts of *Udolpho* may be read.

Radcliffe's Intervention in the Landscaping Debate

Knight's work, a long didactic poem called *The Landscape*, was written in the style of Pope with the purpose of dissuading those who, 'to gratify the jaundic'd eye of taste', were bent on 'shaving' or defacing Nature.[22] Specifically published early in

---

[21] Quoted in Walter John Hipple, Jr., *The Beautiful, the Sublime and the Picturesque in Eighteenth-Century British Aesthetic Theory* (Carbondale: Southern Illinois University Press, 1957), 241.

[22] Richard Payne Knight, *The Landscape, a Didactic Poem in Three Books; Addressed to Uvedale Price, Esq.* (London: W. Bulmer, 1794), bk. 2, lines 17–20. Further references appear in the text.

1794 'to forestall a work in progress by Repton', it was
already well known by the time *Udolpho* came out.[23] Books I
and II contained Knight's theories on landscape gardening,
including his objections to the 'shaven' lawns, woody 'clumps',
and 'prim gravel walks . . . in endless serpentines' of Lancelot
'Capability' Brown and his follower, Repton. Book III concerned the use of trees in gardening: oaks, elms, and chestnuts
were to be given place of honour, while the planting of pop-
lars, which were 'formal, thin and tall', was only to be regretted. Moreover, old decaying trees of the former kind
should not be pruned away:

> If years unnumber'd, or the lightning's stroke,
> Have bar'd the summit of the lofty oak,
> (Such as, to decorate some savage waste,
> Salvator's flying pencil often trac'd);
> Entire and sacred let the ruin stand,
> Or fear the pruner's sacrilegious hand . . .
>
> (II, lines 29–34)

In opposition to Brown, Knight also advocated that trees be
planted close to a mansion; in his view, freedom, variety, and
irregularity in gardening were desirable and analogous to the
free growth of the individual.[24] For him,

> ev'ry shaggy limb and spreading tree
> Proclaimed the seat of native liberty.
>
> (II, lines 39–40)

Stretching his subject, Knight ended his poem by alluding to
the revolutionary confusion in France and commenting optim-
istically on the 'temp'rate order' which, 'fann'd by freedom',
would arise from it.[25]

In *Udolpho*, sentiments on trees and architecture similar to
those of Knight and Price are given to St Aubert, who is

---

[23] Messmann, *Richard Payne Knight*, 64–6. Radcliffe's *Udolpho* was published in May.

[24] Ibid. 83–4.

[25] Knight, *Landscape*, bk. 2, lines 415–16: 'Yet, from these horrors, future
times may see | Just order spring, and genuine liberty.' Knight inserted a long
qualifying note to these lines, claiming that since he had written the poem, the
situation in France had changed for the worse, and that 'all conjectures
concerning the ultimate consequences of it must be vague and unsatisfactory'.

shocked by the insensibility of his brother-in-law, Monsieur Quesnel, now in possession of St Aubert's boyhood home.

The ancestral trappings of this 'gothic hall' have been removed by the new owner, whose 'frivolous ornaments', 'false taste and corrupted sentiments' are in stark contrast with the 'chaste simplicity' of the St Auberts and offensive to them (*Udolpho*, p. 23). In this quasi-ancestral community setting, one in which, according to Madame Quesnel, 'nothing which was past and irremediable ought to prevent the festivity of the present hour', the singular physiognomy of the stranger, Montoni, fails to impress itself on Emily. Already filled with grief for her mother, recently dead, and fearful for the health of her father, she is more preoccupied by the indifference of her aunt and uncle to the loss of their sister.

The Quesnels' snobbery, enjoyment of Parisian political intrigue, and want of familial feeling are matched by their extravagance and lack of aesthetic sensibility. The latter traits have already been demonstrated in an earlier exchange in which M. Quesnel has outlined his plan to 'expend thirty or forty thousand livres on improvements'. This project will necessitate demolition of the whole east wing of the Gothic château to make way for first 'a set of stables' and then 'a *salle à manger*, a *salon*, a *salle au commune*, and a number of rooms for servants; for at present there is not accommodation for a third part of my own people' (*Udolpho* p. 13). As if this were not enough, Quesnel has also signalled his intention to cut down some trees which 'encumber' the grounds, particularly an enormous ancient chestnut which spreads its branches before 'the whole south side of the chateau'. His reason appears to be that the chestnut is excessively large and irregular or unruly in shape—'the hollow of its trunk will hold a dozen men'. 'Your enthusiasm', he tells St Aubert, 'will scarcely contend that there can be either use, or beauty, in such a sapless old tree'. But from St Aubert's point of view, one based on boyhood memories, sentiment, and feeling, there is every reason why this same 'noble chestnut', which has 'flourished for centuries' as 'the glory of the estate', should continue to survive.

St Aubert's protestations to his brother-in-law are to no avail. Quesnel has intentions of planting 'some Lombardy poplars among the clumps of chestnut' that shall be left after all else is removed. Like the 'prim despots' bent on the 'sacrilegious waste | Of false improvement, and pretended taste', whom both Knight and Uvedale Price attack,[26] he is determined to smooth out the surrounds and destroy the old avenue of trees, despite the fact that thus shaven the grounds will be out of character with the 'heavy Gothic mansion' (*Udolpho*, p. 14).

Consistent with the 'retirement' scene at La Vallée with which the novel opens, then, the values being offered nostalgically for the reader to admire are the Sentimental values: 'simplicity', 'moderated wishes', sincerity, freedom, disinterested benevolence—a pastoral order said to stem from the ancestral past: 'times and feelings as old-fashioned as the taste that would spare that venerable tree' (*Udolpho*, p. 13). These values are also offered in those chapters of Volumes III and IV of *Udolpho* which take for their setting the Château-le-Blanc in Languedoc. As the novel makes a long, recursive sweep to 'the year 1584, the beginning of that, in which St. Aubert died', we again find a sensitive and benevolent aristocrat retiring from 'the vexations and tumults of public affairs, which too frequently corrode the heart, and vitiate the taste' (*Udolpho*, p. 465).

Like St Aubert, the Count De Villefort has long cherished the scenery of his youth, and, disregarding his second wife's love of 'gay assemblies' in Paris, he has undertaken repairs and modest improvements to the decaying Gothic mansion which he has inherited. Here once more are the 'spreading chestnuts' and a road, 'overgrown with luxuriant vegetation', marked out by an avenue of trees which winds 'for near half a mile among the woods' before it reaches the château (p. 469). On arrival, the Countess condemns her new home as a 'barbarous spot', desolate', 'gloomy', and 'wild', 'a scene of savage

---

[26] Ibid., line 34; bk. 1, lines 303–4. According to Knight's and Price's criteria, Madame Cheron, with her smooth, monotonous garden of 'straight walks, square parterres, and artificial fountains' (Radcliffe, *Udolpho*, 120), would also qualify as a person of 'pretended taste'. Uvedale Price, *An Essay on the Picturesque, As Compared with the Sublime and the Beautiful; and, on the Use of Studying Pictures, for the Purpose of Improving Real Landscape* (London: 1794), 2–3. Cited in Messmann, *Richard Payne Knight*, 65.

nature', thereby angering her husband, who retorts: 'This place, madam, was the work of my ancestors . . . and you must allow me to say, that your present conversation discovers neither good taste, or good manners' (*Udolpho*, p. 471).

The doubling of narrative space and time extends to the intense, Emily-like imaginative responses of Villefort's natural daughter, Blanche, who observes 'with sublime astonishment, the Pyrenean mountains', and falls into reveries about castles, knights, legends and 'reliques of romantic fiction' (p. 468). Blanche, who has formerly been confined to a convent by her jealous stepmother, is receptive 'to the sweet and gentle emotions, which the hour and scenery awaken', while the Countess, 'shrinking from the prospect of being shut up in an old castle', prepares 'to meet every object with displeasure'. The panoramic landscape, with its woods to the north, 'long tract of plains', and 'towers of a monastery, illumined by the moon, rising over dark groves', soon 'elevate[s] the unaccustomed mind of Blanche to enthusiasm': 'O, who would live in Paris, to look upon black walls and dirty streets, when, in the country, they might gaze on the blue heavens, and all the green earth!' (p. 472).

The novel's recurrent deistic emphasis on the precedence of nature over culture allows what some Britons of the 1790s would have condemned as 'the Jacobinism of taste'.[27] For, like Knight and Price, Radcliffe accommodates a certain heterogeniety, irregularity, and wildness. Early in the novel there is narratorial approval for St Aubert's 'exultation of health, and youthful freedom . . . the wild walks of the mountains, the river . . . the distant plains, which seemed boundless as his early hopes' (*Udolpho*, p. 2). And, in turn, we learn of St Aubert's own indulgent attitude to the 'uncommon vivacity' and incaution of Emily's suitor, Valancourt:

He [St. Aubert] saw a frank and generous nature, full of ardour, highly susceptible of whatever is grand and beautiful, but impetuous,

[27] Anna Seward used this phrase when writing of Knight's *Landscape* in Sept. 1794. Likewise, Horace Walpole, in a letter to Mason, in Mar. 1796, spoke of Knight as a 'pretended and ill-warranted dictator of all taste, who Jacobinically would level the purity of gardens, would as malignantly as Tom Paine or Priestly guillotine Mr. Brown'. Seward and Walpole are both quoted in Messmann, *Richard Payne Knight*, 83.

wild, and somewhat romantic. Valancourt had known little of the world. . . . St. Aubert sometimes smiled at his warmth, but seldom checked it . . .   (p. 41)

When Valancourt actually exercises his warmth and generosity by giving away to a poor shepherd all the money he is carrying 'except a very few louis', his reward is immediate. The thought that he may not be able to return home without privation is cast aside a he experiences a lightness of heart which is of greater value than any riches enjoyed in 'the cold shade of selfishness': 'his gay spirits danced with pleasure; every object around him appeared more interesting, or beautiful, than before' (*Udolpho*, p. 53). To be sure, there is a hint of narratorial irony when St Aubert is made to commend the young chevalier's 'sunshine of benevolence and reason united'; for St Aubert and Emily have both been more prudent in their charity and do not know the extent of Valancourt's gift. But, later, Emily remarks to her father that 'poverty cannot deprive us of intellectual delights . . . so long as we are not in want of necessaries' (p. 60); and, yet later again, she learns to distinguish 'the constant gaiety and good spirits' of Madame Cheron's set from the 'uncommon vivacity' of a Valancourt. 'The feverish animation' of the former does not arise from a 'content as constant and a benevolence as ready', but from 'an insensibility to the cares . . . the sufferings of others, and . . . from a desire to display that appearance of prosperity, which they know will command submission and attention to themselves' (p. 123). Thus it seems that the reader is being asked to accept the notion, generalized from the writings of Shaftesbury, Gerard, Hume, Adam Smith, and others, that aesthetic feelings can become moral principles.[28] 'The best and purest feelings, disposing us to benevolence, pity and friendship' (p. 46) are endorsed by Valancourt and the St Auberts.

For all that, when placed in opposition to those individualistic and materialistic principles for which the Quesnels, Madame Cheron, and the Countess De Villefort stand—worldliness, consequence, selfish ambition, splendour, and the conspicuous consumption associated with middle- and upper-class

---

[28] Mary Poovey, 'Ideology and *The Mysteries of Udolpho*', *Criticism*, 21/4 (1979) 312–14; Murray, *Ann Radcliffe*, 37–8.

city life—these Romantic moral and aesthetic ideals appear initially to have little 'revolutionary' potential. Those who adhere to them can only withdraw from the world, not change it. As St Aubert himself says:

The world . . . ridicules a passion which it seldom feels; its scenes, and its interests, distract the mind, deprave the taste, corrupt the heart . . . Virtue and taste are nearly the same, for virtue is little more than active taste, and the most delicate affections of each combine in real love. How then are we to look for love in great cities, where selfishness, dissipation, and insincerity supply the place of tenderness, simplicity and truth? (*Udolpho*, pp. 49–50)

Moreover, those who have chosen retirement can be seriously disempowered. Faced with further loss because of the failure of a merchant whom he trusted, and Quesnel's self-interested building projects and lack of support, St Aubert's freedom and health are progressively undermined. As he is pushed into poverty, he becomes more than ever 'an insulated being' (p. 24).

Sensibility and distorted perception or instability are shown to be linked when St Aubert deviates from his own precepts about the enervation of excessive grief, the comfort and spiritual elevation provided by nature, and the dangers of impetuosity. Having cautioned Emily against overindulgence in mourning, he secretly gives way at times to his own grief, and is ordered by his physician to travel because perceptible sorrow has 'seized upon his nerves' (p. 25). While travelling through the Pyrenees, he is impressed by Valancourt's 'keen susceptibility to the grandeur of nature'; but caught by his own heightened response to the 'wild', supposedly banditti-infested regions, he rashly wounds the young chevalier in mistake for a bandit. Valancourt is not even given the opportunity to defend himself.[29] The 'romantic' sensibility now begins to look as if it renders the subject more vulnerable in the face of adversity, unless it is strongly governed by the (bourgeois) virtues of prudence and self-control.

Indeed, this is the tenor of St Aubert's deathbed warning to his daughter:

---

[29] Robert Kiely makes this point in *Romantic Novel in England*, 71.

do not indulge in the pride of fine feeling, the romantic error of amiable minds. Those, who really possess sensibility, ought early to be taught, that it is a dangerous quality, which is continually extracting the excess of misery, of delight, from every surrounding circumstance. And, since, in our passage through this world, painful circumstances occur more frequently than pleasing ones, and since our sense of evil is, I fear, more acute than our sense of good, we can become the victims of our feelings, unless we can in some degree command them . . .   (*Udolpho*, pp. 79–80)

St Aubert cautions Emily against both 'a heart that is continually alive to minute circumstances' and 'one that is dead to feeling'. And although he considers that 'apathy is a vice more hateful than all the errors of sensibility', it is the latter which he stresses, thereby signalling that Emily's 'susceptibility' to excessive sensibility will expose her to 'tumult' and 'vicissitude', for which she must develop 'fortitude'. Many of the later incidents and narratorial pronouncements ostensibly augment this theme by accentuating the debility and delusions into which Emily's 'irrational' sensibility leads her, and deeming her recognition and restraint of her own 'excess' necessary to the maintenance of her virtue and growth to maturity. Once 'under the dominion' of the unfeeling Montoni, forcibly separated from Valancourt, promised to another, and confined at Udolpho, Emily is left to test the power which possession of the romantic sensibility entails.

The Interrogation of Sensibility

The view that, through the telling of Emily's adventures, the novel makes a strong case for the balanced union of reason and feeling, sense and sensibility, has been advanced frequently since the novel's initial publication.[30] William Enfield, for example, in the *Monthly Review* for November 1794, approved the 'habit of self command' acquired by Emily, and the 'steady firmness to her conduct': 'Good sense effectually fortifies her against superstitious fear; and a noble integrity and

---

[30] For recent interpretations along these lines see Nelson C. Smith, 'Sense, Sensibility and Ann Radcliffe', *Studies in English Literature*, 13 (1973), 577–90; Roberts, *Gothic Romance*, 154.

sublime piety support her in the midst of ter
gers.'[31] In such interpretations, the sublime, the
the fantastic function to establish, in moral ar
gical terms, the triumph of what, as noted in Ch
Caillois has called 'changeless everyday legalit
'excess' is subsumed by what is ostensibly the n
purpose. In examining the reception of *Udolpho*, it is worth
considering in more detail how these 'common-sense' interpretations can be supported.

To take first the central situation of the confinement of the
heroine by a Gothic villain. While Quesnel resembles the
tyrannical and destructive 'improving' landlords of philosophical novels like Robert Bage's *Man As He Is* (1792) and
Hermsprong (1796)—not to mention Jane Austen's *Northanger Abbey*—Montoni is a descendent of Walpole's 'hyper-
bolized' Manfred.[32] 'Uncommonly handsome', courageous,
and with a singular 'haughtiness of command and quickness
of discernment', the Italian quickly detects and despises vanity,
affectation, and frivolity in others (*Udolpho*, pp. 23, 122, 143,
211). As a result, he enjoys a certain superiority to Quesnel on
whose love of splendour and consequence he plays. By making
Montoni's seat at Udolpho, an ancient, fortified, and isolated
but neglected castle of massive Gothic proportions, Radcliffe
constructs him as an atavistic, fairy-tale tyrant, one with
whom the heroine of sensibility must needs engage if she is to
acquire 'fortitude'.

Emily is first informed by Valancourt of the probability of
Montoni's 'desperate fortune and character' and of his 'castle
situated among the Appenines' (*Udolpho*, pp. 156–7). How-
ever, despite the fact that 'the thought of being solely in
[Montoni's] power, in a foreign land, [is] terrifying to her' (p.
157), she yet refuses immediate marriage to Valancourt.
Instead emphasis is given continually to her need for fortitude:
' "We must part here", said she, stopping, "Why prolong these
moments? Teach me the fortitude I have forgot" ' (p. 160).
Later, Emily's need to seek and encounter the potentially

[31] [William Enfield], unsigned review, 'Mrs. Radcliffe's Mysteries of Udolpho', *Monthly Review*, 2nd ser. 15 (1794), 280.
[32] The phrase is that of David B. Morris, 'Gothic Sublimity', *New Literary
History*, 16/2 (Winter 1985), 302.

..rmful or frightening is described in terms of the 'fascination' of 'the purely sublime', which 'occupies and expands the mind' (p. 248). Overcoming terror engenders energy, activity, and assertiveness. The sexual dimensions which modern psycho-analytic critics see in Emily's fascination with Montoni and Udolpho are not made explicit by Radcliffe.

The virtue of fortitude is contrasted frequently in the novel with sensibility, an opposition appropriated from Edmund Burke's *Enquiry into the Origin of Our Ideas of the Sublime and Beautiful*. For Burke, 'fortitude, justice, wisdom, and the like' are virtues 'of the sublimer kind', producing 'admiration' and 'terror rather than love'. They are, he claims, superior in 'dignity' to the 'amiable', 'softer virtues' of 'easiness of temper, compassion, kindness and liberality'.[33] It is interesting to note that he associates the 'sublime' virtues with male authority and the 'softer virtues' with the weakness of old men and 'feminine partiality',[34] an opposition which *Udolpho* also initially reproduces in its portrayal of Montoni, St Aubert, and Emily.

During Emily's confinement at Udolpho, however, Radcliffe depicts her heroine establishing her own 'sublime' authority, one based on both a clear understanding of the law and certain evidence that the courageous and colourful Montoni is lacking in any sense of justice. Montoni blatantly attempts to cheat Emily of her inherited estates, stressing the while 'the weak-ness' and 'ignorance' of her sex; but she resists his contempt with a quick wit and 'mild dignity', telling him that she 'can endure with fortitude, when it is in the resistance of oppres-sion' (*Udolpho*, p. 381). Having returned to her chamber, she contemplates 'the evil she might expect from opposition to his will', and finds his status in her thoughts much reduced:

his power did not appear so terrible to her imagination, as it was wont to do: a sacred pride was in her heart, that taught it to swell against the pressure of injustice, and almost to glory in the quiet sufferance of ills . . . For the first time, she felt the full extent of her own superiority to Montoni, and despised the authority, which, till now, she had only feared. (pp. 381–2)

[33] Burke, *Philosophical Enquiry into . . . the Sublime*, 110–11.
[34] Ibid. 111.

In Radcliffe's recontextualization of Burke's 'sublime' and 'softer' virtues, the woman, Emily, emerges as custodian of virtues which are not merely the 'softer' ones.

By the same token, the novel also dramatically endorses tenets from Wollstonecraft's *Vindication of the Rights of Woman*. In this work Mary Wollstonecraft had denied 'the existence of sexual virtues' and had discoursed on the grim consequences for women of fostering 'a romantic unnatural delicacy of feeling', 'an overstretched sensibility' which 'relaxes the other powers of the mind'.[35] The answer to 'tyrants and sensualists' who attempted 'to keep women in the dark' lay in a return to reason: 'Strengthen the female mind by enlarging it, and there shall be an end to blind obedience' (Wollstonecraft, p. 36). St Aubert, we remember, had 'endeavoured . . . to strengthen [Emily's] mind; to ensure [his daughter] to habits of self-command' (*Udolpho*, p. 5). Following Wollstonecraft, Radcliffe uses the verbal exchanges between Emily and Montoni to endorse 'such amiable Godlike qualities' as 'gentleness of manners, forbearance and long-suffering' rather than an 'abject' gentleness which assumes 'the submissive demeanour of dependence, the support of weakness that loves, because it wants protection; and is forbearing, because it must silently endure injuries; smiling under the lash at which it dare not snarl' (Wollstonecraft, pp. 46–7). The movement here is away from 'sexed' towards 'human' virtues and 'the harmony which arises from a balance of attributes' (Wollstonecraft, p. 61).

In as much as Montoni has any 'sublime', tyrannical female counterpart, it is his relative, the wild and passionate Signora Laurentini di Udolpho, who is the true owner of the castle she has abandoned. Her story is shrouded in mystery. For most of the novel she is absent, displaced, believed dead. It eventuates that twenty years earlier she had secretly followed her lover, the more prudent Marquis de Villeroi, to France. There, by her 'arts of fascination', she had regained his affections and secured his complicity in poisoning his wife. Subsequently Laurentini had become Sister Agnes and spent the remainder

---

[35] Wollstonecraft, *Vindication of the Rights of Woman*, 46, 79. Further references appear in the text.

of her life in the monastery of St Clair, in a state of intense remorse, melancholia, and frequent derangement. It is there that Emily finally learns the secret of the portrait and papers which her father has kept secret from her. The Marchioness had been her father's other sister, and not his mistress and Emily's mother, as Sister Agnes has intimated. A woman of 'beauty and sensibility', this 'spectral' heiress/nun is well placed to warn Emily of 'the first indulgence of the passions', 'the scorpions' which will 'sting . . . even unto death' (*Udolpho*, pp. 574, 646). Her 'Gothic' past, interpenetrating as it does with Emily's present, accords both with St Aubert's early admonitions to Emily about the vicious 'excess' of feelings indulged at the expense of duty and with Emily's own lessons in the constant need for restraint and fortitude.

One such lesson occurs when her father dies and Emily insists on returning more than once to the chamber where his body lies. There she yields to 'all the anguish of hopeless grief' and is later discovered 'lying senseless across the foot of the bed, near which stood the coffin' (*Udolpho*, p. 87). The relation here between sensibility and insensibility is a very close one; Radcliffe actually refers to Emily's 'state of insensibility' and immediately has her perceive 'the necessity of sparing her spirits, and recollecting fortitude sufficient to bear her through the approaching scene' of her father's funeral.

While she is confined at Udolpho by Montoni, Emily's trials take a more consistently epistemological turn. The prose becomes even less specific and denotative as features of the Burkean sublime are brought into play: obscurity, power, vastness, infinity, magnificence, difficulty and 'general privations' such as 'Vacuity, Darkness, Solitude and Silence'.[36] 'Silent, lonely and sublime', the great Gothic castle, with its 'mouldering walls of dark grey stone' (pp. 226–7), seems to Emily 'to stand the sovereign of the scene, and to frown defiance on all, who dared to invade its solitary reign'; as the twilight deepens, it becomes 'more awful in obscurity'; from 'the massy walls of the ramparts', she is able 'to know' that it is 'vast, ancient and dreary' (*Udolpho*, p. 227). Fearing that she is 'going into her prison', she is confirmed in this belief by the 'gloomy court'

---

[36] Burke, *Philosophical Enquiry into . . . the Sublime*, 58–78.

through which her carriage passes. The pervasive emptiness and 'desolation' of the place engenders an unaccountable conviction of evil—of 'long-suffering and murder'—and at this point the omniscient narrator comments that '[Emily's] imagination, ever awake to circumstance, suggested even more terrors, than her reason could justify' (*Udolpho*, p. 228).

There follows a series of drawn-out events which exemplify this remark. What Emily presumably perceives as the rotting corpse of Laurentini, behind a mysterious black veil, turns out, near the end of the novel, to have been a wax simulacrum. She wrongly believes that Montoni has murdered both her aunt and the Signora Laurentini, and as a result she suffers a temporary loss of reason. Affected by the illusions of 'superstition', she believes that the lute music coming from below her window is her dead father speaking to her in the form of a 'guardian spirit'. Later, believing that this music is played by her lover, Valancourt, she becomes convinced that he is her fellow prisoner, come to rescue her. In fact, her rescuer is an unknown but longstanding admirer, Du Pont, another Frenchman come to Italy in the service of his country and captured by Montoni's men. Clearly, so the narrator's argument goes, 'the influence of superstition' has 'gained on the weakness of her long harassed mind' (p. 355) to such a degree that she is no longer able to distinguish reality from fantasy.

By foregrounding such situations, events, and narratorial pronouncements as those just outlined, the reader or critic can readily interpret *Udolpho* as 'an attack on the cult of sensibility' and a call for return to reason and balance. In recent times Nelson C. Smith has read the novel in this way, as has a feminist critic, Mary Poovey.[37] The latter regards *Udolpho* as Radcliffe's 'intuitive' exposure of both 'the internal instability of sensibility' and the fact that pure aggression or tyranny is immune to its 'socializing reciprocity'. As lived ideology, sensibility thus poses a two fold threat to women: 'Sensibility is dangerous, as Emily's hysteria shows, because it encourages imaginative and libidinal excesses; but its more telling liability

[37] Smith, 'Sense, Sensibility and Ann Radcliffe', 577–90; Poovey, 'Ideology and *The Mysteries of Udolpho*', 307–30.

resides in its inability to resist the masculine version of desire—the lust of unregulated avarice'.[38]

Unlike Smith, however, Poovey admits that Radcliffe continues to affirm sensibility and the sentimental values 'because they do provide women with power'.[39] Where these critics are both at variance with others is in their failure to consider how discourses of the sublime and the fantastic function in the novel. For while it is true that the narrator's moralistic commentaries return the reader to 'everyday legality' and so constitute a critique of the obsessiveness and hysteria which sensibility via 'sublime' fear and superstition can admit, this critique is in turn interrogated by those long and suspenseful passages which bring us close to Emily's consciousness. At such times the omniscient narrator recedes behind Emily's viewpoint and it becomes obvious that the young woman has little concrete information with which to build a framework to make sense of her experience. Thus, if intuition is all she has to go on, she must be given credit for her ingenuity and daring, especially when her fears and 'illusions' have greater interest and plausibility than the supposedly 'real'. As Thomas Noon Talfourd put it in his essay of 1826, 'the impression survives' even after the author has 'dissolved mystery after mystery, and abjured spell after spell'.[40]

The Interrogation of 'Everyday Legality' by the Discourses of the Sublime and Fantastic

Robert Kiely puts Emily's situation precisely when he claims that 'both literally and metaphorically, [she] is unable to see exactly where she is and what is going on around her'.[41] Although the Gothic castle is dark and gloomy, she is given no guidance in respect to its layout. Montoni's terse addresses—

[38] Poovey, 'Ideology and *The Mysteries of Udolpho*', 322.
[39] Ibid. 329.
[40] Thomas Noon Talfourd, 'Memoir of the Life and Writings of Mrs. Radcliffe', in Ann Radcliffe, *Gaston de Blondville or The Court of Henry III*, 2 vols. (London: Henry Colburn, 1826), i, p. cxvii.
[41] Kiely, *Romantic Novel in England*, 74.

when he speaks to her at all—reveal an intention to keep her 'in the dark' and thereby maintain power:

It does not suit me to answer enquiries . . . nor does it become you to make them; time may unfold them all: but I desire I may be no further harassed, and I recommend it to you to retire to your chamber, and to endeavour to adopt a more rational conduct, than that of yielding to fancies, and to a sensibility, which, to call it by the gentlest name, is only a weakness. (*Udolpho*, p. 230)

Forcibly excluded from knowledge and society, Emily is treated by Montoni as an object of contempt in the way that Mary Wollstonecraft had predicted women of sensibility would be treated. Emily, however, is quite aware of the fact that, without any handle on the real, she has only conjecture to go on; she thus explores Udolpho both to assuage her curiosity and to expand her knowledge of her situation. Moreover, she does not see her periodic yieldings to the excesses of sensibility in an entirely negative light; she believes that her present life is a temporary aberration: 'like the dream of a distempered imagination, or like one of those frightful fictions, in which the wild genius of the poets sometimes delighted' (*Udolpho*, p. 296). What is striking, within the figural patterning of the novel, is that Emily's hunches, intuitions, and intense imaginings so often could have been right that they bolster faith in the irrational and threaten to unravel the whole fabric. This is attested by the fact that many readers have felt cheated by Radcliffe's 'rational' explanations, which in some cases seem more improbable than Emily's original fancies.

The *British Critic*, for one, complained that *Udolpho* had 'too much of the terrific' and that 'the endeavour to explain supernatural appearances and incidents, by plain and simple facts, [was] not always happy'.[42] Coleridge, for another, wrote that 'curiosity is kept upon the stretch' and 'is raised oftener than it is gratified; or rather it is raised so high that no adequate gratification can be given it'. He concluded that stretching the novel to a fourth volume was unnecessary and that Emily's adventures did not 'sufficiently point to one centre'.[43] Finally, William Enfield, who early in his review had

[42] *British Critic*, 4 (Aug. 1794), 121.
[43] Coleridge, *Miscellaneous Criticism*, 356–7.

approved the novel's balance, was troubled by the 'alienation of affection' of Valancourt, and remained unconvinced by the substitution of Du Pont as Emily's rescuer. Guided no doubt by the sequencing and transformation, or 'overdetermination', of Radcliffe's imagery, Enfield found the turn of events to be 'unnatural':

The performance would in our opinion have been more perfect, as well as more pleasing, if Du Pont, Emily's unsuccessful admirer, had never appeared; and if Valancourt had been, as Emily expected, her deliverer from Udolpho. The story, we apprehend, might have easily been brought to its present conclusion on this supposition.[44]

For at least some early readers, then, the novel's claims for Emily's intensities of imagination and intuitive feeling were at odds with its moral precepts, and could not be wholly subordinated to the didactic or 'philosophic' frame which, for a recent critic, 'justifies and unifies the tensions of ambivalence in all aspects of the narrative'.[45]

There is also the matter of several minor but seemingly preternatural presentiments and occurrences which are never satisfactorily explained. One of these is the 'small and lambent flame' which by turns appears and vanishes on the point of the lance carried by the soldier, Antonio. This fellow, like Emily, is new to Udolpho, and is himself at a loss to explain the strange light. He can only repeat the claim of his comrade that 'it is an omen . . . and bodes no good' (p. 373). Later that night, Madame Montoni dies and the fantastic conjunction of events takes on a type of validity that is never really refuted. Likewise elements of Fate appear to operate in the strange conveyance of the dying St Aubert to the woods by Château-le-Blanc where his sister was poisoned, and also in bringing back the shipwrecked Emily to the same place after her escape from Udolpho. There is, too, the coincidence of elements of the ghostly 'Provençal Tale' with the facts of Ludovico's disappearance from the late Marchioness's chamber at the château.[46]

    [44] *Monthly Review*, 2nd ser. 15 (Nov. 1794), 281.
    [45] Roberts, *Gothic Romance*, 153.
    [46] For a discussion of Radcliffe's use of Elizabethan-style dramatic scenes of the supernatural, see Clara M. McIntyre, 'Were the "Gothic Novels" Gothic?', *PMLA* 36/4 (Dec. 1921), 646, 652–64.

Similar strange presentiments, confirmed by subsequent events, also occur early in the novel. There is St Aubert's unspoken foreboding that his wife's illness would be 'a fatal one', for example, and the 'superstitious dread' which seizes Emily the night before her father's death. In the latter case, reason has warned Emily that the anecdote told by the peasant, La Voisin, about the 'mysterious music' in the woods coming 'to warn people of their deaths', is only 'ridiculous superstition' (*Udolpho*, p. 68). Even so, she is unable wholly to 'resist its contagion', as St Aubert is indeed sinking fast and dies the next day. Moreover, the music itself, which is produced by a beautiful voice and instrument, is given a sublime, religious connotation: it is 'like the music of the angels' and it arises in the woods near the convent of St Clair (p. 71). Emily listens for it at the window of her chamber, just as she had listened to some music on a previous evening, when, together with her father and Valancourt, she had taken rest for the night in another convent. On that occasion, Emily's thoughts and feelings had gone winging upwards to the 'midnight hymn of the monks' as it 'rose softly from the chapel', and she had become lost in 'adoration of the Deity' (p. 47). This elevation of consciousness, which is not readily relinquished by Emily, is described in tones of approval by the narrator: 'Her eyes were filled with tears of awful love and admiration; and she felt that pure devotion, superior to all the distinctions of human system, which lifts the soul above this world, and seems to expand it into another nature' (p. 48). In the same way, an equivalence between natural and supernatural grandeur is forged in descriptions of Emily's responses to the landscape: 'she loved more the wild wood-walks, that skirted the mountain; and still more the mountain's stupendous recesses, where the silence and grandeur of solitude impressed a sacred awe upon her heart, and lifted her thoughts to the GOD OF HEAVEN AND EARTH' (*Udolpho*, p. 6).

In sum, the reader's confidence in Emily's perceptional powers is wooed early in the novel, where mysterious music, the sublime grandeur of the landscape, and Emily's intense responses and presentiments are intriguing but relatively unproblematic. These 'fantastic' responses anticipate the later extreme conjectures, delusions, and Gothic terrors, but their presence within the protective confines of family and friends is treated more or less as an extension of the 'real'. Shifting to Hoffmann's terminology, we can view them as an 'extension of the finite, an expansion or manipulation of space and time . . . structured in the patterns of "good continuation" '.[47] Thus, when narratorial assertions about Emily's unjustified fears and imaginings are set against superstitions and accounts of the supernatural and unnatural in the later scenes, a conflict of voices occurs. This dialogism is never resolved and reason and reality are revealed as arbitrary, shifting constructs.

Many of Emily's fears and illusions continue to appear justified because they are not altogether disproportionate to the strange appearances and violent events actually occurring. The undercutting of seemingly supernatural events and unnatural events by narratorial revelation or comment does not result in there being no cause for Emily's fears and surmises. The spectral voices which haunt Montoni do actually come from someone—a prisoner (Du Pont) who has discovered hidden passages in the castle. Montoni may not have directly murdered his wife, but his cruelty and neglect do bring about her rapid decline. Likewise, Ludovico may not have been spirited away by supernatural means from the late Marchioness's bedroom at Château-le-Blanc; but his strange removal by banditti by way of a concealed passage is hardly 'natural', either. This complaint was made by the reviewer for the *British Critic* who thought Radcliffe's supposedly natural explanation 'improbable in the extreme'.[48] As Kiely indicates, Emily has a fine sense of danger;[49] if not of the supernatural, then certainly of the unnatural, such as the possible intrusion of someone into her bedroom. Her unwanted suitor, Count Morano, does in fact enter her chamber through the door about which she has complained previously to Montoni. It cannot be locked from the inside, but has been mysteriously bolted from the outside where, winding from it, is a 'steep, narrow staicase . . . between two stone walls' (*Udolpho*, p. 235). Her guardian

---

[47] Hoffmann, 'Fantastic in Fiction', 283–4.

[48] *British Critic*, 4 (Aug. 1794), 121; Howells, *Love, Mystery and Misery*, 48, also comments that too often what is shown is 'a correspondence rather than a contrast between imagined fears and the romance world'.

[49] Kiely, *Romantic Novel in England*, 71.

dismisses the matter as 'trifling' and her fear as 'idle whim', but such is Emily's prescience that, on the night of Morano's sudden appearance, she is 'determined not to undress' and falls asleep in her clothes.

If we ask why Radcliffe employs discourses which make such positive claims for feeling and imagination, we can, of course, point to the fact that many, if not most, of Emily's terrors and imaginings are of sexual violation, confinement, loss of rights and property, and death. We can then claim that the author was using superstitions, presentiments, and hints and tales of the supernatural to acknowledge the powerful desires and fears which lay just below the surface of late eighteenth-century British society.[50] At one point, the narrator comments that the servant, Annette, 'dearly loved the marvellous' (*Udolpho*, p. 235); at another, Montoni is made to say that he is not superstitious, but knows 'how to despise the commonplace sentences, which are frequently uttered against superstition' (p. 291). In as much as the novel uses the fantastic to reproduce and reinforce fears of male domination, endorsing a desire for escape, it can be said to be subversive. Despite the restoration of Emily and the errant Valancourt to the idyllic, pastoral life at La Vallée at the close of the novel, and the conveyance of Udolpho to Emily, the forces of greed, vanity, sexual passion, and death have been shown to be more active in shaping society than St Aubert's benevolence, companionate-romantic love, and 'active virtue'. Modern critics, particularly, find Radcliffe's ending unconvincing, and those of psychoanalytic persuasion have argued that the novel's real theme is the eruption of 'primal' desires repressed by civilized (or middle-class) society.[51]

---

[50] Ibid. 72–8. See also Punter, *Literature of Terror*, 95; 'Social Relations of Gothic Fiction', in David Aers, with Jonathan Cook and David Punter, *Romanticism and Ideology: Studies in English Writing, 1765–1830* (London, Boston, and Henley: Routledge & Kegan Paul, 1981), 110–11, 116–17.

[51] Mary Laughlin Fawcett, 'Udolpho's Primal Mystery', *Studies in English Literature*, 23 (1983), 481–94; Howells, *Love, Mystery and Misery*, 48, 58–61; Cynthia Griffin Wolff, 'The Radcliffean Gothic Model: A Form for Sexuality', in Fleenor, ed., *Female Gothic*, 207–14; Norman N. Holland and Leona F. Sherman, 'Gothic Possibilities', *New Literary History*, 8 (Winter 1977), 285–8, 293.

However, the novel also incorporates a mode of artistic discourse which modern critics find it expedient to ignore. As poetry is particularly conspicuous, its inclusion seems also relevant to our consideration of Radcliffe's ambivalent endorsement of feeling and imagination.

Emily as Sublime Poet

It has generally gone unnoticed that Wollstonecraft qualified at one point her own condemnation of 'the wild emotions that agitate a reed over which every passing breeze has power' (Wollstonecraft, p. 41). 'I do not mean to allude', she says, 'to the romantic passion, which is the concomitant of genius.— Who can clip its wing?' (p. 44). Wollstonecraft was also at pains to deny that a delicate constitution was a necessary concomitant of genius:

People of genius have, very frequently, impaired their constitutions by study or careless inattention to their health, and the violence of their passions bearing a proportion to the vigour of their intellects, the sword's destroying the scabbard has become almost proverbial, and superficial observers have inferred from thence, that men of genius have commonly weak, or to use a more fashionable phrase, delicate constitutions. (p. 52)

The works of Shakespeare and Milton, she continues, 'were not the ravings of imbecility, the sickly effusions of distempered brains; but the exuberance of fancy, that "in a fine phrenzy" wandering, was not continually reminded of its material shackles [i.e. a delicate constitution]' (p. 53). Radcliffe, writing only a year or two later, constructs Emily as a poet of 'romantic passion' and keen awareness of her own need for mental and bodily 'fortitude'.

As we have seen, Radcliffe uses many of the 'sublime' occasions in the novel to celebrate Emily's 'enthusiasm', a creativity which, according to Duff, 'is much more delighted with surveying the rude magnificence of nature, than the elegant decorations of art'. On his view Art produces only 'an agreeable sensation of pleasure', while sublime nature 'throws the soul into a divine transport of admiration and amazement'.[52] As Angela Leighton puts it, for Duff 'the heart is the original speaker, and enthusiasm is the emotional speed with which "the natural dictates of the heart" can be externalized in language'.[53] Thus Emily's psychological energy, which directs her art, authenticates it as 'not fictitious or copied, but original'.[54] During the course of the novel Radcliffe has her compose some fifteen poems. These, along with one or two pieces supposedly by St Aubert and Valancourt, and quotations by Emily and the narrator from Shakespeare, Milton, Thomson, Beattie, Collins, and others, are 'interspersed' with the story. Indeed, in the original 1794 edition, *Udolpho* was subtitled *A Romance; interspersed with some pieces of poetry*. No wonder, then, that literary women enjoyed this aspect of *Udolpho*. Mrs Hester Lynch Piozzi, writing to her daughter in December 1794, commented: 'The reading ladies of Denbigh find our Mysteries of Udolpho a Treasure, I sent for it from London to divert them. Cecilia says that like Emily the moment my Mind or my Teeth are at Ease for an Instant, I sit about arranging a few stanzas . . .'[55]

Robert Kiely comments that Emily 'turns to music and literature for consolation and order, but even art eventually fails her'.[56] However, Radcliffe always makes it clear that Emily is unable to read, draw, or play the compositions of others; and this is because the works are 'utterly discordant with her present state of feelings' (*Udolpho*, p. 319). Emily more than once feels 'how infinitely inferior all the splendour of art is to the sublimity of nature' (p. 189). Just prior to the passage from which Kiely quotes, Emily has witnessed the forcible removal by Montoni's 'ruffians' of her aunt to the east turret. The castle is a scene of 'savage discord' as the vengeful Montoni pursues those responsible for attempting to poison him. Terrified and alone, Emily can find some consolation, but only in nature: 'She sat down, near one of the casements, and, as

[52] Duff, *Essay on Original Genius*, 151.'
[53] Angela Leighton, *Shelley and the Sublime: An Interpretation of the Major Poems* (Cambridge: Cambridge University Press, 1984), 16.
[54] Duff, *Essay on Original Genius*, 156, quoted in Leighton, loc. cit.
[55] James Lowry Clifford, *Hester Lynch Piozzi (Mrs. Thrale)* (Oxford: Oxford University Press, 1957), 379.
[56] Kiely, *Romantic Novel in England*, 77–8.

she gazed on the mountain-view beyond, the deep repose of its beauty struck her with all the force of contrast . . .' (*Udolpho*, p. 318). Consider also the following passage which occurs after Emily's successful resistance of Montoni's first attempt to force her to sign over her estates:

Emily sought to lose the sense of her own cares, in the visionary scenes of the poet; but she had again to lament the irresistible force of circumstances over the taste and powers of the mind; and that it requires a spirit at ease to be sensible even to the abstract pleasures of pure intellect. The enthusiasm of genius, with all its pictured scenes, now appeared cold and dim. As she mused upon the book before her, she involuntarily exclaimed, 'Are these, indeed, the passages, that have so often given me exquisite delight? Where did the charm exist?—Was it in my mind, or in the imagination of the poet? It lived in each', said she, pausing. 'But the fire of the poet is vain, if the mind of his reader is not tempered like his own, however it may be inferior to his in power.' (*Udolpho*, p. 383)

Here, as in late eighteenth-century aesthetic theory generally, the sublime centres on psychological states rather than on 'pictured scenes',[57] which are imitations of nature, no matter how 'original'. Radcliffe's emphasis is always first and foremost on the woman-poet, Emily, as one who sees and feels; *ipso facto*, existing works of art are incommensurate with her own sublime fear and 'sacred pride' at Montoni's injustice.

Radcliffe's re-inscription, in the context of woman's subjection, of the common association between natural creativity, sensibility, and the sublime can be illustrated by passages from the early part of Volume II. Here the author continues to emphasize the richness of Emily's inner life and to contrast it with the shallowness of Madame Cheron (Madame Montoni), who can think only of being mistress of a castle and 'little less than a princess' (*Udolpho*, pp. 166, 177, 190). But there are no narratorial qualifications of the dangers of the imagination. Rather, Emily's feelings of ecstasy and exhilaration,

---

[57] For discussions of the shift from object to subject in the development of theories of the sublime, see Monk, *Sublime*, 75, 110, 132, 204-5. The question is not considered in Malcolm Ware, *Sublimity in the Novels of Ann Radcliffe: A Study of the Influence upon her Craft of Edmund Burke's 'Enquiry into the Origin of our Ideas of the Sublime and Beautiful'* (Uppsala: Lindequist, 1963).

which arise from her solitary contemplation of nature, music, her attachment to Valancourt, and memories of her parents and home, are shown to endow her with a kind of power which includes the possibility of art. Emily employs her thoughts and feelings in composing several poems at this period, the discourse of the sublime being used by the author to convey beforehand the mystical workings of her poetic mind and heart, and the insufficiency of language to the greatness of its object:

they quitted their carriages and began to ascend the Alps. And here such scenes of sublimity opened upon them as no colours of language must dare to paint! Emily's mind was even so much engaged with new and wonderful images, that they sometimes banished the idea of Valancourt, though they more frequently revived it. . . . She seemed to have arisen into another world, and to have left every trifling sentiment, in that below; those only of grandeur and sublimity now dilated her mind, and elevated the affections of her heart. (*Udolpho*, p. 163)

That art could possibly offer a solution to the lack of harmony which all too soon comes to exist between Emily's 'inner' desires and 'outer' existence is suggested by the Carnival scene in Venice. Conveyed abruptly and by stealth to that city by Montoni, Emily watches alone from a balcony of his palazzo, as a colourful procession of gondolas, carrying representations of 'the fabled deities of the city', glides by:

The fantastic splendour of this spectacle, together with the grandeur of the surrounding palaces, appeared like the vision of the poet suddenly embodied, and the fanciful images, which it awakened in Emily's mind, lingered there long after the procession had passed away. She indulged herself in imagining what might be the manners and delights of a sea-nymph, till she almost wished to throw off the habit of mortality, and plunge into the green wave . . . (*Udolpho*, p. 178)

Such is Emily's 'enthusiasm', that she speaks aloud her desires of living 'amidst the coral bowers and crystal caverns of the ocean with [her] sister nymphs'. There would she 'skim on the surface of the waves round wild rocks and along sequestered shores' and be free to soothe the sorrows of 'some pensive wanderer' with her 'sweet music' and 'delicious fruit'.

Drawing on the sublime and on classical myth, the author produces images which give Emily-as-nymph control of her own fate or story. But then, as if there were some impropriety in allowing this wishful fantasy to dominate Emily's thoughts, Radcliffe combines her narratorial perspective with Emily's own and comments ironically, but indulgently, on the young woman's pretensions:

> She was recalled from her reverie to a mere mortal supper, and could not forbear smiling at the fancies she had been indulging, and at her conviction of the serious displeasure, which Madame Montoni would have expressed, could she have been made acquainted with them. (*Udolpho*, p. 178)

Just why Madame Montoni would have been displeased is worth considering. There is, of course, her frequent remark that Emily makes herself miserable indulging in 'affectation of sensibility' (p. 117) and 'fanciful sorrows' (p. 161), and would benefit from a return to common sense. But there is also the content of Emily's reverie, which her aunt is likely to find contrary to propriety, as she understands it; for, as a benevolent sea-nymph, Emily enjoys untrammelled delights and the power of a free agent amidst the companionship of 'sister nymphs'. She is no longer the pensive, sorrowing wanderer; that role is given to a male whom she can comfort after her own fashion. This can be read as both an escape from the tyranny of patriarchal authority in which she now lives—and with which her aunt is complicit—and fulfilment in another mode of being which gives her control of her own sexuality and excludes both marriage and all forms of pecuniary advantage. It is, in short, an oppositional fantasy, and it is significant that, in spite of her disclaimer, Radcliffe later has Emily go on to compose a poem called 'The Sea-Nymph', in which this fantasy is given a coherent and lasting form.

Emily's poetic experience is thus the reverse side of the coin of her earlier 'thick-coming fancies', such as that of her father's ghost sitting in his study at La Vallée. Those 'reveries of superstition' have been discounted by the narrator as 'distempered imaginings' or 'starts of the imagination, which deceive the senses into what can be called nothing less than temporary madness' (*Udolpho*, p. 102). The poem, on the other hand, is valued by the author to the extent that she not only includes it in the text, but uses it to conclude the chapter. She also alludes to it again in Volume III, and inserts a 'peasant' song-version, 'To A Sea-Nymph' (presumably written by herself), in order to contrast the evils of Udolpho with the arcadian happiness and freedom of peasant life in Tuscany (pp. 420–1). The occasion of the poem here is a peasant festival, with old songs, garlands, dancing, and 'sports'.

Radcliffe's poems did not go unremarked by critics of the 1790s, though generally they felt that the inclusion of verses in novels was 'misplaced'.[58] However Coleridge singled out the 'The Sea-Nymph' for particular praise and had it reprinted in full in his review of *Udolpho*, lest it be passed over by readers impatient for the story.[59] And it is not too fanciful to detect in his 'Rime of the Ancyent Marinere' (later subtitled 'A Poet's Reverie') echoes of Mrs Radcliffe's 'air spirits' and sea deeps of 'sapphire blue, | And ruby red and em'rald green' (*Udolpho*, pp. 180–1).

The first four stanzas of 'The Sea-Nymph' describe the nymph's ability to go 'down a thousand fathom deep | Among the sounding seas' where, within 'secret caves', she can hear 'the mighty rivers roar'. From below, she is thus enabled to guide

> streams through Neptune's waves
> To bless the green earth's inmost shore:
> And bid the freshen'd waters glide,
> For fern-crowned nymphs of lake, or brook,
> Through winding woods and pastures wide,
> And many a wild, romantic nook.
>
> (*Udolpho*, p. 179)

For this blessing the fresh-water nymphs dance, sing, and weave her name in gestures of thanks. But there are further wonders with which the sea-nymph 'love[s] to prove [her] charmful pow'r'. Tantalizing 'the sad lover' aboard ship with 'strains as speak no mortal means' is one; guiding 'the lone vessel' through storms, or saving the crew, is another. In these activities Ariel-like spirits of the air obey her 'potent voice they

---

[58] *British Critic*, 4 (Aug. 1794); *Analytical Review*, 19 (1794).
[59] Coleridge, *Miscellaneous Criticism*, 366–9.

love so well', and 'paint visions gay' on the clouds to help her soothe 'the ship-wreck'd sailor's heart'.

Near the end of the poem, Emily's playful nymph makes reference to the periodic punishment meted out by Neptune for her subversion of his sublime will. At such times she is bound 'to rocks below' where she must endure the vain cries of 'drowning seamen'. For all that, the nymph, undaunted, stresses her own freedom and power throughout her 'lay', and reaffirms her call to others in its closing lines.

Through the medium of this poem Radcliffe links Emily's romantic sensibility to freedom, assertiveness, and transgression of propriety, categories about which the narrator is in other places far more ambivalent.

As has already been noted, moralism is often in evidence in *Udolpho*. A representative example occurs when Emily determines to carry out her late father's request to burn some papers hidden at La Vallée. This she does in a state of semi-distraction brought on by a sudden vision of her father's countenance, a state that allows the involuntary fulfilment of her immediate desire. That is, she unwittingly disobeys her father's instructions not to read the papers: 'she was unconscious, that she was transgressing her father's strict injunction, till a sentence of dreadful import awakened her attention and her memory together' (*Udolpho*, p. 103). Having read this much, her imagination is further 'inflamed' and she begins 'to lament her promise'. More subversively still, she begins to doubt that her father's order 'could justly be obeyed, in contradiction to such reasons as there appeared to be for further information'. Emily's self-assertion is, of course, quickly glossed by the narrator as but 'momentary' and a 'delusion'. However, the curiosity aroused in the reader has by now begun to urge Emily's case to such a degree that the young woman's return to the impeccable moralism of filial duty functions as an exposure of its absurdity at the same time as Emily is 'solemnly' underwriting it. Receding behind the first-person voice, the narrator has Emily say: 'I have given a solemn promise . . . to observe a solemn injunction, and it is not my business to argue, but to obey. Let me hasten to remove the temptation, that would destroy my innocence, and embitter my life with the consciousness of irremediable guilt while I

have strength to reject it' (*Udolpho*, p. 103). That this resort
to conduct-book incantation (such as that found in James
Fordyce's *Sermons to Young Women* or Dr Gregory's *A
Father's Legacy to his Daughters*[60]) has frustrated the curiosity
of not only modern-day readers is exemplified by Coleridge's
remark, quoted earlier. Edith Birkhead, writing in 1921, also
complained about Emily's 'disconcerting trait' of 'impregnable
self-esteem' which alienates our sympathies. It would, she
says, have 'exasperated heroes less perfect and more human
than Mrs. Radcliffe's Theodores and Valancourts'.[61]

Here and there are further signs of narratorial impatience
with the convention of having heroines with 'an unfailing
consciousness of their own rectitude'.[62] For example, when it
is plain that St Aubert, in view of his ill health, will need the
attentions of a servant if he is to travel, the narrator excuses
Emily's failure of common-sense assertiveness in this respect
on the grounds that 'Emily seldom opposed her father's wishes
by question or remonstrances' (*Udolpho*, p. 25). Again, when
Emily finds that one of her books has been replaced by a
volume of Petrarch's sonnets belonging to Valancourt, the
narrator comments that Emily 'hesitated in believing, what
would have been sufficiently apparent to almost any other
person' (p. 58). As David Punter notes, '[Emily's] moral perfection is, like her sensibility, sometimes inappropriate and
even silly.'[63]

Certainly it is difficult to believe that Ann Radcliffe was
unaware of these absurdities, or that, in her conscientious
fulfilment of the role of moral educator, she was not also
consciously using the sublime and the fantastic to prejudice
her readers in favour of the power and importance of women's
intuition, 'enthusiasm', and creativity. She may conclude her
novel by commenting modestly and piously on 'the weak
hand' that has recorded her tale, and the usefulness of showing the innocent and patient triumphing over the vicious

---

[60] James Fordyce, *Sermons to Young Women* (London: A. Millar and
T. Cadell, 1767); Dr John Gregory, *A Father's Legacy to his Daughters*
(London: W. Strahan, T. Cadell, 1774).
    [61] Birkhead, *Tale of Terror*, 46.   [62] Ibid.
    [63] Punter, *Literature of Terror*, 87.

oppressor, whose power can only ever be transient (*Udolpho*, p. 672). But she begins her final chapter on a fantastic note, with a quotation from Milton's Comus, exalting the imagination:

> Now my task is smoothly done,
> I can fly, or I can run
> Quickly to the earth's green end,
> Where the bow'd welkin low doth bend,
> And, from thence, can soar as soon
> To the corners of the moon.
>
> (p. 670)

The suggestion here, according to Coral Ann Howells, is that 'the author can "soar" having earned her imaginative freedom, surely a disquieting admission from a novelist whose stated intention is to argue for the claims of decorum and rational self-control'.[64] It can also be added that Comus was a popular masquerade figure during the latter half of the eighteenth century and that by the 1770s it was common practice for women to appear in male attire at masquerades.[65] Attentive readers would have had little difficulty in making a connection between the quotation and Emily's flights of imagination—particularly the Carnival scene in Venice which prompts Emily's subversion of propriety in her poem, 'The Sea-Nymph'.

Dialogism in The Mysteries of Udolpho

Earlier in this chapter, we examined how Radcliffe appropriates the discourses of sensibility and taste to set up the aesthetic and moral norms of La Vallée and Château-le-Blanc. We then saw how sensibility itself is shown to be inherently unstable and hence potentially dangerous because it can lead to vulnerability and extreme insularity, or be subject to 'the riot of its own excess'. The didactic aspect of the novel, uppermost for some readers, develops from this theme, with narratorial stress being placed on the need for reason, restraint, and the acquisition of mental and bodily fortitude. For all that, we

---

[64] Howells, *Love, Mystery and Misery*, 60.
[65] Ribeiro, *Dress Worn at Masquerades in England*, 33.

find reason and order, or 'everyday legality', in turn relativize by the inclusion of superstitions, tales and scenes of the supernatural and unnatural, and the continuing claims for Emily's sublime feelings, imaginings, and presentiments. Moreover, Radcliffe's 'poeticization' of the novel further affirms the value of the romantic sensibility and imagination in contexts which have specific resonances for oppressed women and aspiring women writers.

In addition to constantly questioning the norms of the supposedly real and ideal, this dialogic interaction of discourses reveals the contradictions and dilemmas posed by the privileging of moral and aesthetic sensibility in women. Those very qualities which raised women's authority and allowed ascriptions of 'enthusiasm' and 'genius' to their artistic responses could also be used to constitute them as weak, delicate, and disordered. If the numerous conservative conduct books of the turn of the century are any guide, an increasingly influential, Evangelical, moral code was making 'sedentary' occupations, domestic seclusion, exemplary virtue, and fragility virtually prescriptive for women of sensibility, thus positioning them as a species apart.[66] But in 1794, in the wake of revolutionary excitement and Wollstonecraft's *A Vindication of the Rights of Woman*, Radcliffe was affirming women's poetic sensibility, genius, and fortitude—'sublime' as well as 'soft' virtues— while condemning 'excess', and meeting and occasionally subverting the ever-present but cramping requirements of propriety. Hers was a juggling act of no mean proportions, and one not to be accomplished without a certain amount of slippage.

The Reception of Udolpho

Praise by eighteenth-century readers of both sexes for Radcliffe's picturesque and sublime descriptions and poetry, as well as for her portrayal of Emily's 'steady firmness' of conduct, has been noted at various points during this chapter.

[66] Maurice James Quinlan, *Victorian Prelude: A History of English Manners 1700–1830* (New York: Columbia University Press, 1941), 139–56.

ublication, received reviews from men which ...stic or at the very least favourable. Radcliffe's rld of benevolence and elevated awareness of ...aps satisfied nostalgia for a simpler age, one with- ...iolence and threatened upheavals of late eighteenth- ...city life. Even the *British Critic* saw the work as 'the ven... e of . . . the purest morality'.[67] Critical unease did arise, however, from apparent disjunctions and redundancies in the narrative, departures from the 'natural', and supernatural turns which were unconvincingly explained. For example, the story of Laurentini/Agnes was considered 'extravagant', and the 'strange removal of Ludovico from the chateau of the Count de Villefort . . . improbable in the extreme'.[68] Neverthe-less, the didactic frame still remained uppermost (as it did for Henry Tilney in Jane Austen's *Northanger Abbey*) and Emily's 'visionary' sensibility was not perceived as a threat to the stability of society—except, perhaps by 'feminist' moralists such as Maria Edgeworth, who felt that 'poetic painting', or seeking 'a species of the moral picturesque . . . in every scene of life' was 'not always compatible with sound sense, or with simple reality'.[69]

Familiar with and sensitive to the controversy about women's talents, male critics gave ground to Radcliffe's 'poeticization' of the novel and her talent for suspense. But they still continued to assume implicitly that their own chosen genres and rational understandings were generally superior to those of women.[70] They claimed 'impartiality' and accommod-

---

[67] *British Critic*, 4 (Aug. 1794), 110.   [68] Ibid. 121.

[69] Bridget Hill, *Eighteenth-Century Women: An Anthology* (London: Allen & Unwin, 1984), 61.

[70] This attitude is well exemplified in a review of Wollstonecraft's *Vindication of the Rights of Woman* in the *Monthly Review*, 9 (June 1792), 198: 'Among the most enlightened people of antiquity, Wisdom, as well as Beauty, was deified under a female form; and in modern language it is still usual to give Philosophy and Wisdom a female personification. What is this but a tacit concession in favour of the female part of the species, that they are no less capable of instructing than of pleasing?—and how jealous forever WE might be of our right to the proud pre-eminence which we have assumed, the women of the present age are daily giving us indubitable proofs that mind is of no sex, and that, with the fostering aid of education, the world, as well as the nursery, may be benefited by their instructions.' However, this gesture did not prevent

ated and praised Radcliffe's 'extraordinary powers' as a writer, allowing *Udolpho* 'to rank high in the scale of literary excellence'. But then, in other, more subtle ways, they trivialized her product. As Coleridge put it, 'the trite and the extravagant [were] the Scylla and Charybdis of those who deal[t] in fiction'. Despite its popularity, he regarded fiction as a poor relation of poetry; whereas love of the latter was coupled with 'taste', the intense interest and curiosity inspired by the former was but 'a kind of appetite'.[71] For William Enfield, the curiosity aroused by Radcliffe's 'genius' for story placed readers in a kind of infant thraldom to 'gratifying terror'.[72] At no time did these critics question their own moralistic and evaluative frames. On the other hand, they were more open in expressing their prejudices than have been many twentieth-century formalist critics, who have assumed their own criticism to be objective, non-ethnocentric, and non-gendered.

While we have seen the qualifications and general uneasiness among male critics regarding Radcliffe's use of terror and the supernatural, our examination of the novel's early reception has so far failed to reveal much evidence of specific responses to this aspect of her work from women. When Anna Seward praised Mrs Radcliffe's 'power so to inspirit those fond fancies of the brain', she was careful to distinguish it from the 'matchless ability' and 'highly important morality of Richardson'.[73] Unfortunately, few other women have left us their comments. The time is therefore opportune to consider the context, meanings, and significance of one woman's fictional response

the reviewer from later showing his true colours. He remarks that Wollstonecraft pursues her subject 'with a degree of freedom . . . perhaps . . . thought singular in a female, but with a philosophical air of dignity and gravity, which precludes every idea of indecorum, and almost prohibits the intrusion of a smile' (p. 206).

[71] Samuel Taylor Coleridge, *Critical Review*, 2nd ser. 11 (Aug. 1794), reproduced in Coleridge, *Miscellaneous Criticism*, 356.

[72] William Enfield, *Monthly Review*, 2nd ser. 15 (Nov. 1794), reproduced in Scott, *On Novelists and Fiction*, 393, compares Radcliffe to 'the village matron' who, by the fireside, 'suspends her infant audience'. This sort of comparison is no doubt the source of the lingering nickname, 'Mother Radcliffe'.

[73] Quoted in McIntyre, *Ann Radcliffe in Relation to Her Time*, 55.

to *Udolpho*, Jane Austen's *Northanger Abbey*, alongside that of an 'Anti-Whig, Anti-Jacobin, anti-Sentimentalist, antifeminist writer',[74] Eaton Stannard Barrett. Barrett's burlesque of the Gothic, *The Heroine*, which enjoyed immense popularity when it was published in 1813, is little read today, while Austen's more quietly received 1818 publication has become canonical. Because both of these authors employ forms of parody, an examination of these texts will also extend our discussion of dialogism in the Gothic novel, showing how parody constitutes a specific type of dialogic utterance and differs from Radcliffe's stylization of discourses in *The Mysteries of Udolpho*.

[74] Gary Kelly, 'Unbecoming a Heroine: Novel Reading, Romanticism, and Barrett's *The Heroine*', *Nineteenth-Century Literature*, 45/2 (Sept. 1990), 227.

4

Gothic Parody: Jane Austen's Northanger Abbey *and Eaton Stannard Barrett's* The Heroine

Parody as a Type of Dialogic Utterance

We have seen how Radcliffe's recontextualizations of discourses of sensibility and taste, in circulation at the time of her writing, can be read dialogically as an affirmation of women's poetic sensibility, genius, and fortitude. Here we have drawn attention to a type of 'double-voiced' discourse which Bakhtin called *stylization*, and which involves the appropriation of the utterances of others for the purposes of inserting a new orientation of meaning alongside the original point(s) of view. The general direction and style is the same, but there is a re-nuancing or re-inflection of meaning, the effect of which is to relativize the authority and independence of the prior view. Like all intertextual utterances, stylization is 'best described not simply as an interaction of two speech acts, but as *an interaction designed to be heard and interpreted by a third person* (or second 'second person'), whose own process of active reception is anticipated and directed'.[1] In its dialogism, stylization differs from both imitation and plagiarism which both aim (successfully or otherwise) for a single-voicedness. The intention of the imitator is usually to merge utterances so completely that only one 'voice' is heard, while the plagiarist wishes to deny an original speaker and to attribute the utterance to the second speaker, namely himself or herself.

A parodic utterance, according to Bakhtin, has a different dialogic relation again to the first utterance. In *The Dialogic*

[1] Gary Saul Morson, 'Parody, History and Metaparody', in Morson and Emerson, eds., *Rethinking Bakhtin*, 65.

Imagination he describes parody as 'an intentional dialogized hybrid' within which 'languages and styles actively and mutually illuminate one another'.[2] In Gary Morson's formulation of Bakhtin's view, parody imitates an earlier utterance

in order to discredit it, and so introduces a 'semantic direction' which subverts that of the original. In this way the parodied utterance 'becomes the arena of conflict between two voices . . . the voices here are not only detached and distanced, they are hostilely counterposed' (PDP, 160)—counterposed, moreover, with the second voice clearly representing a higher 'semantic authority' than the first. The audience of the conflict knows for sure with whom it is expected to agree.[3]

At variance with this, however, is Linda Hutcheon's view in *A Theory of Parody*. Again adopting Bakhtin's concept of textual dialogism, but basing her discussion on an examination of modern and post-modern literature, art, and music, Hutcheon denies that parody always discredits its target. 'Both burlesque and travesty do necessarily involve ridicule', she says, while 'parody does not'.[4] In her view, a definition which turns on ridicule is not sufficient to distinguish parody from satire, and although the two styles frequently interact in particular historical periods, for example in the eighteenth- and early nineteenth-century novel, she emphasizes that we must take care to separate the two, 'given their different "targets" (intra- and extramural) and their different affinities with the rhetorical trope most common to both: irony'. While satire 'ridicules the transgression of social norms', parody always targets texts and exhibits what she calls 'a range of pragmatic "ethos" (ruling intended effects), from the reverential to the playful to the scornful'. This model, she claims, has advantages over Bakhtin's 'evaluative distinction between shallow and deep parody'.[5]

Accordingly, for Hutcheon, 'Parody . . . is a form of imitation, but imitation characterized by ironic inversion, not

[2] Bakhtin, *Dialogic Imagination*, 76.
[3] Morson, 'Parody, History and Metaparody', 66–7. He quotes here from Bakhtin's *Problems of Dostoevsky's Poetics*.
[4] Linda Hutcheon, *A Theory of Parody: The Teachings of Twentieth-Century Art Forms* (New York: Methuen, 1985), 40.
[5] Ibid. 26, 78.

always at the expense of the parodied text. . . . Parody is, in another formulation, repetition with a critical distance, which marks difference rather than similarity.'[6] While, in my view, the second of her formulations here does not allow us to distinguish sufficiently between parody and other forms of intertextuality such as stylization, the first, by its inclusion of *ironic inversion* as characteristic of all parody is very useful. It suggests the playful or ludic stylistic element we find in parody, without making it a type of enunciation which is necessarily negative, hostile, and dismissive in relation to its target enunciation, as in Morson's characterization. Operationally, Hutcheon's first formulation will allow us to distinguish between parodic and satiric intent in Austen's partly parodic *Northanger Abbey* and Barrett's thoroughgoing burlesque, *The Heroine*. Both of these novels can be said to parody Gothic and Sentimental fiction, although to different degrees, and both are satiric in tone, although the satiric intent is different in each case.

Hutcheon suggests of *Northanger Abbey* that Austen, under cover of parodying Gothic fiction and so appearing to be 'inoffensive', could take a satiric swipe at 'the literary and social patriarchy'. That is, her parody reveals 'a tension between her desire to exorcize the naive clichés of sentimental "women's" fiction and her inability or unwillingness to do so'. It is not intended to be dismissive of its target texts: 'Austen parodies gothic conventions, while relying on them for her novel's shape. As a result she succeeds in reinvesting the "female gothic" with authority derived from the interaction of parody and satire . . .'[7] Thus *Northanger Abbey* can be considered to challenge literary norms in order to renew and renovate them. On the other hand, the generally accepted view of Barrett's *The Heroine* is that it far exceeds *Northanger Abbey* in its exaggerated mimicking of Gothic conventions and so should be read as 'an effort to laugh Gothic fantasy into disrepute and out of the popular imagination'.[8] However,

---

[6] Ibid. 6, 104.   [7] Ibid. 79.
[8] Paul Lewis, 'Gothic and Mock Gothic: The Repudiation of Fantasy in Barrett's Heroine', *English Language Notes*, 21/1 (Sept. 1983), 44. See also

another reason why *The Heroine* is more radical in its 'critical difference' from the Gothic is that its string of comic episodes draws to a large extent on picaresque satire, bringing to mind Cervantes' *Don Quixote* and the many English novels which participated in this genre, such as Charlotte Lennox's *The Female Quixote* (1752). As a result the overlap between the parodic and satiric intent is far greater than in *Northanger Abbey*.

Because parody, like any other form of textual dialogism, is an enunciative act which involves an entire context of time, place, and prior discursive practices, as readers we need first to examine the climate of literary and social criticism in which *Northanger Abbey* and *The Heroine* appeared. Then we can assess Hutcheon's claims for Austen's reinvestment of 'female gothic' with authority, and the claims of other critics, such as Lewis, for Barrett's trivialization of the genre.

The Literary-Critical Context of Northanger Abbey *and* The Heroine

Although *Northanger Abbey* was not published until 1818, the year after Austen's death, it was largely written during 1797–8.[9] By this time women writers had established the Gothic romance as the dominant fictional mode, and among its many readers was a large group of middle-class women who could afford to purchase books and/or subscribe to established circulating libraries. Audiences were thus assured.

Reading the reviews of the time, however, one is immediately struck by both the severity and condescending indulgence of a coterie of male critics who frequently express contempt for novels *per se*. Works regarded as inferior are sarcastically dismissed in a couple of sentences. For example, of *The Peace-*

Leland Chandler May, *Parodies of the Gothic Novel* (New York: Arno Press, 1980), 73–4, which cites similar statements by Birkhead, *Tale of Terror*, 133 and Varma, *Gothic Flame*, 182.

[9] Jane Austen, *Northanger Abbey, Lady Susan, The Watsons and Sanditon*, ed. John Davie (Oxford: Oxford University Press, 1980), p. vii. Further references appear in the text.

ful Villa, published anonymously in 1793, we read: 'The language is exactly such as we might expect from a young female, whose mind has received little improvement from education, and whose reading has been almost entirely confined to novels.'[10] Such complaints are often accompanied by moans about the hydra-like proliferation of novels and the onerousness of the critic's task.[11] Concern is also expressed about 'the influence that novels have over the manners, sentiments and passions of the rising generation'; works are usually praised only if they are informative, instructive, or 'afford some intellectual improvement'.[12] The 'young and unformed', including 'many a boarding school miss' and those with 'delicate nerves', are felt to be particularly at risk before 'the horrid ideas of supernatural agency' and 'visionary terrors', as well as the murderers, assassins, and robbers, which abound in Gothic fiction.[13] In the writings of these critics, there is often an allegiance to primitive notions about audience identification with character, and young (female) readers are felt to be all too liable to mistake what they read for real life. This view is also evident in a comment by T. J. Mathias in *The Pursuits of Literature: A Satirical Poem in Dialogue*, published in 1797:

Mrs. Charlotte Smith, Mrs. Inchbald, Mrs. Mary Robinson, Mrs. etc., etc. though all of them are ingenious ladies, yet they are too frequently whining or frisking in novels, till our girls' heads turn wild with impossible adventures, and now and then are tainted with democracy . . .[14]

Mathias exempts only 'the mighty magician of The Mysteries of Udolpho' from this charge. Not so 'W.W.', writing in *Scots Magazine* in 1802. For him Gothic novels, including *Udolpho*, are 'literary abortions'; reading them gives rise to 'imbecility of mind', particularly amongst females, as 'the female mind is more readily affected by the tendency of such works'.[15]

---

[10] *Monthly Review*, 2nd ser. 10 (1793), 224.   [11] Ibid. 297.
[12] *Critical Review*, 15 (1795), 63–74.
[13] *Monthly Review*, 81 (1789), 563; *Monthly Review*, 2nd ser. 14 (1794), 464–5; *Critical Review*, 2nd ser. 24 (1798), 236.
[14] Mathias, *Pursuits of Literature*, n. to 1. 100, Dialogue 1.
[15] *Scots Magazine*, 64 (1802), 470–4, 545–8.

This possibility was taken up by Jane Austen in *Northanger Abbey*, and it was into the field of critical practice just outlined, and the controversies over female intelligence, sensibility, and education[16] that, had all gone according to plan, her text was first to have been inserted. Completed in 1803, it was sold to a London publisher for £10, was advertised, and then mysteriously left unpublished.[17] Its suppression led the 'authoress', in 1816, to place an 'Advertisement' at the front of the novel in which she explained that thirteen years had passed since it had been finished, and that this rendered much of the work's allusiveness to 'places, manners, books and opinions' of the time 'comparatively obsolete'.[18]

Barrett, on the other hand, with his novel of 1813, appears to have been deliberately attempting to revive Mathias's 'negative associations of gender, genre and the novel'.[19] In his publication in 1810 of *Woman, A Poem*, he had already rejected the aspirations of middle-class, feminist women, such as Wollstonecraft, to become writers and achieve greater intellectual and social equality. In this work women are relegated firmly to the domestic sphere, as the helpmeets of men:

Hence in each sex, for each peculiar sphere,
Adapted attributes of mind inhere.
. . . .

To Woman, whose best books are human hearts,
Wise heaven a genius less profound imparts.
. . . .

Their very virtues have a sexual line,
And his abroad and her's at home incline.
. . . .

Let Woman, like her sensual master, roam,
Farewell all kindred bonds, all joys of home.[20]

---

[16] For discussions of these controversies see Kirkham, *Jane Austen, Feminism and Fiction*, 10–12, 39–50; Quinlan, *Victorian Prelude*, 139–55; Poovey, *Proper Lady and the Woman Writer*, 15–35.

[17] Kirkham, *Jane Austen, Feminism and Fiction*, 70–1.

[18] Austen, *Northanger Abbey*, p. xxxiii.

[19] Kelly, 'Unbecoming a Heroine', 226. Kelly points out that Barrett's verse satire *All the Talents* of 1806–7 claims kinship with Mathias's *Pursuits of Literature*.

[20] Eaton Stannard Barrett, *Woman, A Poem* (London: Henry Colburn, 1818), 30–1, 33.

Barrett's poem appeared in the wake of successful 'tales' by writers such as Maria Edgeworth, Amelia Opie, and Charlotte Dacre, fiction which gave to women greater autonomy in their affective and social lives. It was not itself well received by critics, as Barrett himself remarked in his Preface to the second edition of 1818. But the continuing Anti-Jacobin fear of the spread of licence and working-class unrest seems to have prompted him to approach once again the topic of public order and the role of women, this time in fiction. In *The Heroine, or Adventures of a Fair Romance Reader*, Barrett burlesques successful novels by women and blatantly attempts to satirize the effects of novel reading altogether, not only by having his novel-reading heroine act in a stupid and disorderly way, but by 'associating novels with a wide range of current and to him, subversive values, practices, and writing'.[21] In notes to the third edition of 1815, now subtitled *The Adventures of Cherubina*, he even quotes specific passages from the novels and other texts he considers to be parodied. These include *The Mysteries of Udolpho, Sir Bertrand, The Italian, The Romance of the Forest, Children of the Abbey, Ida of Athens, Werther, Cecilia, The Sentimental Journey, La Nouvelle Héloïse, Tristram Shandy, The Recess, Corinne, The Novice of St. Dominick, The Wild Irish Girl*, 'Sir Francis Burdett's Address to the Electors of Westminster, Oct. 6, 1812', and 'Buonaparte to the Legislative Body, Sept. 11, 1808'. It will be noted that most of these works are by women, *The Mysteries of Udolpho* being cited nineteen times. Because many of these texts (including Barrett's own) are nowadays rarely read, and the writing of novels by women is not a social issue, much of the intended burlesque in *The Heroine* may no longer be perceived as such. However, the rhetorical flights of the central character do still continually cue us to the ironic discrepancy between what she states is happening and what we see to be the case. Her criticisms of the delusions and follies of others, too, can be read ironically by the reader, as she fails to see that they apply equally to herself.

[21] Kelly, 'Unbecoming a Heroine', 227.

The Heroine *as Burlesque of Gothic Novels and Patriarchal*
Satire on Novel Writing and Reading by Women

Barrett has his protagonist, Cherry Wilkinson, speak in ex-
travagantly inflated language, all the while in inspired imitation, so she thinks, of the novels she has read, particularly *The*
Mysteries of Udolpho, which alone 'escape[s] the conflagra-
tion' when her father orders 'all the novels in the house to be
burnt, by way of purification'.[22] However, with her excessive
infatuation with novels, lack of modesty, indifference to the
suffering of others, and bombastic nature, Cherry is never
more than a caricature of a novelistic heroine. For example, in
her first letter, this prosperous farmer's daughter addresses her
governess as follows:

—O Biddy, what an irreparable loss to the public, that a victim of
thrilling sensibility, like me, should be thus idling her precious time
over the common occupations of life!—prepared as I am, too, by a
course of novels (and you can bear witness that I have read little
else), to embody and ensoul those enchanting reveries› which I
indulge, and which really constitute almost the whole happiness of
my life.
  That I am not deficient in the qualities requisite for a heroine, is
indisputable. I know nothing of the world, or of human nature; and
everyone says I am handsome. My form is tall and aërial, my face
Grecian, my tresses flaxen, my eyes blue and sleepy. (p. 31)

Out of discontent and boredom she rejects her loving parent
and the possibility of marriage to the amiable, middle-class
Robert Stuart in favour of a noble identity as 'Cherubina de
Willoughby', and a life of travelling 'Gothic' heroinism, invol-
ving a long series of ridiculous adventures.
  Within hours of her arrival in London she evades seduction
by the wealthy Betterton whom she has met in the coach, is
tricked by a London prostitute, saves an Irish woollen-draper,
Jerry Sullivan, from imprisonment, and goes to his home for
the night after they have attempted to steal some bonnets from

---

[22] Eaton Stannard Barrett, *The Heroine*, with an introduction by Michael
Sadleir (New York: Frederick A. Stokes, 1928), printed from the third edition
(London: Henry Colburn, 1815), 32. Further references, which appear in the
text, are to this edition unless otherwise stated.

a shopkeeper and created mayhem in the streets. Subsequently, mistaking Covent Garden Theatre for 'a castle of some Marquis or Baron', Cherry seeks protection from a bad actor, Abraham Grundy, who plays on her gullibility by claiming to be really Lord Montmorenci, and like her, 'enveloped in a cloud of mysteries' (p. 74). Posing as Grundy's orphan cousin, she is allotted a sleeping room by his landlady and becomes a frequenter of the establishment's parlour, where she meets Higginson, a poet. Barrett takes the opportunity for further burlesque of particular literary discourses by having both men tell her their life stories, the duplicitous Montmorenci continuing to play the Gothic hero with great melodrama, wearing a suit of tin armour and plumed helmet. When the action shifts to the country, Cherry is rescued by Stuart from a further seduction attempt before she arrives at Gwyn Castle, which she intends to reclaim as her rightful inheritance from Lady Gwyn, who indulges Cherry's inclination for romance by pretending to be her aunt. In the last third of the novel, Cherry attempts to restore a ruin, Monkton Castle, assisted by a gang of Irish labourers, her 'vassals', including Jerry Sullivan. In this section Barrett burlesques the discursive practices of English Jacobins and satirizes Cherry's pretensions to be 'a Patriot'. The burlesque of Gothic excesses reaches a crescendo when her castle is attacked by Betterton and Montmorenci, who abduct her and gull her into believing, not only that she is in the company of characters from well-known novels, but also that she is the subject of threatening spectral visitations. At the point of her discovery of this plot to divest her of virtue and money, she is rescued by Stuart with 'a posse of constables', and British law and order are restored.

Thus, for almost three hundred pages, Cherry authors her life, fabricating a long series of supposedly 'Gothic' episodes which often bring harm to others and make her appear very stupid in her obliquity. But then, with obvious irony, Barrett has set her up in Letter IV to remain stupid, by having her remark à propos of the formulaic nature of novels:

Since, therefore, an established series of incidents are fated to befal all heroines, and since I am a heroine, it follows that I need not so much consider whether my conduct be prudent or indiscreet, as

whether it be graceful, and fit for immortality. The grand criterion
is, 'how will it read?'

Occupied with these observations, the result of natural good sense,
and an intimate knowledge of romances, I walked four long and
toilsome miles. (p. 45)

The use of such farcical self-reflexivity and irony to ridicule
Cherubina and women's novels is constant, making *The Heroine* close at times to travesty. For example, early in the novel,
having come upon Stuart wounded by robbers, she reasons
that in such a situation a heroine 'either faints on the spot or
exhibits energies almost superhuman'. She then avowedly attempts to 'surpass' Elinor in *The Recess* by strewing a train of
gunpowder as she walks towards Stuart, lighting the powder
with a candle from the lantern, and withstanding the shock of
'the tremendous explosion' which takes place. Timbers fall,
the robbers scamper off, and she whispers to Stuart, who has
also somehow miraculously survived the blast, 'There! . . .
there is an original horror for you; and all my own contriv-
ance' (p. 49). Such incidents straining credibility are frequent,
as are those which show Cherry to be insensitive to the feelings
of others. For example, because he is only 'a fat funny farmer',
Cherubina rejects her father as the true villain in her life and
aids his commitment to a madhouse: 'Remain, then, my good
man, what nature made you; ply your plough; whistle Spin-
ning Jenny; fatten your pigs and the parson; but never again
attempt to get yourself thrust into the pages of a romance' (pp.
95–6). Likewise, the family which kindly offers her breakfast
after she has spent a cold night in a haystack are considered
unworthy of her company because they have 'flat noses and
thick lips without mercy' (p. 50), while her actor-friend, Abraham Grundy, cannot qualify as her hero once he has lost his
two front teeth because a 'perfect set of teeth are absolutely
indispensable to a Hero' (pp. 285–6). This is a crude inversion
of Emily's care and concern for her father and others in *Udolpho*. Further examples abound, such as the occasion when
Cherry selects a new bonnet in a shop and attempts to walk
away without paying, addressing the shopkeeper as follows:

'My sweet friend,' said I, 'a distrest heroine, which I assure you I am,
runs in debt every where. Besides, as I like your face, I intend

implicating you in my plot. Who knows but you may turn out to be my mother's nurse's daughter? happen that may, however, I give you my word I will reward you at the *dénouement*, along with the other characters; and meantime, to secure your acquaintance, I must insist on owing you money.' (p. 67)

This is not simply a parody of the incident in *Udolpho* in which Emily buys a new bonnet,[23] but a frivolous debasement of it. We find none of the ambiguity which Hutcheon sees as characteristic of the ironic inversion constituting parody. Rather, we are left in no doubt of the joke against Cherry, that her supposedly 'Gothic' view of life not only bears no relation to reality, but is often destructive and unscrupulous. Assertive rather than passive in her heroinism Cherry may be, but Barrett trivializes her to such a degree that she becomes a tedious character with whom we can have little sympathy. As Paul Lewis comments, 'it is difficult to take Cherry seriously' because Barrett has not created 'a plausible psychological history for her'; instead he 'treats her as the *reductio ad absurdum* of Gothic readers, a target for his humor only'.[24] It is not surprising that some readers have perceived *The Heroine* as simply a satire on women.[25] Certainly, Barrett credits women with little intelligence or discrimination. It is merely assumed that, without male intervention, all women who read novels will act as Cherry does.

The Heroine ends with Cherry's restoration to her father, and, for the sake of decorum, a period of delirium before she rises from her bed 'an altered being'. The loyal, sensible Bob Stuart then takes charge to perfect 'the mental reformation' of the wandering, self-styled heroine before ultimately becoming her husband. Of all the different characters whose 'conversations' Cherry has attempted to reproduce 'word for word' in the manner of 'all heroines' (pp. 36–7), Stuart is the only one whose speeches correspond to standard written English.[26] It is

[23] Radcliffe, *Udolpho*, 454–5.
[24] Lewis, 'Gothic and Mock Gothic', 48.
[25] Walter Alexander Raleigh, *The English Novel: A Short Sketch of its History from the Earliest Times to the Appearance of 'Waverley'* (London: Murray, 1904), 272, cited in May, *Parodies of the Gothic*, 76.
[26] Kelly, 'Unbecoming a Heroine', makes this point also on p. 240: 'Usually Cherry's language is burlesque novelese . . . Betterton speaks in genteel slang

here that we can locate the authorial position, as it is Stuart's authoritative 'voice' which takes over from Cherry's narration in the form of a lecture about the pernicious influence of novels:

In a country where morals are on the decline, sentimental novels always become dissolute. For it is their province to represent the prevalent opinions; nay, to run forward and meet the coming vice, and to sketch it with an exaggerating and prophetic pencil. Thus, long before France arrived at her extreme vicious refinement, her novels had adopted that last master-stroke of immorality, which wins by the chastest aphorisms, while it corrupts by the most alluring pictures of villainy. (p. 350)[27]

Only very few novels meet with Stuart's approval. Significantly, the first one he gives her to read is *Don Quixote*; but *The Vicar of Wakefield*, *Cecilia*, *O'Donnel*, *The Fashionable Tales*, and *Coelebs* he declares to be 'both instructive and entertaining' because they 'draw man as he is, imperfect'. In contrast, romances, such as *The Mysteries of Udolpho* and *The Italian*, 'which address our imagination alone', are 'so seductive' that people become 'too fond' of them to the neglect of 'more useful books'. Moreover, he continues:

Romances, indulged in the extreme, act upon the mind like inebriating stimulants; first elevate, and at last enervate it. They accustom it to admire ideal scenes of transport and distraction; and to feel

---

or burlesque revolutionary rhetoric, Montmorenci in melodramatese, Higginson in vulgarisms and poeticisms, Jerry in brogue, Lady Gwyn with elevated formality, and so on. . . . In short, all of the 'voices' in *The Heroine* are recognisably in nonstandard English except one . . . that of Robert Stuart . . .'.

[27] Interestingly, in the 1813 edition of the novel, this passage describes the immorality of novels as an effect rather than a harbinger of vice and corruption: 'In a country where morals are on the decline, novels always fall several degrees below the standard of national virtue. . . . For as these works are an exaggerated picture of the times, they represent the prevalent opinions and manners with a gigantic pencil. Thus, since France became depraved, her novels have become dissolute; and since her social system arrived at its extreme vicious refinement, they too have adopted that last master-stroke of refined vice, which wins the heart by the chastest of aphorisms, and then corrupts it by the most alluring pictures of villainy.' Eaton Stannard Barrett, *The Heroine, or Adventures of a Fair Romance Reader*, 3 vols. (London: Henry Colburn, 1813), iii. 290. Quoted in Kelly, 'Unbecoming a Heroine', 232.

disgusted with the vulgarities of living misery. They likewise incapacitate it from encountering the turmoils of active life; and teach it erroneous notions of the world, by relating adventure too improbable to happen, and depicting characters too imperfect to exist. (pp. 349–50)

Foremost amongst 'superior' novels he ranks *Rasselas* and *A Picture of Society*, which, 'gratifying our reason more than our imagination, and interesting us, not so much by story as by morality, are at once a test and source of national virtue'. However, the majority, he concludes, have had a bad influence, creating disorder and corrupting manners as they have Cherry's, because they 'indulge in a certain strain of overwrought and useless, if not pernicious sentimentality' (p. 351). Cherry, of course, has constantly referred to characters and incidents in novels by women, such as *Udolpho*, *The Italian*, *Corinne*, *The Recess*, *Camilla*, *Cecilia*, *Evelina*, *Children of the Abbey*, and so on, making little distinction between them, and appropriating phrases here and there from a wide range. But from henceforth she will have a 'counsellor' and 'companion' who will 'guide', 'encourage', and 'correct', for she avowedly still retains 'some taints' of her 'former follies and affectations' in her language and behaviour. Indeed, she explains, the new regimen has already begun: 'Morality, history, languages, and music, occupy my mornings; and my evenings are enlivened by balls, operas and familiar parties' (p. 351). Even though Cherry remonstrates with Stuart for making her terminate her adventures with an ending imitated from romance, his deliberate refusal to provide the conventional 'moral' in the form of 'some flourishing sentence' points back to his earlier pronouncements and attempts to remove *The Heroine* from the genre in which it has participated. Gary Kelly puts it neatly when he concludes: 'The closure of *The Heroine* is meant to remove the novel and the reader, as it removes the heroine, from the vitiated moral, ethical, literary, and political culture of novel reading.'[28]

In effect, then, *The Heroine* seeks to silence alternative views to those of Stuart regarding the Gothic, as it offers only one other position in regard to novels, that of Cherry herself. This

[28] Kelly, 'Unbecoming a Heroine', 241.

also takes the form of a lengthy speech—at her mock coronation in imitation of 'Corinne [who] was crowned in the capi-
tol' (p. 195). Arranged by Lady Gwyn, who plays up to what
she considers to be Cherry's madness, this celebratory occasion enables Cherry to speak publicly as 'patroness of the arts,
the paragon of charms and the first of heroines' (p. 198):

England, my friends, is now the depository of all the virtue which
survives. She is the ark that floats upon the waters of the deluge. But
what preserves her virtuous? Her women. And whence arises their
purity? From education.
   To you, then, my fair auditory, I would enjoin a diligent cultivation
of learning. But oh! beware what books you peruse; for, trust me,
some are as injurious as others are salutary. I cannot point out to you
the mischievous class, because I have never read them; but indubit-
ably, the most useful are novels and romances. Such as I am, these
alone have made me. These, by depicting heroines who were sublim-
ated almost above terrestriality, teach the less gifted portion of
womankind to reach what is uncommon, in striving for what is
unattainable; to despise the follies and idleness of the mere worker
of samplers, and to entertain a taste for that sensibility, whose tear
is the melting of pearl . . . (p. 199)

As a whole, this incident is a merciless burlesque of Corinne's
coronation with the laurel wreath of genius in the popular
novel by Mme de Staël (1807), although to contemporary
readers Cherry's improvised speech may have seemed insignificant beside the throbbing sentiments of Corinne's almost
chapter-length oration on 'The Glory and Happiness of
Italy'.[29] Even if it were not parodic in this way, Cherry's view
on novels and romances is presented ironically, being 'vitiated'
by her own continuing insensitive and stupid behaviour as she
adheres to novelistic conventions. Hence the irony leaves us in
no doubt which 'voice' here is intended to have superiority,
Stuart earlier having told Cherry that 'the heroes and heroines
of romance . . . are useful certainly; but in teaching us what we
should shun, not what we should imitate' (p. 113).

[29] 'Cradle of Letters! Mistress of the World! | Soil of the Sun! Italia! I salute
thee! | How oft the human race have worn thy yoke, | The vassals of thine
arms, thine arts, thy sky!' Madame De Staël, *Corinne; or, Italy*, trans. Isabel
Hill with metrical versions of the Odes by L. E. Landon; and a Memoir of the
authoress (London: Richard Bentley, New Burlington Street, 1847), 25–31.

In conclusion, we can agree with Paul Lewis that Barrett's epistolary novel is an 'attempt to hoist popular fiction on its own petard, to expose and ridicule the distorted fancies of a young woman whose head is filled more with the conventions of romance than with the realities of life'. The only possibility for a more positive reading of Barrett's intentions would be to emphasize the main point of difference of his burlesque from its target text, Udolpho, Cherry's wilful and bombastic assertiveness contrasting greatly with Emily's restraint and caring demeanour. Cherry's quest could then perhaps be interpreted positively 'as a flight from the normal oppression of controlling but unexciting men (her father and Stuart) in pursuit of an honest confrontation with a straightforward, brutal and thrilling villain'. However, the ending precludes such a reading. Cherry does not merely fail in her quest. Nor is she merely restrained. She allows herself to be transformed 'according to socially accepted ideas of the proper role for a young woman'. Thus, as Lewis concludes, The Heroine demonstrates 'an unquestioning faith in patriarchy and repression'. For Barrett's novel not only denigrates women's intelligence but is 'a repudiation of fantasy so extreme that it seeks to regulate daydreams and structure whimsies'. The Heroine denies mystery, doubt, fear, what Lewis calls 'the adventurous exploration of the fantastic at the center of the Gothic'.[30]

At no point does Cherry become submerged in the strange and fantastic and begin to question what is real, as does Emily in Udolpho, or even Catherine in Northanger Abbey. When she is visited by the supposed Baron Hildebrand, she is preoccupied with all the melodramatic Gothic trappings of the scene, his 'Schedonaic scowl', 'black plume', 'Persian sash', 'Spanish cloak', and so on, rather than with any real threat he might present. The same is true of the scene in which she is visited by the ghost. Rather, as a character in a picaresque novel, Cherry charges on, tilting at windmills, encouraging duplicity in others, and attracting disorder wherever she goes. Even in her humiliation, when all the pranks played upon her are revealed, Cherry's language remains inflated novelese. Her 'slavish adherence' to purely literary conventions so thoroughly

[30] Lewis, 'Gothic and Mock Gothic', 44–5, 47–8, 51–2.

pre-empts any raising of the epistemological, psychological, and theological questions commonly found in the Gothic that it trivializes the genre.[31] *The Heroine*, by its constant resort to ridicule, as well its privileging of Stuart's speeches, seeks to suppress alternative views. Nevertheless, *Udolpho*, as a parodied text, can be deemed to offer some internal dialogic resistance to Barrett's parodying intentions. And so we find Jane Austen, with considerably more subtle parody and irony, using it to create Catherine and offer a more democratic position in relation to the politics of reading and the status of (women's) novels, including the Gothic.

Northanger Abbey *as Parodic Defence of Novel Reading and Writing by Women*

As mentioned earlier, in 1816 Austen feared that *Northanger Abbey* was outdated. On the one hand, in its parodic aspect— the one most often taken up by modern critics—it does not appear to have been outmoded, as Thomas Love Peacock's *Nightmare Abbey* also appeared in 1818 and the third edition of *The Heroine* in the previous year. On the other hand—and this asect has received but scant attention—the novel also satirizes the overly moralizing and chauvinistic interpretative framework brought to bear on women's novels by those male critics who regarded themselves as guardians of middle-class taste. Perhaps, then, it was a certain type of pronouncement which Austen was claiming had lost its immediacy for readers of 1816. For the novel will certainly support a 'historical' reading which foregrounds the conspicuous denigration by some late eighteenth-century critics of women's intelligence and writing, a denigration which, as we have seen, is also found in *The Heroine*.

First of all, *Northanger Abbey* strongly defends popular fiction by women. Early in the novel, the reader is informed of the intentions of Catherine and Isabella to 'shut themselves up to read novels together' (p. 21). Then, via a lengthy aside about the 'contemptuous censure' of reviewers and those

---

[31] Ibid. 51–2.

novelists and readers who are complicit with them, the narrator addresses the reader directly in the following extraordinary outburst:

Let us leave it to the Reviewers to abuse such effusions of fancy at
their leisure, and over every new novel to talk in threadbare strains
of the trash with which the press now groans. Let us not desert one
another; we are an injured body. Although our productions have
afforded more extensive and unaffected pleasure than those of any
other literary corporation in the world, no species of composition
has been so much decried. From pride, ignorance, or fashion, our
foes are almost as many as our readers. And while the abilities of the
nine-hundredth abridger of the History of England, or of the man
who collects and publishes in a volume some dozen lines of Milton,
Pope, and Prior, with a paper from the Spectator, and a chapter on
Sterne, are eulogized by a thousand pens,—there seems almost a wish
of decrying the capacity and undervaluing the labour of the novelist,
and of slighting performances which have only genius, wit, and taste
to recommend them. 'I am no novel reader—I seldom look into
novels—Do not imagine that *I* often read novels—It is really very well
for a novel'.—Such is the common cant.—'And what are you reading,
Miss—?' 'Oh! it is only a novel!' replies the young lady; while she lays
down her book with affected indifference or momentary shame.—'It
is only Cecilia, or Camilla, or Belinda;' or, in short, only some work
in which the greatest powers of the mind are displayed, in which the
most thorough knowledge of human nature, the happiest delineation
of its varieties, the liveliest effusions of wit and humour are conveyed
to the world in the best chosen language. (pp. 21–2)

There is a strong sense here that novelists and their readers
constitute a beleaguered community—not because the works
which circulate amongst them are necessarily inferior, but
because the community itself largely consists of females, who
are *themselves* considered inferior. It is on this account that
their intellectual labours are 'undervalued'.

Austen's lengthy narratorial address has often been remarked, but seldom considered as a contract with the reader
and cue for interpreting other passages in the novel. Margaret
Kirkham, for example, sees it as important but 'uncharacter-
istic of the author in that it amounts to an interpolation in her
work of matter not strictly to the point of the "story" '.[32]

---

[32] Kirkham, *Jane Austen, Feminism and Fiction*, 67.

Overall, modern (mostly male) critics have been so preoccupied with attempts to impose a formal unity on the text, that
its allusions to 'the woman question' have been largely ignored
in favour of evaluative comments which relegate the novel to
an inferior position in the Austen canon.[33]

Yet the novel's discourses of the real and the fantastic—in
the latter case, a mood-invested situation, the uncanny—are
under the dominance of a shifting satiric perspective which
relativizes both the Sentimental/Gothic world and the normative, 'common-sense' fictional world. Gothic conventions are
clearly mocked when Catherine's feelings are 'wound up . . .
to the highest point of extasy' at the sound of the name,
Northanger Abbey, and Henry Tilney attempts to frighten her
with a teasing tale of what she will find there. With her recent
reading of *The Mysteries of Udolpho* in mind, he tells her that
it is 'just like what one reads about'. There are 'sliding pannels
and tapestry', 'a hall dimly lighted', 'Dorothy the ancient
housekeeper', 'gloomy passages', 'the portrait of some handsome warrior' above the fireplace, a bedroom door without a
lock, a hidden manuscript containing 'memoirs of the
wretched Matilda', 'unconquerable horror', and so on (*Northanger Abbey*, pp. 124–6). However, at the same time, such
conventions are also exploited; and nowhere better, perhaps,
than in the description of Catherine's first (stormy) night at
Northanger, with all its uncanny coincidences (pp. 132–6); or
in the passage in which the narrator informs us that Catherine's 'visions of romance' are over. In the statement, 'The
anxieties of common life began soon to succeed to the alarms
of romance' (*Northanger Abbey*, p. 161), we have a reworking
of Radcliffe's narratorial comment in *Udolpho* about Emily:
'from imaginary evils she awoke to the consciousness of real
ones' (*Udolpho*, p. 161). Thus, when Catherine Morland's
'fantastic' deformation of reality is revealed to contain some

---

[33] Martin Mudrick, *Jane Austen: Irony as Defense and Discovery* (Princeton, NJ: Princeton University Press, 1952), 59; A. Walton Litz, *Jane Austen:
A Study of Her Artistic Development* (New York: Oxford University Press,
1965), 59. For a defence of the structural coherence of *Northanger Abbey* see
Frank J. Fearful, 'Satire and the Form of the Novel: The Problem of Aesthetic
Unity in *Northanger Abbey*', *Journal of English Literary History*, 32 (Dec.
1965), 511–27.

correspondence to reality after all, this further relativizes the 'common-sense' perspective to which she (for the most part) and Henry Tilney adhere, and actually partially reinstates the Gothic fantasy which has been mocked. This 'reinstatement' has certain links with those passages in the novel which specifically deal with the value of reading novels—and all of the main characters read novels.

Northanger Abbey's heroine, 'almost pretty' Catherine Morland, daughter of the Revd Richard and Mrs Morland, is 'in training for a heroine'. But no one, least of all herself, has consciously thought of her in this way, because to all appearances she is quite the opposite, an anti-heroine in fact. She is one of ten children, and in the way that Wollstonecraft approved, she has been allowed to rough it like a boy.[34] Until the age of 14 'noisy and wild' and with 'a hatred of confinement and cleanliness', she has acquired no misconceived notions of female frailty, timidity, or propriety. However, 'she never could learn or understand anything before she was taught' and even then 'she was inattentive and occasionally stupid' (*Northanger Abbey*, p. 2).

The reason for Catherine's intractability is not hard to see. Her education at home at Fullerton Parsonage has been a trivial, hit-and-miss affair, one which has not inculcated any active interest in learning; she has had no objection to books 'provided they were all story and no reflection' (*Northanger Abbey*, p. 3).

The advance of puberty changes all that. She becomes aware of the importance of sensibility for women and a new 'feminine' but superficial awareness governs her reading: 'she read all such works as heroines must read to supply their memories with those quotations which are so serviceable and so soothing in the vicissitudes of their eventful lives' (p. 3). This passage, it should be noted, mocks not only the conventions of the Sentimental novel. More broadly, it mocks the notion made popular by Dr Johnson that novels and other literary works should serve as 'lectures of conduct', as well as the expectation that women should conform to a didactic paradigm. To acquire the right moral precepts and sentiments,

[34] Wollstonecraft, *Vindication of the Rights of Woman*, 58.

Catherine acquaints herself with 'improving' works—Pope, Gray, Thomson, Shakespeare, and Richardson's Sir Charles Grandison, a novel read often by her mother, as 'new books do not fall in [their] way' (*Northanger Abbey*, p. 25). For all this, Catherine remains as open, unaffected, candid, and guileless as she has always been. Because she has lived all her life in a secluded village in Wiltshire, she lacks first-hand experience of the ways of the world, and, being good-hearted herself, she is naïvely confident in the goodness of others. In all, her mind remains 'about as ignorant and uninformed as the female mind at seventeen usually is' (p. 5). The irony here is consistently unstable; Catherine falls short of what a character must be if she is to conform to the Sentimental/Gothic mode, she reads the 'improving' works that critics expect of young women—and she remains what she 'really' is.

Her stay at Bath with the Allens marks her introduction to the world, and when she begins her first Gothic novel, Radcliffe's *Udolpho*, she is extremely susceptible to the excitement of its subjectivity, mysteries, and terrors. We find that she has taken in nothing of the novel's moralistic warnings about the dangers of excessive sensibility. And 'having no notion of drawing', she also fails to gain much from Radcliffe's frequent passages of nature description—the picturesque and the sublime. She delivers 'a very warm panegyric' on Mrs Radcliffe's merits, but when Henry and Eleanor Tilney begin to view the landscape of Bath 'with the eyes of persons accustomed to drawing' (p. 86), Catherine is unable to participate in their conversation and feels ashamed of her ignorance and lack of taste. Catherine, it seems, reads *Udolpho* primarily as a suspense novel, indulging, in the quiet of her room, in 'the luxury of a raised, restless, and frightened imagination' (*Northanger Abbey*, p. 34).

Her enthusiasm for the work is further encouraged by the new-found friend, Isabella Thorpe, who has lent her the novel and with whom she discusses 'the dreadful black veil' incident. Isabella promises her some ten or twelve more novels 'of the same kind' and subsequently, when Catherine is invited by the domineering General Tilney to stay at Northanger Abbey, she attempts to map Gothic co-ordinates on to her own rapidly expanding life experiences. She is thus an easy target for humour: the anticipated 'Gothic' Abbey is disappointingly modern, a 'mysterious chest' contains nothing other than a white cotton counterpane, a 'mysterious manuscript' turns out to be a set of laundry bills, and General Tilney himself fails to be a wicked Montoni who has secretly locked up and some-how contrived to dispose of his wife. Indeed, it can be argued that this type of deflation of expectations is the only form of humour that *Northanger Abbey* and *The Heroine* share. We can draw parallels with Catherine when Cherry wanders into the music room of Lady Gwyn's mansion and hears music coming from the piano, 'as if all its chords were agitated at once, by the hand of some invisible spirit'. For, upon lifting the lid and thinking of Emily, 'who drew aside the black veil', she is confronted by a mouse, rather than the skeletal hands she had been expecting (*The Heroine*, p. 177).

Nevertheless, however much *Northanger Abbey* laughs at Catherine's excesses of imagination, it is also abundantly clear that this projection of a Gothic framework on to a situation in her life is no more than a temporary fantasy in the course of her assimilation of the new and unknown. It is subject to revision and will by no means, as J. M. S. Tompkins puts it, 'incapacitate her for mature life'.[35] On the contrary, as a result of her mistaken projection, she is sobered considerably and remembers 'with what feelings she had prepared for a know-ledge of Northanger' (*Northanger Abbey*, p. 160). Unlike Cherry in *The Heroine*, Catherine is a credible character, capable of reflection and growth. Recognizing that 'the infatu-ation' has been 'created by her reading', she also begins to approach novels with a greater awareness of their conven-tional nature, and to reflect on the codes and conventions operating in both them and her society:

Charming as were all Mrs. Radcliffe's works, and charming as were the works of all her imitators, it was not in them perhaps that human nature, at least in the midland counties of England, was to be looked for. . . . in the central part of England there was surely some security for the existence even of a wife not beloved, in the laws of the land, and the manners of the age. Murder was not tolerated, servants were not slaves, and neither poison nor sleeping potions to be procured,

---

[35] Tompkins, *Popular Novel in England*, 218.

like rhubarb, from every druggist. Among the Alps and Pyrenees, perhaps, there were no mixed characters. There, such as were not as spotless as an angel, might have the dispositions of a fiend. (*Northanger Abbey*, pp. 160–1)

Written in *style indirect libre*, this long passage gives us Catherine's revaluation of *Udolpho* in relation to contemporary life in England and Europe. Catherine's perspective is still limited in the way she employs literary categories and excludes the possibility of 'mixed characters' living in southern Europe. But her previous assumptions are subject to radical questioning, and she is later to be more than vindicated in her conclusion that Henry's father is 'not perfectly amiable'. He may not be a Montoni, but his heartlessness, materialism, and duplicity do make of him something like a Quesnel. In the belief that Catherine's family is wealthy, the tyrannical General has invited her to Northanger Abbey, hoping subsequently to marry her off to his son. But he abruptly and rudely sends her home unchaperoned when he learns that she is without a fortune. On reflection, therefore, Catherine finds that 'in suspecting General Tilney . . . she had scarcely sinned against his character or magnified his cruelty' (*Northanger Abbey*, p. 201). As in *Udolpho*, after the misapprehensions have been cleared, Catherine has still had something real to fear and combat— patriarchal tyranny.

To Catherine's delight, unlike the devious and hypocritical John Thorpe, Henry Tilney eschews 'common cant' and owns enthusiastically to reading many novels. These include all of Mrs Radcliffe's works, most of which he has read 'with great pleasure' (*Northanger Abbey*, p. 82). While he quips that he finished *Udolpho* in two days, his 'hair standing on end the whole time', he does not allow the work or others like it to disturb his 'common-sense' upper-middle-class conception of an ordered and stable British society; for him the didactic frame of *Udolpho* appears to be finally uppermost. When he discovers that Catherine has entertained bizarre conceptions about the integrity of his father, General Tilney, he remonstrates:

Dear Miss Morland, consider the dreadful nature of the suspicions you have entertained. What have you been judging from? Remember the country and age in which we live. Remember that we are English, that we are Christians. Consult your own understanding, your own sense of the probable, your own observation of what is passing around you—Does our education prepare us for such atrocities? Do our laws connive at them? Could they be perpetrated without being known, in a country like this, where social and literary intercourse is on such a footing; where every man is surrounded by a neighbour-hood of voluntary spies, and where roads and newspapers lay every-thing open? Dearest Miss Morland, what ideas have you been admitting? (*Northanger Abbey*, p. 159)

If Radcliffe's distancing devices—the historic southern Euro-pean settings, the fairy-tale stylization—have been initially 'flattened out' altogether by the inexperienced Catherine, they have perhaps figured too conspicuously for the scholarly and often judiciously ironic Henry. In making him overstate his case, Austen treats such blinkered avowals of an ordered society and security from threat with some irony. Further-more, Henry's pleasure in feeling superior to Catherine, whom he loves for her freshness, honesty, teachability, and 'very ignorant mind' both undercuts and limits his perceptions. While it is evident that Catherine's particular imaginings are wide of the mark, it is not the case that a concealed murder is unthinkable in Christian England, or that women are neces-sarily always safe.

Henry's rebuke to Catherine is in effect a transformed repetition of his mock rebuke to his sister about the 'riot' in her mind, in Volume I. And, in both cases, it can be argued that Henry is not entirely correct in ascribing 'confusion' simply to the minds of the women he addresses. These 'riot' and 'spy' passages are more or less ironic, depending very much on the reader's ideological stance and knowledge in relation to the late eighteenth-century riots and social disturb-ances in the English Midlands and elsewhere, and to the repressive practices, including readings and writings, promul-gated in response to fear of domestic Jacobinism.[36] In their lack of stability these passages are quite different in orienta-tion from Robert Stuart's authoritative lecture in *The Heroine*.

[36] For an account of these disturbances and practices see Warren Roberts, *Jane Austen and the French Revolution* (London and Basingstoke: Macmillan, 1981), 105.

There are several other passages in *Northanger Abbey* which satirize dominant assumptions by men about women's intellectual powers and education, and the argument can be developed further. Catherine's ignorance in matters of drawing and taste, for example, is given mock approval by the narrator:

> She was heartily ashamed of her ignorance. A misplaced shame. Where people wish to attach, they should always be ignorant. To come with a well-informed mind, is to come with an inability of administering to the vanity of others, which a sensible person would always wish to avoid. A woman especially, if she have the misfortune of knowing any thing, should conceal it as well as she can. (*Northanger Abbey*, p. 86)

Here Austen parodies with satiric intent the sort of conduct-book discourse which promulgated such moralistic and sexist notions in all seriousness—'Dr. Gregory's Legacy to his Daughters', for example: 'But if you happen to have any learning, keep it a profound secret, especially from the men, who generally look with a jealous and malignant eye on a woman of great parts, and a cultivated understanding.'[37]

Commenting on how 'the General's unjust interference' was finally conducive to the happiness of Catherine and Henry, the narrator ends *Northanger Abbey* with a playful challenge to the moralizing critic and reader: 'I leave it to be settled by whomsoever it may concern, whether the tendency of this work be altogether to recommend parental tyranny, or reward filial disobedience' (*Northanger Abbey*, p. 205). In defiance of the pontifications of critics and moralists (the suffix, 'anger', in 'Northanger' is perhaps significant), readers are introduced to the notion of there being radical differences in readers' responses. Privy to the responses to Gothic novels of Catherine, Isabella Thorpe, her brother, John, and Henry Tilney, we are invited to evaluate their readings of *Udolpho* in the light of characters, events, and our own knowledge of the situation in England during the 1790s. Due to the (at times proleptic) play of irony, what we find is a series of perspectives

---

[37] Quoted in David Monaghan, ed., *Jane Austen in a Social Context* (London and Basingstoke: Macmillan, 1981), 105.

which continually turn back on themselves—in short, 'the liveliest effusions of wit and humour' and a demonstration of the imaginative power of (Gothic) fiction. The *British Critic* of March 1818, emphasizing the humour of Catherine's mistakes, thought *Northanger Abbey* 'the very best of Miss Austen's productions', but (predictably) found the 'want of delicacy' and 'improbability' in the presentation of Catherine's visit to Northanger Abbey and the General's character disquieting. 'Drawn from imagination, it is . . . not pourtrayed [*sic*] with our authoress's usual taste and judgement'.[38] One cannot help smiling, as the narrator, in her ironic disclosure that Henry's love originated in his 'gratitude', seems to have anticipated such a judgement: 'if it be as new in common life, the credit of a wild imagination will at least be all my own' (*Northanger Abbey*, p. 198).

Finally, scores of modern readers have continued to be teased by the novel's ambiguities. Marvin Mudrick finds the irony 'always somewhat excessive for its material',[39] while a recent feminist critic comments that in correcting the schema of 'making [a] heroine the subject of absurd delusions following on the reading of romantic novels, Austen ran the risk of confusing readers'.[40] The novel can do just that. Strongly dialogic, *Northanger Abbey* is a self-reflexive unsettling of fixed notions of the real and the romantic and does indeed have the renewing, revitalizing effect on the Gothic which Hutcheon claims for it.

Reading Subversion of Patriarchal Values in Northanger Abbey *and* The Mysteries of Udolpho

Mikhail Bakhtin has argued that 'The primary stylistic project of the novel as a genre is to create images of languages. . . . it is an intentional and conscious hybrid, one artistically organized . . .'.[41] Working with Bakhtin's notion that discourse

---

[38] Brian Charles Southam, *Jane Austen: The Critical Heritage* (London: Routledge & Kegan Paul, 1968), 92.

[39] Mudrick, *Jane Austen: Irony as Defense and Discovery*, 52.

[40] Kirkham, *Jane Austen, Feminism and Fiction*, 90.

[41] Bakhtin, *Dialogic Imagination*, 366.

in the novel is not homogeneous but an ensemble of 'images of language'—secondary representations of prior discourses—I have argued that Radcliffe and Austen expropriate familiar late eighteenth-century discourses in ways which question and challenge 'official' patriarchal values.

Northanger Abbey, for example, can be perceived as situating itself not only in relation to *The Mysteries of Udolpho* and other Gothic and Sentimental fiction, but to contemporary criticism of novels, including *The Heroine*, treatises on female education, political tracts, and conduct-book moralizing. With its self-conscious parody and exploitation of romance and novelistic conventions, its mockery of both romantic effusiveness and unimaginative, chauvinistic moralizing about women and a traditional, stable, British social order, the novel can seem extremely ambivalent. Its discursive tensions are many and tied to divisions between gender, class, occupational, and political groups in the late eighteenth-century British middle- and upper-class population: for example, those between male reviewers/moralists (and those complicit with them)[42] and women writers and readers; those between Rousseauistic supporters of female 'taste' and delicacy and detractors such as Wollstonecraft; those between 'serious writers' and the supposed tribe of sensation-mongers and their publishers who were cashing in on the wide currency of the Gothic; and those between supporters of a closed society, based on wealth, privilege, and primogeniture, and advocates of political and social reform. In drawing attention to these tensions I have privileged the defence passage because historically and textually it is such a striking marker of the conditions which give *Northanger Abbey* point. However, as stated earlier, modern readers have on the whole not perceived it as such and an important dimension of the novel has been

---

[42] Austen appears to have Edgeworth in mind when she reproaches novel writers with their 'ungenerous and impolitic custom' of 'degrading . . . the very performances . . . to which they themselves are adding' and so 'joining their greatest enemies in bestowing the harshest epithets on such works'. Maria Edgeworth's 'harshest epithets' appeared in the advertisement to *Belinda* (1801). See Frank W. Bradbrook, *Jane Austen and her Predecessors* (Cambridge: Cambridge University Press, 1966), 113.

lost. Furthermore, even when the passage has been highlighted, its inscribed female/male opposition has usually been overlooked.

Robert Kiely, for one, uses the defence passage to open his discussion of what he sees as Jane Austen's belief in the considerable 'capabilities of language, correctly used'.[43] Kiely is impressed by the ways in which several characters in the novel repeatedly misuse language. Their conversation is either imprecise or in excess of what the situation demands. From innocence and/or ignorance (Catherine, Mrs Allen) or from a disposition to affectation, braggadocio, or deviousness (Isabella and John Thorpe, General Tilney), characters use words 'as adornments . . . rather than as a means of communication'.[44] Only Henry Tilney is keenly aware of the absurdity and dangers of imprecision and fashionable, 'excessive' ways of talking. By way of some judicious teasing, he acts as mentor to the inexperienced Catherine, but in his well-known remonstration, it is revealed that even he is not infallible. Thus, for Kiely, Austen's novel is about the value and limitations of social and verbal convention; but primarily it is a critique of those 'poses and excesses of Romanticism' which fail to approximate reality.[45]

In constructing this interpretative frame, however, Kiely actually rewrites[46] the narrator's defence of novels as a defence of 'what a novel *might* be' if it were not given to romantic excess. In so doing he ignores completely the undervaluing of women's reading and writing (Fanny Burney's *Cecilia* and *Camilla*, Maria Edgeworth's *Belinda*) and the overvaluing of men's writing (Goldsmith's *History of England*, editors of anthologies of works by men such as Milton, Pope, Prior, Sterne, or some contributor to the *Spectator*). Mary Ann Caws has truly observed, 'to frame in is to frame out';[47] we tend to

<hr/>

[43] Kiely, *Romantic Novel in England*, 122.   [44] Ibid. 124–5.
[45] Ibid. 122–6, 134–5.
[46] I realize that every reading or interpretation is in a sense a 'rewriting'. However, while quoting Austen, Kiely, *Romantic Novel in England* at p. 122 actually interpolates words of his own, viz. '[A novel at its best can be a] work in which the greatest powers of mind are displayed . . .'.
[47] Mary Ann Caws, *Reading Frames in Fiction* (Princeton, NJ: Princeton University Press, 1985), 3.

'flatten out' differences and employ various forms of slippage in order to homogenize and grasp more firmly our version of the whole.[48] In Kiely's case, the issue of gender styles simply does not arise and he overlooks the fact that his 'heroic' Henry Tilney is also given to clichéd talk—a supposedly 'common-sense' moralizing about women's nature that is ironically deflated by Catherine's ingenuous replies.

Consider Henry's response to Catherine's comment that she is learning to like flowers: 'a taste for flowers is always desirable in your sex, as a means of getting you out of doors, and tempting you to more frequent exercise than you would otherwise take' (*Northanger Abbey*, p. 138). When Catherine upsets his stereotype by objecting that she does not need 'any such pursuit to get [her] out of doors', that 'the pleasure of walking and breathing fresh air is enough', and that 'in fine weather' she is 'out more than half [her] time', he falls back on yet another platitude: 'At any rate, however, I am pleased that you have learnt to love a hyacinth. The mere habit of learning to love is the thing; and teachableness of disposition in a young lady is a great blessing' (p. 139). This patronizing talk is a stylization of those authoritative, male-authored pronouncements addressed to young women in conduct books and reviews. Moreover, Austen is again aiming a dart at those of her sex who are complicit with such pomposity. This is evident when Henry approves Catherine's new-found love of hyacinths because, though 'rather domestic', it will help her 'to have as many holds upon happiness as possible'. The intertext here is from Maria Edgeworth, this time a passage on novel-reading in her *Practical Education* (1798): 'This species of reading cultivates what is called the heart prematurely, lowers the tone of the mind, and induces indifferences for those common pleasures and occupations which, however trivial in themselves, constitute by far the greatest portion of our daily happiness . . . '.[49] That such talk has an affinity with the style of 'common cant' pilloried by the narrator in the defence passage cannot be denied.

---

[48] These processes are described as aspects of perception and intelligence by Douglas R. Hofstadter, in *Godel, Escher, Bach: An Eternal Golden Braid* (New York: Vintage Books, 1980), esp. 646–62.

[49] Hill, *Eighteenth-Century Women*, 60–1.

Other critics ignore the defence passage completely or see it as an anomaly. With its sudden change in register and suspension of focus on Catherine, it is by some deemed to be complete within itself, an intrusive, somewhat aberrant piece of writing on Austen's part.[50] As mentioned earlier, even Margaret Kirkham, who emphasizes its historical importance as a defence of women's writing, sees it in this way. Yet, as we have seen, the passage can be perceived as very much 'to the point' if we treat it as a synecdochic or metonymic utterance connected with the whole by relations of similarity.[51] Seen from a historical, Bakhtinian perspective, the passage is a very strong reply to the mode of deprecatory critical discourse which it incorporates as reported speech—' "I seldom look into novels—Do not imagine that *I* often read novels" . . . "And what are you reading, Miss—?" "Oh! it is only a novel!" ', etc. The subject-matter of the passage ranges wide: not only late eighteenth-century attitudes to novels and the undervaluing of women's writing compared to that of men are mentioned, but also the 'improbable circumstances, unnatural characters, and topics of conversation' in the history, poetry, and reporting produced by men—those works valorized in eighteenth-century England as 'The Tradition'. Given that opinions about novels, poetry, history, aesthetics, reading, and reporting (often with overt references to titles and events) also recur later in the conversations of Catherine with the Thorpes and with the Tilneys, there is strong justification for reading the passage as in some way a 'model' for the text.[52]

---

[50] See Jane Aiken Lodge, *Only a Novel: The Double Life of Jane Austen* (London: Hodder & Stoughton, 1972), 62; Bradbrook, *Jane Austen and her Predecessors*, 114; Mudrick, *Jane Austen: Irony as Defense and Discovery*, 54. Mudrick would no doubt include the defence passage among the authorial intrusions of which he complains.

[51] For an account of text-specific modes of making meaning, see Ross Chambers, *Story and Situation: Narrative Seduction and the Power of Fiction* (Minneapolis: University of Minnesota Press, 1984), 28–35.

[52] Jacqueline Howard, 'Repetition and Revision: Structure in Christina Stead's *Salzburg Tales*', MA Preliminary thesis (Deakin University, 1982), 6: 'images . . . can be imprinted so strongly in memory that they are later used as models for other images which are clearly like them in some way; that is, a specific image serves as a general example of a class of images.' Hofstadter, *Godel, Escher, Bach*, 352, calls this use of a model 'the prototype principle'. Chambers, *Story and Situation*, 29, also adopts the term 'model'.

For example, on one occasion Catherine presents a significant case for the female novelist's more inclusive craft when she frankly admits to Henry and Eleanor that history 'tells [her] nothing that does not either vex or weary [her]. The quarrels of popes and kings, with wars or pestilences, in every page; the men all so good for nothing, and hardly any women at all . . .' (*Northanger Abbey*, p. 84). She then goes on to problematize both the 'invention' and sensationalism employed by writers of history. Later, the learned Henry gives her 'a lecture on the picturesque', obviously culled from Gilpin,[53] in which he talks of 'fore-grounds, distances, and second-distances—side-screens and perspectives—lights and shades' (*Northanger Abbey*, p. 86). But when, from the top of Beechen Cliff, his apt pupil delights him by rejecting 'the whole city of Bath, as unworthy to make part of a landscape', we may suspect that the jargon of Gilpin (whose work had been criticized by Sir Uvedale Price), and by extension that of Henry, are the targets for fun, rather than Catherine's untutored imagination.[54] On yet other occasions, parodies of readerly and critical talk, such as Isabella's ignorant effusions about 'horrid novels' and her brother's proud adoption of the 'common cant' ('Udolpho! Oh, Lord! not I; I never read novels; I have something else to do') function as 'ventriloquized' illustrations of the sort of discourse attacked by the narrator in her 'Defence'.

The repeated parodying and deflation of familiar male-authored critical and scholarly styles is thus a basic aspect of Austen's work. *Northanger Abbey* can be seen as a reply and challenge to those who would denigrate women's intelligence, undervalue their reading, writing, range of feeling and imagining, restrict their education, and everywhere impose stereo-

---

[53] Gilpin defined the picturesque in terms of roughness: 'that particular quality which makes objects chiefly pleasing in painting'. Rough objects alone yield the 'effect of light and shade'. William Gilpin, *Three Essays: On Picturesque Beauty; On Picturesque Travel; and on Sketching Landscape: to Which is Added a Poem, On Landscape Painting* (London: R. Blamire, 1794), 6–7, 19–21.

[54] Gilpin's definition of picturesque beauty was made solely in terms of 'objects which please from some quality capable of being illustrated in painting'. For Price's criticism, see his *Essay on the Picturesque*, nn. to 42, 44, 55, 59.

typed expectations and responses—as if interpreting aspects of life and art and their interconnectedness were not part of an ongoing process, different for each individual.

However, this reading of the novel remains, like Kiely's, a partial one. In the words of Ian Reid, 'metonymic substitutions . . . also release differential meanings that are not entirely subsumed by their resemblance'.[55] I would add that the difference which is logically necessary to similarity is not the only source of alterity or otherness in a narrative. The 'differential meanings' of which Reid speaks are produced from within a text's own repetitions and figurative transformations—its own recontextualizations of the 'same' images, figures, and motifs. And while both he and Ross Chambers recognize that intertextual reference also 'guides the reader's identification and comparison of significant repetitions and equivalences',[56] in practice they give primacy to a text's own 'situational self-reflexivity'. Yet, as we have seen, there are other differential meanings, dense traces of other historical uses, which are generated from without—from the incorporation of snatches of other texts and discursive styles, what M.-Pierrette Malcuzynski calls 'fragments of other, autonomous ensembles'.[57] As various words, phrases, or whole blocks of text interanimate each other, recontextualizing various class, gender, and occupational styles, other 'already said' meanings emerge and these, too, cannot be entirely suppressed. In *Northanger Abbey*, particularly, parodic echoes and waggish renditions of the words of others jostle against each other, producing a welter of meanings and frustrating attempts at interpretative closure. Thus Reid's principle, that a narrative's controlling voice 'can neither subsume without residue all that is told nor silence entirely all that is not told',[58] needs to be seen as doubly valid.

For instance, what are we to make of the quick and 'easy transition' made by Henry Tilney from his lecture on the

---

[55] Ian Reid, ' "Always a Sacrifice": Executing Textual Unities in Two Stories by Katherine Mansfield', *Journal of the Short Story in English*, 4 (Spring 1985), 80.

[56] Chambers, *Story and Situation*, 31.

[57] M.-Pierrette Malcuzynski, 'Mikhail Bakhtin and Contemporary Narrative Theory', *Revue de l'Université d'Ottawa*, 53/1 (1983), 63.

[58] Reid, 'Always a Sacrifice', 83.

picturesque 'to oaks in general, to forests, the inclosure of them, waste lands, crown lands and government', to politics, and 'from politics . . . to silence' (*Northanger Abbey*, p. 87)? In these words are traces of innumerable aesthetic treatises, political tracts, reports, and debates known to Austen's audience, and the 'general pause' which follows seems of the proverbial pregnant sort. No doubt here is one of those occasions when 'the common ideological purview' of the author and her late eighteenth- and early nineteenth-century readers would have 'worked toward discernment of patterns in the unsaid'.[59] Does Henry fall silent about politics because he is in the company of women or because of tension at large about the state of the nation? Or is there another reason?

Catherine breaks the silence with her 'solemn' but vague claim to have heard that 'something very shocking indeed, will soon come out in London'. She does not know its nature or author, only that it is 'to be more horrible than any thing we have met with yet'. Still thinking along political lines, Eleanor replies by expressing faith in the 'proper measures' which will be taken by the government. Her assumption is that Catherine alludes to the possibility of riots and rebellion in London. But Henry soon makes her aware of her mistake—Catherine has again been speaking of Gothic novels: 'a new publication which is shortly to come out, in three duodecimo volumes, two hundred and seventy-six pages in each, with a frontispiece to the first, of two tombstones and a lantern' (*Northanger Abbey*, p. 88). Together with Catherine's prediction, this sentence echoes John Aikin's satirically amusing 'Literary Prophecies for 1797'. Aikin's short piece, written in 1796—the year of publication of *The Monk*—itself appears to have parodied literary scandal and gossip while mocking various literary trends, including the practice of anonymity and the fashion for the sensationally morbid and horrible: 'A novel, by a lady, will make some noise; in which the heroine begins by committing rape, and ends with killing her man in a duel.'[60]

    [59] Susan Stewart, 'Shouts on the Street: Bakhtin's Anti-Linguistics', *Critical Inquiry*, 10/2 (Dec. 1983), 278.
    [60] John Aikin, 'Literary Prophecies for 1797', in id., *Miscellaneous Pieces*, 292–3.

Several subjects begin to vie for our attention in this episode: Eleanor's confusion of a book with an event (which Henry fictionalizes in the form of a sensational, mock-historical report), wild fears and rumours (or is it complacency?) about riot and disorder in London, Catherine's untutored imagination, literary gossip and scandal, and, of course, sensational Gothic novels, several amusing allusions to which have already occurred. Where in all this are we to locate the narrative's dominant voice or perspective?

My own impulse is to return to Mary Wollstonecraft's point about the expectations, attitudes, and 'false system of education' which were perpetuating in women what she called a 'barren blooming'.[61] The debate which she stirred over women's talents and education is implicit in Henry's teasing reply to his sister; like Aikin's 'Literary Prophecies', this reply plays on those common assumptions of a natural, male intellectual superiority[62] which Wollstonecraft was at pains to attack:

I will be noble. I will prove myself a man, no less by the generosity of my soul than the clearness of my head. I have no patience with such of my sex as disdain to let themselves down to the comprehension of yours. Perhaps the abilities of women are neither sound nor acute—neither vigorous nor keen. Perhaps they may want observation, discernment, judgement, fire, genius, and wit. (*Northanger Abbey*, p. 88)

Despite the obvious playfulness, in clearing up his sister's 'confusion' Henry is made to speak from that position of male superiority which his education, profession, broader experience, relative independence, and seniority in years have bestowed. He *expects* and gains amusement at the expense of Catherine and Eleanor—a proclivity we see again in his protracted burlesque of Gothic novels on the way to Northanger. On that occasion he cannot resist taking control of Catherine's eager credulity. So perhaps we are to take it that he did, after all, fall silent about politics out of deference to 'the ladies'. If

[61] Wollstonecraft, *Vindication of the Rights of Woman*, 15–20.
[62] Aikin, *Miscellaneous Pieces*, 290–1: 'The controversy about the talents of women will give birth to two bulky volumes, from a female pen; which will, at least, prove that lightness and vivacity are not, as has been supposed, characteristic of the writers of that sex.'

so, we can locate the text's dominant voice in the recurrent exposure of masculine vanity and assumed authority. Nevertheless, it remains true that whichever perspective we finally decide to privilege it is relativized by the dialogic play of those other historic voices echoing in the background.

This point applies equally to *The Mysteries of Udolpho*, which is a much less self-conscious book than *Northanger Abbey*. With its celebration of the ancestral home, family virtues, intuition, and 'fortitude', its critique of 'improving' landlords, arbitrary power, 'apathy', excessive sensibility, superstition, greed, and lust, Radcliffe's romance can also be seen as situating itself in relation to broad movements for political reform and to controversies about women's rights, talents, and authorship. Without Austen's irony and facetiousness, Radcliffe brings together, into a vast dialogic relationship, heterogeneous styles of discourse: superstitions, scenes and tales of the supernatural, poems, conduct-book moralizing, and the aesthetic discourses of sensibility, the picturesque, and the sublime. Repeated moral precepts and *a posteriori* explanations of seemingly supernatural and strange occurrences interrogate the excesses of sensibility. But they leave unexplained various coincidences or elements of fate and Emily's constant predilection to reach out beyond the tangible and the visible, an intuitive capacity which is tied closely to notions of poetic/painterly 'enthusiasm', creativity, virtue, and 'a contempt for what is mean'. As a result, 'everyday legality' is relativized by the comparative validity of the heroine's intuitive fears and imaginings and by the implausibility of what are offered as 'natural' explanations.

The recurrent emphasis on Emily's aesthetic responses to her situation indicates that more is being claimed for this 'visionary' aspect of her sensibility than mere 'lady-like accomplishments' with pen, water-colours, or lute. Yet Emily's creativity has been all too frequently dismissed as such by critics.[63] Textual support for their stance can be adduced from one or two Gilpinesque passages,[64] particularly the following:

[63] See e.g. Birkhead, *Tale of Terror*, 46.
[64] Cf. John Gilpin, *Observations, relative chiefly to Picturesque Beauty, made in the year 1772, on several parts of England, particularly on the Mountains and Lakes of Cumberland and Westmorland* (London: Blamire,

she was thus enabled to amuse herself with selecting some of the lovely features of the prospect, that her window commanded, and combining them in scenes, to which her tasteful fancy gave a last grace. In these little sketches she generally placed interesting groups, characteristic of the scenery they animated, and often contrived to tell, with perspicuity, some simple and affecting story, when, as a tear fell over the pictured griefs, which her imagination drew, she would forget, for a moment, her real sufferings. (*Udolpho*, p. 418; see also p. 276)

On the other hand, David S. Durant has noted that this particular description of Emily drawing would seem to offer a 'metaphor' for Radcliffe's own fiction, in which 'people are only functions of the setting' and 'characterization is a product . . . of appearance'.[65] Because Radcliffe uses the pictorial technique throughout her romance and we often share Emily's perspective, 'we are gradually manipulated into taking this [visual] sense data as thought'. We accept, in short, an 'implicit pictorial theory of the mind'. The novel's insistent emphasis on 'what is fine in aesthetic response' thus points toward itself: 'how one reacts to an art object is as important as how one interacts with the world. So Emily supersedes the normal heroine by becoming a model for the reader's correct response to what he [*sic*] reads.'[66] Durant thus argues that Emily's 'visual mind' is a model for the 'proper reading' of *The Mysteries of Udolpho*; if one can appreciate her vision, one has become 'heroic'.

Although he does not say so, Durant appears to be working here with Ricardou's hypothesis that any narrative is ultimately 'a vast metaphor of its narration'.[67] But as Lucien Dällenbach

1786), vol. ii, particularly statements such as the following on p. 219: 'It is impossible to view such scenes as these without feeling the imagination take fire. . . . We are carried at once into fields of fiction, and romance. Enthusiastic ideas take possession of us; and we suppose ourselves among the inhabitants of fabled times. . . . The transition indeed is easy and natural, from romantic scenes to romantic inhabitants.'

[65] David S. Durant, 'Aesthetic Heroism in the Mysteries of Udolpho', *Eighteenth Century: Theory and Interpretation*, 22/2 (Spring 1981), 178–9.

[66] Ibid. 185.

[67] Jean Ricardou, *Pour une theorie du nouveau roman* (Paris: Editions du Seuil, 1971), 220: 'En un sens, la fiction est une immense metaphore du sa narration.'

has argued in *Le Récit spéculaire*, if all texts can be said to be self-reflexive, 'they do not display this feature in the same way, nor to the same extent'.[68] Just as, in *Northanger Abbey*, Henry Tilney's telling of a parodic Gothic tale might be seen as mirroring to some extent Austen's own narration, so *Udolpho* is undeniably self-reflexive to the extent that the Gilpinesque description of Emily drawing appears to replicate the author's 'visual style' or penchant for landscape description. However, Durant's homogenization of Emily's and the reader's 'correct' response begins to come apart when we remember that Emily herself is never more the 'heroic' poet/artist than when she is actively experiencing at first hand not so much picturesque beauty as the Burkean sublime—that elevation of mind or 'indescribable awe' (*Udolpho*, p. 226) which cannot be captured in language.

Ross Chambers has remarked that 'texts very frequently incorporate in their structure a true antimodel' of their own narrative situation.[69] The passage quoted by Durant seems to be of this order. It occurs quite late in *Udolpho* and so needs to be evaluated in terms of its difference from those passages in which Emily puts her reading or drawing aside. At times of crisis, 'the genius, the taste, the enthusiasm of the sublimest writers [are] felt no longer' (*Udolpho*, p. 248). Only sublime nature itself can instil 'enthusiasm' and enable Emily, confined within her castle 'prison', to transcend fear and anxiety, while her ambiguous psychological states, her ability to recollect them and later to write poetry or draw in moments of comparative tranquillity, are presented as marks of her virtue, inner strength, sensibility, and genius. Emily's moral aestheticism, poetry, and other artistic endeavours may be offered for the reader's admiration and indulgence, but Art is declared inferior to nature and merely reading about the aesthetic response of others cannot make Emily, or the reader, 'heroic'.

To summarize, then, this review of our dialogic readings so far. The authors of *Northanger Abbey* and *Udolpho* situate their Gothic narratives for readers in a twofold way. First, we

[68] Phillipe Carrard, 'From Reflexivity to Reading: The Criticism of Lucien Dällenbach', *Poetics Today*, 5/4 (1984), 846.
[69] Chambers, *Story and Situation*, 29.

find the recontextualizing of familiar contemporary discourses and discursive styles, either as parody or stylization, often with overt references to other known authors and texts. Secondly, we find various 'models'—forms of self-quotation, repetition, duplication, or recursion, called 'figurative substitutions'—which enable the reader to perceive parts as similar to each other and to relate them to the text as a whole, even though these 'models' can also be seen as ultimately disjunctive, that is, working against holistic interpretations of the text.[70]

This inter- and auto-textuality has provided us with hypotheses about authorial intention, a historical, female-gendered framework in which to read each work. But neither narrative on that ground can be reduced to a single, unified 'woman's voice' or, for that matter, to any single authorial voice or individuality. In both cases a surplus of meaning can be seen to spill over and out of the frames that readers construct.

Moreover, as was argued in Chapter 1, Julia Kristeva and Rosemary Jackson to the contrary, instability in generic, semantic, or syntactic form does not make a novel inherently subversive or transgressive in the political sense. The question of subversion in this sense is a historical one, depending on the presence and semantic orientation of 'voices' in the text which challenge authoritative languages, the degree of dissent and transgression in literary works being accommodated by the author's or reader's society and the position from which the text is read.

In their different ways, *Udolpho* and *Northanger Abbey* can both be seen as interrogating common-sense, 'everyday legality'. To varying degrees, they expose the ruses of patriarchal power and recontextualize common 'official' languages which represent women as naturally weak in constitution and understanding. Above all, they celebrate the 'powers of mind' of women authors. Significantly, early male critics did not describe either novel explicitly in terms of subversion of patriarchal authority, although some aspects, as we have noted, did give cause for unease. Moreover, we should remember that *Northanger Abbey* was suppressed by its first publisher and

[70] Reid, 'Always a Sacrifice', 78.

did not appear until fifteen years later. And when we consider Barrett's response to *Udolpho* in *The Heroine*, the fact that Cherry, a farmer's daughter, lives out what she conceives to be the conventions of the Gothic novel by having her father committed to an asylum, by claiming to be wrongly cheated of her aristocratic inheritance and by running off unchaperoned, we can take it that, by 1813, Tory conservative male readers of Barrett's ilk were treating *Udolpho* as part of a general novelistic threat to patriarchal order in society.

The question now is whether, and if so, how, gender can equally be read as a determinant in the production and reception of those texts historically designated 'Gothic' and written by men. We can begin to map out an answer by examining the type and inflection of the discourses which constitute the world of *The Monk* by Matthew Lewis and the ways in which these discourses, too, have been received.

5

Anticlerical Gothic: Matthew Lewis's The Monk

The Difference of The Monk

Turning to Lewis's romance, we readily find a string of differences from *Udolpho* in emphasis. Coral Ann Howells comments that *The Monk* 'is much more aggressive than *Udolpho* with striking extensions into criminal pathology as Lewis explores male sexual guilts rather than female sexual fears'.[1] Undoubtedly, more attention and sympathy are given to the male victimizer, whose fantasies, emotions, and 'thousand opposing sentiments' are closely delineated. Moreover, the villain's fierce desires are no longer fixed, like Montoni's, on the acquisition of property; Ambrosio's passion is sexual, and his victim, a modest and virtuous young woman without Emily St Aubert's spirit, is made abject by his monstrous will-to-power. His often impersonal attitude to Antonia, coupled with her ineffectual but 'incessant opposition' to his sexual advances (an opposition which serves 'only to inflame [his] desires, and supply his brutality with additional strength'),[2] leads ineluctably to her sadistic rape and murder. In Lewis's Gothic world, the supernatural realm offers no succour to the persecuted; his ghosts are not limited to haunting single chambers or buildings as in Walpole, Reeve, and Radcliffe, but neither are they concerned with bringing about justice in the world.[3] The mythical Madrid of the narrative is

---

[1] Howells, *Love, Mystery and Misery*, 67.

[2] Matthew Gregory Lewis, *The Monk*, ed. James Kinsley and Howard Anderson (Oxford: Oxford University Press, 1980), 383. Further references to this edition will appear in the text.

[3] Syndy M. Conger, 'Matthew G. Lewis, Robert Charles Maturin and the Germans: An Interpretative Study of the Influence of German Literature on

a place in which decadence, hypocrisy, and perversity hold sway. As a result, *The Monk* ends as tragedy rather than romance, and the moral sensibility of Antonia is treated with a cynicism and sadistic harshness beyond anything found in Radcliffe.[4] Indeed, the positive, visionary, and creative aspects of aesthetic sensibility stressed in *Udolpho* and *The Italian* are neglected almost entirely.

In this chapter I will argue that one factor underlying these differences is Lewis's bid for authorship, which is founded on an ideal of the author as unconventional, eccentric, extreme— a risk-taker prepared to shock the complacency of respectable elders in order to gain a reputation for genius. Accordingly, he appropriates styles and stories from German and French literature to give his brand of Gothic a quite different flavour of sensational anticlericalism.

The Preface to The Monk *and Lewis's Claim to Authorship*

Lewis's orientation is first noticed in his 'Imitation of Horace', the verses with which he chose to preface his self-styled romance. Here we find him wittily displacing his own desire for fame on to his text, whose supposed pretensions provide the occasion for both prophecies of the book's reception and some significant disclosures about the author's 'condition'—his 'apartness', his unattractive, almost freakish appearance, his extremes of feeling and behaviour, and his extreme youth.

Lewis first addresses *The Monk* from the position of a wise but indulgent parent:

> METHINKS, Oh! vain ill-judging Book,
> I see thee cast a wishful look,
> Where reputations won and lost are
> In famous row called Paternoster.
> Incensed to find your precious olio

Two Gothic Novels', *Salzburg Studies in English Literature: Romantic Reassessment*, 67 (1977), 2.

[4] Punter, *Literature of Terror*, 75, argues that 'in their portrayals of the continual defeat of . . . poetic justice Radcliffe and Lewis become cruel to the point of sadism'.

> Buried in unexplored port-folio,
> You scorn the prudent lock and key,
> And pant well bound and gilt to see
> Your Volume in the window set
> Of Stockdale, Hookham, or Debrett.
>
> Go then, and pass that dangerous bourn
> Whence never Book can back return:
> And when you find, condemned, despised,
> Neglected, blamed, and criticised,
> Abuse from All who read you fall,
> (If haply you be read at all)
> Sorely will you your folly sigh at,
> And wish for me, and home, and quiet.

Then, assuming 'a conjuror's office', he prophesies that *The Monk* will be ignominiously thrown into some dark corner,

> Or sent to Chandler-Shop away,
> And doomed to suffer public scandal.

Unlike Horace, who seems confident that his book will be 'loved in Rome', becoming 'food for vandal moths' and confined to the provinces only in middle age, Lewis foretells a less favourable reception. Notably, too, he makes no allusion to the ultimate fate which Horace announces for the *Epistles*: 'stammering age will come upon you as you teach boys their A B C in the city's outskirts.'[5] Presumably, 'public scandal' will preclude the possibility of any such pedagogic use for *The Monk*. However, should his 'dear book' by chance 'meet with approbation', and someone 'by natural transition' ask after its author, Lewis would have it impart some information. So he directs it what to say, thereby constructing the following portrait of himself as author:

> That I am one, the enquirer teach,
> Nor very poor, nor very rich;
> Of passions strong, of hasty nature,
> Of graceless form and dwarfish stature;
> By few approved, and few approving;
> Extreme in hating and in loving;

---

[5] Horace, *Satires, Epistles and Ars Poetica*, with an English translation by H. Rushton Fairclough (London: W. Heinemann, 1961), 'Epistle 20', 389.

> Abhorring all whom I dislike,
> Adoring who my fancy strike;
> In forming judgements never long,
> And for the most part judging wrong;
> In friendship firm, but still believing
> Others are treacherous and deceiving,
> And thinking in the present aera
> That Friendship is a pure chimaera:
> More passionate no creature living,
> Proud, obstinate, and unforgiving,
> But yet for those who kindness show,
> Ready through fire and smoke to go.
> Again, should it be asked your page,
> 'Pray, what may be the author's age?'
> Your faults, no doubt, will make it clear,
> I scarce have seen my twentieth year,
> Which passed, kind Reader, on my word,
> While England's Throne held George the Third.

A glance at the corresponding section of Horace's Epistle[6] shows Lewis's claims to be more elaborate, more extreme, the tone more emphatic, and one assumes that he found his romantic description of himself congenial.

Indeed, in a letter to his mother, Lewis had already drawn attention to what he considered his 'resemblance' to the villainous Montoni.[7] Not for him Radcliffe's emphasis on aesthetic and moral sensibility: the delicate balancing of intense, romantic feeling against behavioural restraint, of 'soaring' poetic imagination against pedagogic intent. Rather, he lays claim to the passionate feeling, energy, and boldness exhibited by the *Sturm und Drang* writers of the previous decades in Germany. And, like them, he quickly gets down to the business of dramatizing such qualities for his audience, though without their very specific socio-political programme or interest in nature.[8] As David Punter says of *The Monk*: 'The reader is . . .

---

[6] Ibid. 391.

[7] Letter dated 18 May 1794, reproduced in Louis F. Peck, *A Life of Matthew G. Lewis* (Cambridge, Mass.: Harvard University Press, 1961), 209.

[8] Although the *Sturm und Drang* authors eschewed any form of political organization, they challenged Church and State 'in the name of personal and social culture'. See Roy Pascal, *The German Sturm und Drang* (Manchester: Manchester University Press, 1953), esp. 300–9.

required to see himself [*sic*] as a spectator at a dramatic entertainment which deliberately highlights and parades the more spectacular aspects of life.'[9]

Lewis also seems bent on boldly demonstrating his range and versatility. Like Radcliffe, he begins each of his chapters with an epigraph, most often from Shakespeare or one of the 'melancholy' poets, such as Blair, Strode, Cowper, or Thomson. Unlike Radcliffe, however, he doesn't scruple to include a 'Table of the Poetry', in which his own ten songs and ballads are listed—or to have these poems advertised in pre-publication announcements. And he inserts at the beginning of the novel an 'Advertisement', in which he acknowledges various 'plagiarisms' (translations, adaptations) from European folklore and balladry. Add to that his penchant for myth and interpolations of colourful *Germanisch* folk-tales—of Marguerite, of the Bleeding Nun, and of the Wandering Jew, all within 'The History of Don Raymond', itself an interpolated tale—and we begin to form a picture of an author determined to draw attention to his many talents.

In Chapter 2, I mentioned the high repute of Edward Young's *Conjectures* in Germany and the rapidity with which the notion of 'original genius' was taken up and theorized there. Johann Gottfried Herder, for example, publicly defended the *Conjectures*, extolled the genius of Shakespeare, and argued for the dramatist's right to be judged by a standard set by himself and his times, rather than by modern literary rules and technical refinements.[10] Exalting Nature over art, letters, and learning, he claimed that more primitive languages were 'richer in expressiveness, closer to the source of the creative act', than the sophisticated writing of his own time.[11] In the belief that a revival of simple folk-song could

[9] Punter, *Literature of Terror*, 90.

[10] Lawrence Marsden Price, *The Reception of English Literature in Germany* (Berkeley: University of California Press, 1932), 291, 295; Henry Burnand Garland, *A Concise Survey of German Literature* (London and Basingstoke: Macmillan, 1976), 70–1; Pascal, *German Sturm und Drang*, 219.

[11] Johann Gottfried Herder, 'Über Ossian und die Lieder alter Volker', cited in J. D. Stowell, 'Englightenment and Storm and Stress', in J. M. Ritchie, ed., *Periods in German Literature: A Symposium* (London: Oswald Wolff, 1968), 88.

stimulate a renaissance in German writing on a par with that of Shakespeare's England, he collected and published folksongs, urging others to do the same. Along with Johann Georg Hamann, he fostered the notions of originality and the *Genie*.[12]

By the early 1770s, small, compact groups of self-styled 'geniuses', primarily students associated with the Universities of Strasburg and Göttingen, had begun the *Geniebewegung*, usually referred to as *Sturm und Drang*. Exalting the genius of Shakespeare, and seeking to overturn accepted rules and conventions in both life and art, these youths 'stressed primeval energy as the chief ingredient of genius'.[13] Although the movement was sporadic and is said to have come to an abrupt end once its principal figure, Goethe, moved to Weimar, its public, according to H. B. Garland, was 'widely and well distributed'.[14] The literary output of the *Genies* was also considerable. In addition to *Werther* (1774), a novel of obsessive love and suicide, Goethe wrote powerful poems and two tragedies, *Götz von Berlichingen* (1773) and the early *Faust*, while Lenz, Klinger, Müller, and Wagner all made their names primarily as playwrights. Schiller's play, *Die Räuber* (1781), and his mystery tale, 'Der Geisterseher' (1787-9), both of which later became popular in England, were delayed additions to this literature of revolt.[15]

During the early 1790s, Lewis, an avid theatre-goer, spent considerable time on the Continent. Peck notes that while in Paris in 1791, 'Matthew familiarized himself with the French drama of the day and probably with German *Sturm und*

---

[12] Price, *Reception of English Literature in Germany*, 293; Henry Burnand Garland, *Storm and Stress* (London: George Harrap, 1952), 139-40; Joe K. Fugate, *The Psychological Basis of Herder's Aesthetics* (The Hague: Mouton, 1966), 90-3, 185-9, 213-14, 222-3.

[13] Werner Kohlschmidt, *A History of German Literature 1760-1805* (London and Basingstoke: Macmillan, 1975), 139. According to Garland, *Concise Survey of German Literature*, 72, 'the genius was an original personality, and whether or not he could write or paint, he had to act according to his own laws in disregard of accepted patterns and conventions'.

[14] Ibid. 75.

[15] Garland, *Storm and Stress*, 138; id., *Concise Survey of German Literature*, 78; Pascal, *German Sturm und Drang*, 38-9.

Drang productions, many of which had been translated into French'.[16] Then, in 1792, in order to learn German (a language for which he appears to have had a singular propensity), Lewis spent six months in Weimar, where he read and translated 'the most difficult poets' and met Goethe and Wieland.[17] Yet later again, he spent nearly seven months as an attaché to the British Embassy in The Hague, where his own fever for writing seems to have continued unabated.[18]

Here a link can be made with *The Monk* in which at one point Lewis has Don Raymond contemplate such compulsion to authorship. Having just discovered that his young manservant, Theodore, is a closet poet, Raymond offers him encouragement and the following advice:

An Author, whether good or bad . . . is an Animal whom every body is privileged to attack; For though All are not able to write books, all conceive themselves able to judge them. . . . In short to enter the lists of literature is wilfully to expose yourself to the arrows of neglect, ridicule, envy, and disappointment. Whether you write well or ill, be assured that you will not escape from blame . . . Authorship is a mania to conquer which no reasons are sufficiently strong; and you might as easily persuade me not to love, as I persuade you not to write. (*The Monk*, pp. 198–9)

In a section which Peck sees as an 'intrusive' break in Raymond's narrative,[19] Lewis reminds his readers of the authorial risk-taking and driving energy alluded to in his Preface. Significantly, the 13-year-old Theodore, for all his apparent humility and 'delicacy of . . . features', is a precocious and enterprising young man. His capacity for outrageous exploits, disguises, and stories echoes accounts of the extravagant pranks of the *Sturm und Drang* authors.[20] This image of an author is thus very different from that constructed by Radcliffe. Lewis, it seems, consciously sought to give the impression of youth, boldness, unconventionality, and extraordinary

---

[16] Peck, *Life of Matthew G. Lewis*, 9.   [17] Ibid. 11–12.
[18] See letter dated 23 Sept. 1794, reproduced in Peck, *Life of Matthew G. Lewis*, 213.
[19] Ibid. 39.
[20] Garland, *Concise Survey of German Literature*, 72; Kohlschmidt, *History of German Literature 1760–1805*, 140.

energy; among other things, he claimed to have written *The Monk* in ten weeks.[21]

We should also note that, in some of his letters to his mother, Lewis wrote of female authorship with some disdain: 'Our opinions certainly . . . seem to differ; for I hold that a Woman has no business to be a public character, and that in proportion that She acquires notoriety, She loses delicacy: I always consider a female Author a sort of half-Man . . .'.[22] Moreover, in his first (unpublished) novel, *The Effusions of Sensibility; or Letters from Lady Honorina Harrow-heart to Miss Sophonisba Simper—a Pathetic Novel in the Modern Taste, Being the First Literary Attempt of a Young Lady of Tender Feelings* (1792), he held the conventions of sensibility up to ridicule.[23] The burlesque in *The Monk*, of Leonella's attempts to banish the image of Don Christoval from her 'too susceptible heart', is hardly less crude. A 'love-sick Virgin' (who has neither youth nor beauty), Leonella heaves 'lamentable sighs', utters 'long soliloquies', and, in snatches of poetry, 'declare[s] herself a violent Admirer of murmuring Streams and Nightingales' (pp. 245–6). It is perhaps not surprising, then, that in 1794 Lewis wrote of the early chapters of *Udolpho* as 'dull'. Only when he reached 'the part when Emily returns home after her Father's death' did Radcliffe's romance become 'one of the most interesting Books that have ever been published', one which avowedly inspired him to complete *The Monk*, his own 'Romance in the style of the Castle of Otranto'.[24] This points to Lewis's interest in Radcliffe's more definite strokes of the supernatural, the persecution of Emily and her confinement at Udolpho by Montoni.

Certainly, serious treatment of the beauties and terrors of the natural landscape scarcely figures in *The Monk*, apart from descriptions of the environs of Lindenburg Castle, home of the Bleeding Nun, and the jagged precipices of the Sierra Morena, from which Lucifer hurls Ambrosio to a dreadful death. Nor

[21] Letter dated 23 Sept. 1794, in Peck, *Life of Matthew G. Lewis*, 213.
[22] Letter dated 18 Mar. 1803, in ibid. 220. See also 221–3.
[23] 'The Effusions of Sensibility', in Mrs Margaret Baron Wilson, *The Life and Correspondence of M. G. Lewis, with Many Pieces in Prose and Verse Never Before Published* (London: Henry Colburn, 1839), 241–70.
[24] Letter dated 18 May 1794, in Peck, *Life of Matthew G. Lewis*, 208.

does Lewis's romance share *Udolpho's* benevolist viewpoint. The world which *The Monk* constructs through its 'mutually self-validating fictions'[25]—the story of the monk, Ambrosio, and the long sub-plot of Raymond and Agnes, with its various intercalations—is one in which unpredictable diabolical forces lurk beneath the phenomenal, constantly upsetting appearances and interrogating the real, so that reality itself becomes a very shifty notion indeed. In these circumstances, such qualities as excessive modesty, sensibility, innocence, and virtue not only render men and women vulnerable to exploitation; they are also regarded as in some sense bogus, a veil or mask of demonic passions within.

Discourses of Taste and Sensibility in The Monk

From the start, Lewis's romance eschews a tranquil, pastoral world where nature functions as source of visions of a divine realm—the 'Deity' which so comforts and strengthens Emily St Aubert. Instead, *The Monk* is set in a city, Madrid, 'where superstition reigns with . . . despotic sway' along with all those other vices for which city-dwellers are arraigned by Radcliffe: hypocrisy, pride, ignorance, greed, lust, vanity, and vulgarity. Having stated in the first sentence that Auditors have flocked to the Church of the Capuchins, filling it to capacity within five minutes, the narrator is concerned to dispel any expectations of 'true devotion' or of a virtuous congregation of citizens:

Do not encourage the idea that the Crowd was assembled either from motives of piety or thirst of information. But very few were influenced by those reasons. . . . The Women came to show themselves, the Men to see the Women: Some were attracted by curiosity to hear an Orator so celebrated: Some came because they had no better means of employing their time till the play began; Some, from being assured that it would be impossible to find places in the Church; and one half of Madrid was brought thither by expecting to meet the other half. (*The Monk*, p. 7)

---

[25] A phrase used by Punter, *Literature of Terror*, 70.

This direct address to the reader is the opening gambit in a sustained attack throughout *The Monk* on the hypocrisy, superstition, and moral corruption of the Catholic Church— an attack which Lewis could have expected to be accepted uncritically by his English audience.[26]

Lorenzo de Medina, a young nobleman, is made to share this seemingly Protestant viewpoint. When one of the few truly virtuous auditors, Antonia, enthuses about the preacher's 'powers of eloquence', he warns her of monkish hypocrisy and the hidden perils of the cloistered life:

Your heart new to the world, and full of warmth and sensibility, receives its first impressions with eagerness. Artless yourself, you suspect not others of deceit . . . What pity, that you must soon discover the baseness of mankind . . . a Man who has passed the whole of his life within the walls of a Convent, cannot have found the opportunity to be guilty . . . But now, when . . . he must enter occasionally into the world . . . The trial is dangerous.' (*The Monk*, p. 21)

Later in the novel, Lorenzo again reflects upon the falsity of the Catholic sensibility, but from a slightly different standpoint:

Universal silence prevailed through the Crowd, and every heart was filled with reverence for religion. Every heart but Lorenzo's. Conscious that among those who chaunted the praises of their God so sweetly, there were some who cloaked with devotion the foulest sins, their hymns inspired him with detestation at their Hypocrisy. He had long observed with disapprobation and contempt the superstition, which governed Madrid's Inhabitants. His good sense had pointed out to him the artifices of the Monks, and the gross absurdity of their miracles, wonders, and supposititious reliques. He blushed to see his Countrymen the Dupes of deceptions so ridiculous, and only

---

[26] Bernard Ward, *The Dawn of the Catholic Revival in England 1781–1803* (London: Longmans, Green, 1909), 5–6. In a letter to the Catholic Committee in 1788, Bishop Walmesley wrote, 'it is well known that a great share of prepossessions and prejudices remain still in the breasts of Protestants against the Catholic Religion, not confined among the common people, but prevail even with those of higher class and more improved state of knowledge. These prepossessions and prejudices are imbibed in their youth, and make a common part of their early education, nor do they afterwards examine into the grounds of them, but implicitly retain them as genuine truth. Such undoubtedly is the case of a great number of members of Parliament in both Houses.'

wished for an opportunity to free them from their monkish fetters. (p. 345)

Believing rightly that the true fate of his sister, Agnes, has been determined and concealed by the wicked Prioress of the Convent of St Clare, Lorenzo resolves 'to set before the People in glaring colours, how enormous were the abuses but too frequently practised in Monasteries'. The focus of the novel's indictment has shifted from hypocrisy and the falsity of cloistered virtue to the Church's adherence to superstition, deception, and what is soon to be revealed as its monstrous abuse of power.

If *The Monk* were simply a polemic against Catholicism, concerned with exposing institutional despotism and contrasting Lorenzo's virtue and 'good sense' or rational sensibility with religious hypocrisy, it would be a much less complex and paradoxical book than it is. However, the novel also explores the implications for the individual of an abandonment of conventional restraints and, in the case of Ambrosio, of a Faustian bid for superhuman freedom and sensual gratification. Here, as already indicated, Lewis demonstrates a self-conscious interest in writing for the stage, in Shakespeare, and in contemporary German expropriations of European folklore and legend. His dramatic and often sensational scenes resonate with traces of German plays, tales, and folk- and spirit-ballads, such as Goethe's *Faust*, Schiller's 'Der Geisterseher', Musäus's 'Die Entführung', Bürger's 'Lenore', and Schubart's 'Der Ewige Jude'.[27] Thus diverse and contradictory patterns of tone and meaning problematize any attempt to read Lorenzo's combination of 'Protestant' rationalism and sensibility as morally normative or ideal.

Consider first the outcome of Lorenzo's love for Antonia. Symbolically, his restraint and obedience to social conventions are punished by her death. In a sensationalized expropriation of the final scenes of Shakespeare's love tragedy, *Romeo and Juliet*, Lewis has Antonia drugged and placed in the funeral vaults beneath the convent. There, amidst putrescent corpses, she is raped on waking by the frenzied monk and then

[27] See Conger, 'Matthew G. Lewis, Robert Charles Maturin and the Germans'.

murdered—a fate which Lorenzo could perhaps have prevented had he not been so precise in observing the etiquette of courtship. As it happens, he arrives only by accident on the murder scene and only just in time to converse with Antonia in her last moments. But these are not the only ironies. The poignancy of the scene is undercut by Lewis's parodic manipulation of Sentimental conventions:

She lay, her head reclining upon Lorenzo's bosom, and her lips still murmuring to him words of comfort. She was interrupted by the Convent-Bell, as tolling at a distance, it struck the hour. Suddenly Antonia's eyes sparkled with celestial brightness; Her frame seemed to have received new strength and animation. She started from her Lover's arms. 'Three o'clock!' She cried; 'Mother, I come!' She clasped her hands, and sank lifeless upon the ground. Lorenzo in agony threw himself beside her: He tore his hair, beat his breast, and refused to be separated from the Corse. (*The Monk*, p. 393)

The melodramatic gestures of the lovers and the burlesqued biblicism of 'Mother, I come!' unsettles the reader's involvement in the fulfilment of earlier prophecies concerning the separation of Lorenzo and Antonia and the latter's saintly 'ascension'. A little later the narrator even cruelly suggests that Lorenzo's illness and melancholia are not to be taken very seriously:

His Attendants expressed serious apprehensions for his life; But the Uncle entertained not the same fears. He was of opinion, *and not unwisely*, that 'Men have died, and worms have eat them; but not for Love!' . . . He allowed that He could not but feel shocked at an event so terrible, nor could He blame his sensibility; But He besought him not to torment himself with vain regrets . . .' (*The Monk*, p. 399; my italics)

The misquotation here from *As You Like It*[28] implies that Lorenzo's genuine self in matters of love is different from that which his illness and remorse suggest, that in fact he is again living out a conventional role, and that it is only a matter of time before Antonia's image is 'effaced from his bosom'.

Such cynical questioning of his characters' 'true' selves is a feature of Lewis's romance, from the minute narratorial atten-

[28] William Shakespeare, *As You Like It*, ed. Albert Gilman (Signet Classic; New York: New American Library, 1963), 110.

tion to costume and demeanour which interrogates the virtuous Antonia's 'sensibility of Countenance' to that which un-
masks the sweetness, 'gentle demeanour', and 'profound
melancholy' of the heavily cowled novice, Rosario. In the case
of Antonia, it is her imperfectly veiled physical or sexual
charms that, from the outset, are made the real objects of her
admirers' (and the reader's) curious gaze:

Her features were hidden by a thick veil; But struggling through the
crowd had deranged it sufficiently to discover a neck which for
symmetry and beauty might have vied with the Medicean Venus. It
was of the most dazzling whiteness, and received additional charms
from being shaded by the tresses of long fair hair, which descended
in ringlets to her waist. Her figure was rather below than above
middle size: It was light and airy as a Hamadryad. Her bosom was
carefully veiled. Her dress was white . . . (p. 9)

Skin, eyes, lips, hair, waist, throat, hand, and arm become the
objects of a lip-smacking male gaze which seems bent on
discovering the erotic in the declaredly innocent. And indeed,
finally, 'an arch smile, playing round her mouth', declares
Antonia 'to be possessed of liveliness, which excess of timidity
at present represt' (p. 12).

This description occurs in the opening scene of *The Monk*—
in a first chapter which is light-hearted, almost a burlesque, in
its overturning of conventional 'Romance' expectations of
sensibility and manners. The crowd is rude and jostling (boys
are suspended on the wings of cathedral statuary) and the
costumes and dialogue are colourful. There are echoes, in the
character types and characteristic banter, of comic scenes in
Shakespeare's *Romeo and Juliet* and the scene in Marthe's
garden in Goethe's *Faust: Ein Fragment* (1790).[29] Humour
prevails as two women—one old, one young, both obviously
strangers to Madrid—search for seats in the church and unwittingly attract the attention of two Cavaliers.

The younger man, Lorenzo, instantly offers his seat to the
beautiful Antonia, while the worldly Don Christoval offers his
to Leonella, the maiden aunt, whose attention he diverts so
that Lorenzo can make the younger woman's acquaintance.

[29] Conger, 'Matthew G. Lewis, Charles Robert Maturin and the Germans',
13–42, considers in detail the ways in which Lewis has drawn on Goethe's
Faust.

But like Juliet's nurse in *Romeo and Juliet*, Leonella is garru-
lous and 'totally devoid of taste'. Vain, foolish, and easily
duped by insincere flattery, she is transparently a husband-
hunter and in no time is wrongly assuming that Don Christoval wishes to marry her. So, like Mephistopheles' role in
entertaining Marthe, Margarethe's widowed neighbour in
Goethe's *Fast*, Don Christoval's allotted task becomes comic-
ally painful,[30] as afterwards he jests to Lorenzo:

> at the end of an hour I find myself upon the brink of Matrimony! How
> will you reward me for having suffered so grievously for your sake?
> What can repay me for having kissed the leathern paw of that
> confounded old Witch? Diavolo! She has left such a scent upon my
> lips, that I shall smell of garlick for this month to come! As I pass
> along the Prado, I shall be taken for a walking Omelet, or some large
> Onion running to seed. (*The Monk*, pp. 23-4)

If Leonella's forwardness and foolish vanity are the occasion
for masculine fun, however, there also seems to be mockery of
Antonia's extreme modesty and passive sensibility and Lorenzo's uncritical endorsement of this 'feminine' ideal.

First, there is the fuss made by Leonella when Antonia shows
reluctance to remove her veil in church because 'it is not the
custom in Murcia'. Then, when Don Christoval suggests to
Lorenzo that, as the granddaughter of a shoemaker, Antonia
might be more suitable as mistress than wife, the following
exchange ensues between the two men:

> 'I should be a Villain, could I think of her on any other terms than
> marriage; and in truth She seems possessed of every quality requisite
> to make me happy in a Wife. Young, lovely, gentle, sensible. . . .'
> 'Sensible? Why, She said nothing but "Yes" and "No".' 'She did not
> say much more, I confess—But then She always said "Yes" or "No"
> in the right place.' 'Did She so? Oh! your most obedient! . . .' (*The
> Monk*, pp. 24-5)

The question for the reader here is where to locate the narrative's controlling voice. Don Christoval's critique of a
passive 'feminine' sensibility might be thought to be vitiated
by his commitment to a masculine and upper-class double
standard regarding women. But Lorenzo himself has earlier
gently criticized Antonia's untried sensibility, and the short-

---

[30] Ibid. 22-3.

comings of her moral rectitude are later made patently clear by the narrator. For example, when Antonia naïvely confides in Ambrosio, the narrator comments with mock approval that

She thanked him for his goodness with all the genuine warmth, which favours kindle in a young and innocent heart. Such alone know how to estimate benefits at their full value. They who are conscious of Mankind's perfidy and selfishness, ever receive an obligation with apprehension and distrust: They suspect, that some secret motive must lurk behind it . . . (*The Monk*, p. 249)

Again, when Lorenzo takes to serenading Antonia from the street, in her innocence the young woman cannot believe 'that this nightly music [is] intended as a compliment to her'. Her extreme modesty prevents her from thinking 'herself worth such intentions' (p. 297). One is reminded of those occasions when Emily St Aubert demonstrates a similar modesty. But in the case of Antonia, this moral perfection is not only silly; it reduces her to a virtual puppet, at the mercy of Ambrosio's lust. 'Extreme simplicity', the narrator tells us, 'prevented her from perceiving the aim to which the Monk's insinuations tended' (p. 257). Although Antonia's simple moral precepts allegedly overthrow Ambrosio's 'sophistical arguments', he in turn overpowers her with 'a torrent of Philosophical paradoxes' which are beyond her understanding.

   In contrast, Lewis has an alert and wise young nun, Agnes de Medina, make a spirited defence to Ambrosio of her own unconventional behaviour in love: 'Tax me not with impurity, nor think that I have erred from the warmth of temperament. Long before I took the veil, Raymond was Master of my heart: He inspired me with the purest, the most irreproachable passion . . .' (*The Monk*, p. 47). Having spoken of how she came to violate her vows of chastity, Agnes implies that her virtue— now tried—is greater than Ambrosio's much vaunted, but untried, sanctity. She even argues that he is the real criminal; for, by ensuring that she is placed in prison, he may be the murderer of her unborn child. Later, too, we find a defence of illicit love offered by another rebellious young woman. In her interpolated tale, Marguerite, wife of a robber, tells Don Raymond: 'A villain made himself Master of my affections, and to follow him I quitted my Father's House. Yet though my

passions over-powered my virtue, I sank not into that degeneracy of vice, but too commonly the lot of Women who make the
first false step. I loved my Seducer; dearly loved him!' (*The
Monk*, p. 122). Her 'nature', she argues, 'was licentious and
warm, but not cruel', her conduct 'imprudent' but her heart
'not unprincipled' (p. 124).

Following these assertions by Agnes and Marguerite, and the
critique of Antonia's innocence and sensibility, one is tempted
to posit a narrative voice sympathetic to women's freedom and
spontaneity in love over and against the demands of conventional morality and religion—a voice reminiscent, in fact, of
the *Sturm und Drang* sentiments operating in Goethe's portrayal of Gretchen's love for Faust in what is now known as
the *Urfaust*.[31]

Needless to say, such a voice is not consistently present in
The Monk. Agnes's vivacity and talents, her genuine love for
Raymond, her pregnancy and terrible suffering at the hands of
the wicked Domina, may all be presented with sympathy; but
at other times the narrator comes perilously close to contempt
of women and what he envisions as their intelligence and
sexuality. Some of his narratorial asides, for example, attempt
humour at the expense of women. One instance occurs near
the end of the first chapter when the narrator suddenly com-
mends Antonia for not contradicting Leonella's vain conjectures about Don Christoval: 'She was wise enough to hold her
tongue. As this is the only instance known of a Woman's ever
having done so, it was judged worthy to be recorded here'
(*The Monk*, p. 34). If this is burlesque, it has a distinctly male
chauvinist ring! Other representations of women and male–
female relationships are even more disturbing. We have already noted how Antonia is objectified by the insinuative look
of her male admirers, Lorenzo and Don Christoval, and how
the narratorial tone here is at odds with the conventional
morality which is asserted for Lorenzo. Antonia's charms are
again compared to those of the Venus de Medici when a vision
of her 'undressing to bathe herself' appears to Ambrosio in
Matilda's magic mirror:

[31] Ibid. 36–9. Conger draws parallels between the situations of Gretchen
and Agnes. Like Gretchen, Agnes becomes 'a fearful unwed mother who has
just lost a parent and seems to be abandoned by her lover'.

Though unconscious of being observed, an in-bred sense of modesty induced her to veil her charms; and She stood hesitating on the brink, in the attitude of the Venus de Medicis. At this moment a tame Linnet flew towards her, nestled its head between her breasts, and nibbled them in wanton play. The smiling Antonia strove in vain to shake off the Bird, and at length raised her hands to drive it from its delightful harbour. (*The Monk*, p. 271)

Here the 'voluptuous contours and admirable symmetry of [Antonia's] person' are the specular object of a frankly lustful gaze. But the difference in focalization of this description, compared with the earlier one quoted, seems a matter only of the degree of lewdness employed by the narrator. Irrespective of who sees, Antonia's sexuality is foregrounded. As Coleridge noted, 'the trembling innocence of Antonia' is seized upon as vehicle 'of the most voluptuous images'.[32]

Contrasting the monk's attraction to Antonia with his 'voluptuous desires' for Matilda, the narrator at first draws on the language of sensibility to gain sympathy for his male protagonist:

what He now felt was a mingled sentiment of tenderness, admiration, and respect. A soft and delicious melancholy infused itself into his soul . . . His thoughts were all gentle, sad, and soothing, and the whole wide world presented him with no other object than Antonia. (*The Monk*, p. 242)

Yet, despite this intimation of Ambrosio's tenderness and honour, the final comment even here signals that the monk does not see Antonia as real and autonomous, but more as an extension of his own consciousness. Predictably, her modesty soon fails to command his 'respect and awe', and he becomes 'anxious to deprive her of that quality, which formed her principal charm' (p. 257). The monk's fantasies immediately prior to the rape finally deny Antonia-as-woman any existence as a free, active, and independent feeling agent. Instead, they affirm a Sadeian 'power and will-to-power' which are felt to be 'erotically indissociable' from his own sexuality and which

[32] Samuel Taylor Coleridge, *Critical Review*, 19 (Feb. 1797), reproduced in Coleridge, *Miscellaneous Criticism*, 374.

justify his sadistic actions:[33] 'Society is ever lost to you. I possess you here alone; You are absolutely in my power, and I burn with desires, which I must either gratify, or die . . . Nay, this struggling is childish . . .' (*The Monk*, p. 382). The monk, we are told, then treats Antonia with all the violence of 'an unprincipled Barbarian'. Almost immediately, she becomes for him an object of disgust, inspiring 'no other sentiment in his heart than aversion and rage' (*The Monk*, pp. 383–6). She is no longer 'the sleeping Beauty' but a 'Wretched Girl' and 'Fatal Witch' (pp. 379, 385). Her beauty and innocence have 'plunged [his] soul into infamy', have trapped him in the damned roles of 'perjured Hypocrite', 'Ravisher', 'Assassin'; and even now her 'angel look' bids him 'despair of God's forgiveness'.

Earlier in the novel, Matilda has likewise been regarded as an object of disgust once she has thrown off her novitiate role of 'brotherly' affection and purity. Having declared that she is prey to 'the wildest of passions' because 'the Woman reigns in [her] bosom', she initiates Ambrosio into the pleasures of sex. Thereafter she is referred to as 'wretched Matilda', 'Dangerous Woman', 'Wanton', 'Syren', 'Prostitute', and 'Concubine' (pp. 89, 223–5, 244). Here the amorous monk is described as regretting the sudden change in her character from submissiveness to assertiveness:

But a few days had past, since She appeared the mildest and softest of her sex, devoted to his will, and looking up to him as to a superior Being. Now She assumed a sort of courage and manliness in her manners and discourse but ill calculated to please him. She spoke no longer to insinuate, but to command: He found himself unable to cope with her in argument, and was unwillingly obliged to confess the superiority of her judgement. Every moment convinced him of the astonishing powers of her mind: But what she gained in the opinion of the Man, She lost with interest in the affection of the Lover. He regretted Rosario, the fond, the gentle, and submissive: He

---

[33] The phrases quoted are used by Allon White in his analysis of 'compulsive erotic cruelty in well-known transgressive writers of modernism'. He also uses the term 'model of abjection' to refer to the 'compulsive return to instrumental scenes of erotic violence' in the work of these writers. See Allon White, 'Pigs and Pierrots: The Politics of Transgression in Modern Fiction', *Raritan*, 2/2 (1982), 65.

grieved that Matilda preferred the virtues of his sex to those of her own . . .   (pp. 231–2)

Female sexuality is thus construed as dangerous, while initiative, courage, and 'powers of mind' are deemed masculine qualities which can only be unnatural and threatening in a woman.

Now, it might be argued that this, after all, is Ambrosio's perspective, that we are warned by the narrator of the monk's warped sensibility, and that we are being shown the slide from spirituality to demonic sensuality which his pride and desire for superhumanity—first as 'Man of Holiness' and then as consort for the Holy Virgin—are taking him. Or it might be said that Matilda herself is an extreme case—a whore who tricks Ambrosio by having her portrait painted in the conventional style of the chaste Madonna, knowing full well that this icon will be adored for its erotic component—the graceful turn of head, the blushing cheek, 'golden ringlets', and 'snowy bosom' (*The Monk*, pp. 40–1). In fact, with her diabolical conjurations and her scorn for Ambrosio's guilt and fear of transgression, Matilda does turn out to be some sort of Antichrist figure. She rejects Ambrosio's belated impulse to assist Agnes, and, after Ambrosio has murdered Antonia's mother, Elvira, tells him that he has 'only availed himself of the rights which Nature allows to everyone, those of self-preservation' (*The Monk*, p. 306). Like Mephistopheles in the *Urfaust*, Matilda uses a magic mirror to tempt her victim. She also obtains for Ambrosio the magic myrtle and goads him into signing a devil's pact (*The Monk*, pp. 271–9, 427–30). Her early history of genius and learning, her appropriation of male attire and secret retreat into the monastery in order to pursue her passion for Ambrosio, her feigned sanctity, powers of ratiocination and destructive influence, are all also reminiscent of the legend of Pope Joan, a scandalous anti-Catholic tale most fully developed by seventeenth-century German and French Protestant controversialists in order to mock the established order.[34] That this tale was still being

[34] Sabine Baring-Gould, *Curious Myths of the Middle Ages* (London: Rivington, 1888), 171–89; Giovanni Boccaccio, *Concerning Famous Women*, trans. Guido A. Guarino (London: George Allen & Unwin, 1964), 231–3.

reworked late in the eighteenth century, in order to disseminate anti-Catholic sentiment, is attested by the anonymous publication in Leipzig in 1783 of a romance entitled *Die Päbstinn Johanna, Romantisch behandelt fon Fr. Antonius von Padua, Bibliothekar des Kapuzinerklosters zu St. Vincenz.* This work was recognized by its reviewers as 'a distortion and diatribe on religion'.[35]

But neither of these argumentative ploys can save Lewis's romance from charges of sexism, as the narrator is too frequently given to affirming various essentialist statements about women. According to the narrator of *The Monk*, it is 'difficult for Woman to keep a secret' (p. 240) and 'Possession, which cloys Man, only increases the affection of Woman' (p. 235). Moreover, he claims that Burke's 'soft' virtue, pity, 'is a sentiment so natural, so appropriate to the female character, that it is scarcely a merit for a Woman to possess it, but to be without it is a grievous crime' (p. 232).

As we have seen, Ambrosio's response to the sexual and intellectual dominance of Matilda is to pursue a 'feminine' ideal of chastity and submissiveness in the form of Antonia. But, equally, the narrator makes much of the point that Virginia de Villa Franca, the woman who replaces Antonia in Lorenzo's affections, has in abundance Antonia's same fairy-tale beauty, 'sweetness', 'gentleness of manners', and 'tender concern' (pp. 348, 395, 400). Virginia, we are told, 'laid herself out to please' Lorenzo, while he 'was also much flattered by her prejudice in his favour, which She had not sufficient art to conceal' (p. 419). Again, it seems, a virtuous woman—Virgin(ia)—is presented as little more than a passive object for male comfort and recipient of his desire.

According to Boccaccio, once Joan 'had risen to the lofty pontificate', she 'fell prey to the ardor of lust' and became pregnant. Having miscalculated her time of delivery, she gave birth during a sacred procession. As a consequence, the cardinals threw her into a dungeon where she 'died in the midst of her laments'. There are further interesting parallels here with *The Monk*: the wicked Domina of the Convent of St Clare, although not pregnant, is exposed during a procession while Agnes, having previously given birth to a child, lies close to death in a dungeon.

[35] Michael Hadley, *The Undiscovered Genre: A Search for the German Gothic Novel* (Berne, Frankfurt, and Las Vegas: Peter Lang, 1978), 115.

Finally, even the rebellious Agnes, once she is reunited with Raymond, is made to take a more conservative stance. She speaks of having 'trembled with all a Woman's weakness' while in the dungeons beneath the Convent of St Clare, and sees her 'past sufferings' as a purchase of pardon from heaven. Granting that she has 'offended greatly and grievously', she also enjoins her husband, 'because he once conquered [her] virtue', not to 'doubt the propriety of [her] future conduct', which shall be 'exemplary' (*The Monk*, p. 417). Although Agnes does not exonerate her lover from all blame, her logic is akin to that which compels the dying Antonia to tell Lorenzo, in tones reminiscent of Richardson's Clarissa, 'that had She still been undefiled She might have lamented the loss of life; But that deprived of honour and branded with shame, Death was to her a blessing: She could not have been his Wife, and that hope being denied her, She resigned herself to the Grave without one sigh of regret' (*The Monk*, p. 392).

In short, although the novel offers sympathetic and respectful representations of sexually active women whose lives are being ruined by the corruption and small-mindedness of society, it is difficult to maintain that *The Monk* champions a liberated attitude to women's sexuality. Agnes and Raymond's affair may end relatively happily, but only after both have been subjected to prolonged terrors and brought close to death. Lewis's romance not only portrays human sexuality as fraught with danger but also comes close to rejecting female sexuality as an active, independent force altogether.[36]

Other inconsistencies in voice occur as *The Monk* alternates between comic burlesque of Sentimental conventions and their exploitation. In order to stage melodramatic scenes of violent passions and include interpolated tales and ballads of the supernatural and physically gruesome, Lewis occasionally finds it necessary to resort to a Radcliffean style in which church or landscape acts as catalyst to romantic yearnings.

For example, after Don Christoval has taken his flamboyant and teasing farewell of Lorenzo in the opening chapter, a rare

---

[36] David Morse, *Romanticism: A Structural Analysis* (London and Basingstoke: Macmillan, 1982), 60, claims that *The Monk* can be read as 'an allegory of the rejection of female sexuality by Monk Lewis'.

description of the church in the picturesque style is given. The passage is used to frame the first omen of Antonia's impending violation and death. Ambrosio, Abbot of the Capuchin monastery, has left the Cathedral, having delivered the latest of the weekly sermons for which he is famed. The aisles are virtually deserted, save for Lorenzo, newly returned to the city after a long absence. His principal purpose is to see his sister, Agnes, who has recently taken her vows as a nun in a nearby convent. But in the preceding hour of the service, he has met Antonia; so he lingers a while in the stillness of the church, his thoughts bent on marriage. It becomes a mark of his virtue and sensibility that, as evening approaches, he falls victim to 'a pleasing melancholy' not unlike that of which Ann Radcliffe writes:[37]

The night was now fast advancing. The lamps were not yet lighted. The faint beam of the rising moon scarcely could pierce through the gothic obscurity of the Church. Lorenzo found himself unable to quit the Spot. The void left in his bosom by Antonia's absence, and his Sister's sacrifice which Don Christoval had just recalled to his imagination, created that melancholy of mind, which accorded but too well with the religious gloom surrounding him. He was still leaning against the seventh column from the Pulpit. A soft and cooling air breathed along the solitary Aisles: The Moon-beams darting into the Church through painted windows, tinged the fretted roofs and massy pillars with a thousand various tints of light and colours . . . (*The Monk*, p. 26)

Nourished by this awesome calm and solitude, Lorenzo's 'disposition to melancholy' causes him to forget his immediate purpose entirely. Taking a nearby seat, he 'abandon[s] himself to the delusions of his fancy.' As he thinks of 'his union with Antonia' and 'the obstacles which might oppose his wishes', a thousand visions present themselves until, at length, 'sleep insensibly [steals] over him' and he moves in a surreal world which is at first pleasantly contiguous with his waking fancies.

In answer to a question from the preacher, Ambrosio, Antonia claims Lorenzo as her 'destined Bridegroom'. Lorenzo's surge of joy is shortlived, however. His wish-fulfilling dream changes instantly to grotesque nightmare when a terrible 'Un-

---

[37] See, in particular, Radcliffe, *Sicilian Romance* (in *Limbird's edition of The British Novelist*, vol. i), 43, 50.

known' of 'gigantic form' rushes between him and his bride. The eyes of this 'Monster' are 'fierce', his skin is 'swarthy', from his mouth issue 'volumes of fire', and on his forehead are inscribed the words, 'Pride! Lust! Inhumanity!' Grasping Antonia, the creature springs with her on to the altar and tortures her with 'his odious caresses'. Just as suddenly, the Cathedral seems to begin crumbling and the Altar sinks down into 'an abyss vomiting forth clouds of flame'. Into this 'Gulph' the monster plunges, attempting to drag Antonia with him. However, 'animated by supernatural powers', she disengages herself and soars to heaven on wings of 'brilliant splendour' and amidst 'rays of dazzling brightness', as Lorenzo sinks helpless to the ground (*The Monk*, p. 28).

So dramatic a turn in the dream narrative alerts readers to its possible predictive function, an expectation reinforced a few pages later by the Gypsy's prophecy of Antonia's destruction by 'lustful Man and crafty Devil' (p. 38). Indeed, by the end of the novel, every detail of Lorenzo's dream can be read as referring out to the larger text. However, although at first Lorenzo cannot believe that what he has just witnessed is a dream, 'a little recollection convince[s] him of its fallacy' and soon he is made to forget the episode entirely. Lorenzo is, it seems, a sensitive but rational man; he is not susceptible to superstition. In this way Lewis employs the discourse of sensibility both to suggest the virtue of Lorenzo and to begin a progressive modulation into a lurid world in which supernatural forces will take on a real and oppressive existence. In so doing, he performs a confidence trick, cynically rendering Lorenzo's ostensive virtue ineffectual and ambiguous.

To a similar end, the discourses of sensibility and the picturesque are also woven into the interpolated 'History of Don Raymond, Marquis de las Cisternas', a long tale of misadventure, love, and horror, related by Raymond himself to Lorenzo. Challenged by Lorenzo for conducting a clandestine correspondence with Agnes, Don Raymond tells his tale in the hope of vindicating himself. Thus he first establishes the honour, nobility, and benevolence of his family by recounting how his father and the Duke of Villa Hermosa had together sent him on his 'Travels' (the 'Grand Tour' customary in the eighteenth century for young men of wealth and position) with the

charge to mix with 'the classes below him' and become 'an
eye-witness of the sufferings of the People'. For, having observed 'how the vassals of foreigners were treated', he would
'learn to diminish the burthens, and augment the comforts of
[his] own' (*The Monk*, p. 96). Raymond then furthers the
claim for his own sensibility and virtue by referring to the
extravagances of city life. Like Valancourt in *The Mysteries of
Udolpho*, he has both fallen under and rejected the corrupting
influence of Paris: 'I grew sick of dissipation: I discovered, that
the People among whom I lived, and whose exterior was so
polished and seducing, were at bottom frivolous, unfeeling
and insincere. I turned from the Inhabitants of Paris with some
disgust, and quitted that Theatre of Luxury without heaving
one sigh of regret' (*The Monk*, pp. 96–7).

As Raymond continues his narrative, it is explained that he
first met and fell in love with Agnes when invited to stay at
Lindenberg Castle by her aunt, the Baroness Lindenberg,
whom he had saved from certain death at the hands of bandits
in the thick woods near Strasburg. Unfortunately, the Baroness's ill-conceived passion for him had turned to hatred when
she learned that Agnes, not herself, was his true love.
Threatening vengeance, she had requested him to leave the
castle immediately. In an effort to escape her aunt's resent-
ment, Agnes had then planned to elope with Don Raymond by
disguising herself as the ghost of the Bleeding Nun, a legendary figure whose story she had previously related to her lover
in a tone of 'burlesqued gravity'.

On a certain night the servants were to leave open the gates
for the ghost's quinquennial wanderings and then retire, thus
unwittingly assisting the pair to escape. Don Raymond had
provided a carriage, concealed in 'a spacious Cavern of the
Hill, on whose brow the Castle was situated' (p. 153), and
finally midnight had come. The 'massy gates' were unbarred
and the castle was 'wrapt in darkness'. As Raymond waited
for one o'clock, his propensity to melancholy had induced a
preternatural awareness, quite in contrast to his usual mockery of the spirit world:

While I sat upon a broken ridge of the Hill, the stillness of the scene
inspired me with melancholy ideas not altogether unpleasing. The
Castle which stood full in my sight, formed an object equally awful

and picturesque. Its ponderous Walls tinged by the moon with solemn brightness, its old and partly-ruined Towers lifting themselves into the clouds and seeming to frown on the plains around them, its lofty battlements oërgrown with ivy, and folding Gates expanding in honour of the Visionary Inhabitant, made me sensible of a sad and reverential horror. (p. 154)

This passage, with its traces of graveyard poetry, exploits, as Peter Brooks has noted, 'a delectation in chiaroscuro, in the experience of ruin, mystery, awe—in order to imply the capacity and aptitude of the natural world to receive and produce the supernatural. Nature is primed, readied to produce things beyond its phenomenological appearances.'[38] No longer do we find the earlier jaunty prose, in which references to 'old Spanish romances' and lovers' jokes about 'her ghostship', the Bleeding Nun, promised a farcical romp at the expense of Agnes's superstitious relatives. With Raymond's sudden chanting of his strange, ballad-like pledge, his embrace of the Bleeding Nun and her entry into his coach, there begins a terrifying and preternaturally fast ride. It seems that, from the moment Raymond's elevated sensibility gives admittance to ideas and feelings of a transcendent state, he is vulnerable. But it is his rash pledge to the ghostly figure that actually places him in her thrall.

From the plan for the elopement to the ghost's eventual banishment, Don Raymond's narrative exhibits close similarities in content, if not always in tone, to Johann Musäus's comic fairy-tale, 'Die Entführung', from his *Volksmärchen der Deutschen* (1782–6).[39] Like Fritz in that tale, Raymond escapes from the shattered carriage alive, but injured, and frantic for news of Agnes, who has disappeared. Not until he is visited that night by the spectre of the Bleeding Nun does he realize the truth—that it was not Agnes whom he greeted at the rendezvous. The ghost cannot be seen by anyone but Raymond, and the increasing horror which her nightly visits

[38] Peter Brooks, 'Virtue and Terror: *The Monk*', *ELH* 40/2 (Summer 1973), 255.

[39] Conger, 'Matthew G. Lewis, Charles Robert Maturin and the Germans', 93–105. Conger claims that Lewis 'transforms a comic fairy tale which spoofs both superstition and young love into a graveyard melodrama which does neither' (99).

inspire begins to undermine his health. He becomes 'the prey
of habitual melancholy' and is long confined to bed. The
'profound sadness' which oppresses him 'without remission'
leads his physician to consider him 'an hypochondriac' (*The
Monk*, pp. 161–3). Only after Theodore has arranged for the
Wandering Jew to visit Raymond and exorcize the ghost does
Raymond recover his health 'so rapidly as to astonish [his]
physicians'. However, unlike Fritz in Musäus's tale, he is not
speedily reunited with the woman he loves. Both Raymond
and Agnes undergo much further suffering before their eventual reconciliation.

Lewis also has the Wandering Jew[40] complete the ghost's
own tale of how, as Beatrice de las Cisternas (the great-aunt of
Raymond's grandfather), she was forced into convent life.
Subsequent upon this early repression, she became depraved:
'a Prostitute', 'an Atheist', and 'Murderess' (*The Monk*, pp.
172–6). There are clear parallels here with the development of
Ambrosio, whose interventions also separate and harm young
lovers; and the effect of all this is again cynically to cast doubt
on the effectiveness or point of the sensibility and virtue of
Raymond and Agnes. As Kiely points out, the lovers have,
after all, been 'guilty of no crime other than their desire to be
together'.[41] Yet their love is strongly linked to the demonic,
Raymond being required inexplicably to consign his ghostly
ancestor's unburied bones to the 'family vault of his Andalu-
sian Castle' (*The Monk*, p. 172).

It is instructive to contrast Raymond's exercise of sensibility
with that of Vivaldi, the virtuous lover of Ann Radcliffe's last
Gothic novel, *The Italian* (1797), which in many ways can be
considered a reply to *The Monk*. A prisoner of the Inquisition,
Vivaldi is enmeshed in a mysterious set of circumstances. At
one point, a stranger, who has previously inexplicably gained
admittance to his cell, and who refuses to disclose his identity,
appears before the tribunal to accuse the villainous monk,

[40] Conger, ibid. 71, points out that Lewis's Jew bears strong resemblances
to Schiller's Armenian in 'Der Geisterseher' and Schubart's eternal wanderer
in 'Der ewige Jude', as well as to such legendary figures as Faustus and Cain.
Tales about the contemporary magician, Cagliostro, could also have been
appropriated by Lewis.
[41] Kiely, *Romantic Novel in England*, 111.

Schedoni, of murder. Vivaldi looks upon 'the wild physiognomy' of this stranger and 'almost fancie[s], as he ha[s] formerly done, that he be[holds] something not of this earth'. The qualification 'almost' is important, and the narrator of *The Italian* goes on to underline her hero's restraint:

'I have heard of the spirit of the murdered,' said he, to himself— 'restless for justice, becoming visible in our world—.' But Vivaldi checked the imperfect thought, and, though his imagination inclined him to the marvellous, and to admit ideas which, filling and expanding all the faculties of the soul, produce feelings that partake of the sublime, he now resisted the propensity, and dismissed, as absurd, a supposition, which had begun to thrill his every nerve with horror.'[42]

For Raymond, the full exercise of his elevated sensibility banishes scepticism, induces a peculiar rashness which puts him in touch with the realm of spirits, and almost sends him mad. Once the ghost has been admitted, there can be no simple reprieve from anxiety via a return to common sense.[43] On the other hand, for Vivaldi, faced with a similar situation, the exercise of sensibility is mingled with restraint, a holding back and return to the rational. He senses the potential for harm of his fervent imagination, while yet venerating his imaginative capacity. This difference in appropriation by the two authors of the discourse of sensibility goes a considerable way towards clarifying Lewis's ability to incorporate the marvellous so boldly in his work as against Radcliffe's often ambiguous use of the 'explained supernatural'.

It is also interesting to note in Lewis's description of Lindenberg Castle and its environs the departures from Radcliffe's description of the Castle of Udolpho. The latter is darker, more massive, rugged, isolated, and uncompromising, than the relatively domesticated and picturesque but decadent Castle of Lindenberg. Avoiding the positive associations of freedom which Radcliffe had developed for sublime landscapes and the mountainous or wooded setting of the ancestral

---

[42] Ann Radcliffe, *The Italian: or The Confessional of the Black Penitents* (Oxford: Oxford University Press, 1981), 347. Further references appear in the text.
[43] This point is made by Sydney L. W. Lea, *Gothic to Fantastic: Readings in Supernatural Fiction* (New York: Arno Press, 1980), 26.

Gothic home, Lewis concentrates on their inversion in the claustrophobic terrors of sublime ecclesiastical architecture—the dark underground passage, narrow cell, evil-smelling tomb, and dank dungeon. As places of death and imprisonment, these airless spaces can be read as images of the monk's 'tortuous psychology', the perversion of his sexual impulses into 'a dark destructive lust for power'.[44] Even the picturesque and beautiful monastery garden is constrictive and, as a site of temptation, is described with the tinsel and crêpe theatricality which pervades so much of *The Monk*.

Ambrosio descends into the garden when he wishes to find peace after Agnes has cursed his pride and severity and prophesied his own 'day of Trial'. From the outset we are made aware of the garden's artificiality, as it is described by the narrator as the most beautiful and 'regulated' spot in Madrid:

It was laid out with the most exquisite taste; The choicest flowers adorned it in the height of luxuriance, and though artfully arranged, seemed planted only by the hand of Nature: Fountains, springing from basons of white Marble, cooled the air with perpetual showers; and the Walls were entirely covered by Jessamine, vines and Honeysuckles. The hour now added to the beauty of the scene. The full Moon ranging through a blue and cloudless sky, shed upon the trees a trembling lustre, and the waters of the fountains sparkled in the silver beam: A gentle breeze breathed the fragrance of Orange-blossoms along the Alleys; and the Nightingale poured forth her melodious murmur from the shelter of an artificial wilderness. (*The Monk*, p. 50)

The grove with its 'rustic Grotto, formed in imitation of a Hermitage' communicates its 'universal calm' to Ambrosio, but there always remains the hint of the deceptive nature of both the place and the monk's sensibility. Ambrosio's tranquillity is described as 'voluptuous', one which 'spread[s] languor through his soul'. And, indeed, it is in this place that the novice, Rosario, tells a seductive tale about his sister, Matilda, only to fall at the monk's feet and reveal melodramatically that 'he' is she—'Father . . . I am a Woman! . . . I acknowledge my Sister's story to be my own! . . . You are her

---

[44] Howells, *Love, Mystery and Misery*, 68–9.

Beloved' (p. 58). In the seclusion of the Grotto, Rosario turns into the temptress, Matilda, the moonbeams revealing the 'dazzling whiteness' of her breast as she threatens to stab herself if Ambrosio will not allow her to remain in the monastery.

For Ambrosio, the step from 'voluptuous tranquillity' to 'insatiable avidity' is but a short one: 'A sensation till then unknown filled his heart with a mixture of anxiety and delight: A raging fire shot through every limb; The blood boiled in his veins, and a thousand wild wishes bewildered his imagination' (*The Monk*, p. 65). Here, in graphic terms, is the 'excess' of which Radcliffe warns through her interpolated story of Laurentini in *Udolpho*—the scorpions of lust which 'sting . . . even unto death'. Lewis actually symbolizes Ambrosio's awakening to lust by having a serpent sting him in the garden when Matilda asks him to pluck her a rose—an incident with strong biblical overtones of the Fall. Ambrosio's religiosity is not proof against evil. Rather, as Ann Radcliffe might have argued, the monk's 'life of abstinence and prayer' has been a self-centred one of 'mere negative' rather than 'active virtue'.[45] Nor has he been nurtured on that awful magnificence in nature, that 'pleasing dread' or terror, which for Radcliffe always carries a concomitant moral vision.

'Virtue and taste are nearly the same, for virtue is little more than active taste, and the most delicate affections of each combine in real love', St Aubert tells Emily. But unlike the St Auberts or Goethe's Faust, Ambrosio is no lover of nature. As the narrator of *The Monk* makes clear, his 'natural' sensibility has been distorted by his conventual upbringing:

His Instructors carefully repressed those virtues, whose grandeur and disinterestedness were ill-suited to the Cloister. Instead of universal benevolence He adopted a selfish partiality for his own particular establishment: He was taught to consider compassion for the errors of Others as a crime of the blackest dye: The noble frankness of his temper was exchanged for servile humility; and in order to break his natural spirit, the Monks terrified his young mind, by placing before him all the horrors with which Superstition could furnish them . . . (p. 237)

---

[45] Phrases used of a monk in Ann Radcliffe, *Romance of the Forest* (in *Limbird's edition of The British Novelist*, vol. i), 31.

Tales of monastic cruelty and of monks and nuns involved in illicit sexual relations had been in circulation since at least the fourteenth century when Baccaccio wrote *The Decameron*. In the sixteenth century Protestant writers and historians, particularly in France and Germany, often distorted and sensationalized—either from ignorance or wilfully—the doctrines and practices of the religious orders.[46] The prototype of the wicked cleric in English fiction was Reginald, the monk in Thomas Leland's *Longsword* (1762). But by the time Lewis's romance was published, the type had also been commonly revived and extended elsewhere—by the *Sturm und Drang* writers, by authors of convent tales and *Ritter-*, *Räuber-*, and *Geisterromane*, and by anticlerical dramatists and philosophers in revolutionary France. Hadley points out that 'even a Roman Catholic writer like Leopold Alois Hoffmann in *Mönche und der Teufel*' (Vienna, 1782) could malign the monk 'for his "feigned" poverty, chastity and obedience'.[47] And in Citoyen Jacques M. Boutet de Monvel's *Les Victimes cloîtrées* (1791), the heroine, Eugenie, is sexually harassed and imprisoned in the abbey vaults by a priest, the tyrannical Père Laurent, and his accomplice, the Abbess.[48] Yet another instance of the type occurs in Schiller's 'Der Geisterseher', in which the sensibility of an ascetic Prince has been so distorted by his repressive, Protestant religious education, that his faith and morality are readily undermined by the spooky machinations of a wandering, Catholic, Armenian

[46] Baring-Gould, *Curious Myths of the Middle Ages*, 177, 185. For a survey of the expropriation of Catholic doctrines and history by writers of Gothic fiction, see Sister Mary Muriel Tarr, *Catholicism in Gothic Fiction: A Study of the Nature and Function of Catholic Materials in Gothic Fiction in England (1762–1820)* (Washington: Catholic University of America Press, 1946). Montague Summers, in *Gothic Quest*, 211, details the errors which show Lewis's 'farcical ignorance of the religious orders, of convents, and of the enclosed life'.

[47] Hadley, *Undiscovered Genre*, 116.

[48] Jacques M. Boutet de Monvel, *Les Victimes cloîtrées* (Paris: Barba, 1803), cited by Conger, 'Matthew G. Lewis, Charles Robert Maturin and the Germans', 110–11, 157. See also Robert Shackleton, 'The Cloister Theme in French Pre-Romanticism', in Will Moore with Rhoda Sutherland and Ruth Starkie, eds., *The French Mind: Studies in Honor of Gustav Rudler* (Oxford: Clarendon Press, 1952), 170–86.

priest.[49] Religious and political institutions and bourgeois morality in general were often portrayed in Germany at this time as denying the individual's rights and natural impulses or feelings. But the belief that monks were prey to sexual obsession and illicit desire was also commonly held in England. Notably, it is stated in Richard Payne Knight's poem, *The Landscape*:

> The Monk, secluded by his early vow,
> The blessings of retreat can never know:
> Barren of facts and images his mind
> Can no materials for reflection find;
> Dark rankling passions on his temper prey,
> And drive each finer sentiment away;
> Breed foul desires; and in his heart foment
> The secret germs of lurking discontent:
> Long weary days and nights successive roll,
> And no bright vision dawns upon his soul;
> No gleams of past delight can mem'ry bring,
> To stimulate the flight of fancy's wing:
> In vain to distant Hope, Religion calls,
> When dark vacuity his mind appalls:—
> Without, a dismal sameness reigns around;
> Within, a dreary void is only found.[50]

Lewis claimed in his 'Advertisement' to have got 'the first idea' for *The Monk* from 'the story of Santon Barsisa in *The Guardian*'—a tale printed in 1713 about 'a holy man led by the devil into seduction and murder and tricked at the point of death into forfeiting his soul'.[51] Obviously, however, he also appropriated contemporary humanistic and anticlerical writings—English, French, and German—about the unnaturalness of the ascetic life.

Ambrosio is invested with 'natural good qualities' (p. 237) which, like those of Schiller's prince, have been suppressed by his upbringing—the monks have busied themselves in 'rooting out his virtues and narrowing his sentiments'. And, like the monk of Knight's poem, Ambrosio has been long absent 'from

---

[49] Conger, 'Matthew G. Lewis, Charles Robert Maturin and the Germans', 54–6.

[50] Knight, *Landscape*, bk. 1, lines 377–92, pp. 21–2.

[51] Peck, *Life of Matthew G. Lewis*, 21.

the great world'; his 'inborn genius' has been plunged into
'darkness' by superstition. Ignorance of women and 'a spare
diet, frequent watching and severe penance' have 'cooled and
represt the natural warmth of his constitution'. But his dormant passions are easily overcome by a single glimpse of 'joys till
then unknown to him' and soon he looks 'with disgust on the
monotony of the convent'. His religious devotion is 'too feeble
to resist the over-whelming torrent of his desires' and 'all
impediments [yield] before the force of his temperament, warm
sanguine, and voluptuous in the excess' (*The Monk*, pp. 67, 86,
239). Other passions, we are told, only need to be awakened
'to display themselves with violence as great and irresistible'.

Here, then, is an explicit psycho-biographical explanation of
the ease with which the crafty Matilda is able to seduce
Ambrosio. Once he has tired of her, only pride in his image of
sanctity and fear of losing his reputation prevent the monk
from satisfying his desires in relation to the numerous female
penitents for whom he is Confessor. Ambrosio's pride, as one
of Lewis's earliest critics pointed out, is in fact the real 'arch-
devil' which betrays him.

Writing for the *Analytical Review* in October 1796, this
critic felt that 'the calling up a spirit from Hell to borrow a
female shape' was redundant, even an act of bad faith on the
author's part:

Ambrosio, the monk, it is true dies, but fancy follows him to Hell,
and wishes to see him meet the treacherous Matilda in her proper
person, and hear his bitter upbraidings. The monk, in fact, inspires
sympathy because foiled by more than mortal weapons; yet nothing
was done by Matilda which could not have been achieved by female
wiles . . .[52]

The reviewer is referring to Satan's final disclosure that he had
'bade a subordinate but crafty spirit assume a similar form' to
the picture of the Madonna so blindly idolized by Ambrosio.
It is a detail which again (and very obviously) renders *The
Monk* resistant to any unifying frame; as David Punter suggests, it appears to be 'a piece of deliberate extremism' on
Lewis's part.[53]

[52] *Analytical Review*, 24 (Oct. 1796), 403.
[53] Punter, *Literature of Terror*, 90.

Indeed, the entire ending with its shocking revelations and grand, metaphysical dimensions—Ambrosio's Oedipal past, the Faustian pact and damnation, the triumph of disorder and chaos—suffers from mythical 'overload' and seems once more a deliberate attempt to upset the security of the reader. In the mention of mountain eagles, and the figural prominence given to the Rock to which Ambrosio is delivered, for example, are traces of the myth of the archetypal overreacher, Prometheus, whose daily torture by an eagle is again echoed in the description of the monk's protracted dying: 'The Eagles of the rock tore his flesh piecemeal, and dug out his eye-balls with their crooked beaks' (*The Monk*, p. 442). The implication is, perhaps, that Ambrosio is an anti-Prometheus figure who, by imagining himself beyond the limits of society and becoming demonic, has 'made a travesty of human aspiration'.[54] Freedom can never be a simple rejection of limits; Ambrosio's belief in such liberty is naïve and results in newer forms of subjection to unsuspected forces. Following closely the description of the death of Francesco, the villain in Veit Weber's 'Die Teufelsbeschwörung',[55] Lewis has Ambrosio die a long and agonizing death after being cast down (ironically, somewhat like Satan) by Lucifer from a great height on to the rocks below. The monk's drawn-out death then 'seems to put the order of Genesis itself into reverse':[56]

six miserable days did the Villain languish. On the Seventh a violent storm arose: The winds in fury rent up rocks and forests: The sky was now black with clouds, now sheeted with fire: The rain fell in torrents; It swelled the stream; The waves overflowed their banks; They reached the spot where Ambrosio lay, and when they abated carried with them into the river the Corse of the despairing Monk. (*The Monk*, p. 442)

Yet if Ambrosio's fall was all along due to demonic possession rather than psychological obsession, and Matilda was in the employ of Satan from the first, much of the earlier

[54] Conger, 'Matthew G. Lewis, Charles Robert Maturin and the Germans', 91.
[55] For a close textual comparison of the ending of *The Monk* with this work, see ibid. 89–92.
[56] Kiely, *Romantic Novel in England*, 117.

narrative loses point.[57] As Syndy M. Conger comments, Lewis
at times gives Ambrosio some tragic stature by suggesting that
his nobility and capacity for love have been distorted and 'his
fine mind ruined . . . by an oppressive Capuchin education'.[58]
Ambrosio is also given moments of self-reproach; even after
the rape, as the monk's 'gloomy rage' and disgust abate, Lewis
suggests that he is still capable of compassion (*The Monk*,
pp. 386–7). But then, finally, our author affords his creation
little respect. Representing Ambrosio as a sensualist and
proud, sinful overreacher, an easy mark for the Devil, he
punishes him horribly.

Critics such as Frederick Garber would argue here that
Lewis was refusing to face the full implications of his move to
internalize evil.[59] Elizabeth R. Napier postulates that 'Lewis's
writing . . . reflects the turbulence of a novelist doubting, de-
fying, or perhaps insufficiently intrigued by his own moralistic
messages of truth, candour and mercy'.[60] But it is just as
plausible that Lewis's modern and mythical reworkings of the
Barsisa tale, his self-consciously 'authorial' allusiveness and
bold mixing of discourses and styles, had involved him in
unavoidable contradictions. As we have seen, he includes both
anticlericalism and serious censure and burlesque of superstition in a narrative which aims from the outset to represent the
supernatural manifestations of superstition as sensationally
real.

This throws up the question of the function of discourses of
the fantastic and the sublime in *The Monk*. Together with the
psycho-biographical explanation of Ambrosio's distorted sensibility and false virtue, these discourses are nowadays often
considered to constitute a pre-Freudian discourse of psycho-

[57] Punter, *Literature of Terror*, 69, comments that if Matilda has been a
demon all along, this makes 'nonsense of the earlier part'. Peck, *Life of
Matthew G. Lewis*, 39, quotes Byron, who suggested that Lewis should have
made the demon 'really in love with Ambrosio'. See also Summers, *Gothic
Quest*, 220–1.
[58] Conger, 'Matthew G. Lewis, Charles Robert Maturin and the Germans',
40.
[59] Frederick Garber, 'Meaning and Mode in Gothic Fiction', in H. E. Pagliaro,
ed., *Studies in Eighteenth Century Culture* (Cleveland: Case Western Reserve
University Press, 1973), iii. 168.
[60] Napier, *Failure of the Gothic*, 132.

analysis. Mark Madoff, for instance, asserts that Lewis showed the Goths as 'not so much strange, savage ancestors as alienated parts of the so-called normal personality'. The Goths are thus 'removed from the rational world of the eighteenth-century reader not by time but by denial'. Peter Brooks, too, claims that 'the epistemology of the irrational' in *The Monk* 'puts us in touch ... with the unconscious'; while Syndy Conger argues that Lewis 'intuited ... what Freud was to conclude a century later'.[61] On the other hand, Robert Kiely argues that 'despite patterns which correspond to Freudian theory, *The Monk* is not interesting primarily as a precursor of early twentieth-century psychology. It is not sufficiently optimistic, mechanistic, or deep.'[62] In order to assess these claims, we need to examine more closely Lewis's expropriations of myth, legend, balladry, folk- and fairy-tale, and discourses of the sublime.

The Function of the Discourses of the Sublime and Fantastic *in* The Monk

At the end of Lewis's romance, there is a striking description of the terrain perceived by Ambrosio from the 'Precipice's brink' to which his 'infernal Conductor', Lucifer, has brought him:

The Objects now before his eyes, and which the full Moon sailing through clouds permitted him to examine, were ill-calculated to inspire that calm, of which He stood so much in need. The disorder of his imagination was increased by the wildness of the surrounding scenery; By the gloomy Caverns and steep rocks, rising above each other, and dividing the passing clouds; solitary clusters of Trees scattered here and there, among whose thick-twined branches the wind of night sighed hoarsely and mournfully; the shrill cry of mountain Eagles, who had built their nests among these lonely Desarts; the stunning roar of torrents, as swelled by late rains they rushed violently down tremendous precipices; and the dark waters

[61] Madoff, 'Useful Myth of Gothic Ancestry', 345; Brooks, 'Virtue and Terror: *The Monk*', 262; Conger, 'Matthew G. Lewis, Charles Robert Maturin and the Germans', 124.
[62] Kiely, *Romantic Novel in England*, 107.

of a silent sluggish stream which faintly reflected the moon-beams, and bathed the Rock's base on which Ambrosio stood. The Abbot cast round him a look of terror.　(pp. 438-9)

Darkness, solitude, power, magnitude, terror—here are all the marks of Burke's sublime. But they are not given a Radcliffean inflection. The difference between the two authors' expropriations of Burke can readily be seen by comparing the passage just quoted with one from *The Italian* in which the abducted heroine, Ellena, takes strength and courage from gazing at the wild, forsaken regions through which she is being transported. She, too, is a prisoner and, though not about to perish in an Inquisitional *auto-da-fé*, like Ambrosio, she is filled with despair at the horrors to which she might be subjected. However, as soon as she is permitted to view the natural scenery, her feelings and outlook change dramatically:

Ellena after having been so long shut in darkness, and brooding over her own alarming circumstances, found temporary, though feeble relief in once more looking upon the face of nature; till, her spirits being gradually revived and elevated by the grandeur of the images around her, she said to herself, 'If I am condemned to misery, surely I could endure it with more fortitude in scenes like these, than amidst the tamer landscapes of nature! Here, the objects seem to impart somewhat of their own force, their own sublimity, to the soul. It is scarcely possible to yield to the pressure of misfortune while we walk, as with the Deity, amidst his most stupendous works.' (*The Italian*, pp. 62-3)

Even more evidently than in *Udolpho*, sublime nature in *The Italian* always connotes the possibility of freedom and autonomy, and 'enthusiasm' remains the greatest of virtues, often contrasted with the meanness, 'selfish prudence', and 'apathy' engendered by the doctrines and practices of the Catholic Church. Indeed, as David Morse points out, Radcliffe 'argues so strongly for enthusiasm and generosity of spirit that she even questions the conduct of her heroine'.[63] Urged by Vivaldi to marry him against his parents' wishes, Ellena is at first reluctant to infringe propriety, only to become convinced of the narrowness of her position: 'Her very virtues, now that

---

[63] Morse, *Romanticism: A Structural Analysis*, 65.

they were carried to excess, seemed to her to border upon
vices; her sense of dignity, appeared to be narrow pride; her
delicacy weakness; her moderated affection cold ingratitude;
and her circumspection, little less than prudence degenerated
into meanness' (*The Italian*, p. 181). As Morse has rightly
perceived, it is through descriptions of Ellena's responses to
the sublime in nature that her developing subjectivity is
presented: 'the progressive revelation to Ellena of herself as a
free and autonomous human being rather than a helpless and
abject dependent'.[64]

Lewis, on the other hand, as we have seen, excludes con-
siderations of nature and associates the only sublime and open
landscape in his novel with the devil's omniscience and omnipotence. Far from infusing Ambrosio's soul with strength and
calm, the scene increases 'the disorder of his imagination', as
do the ironies of the Fiend's sensational revelations—that the
crimes of incest and matricide are amongst the monk's many
offences and that the Inquisition had actually decided to pardon him. Evil seemingly becomes absolute when the devil
claims to have controlled the dreams of even the virtuous
Elvira, Ambrosio's mother. Only for a fleeting moment is there
a hint of a force for good, when Ambrosio sinks to his knees
and raises his hands 'towards heaven'. But this suggestion is
quickly suppressed. The monk's intention to 'implore the
Eternal's mercy' is discerned by the Fiend and prevented. A God
of love and order, it seems, is absent from Lewis's world, a fact
which throws in doubt the novel's earlier 'Protestant' positional-
ity and suggests a free-thinking stance—a strong shift to the
moral and epistemological uncertainty of a primeval Gothic
world. Moreover, this uncertainty can be seen to replicate that
suggested by the poems which Lewis inserted in the narrative.

The folk- or spirit-ballads included in *The Monk*, such as
'The Water-King' and 'Alonzo the Brave and Fair Imogene',
like the intercalated tale of the Bleeding Nun, describe a world
in which there is no universal rational and moral order. As one
critic has put it,

the Gothic poet asserts the intuition that . . . there exists radical evil
which cannot be justified or explained; that outside the tiny ordered

areas of our experience there are fates or destinies or even conscious-
nesses which are inscrutable in their designs, and at best capricious
or at worst actively malevolent in their designs on human lives.[65]

For example, in 'The Water-King' (an explicit and eroticized
version of Herder's 'Der Wassermann'),[66] a water-fiend spies a
lovely maid walking to church and, aided by 'his Mother-
witch', disguises himself as a knight in white armour in order
to follow and 'obtain' the maid. The priest questions the
presence of 'the white Chief' in the crowded church, but

> The lovely Maid She smiled aside;
> 'Oh! would I were the white Chief's Bride!'

When the knight approaches the maid, she willingly consents
to go with him, and, little thinking that he is the water-sprite,
she is led to her death by drowning. From one perspective, she
has pledged herself to a demon unwittingly, and is absurdly
punished for some infraction which makes no moral sense;
from another, she has activated a sudden and spontaneous
wish, which, in its rashness, can be seen as almost daemonic.
Although one can think of exceptions (for example, Goethe's
'Erlkönig'), there does seem to be some truth in Sydney Lea's
observations that 'it is a commonplace of the *Volksballade*
that, in order to carry a mortal off, the spright must have the
mortal's cooperation', and that the sudden, unpremeditated
wish 'seems to be the *only* signal which the demon needs in
order to seize his victim'.[67] Thus the maid's drowning can be
interpreted as both a fulfilment of her reckless wish and its
punishment, in which case, the explicit moral at the end of the
poem ('To whom you give your love beware!'), apposite as it
may sound, is really problematic. For, by metonymic association or slippage, the sudden or isolated spontaneous wish or
desire *becomes* the demonic force—an internalized force
which carries all before it and so is not subject to conscious
control.

[65] Peter Larsen Thorslev, Jr., *Romantic Contraries: Freedom versus Destiny*
(New Haven, Conn. and London: Yale University Press, 1984), 131.

[66] Johann Gottfried Herder, *Werke in Zwei Banden* (Munich: Carl Hanser
Publishing House, 1953), i. 319–20; Conger, 'Matthew G. Lewis, Charles
Robert Maturin and the Germans', 45–7.

[67] Lea, *Gothic to Fantastic*, 19–20.

We can discern a similar pattern in Lewis's adaptation of Bürger's popular ballad 'Lenore',[68] which he called 'Alonzo the Brave and Fair Imogene'. Here, as Syndy M. Conger points out, Lewis's disregard for the *Sturm und Drang* elements of his model is even more obvious than in his adaptation of 'Der Wassermann'. Unlike Lenore, Imogene is not a rebel against an unkind God,[69] but a woman untrue to her rash promise to her lover, Alonzo:

> For if ye be living, or if ye be dead,
> I swear by the Virgin, that none in your stead
> Shall Husband of Imogene be.

Some strange impulse causes Imogene even to vow that if she forgets Alonzo and marries another, God may punish her 'falsehood and pride' by sending Alonzo's ghost to the marriage ceremony:

> Your Ghost at the Marriage may sit by my side,
> May tax me with perjury, claim me as Bride,
> And bear me away to the Grave!

And, of course, this is what happens; her head turned by the riches and generosity of a baron who comes courting, Imogene soon weds him, only to find his place at her side usurped by a strange armoured knight whose presence rapidly alarms all of the guests. The stranger lifts his visor to reveal a skeleton's head before taxing Imogene with her faithlessness, winding his arms around her, and sinking with her 'through the wide-yawning ground'. Again, a peculiar wish for communion with some other mode of being is both fulfilled and punished.

Raymond's rash vow to the ghost of the Bleeding Nun is an obvious repetition of this narrative pattern. Another parallel can be discerned in the peculiar avidity with which Ambrosio buys the Galuppi portrait of the Madonna/Matilda and henceforth addresses his supplications 'to no other Saint' (*The Monk*, pp. 81–2). Yet again, Antonia's first glimpse of Ambrosio arouses an inexplicable feeling of attraction towards the monk:

[68] Gottfried August Burger, *Gedichte*, ed. Arnold E. Berger (Leipzig and Vienna, 1891), 64–71.
[69] Conger, 'Matthew G. Lewis, Charles Robert Maturin and the Germans', 49.

Antonia, while She gazed at him eagerly, felt a pleasure fluttering in
her bosom which till then had been unknown to her, and for which
she in vain endeavoured to account. She waited with impatience till
the Sermon should begin; and when at length the Friar spoke, the
sound of his voice seemed to penetrate into her very soul. (*The
Monk*, p. 18)

Although Antonia's instinctive affinity (later, shared by her
mother, Elvira) is eventually 'explained' by facts from the
hidden past—that Ambrosio is her lost brother[70]—her sudden
acute feelings can be read as a strange (incestuous) desire for
communion which conventional morality cannot contain—
one very like the spontaneous imaginings which seal the doom
of victims of supernatural forces in the *Volksballade*. Moreover, it seems to have gone unremarked that, like the maid in
'The Water-King', Antonia unwittingly reveals her feelings to
her pursuer. While visiting her at her home, Ambrosio asks,

Have you seen no Man, Antonia, whom though never seen before,
you seemed long to have sought? Whose form, though a Stranger's,
was familiar to your eyes? The sound of whose voice soothed you,
pleased you, penetrated to your very soul? In whose presence you
rejoiced, for whose absence you lamented? With whom your heart
seemed to expand, and in whose bosom with confidence unbounded
you reposed the cares of your own? Have you not felt all this,
Antonia? (*The Monk*, p. 261)

To this Antonia gives an unqualified answer in the affirmative:
'Certainly I have: The first time I saw you, I felt it.' She thus may
be thought to give the signal of 'co-operation' which spurs the
monk to take sexual liberties. Again and again, we find Lewis
blurring the distinctions between 'good' and 'bad' subjectivity as
constructed by Radcliffe. We can hypothesize that he thereby
attempts to subvert her claims for feminine prescience and
awareness of a benevolent Deity in control of nature.

It does appears then, as Madoff claims, that Lewis is indicating that 'the same chaotic subconscious forces' drive both the

[70] The notion that 'sympathies' exist between 'far-distant, long-absent,
wholly estranged relatives' is discussed by Jane, the heroine in Charlotte
Brontë, *Jane Eyre* (1847; Oxford: Oxford University Press, 1973), 222. According to Jane, the workings of such sympathies 'baffle mortal comprehension', but they assert 'the unity of the source to which each traces his origin'.

virtuous and the villainous. In this respect, too, we have seen how 'normally pure actions'—Ambrosio at prayer, Lorenzo's purity in courtship, Raymond's attempted rescue of Agnes—'are crossed with ambiguities'.[71]

Further parallels can also be drawn between the ballads and the prose sections of the novel in relation to the use of motifs, particularly the prominent association of grave and bridal bed, sex and death. Ambrosio, for example tells the terrified Antonia that the sepulchre in which he holds her captive seems to him 'love's bower'; and the repeated references in the rape scene to 'putrid half-corrupted bodies' (*The Monk*, pp. 379, 385, 388) are recalled in the gruesome details of Agnes clutching her decaying child in the dark and narrow dungeon below the statue of St Clare (p. 415). Both prospective brides, Antonia and Agnes, are virtually buried alive, as is the fair Imogene, who is presumably borne to the grave by her skeleton-knight. Moreover, Alonzo, unlike the ghost of the lover in Bürger's 'Lenore', is no pure, clean skeleton:

> The worms, They crept in, and the worms, They crept out,
> And sported his eyes and his temples about . . .

Conger comments on the ludicrousness of these 'grisly' descriptions which Lewis employs in the final stanzas of his ballad, and suggests that they border on parody.[72] Taking up her point, one might argue that the images of the skeleton-knight cannot be regarded merely as 'an incitement premium' (to use Freud's term) to a terror that has its origin in strange, unfathomable, and pre-ethical desires. Nor, in so much as these images are exaggerated or parodic, can they be read allegorically as representing Death, as in earlier literature. Rather, perhaps, we should view them as 'non-signifying signs', jokey deferrals or substitutes for the terror of what cannot be known, grotesque reminders of our inability to represent death.[73]

It is on grounds like these that *The Monk* has been read as an exploration of the workings of repressed and conflicting

[71] Madoff, 'Useful Myth of Gothic Ancestry', 345–6.
[72] Conger, 'Matthew G. Lewis, Charles Robert Maturin and the Germans', 50.
[73] Jackson, *Fantasy*, 40–1, 69, discusses 'signifiers which are superficially full, but which lead to a terrible emptiness'.

fears and desires, of the unconscious, or of what lies outside of direct representation. By utilizing one or more thematic or structural patterns which appear to correspond to a particular version of Freudian or neo-Freudian psychoanalytic theory, the reader can quite readily interpret the claustrophobic Gothic world of *The Monk* as a symbolic representation of the human mind or as a cryptic inscription of its 'libidinal economy'. The numerous rapid transformations which Ambrosio and Matilda undergo, for example (and which Kiely sees simply as the self-consciously 'trivial and charade-like quality of [Lewis's] art'),[74] may be seen as undermining notions of psychic unity, whether these transformations are read simply as symbolic of a fragmented, unstable self, or, in a more complex Lacanian mode, as 'attempting to depict a *reversal* of the subject's cultural formation'.[75]

Such interpretations may be illuminating but need to be acknowledged as partial. After all, Lewis did validate the existence of the supernatural and the marvellous in his novel, thereby contradicting his own earlier psychologizing of ghosts and demons. And for his eighteenth-century readers, if not for us, this validation raised disturbing metaphysical as well as psychological questions about the nature of evil—questions which could not be answered by eighteenth-century associationist psychology.[76] Again, irrespective of whether the marvellous is read in terms of the absurd, pre-moral workings of metaphysical evil, or in terms of internalized interdictions and taboos—'the return of the repressed'—we need to remember that the discourses of the fantastic in *The Monk* were not the only sources of disquiet about the novel. The novel's social and political meanings also affronted and polarized readers.

The Reception of The Monk

'Have you ever read Udolpho, Mr. Thorpe?'
'Udolpho! Oh, Lord! not I; I never read novels; I

---

[74] Kiely, *Romantic Novel in England*, 107.
[75] Jackson, *Fantasy*, 179.
[76] Conger, 'Matthew G. Lewis, Charles Robert Maturin and the Germans', 118.

have something else to do. . . . Novels are all so full
of nonsense and stuff; there has not been a tolerably
decent one come out since Tom Jones, except the Monk;
I read that t'other day . . . ' (*Northanger Abbey*, pp. 31–2)

During 1797–8, when Jane Austen was first writing *North-anger Abbey*, *The Monk* was under heavy fire from reviewers and critics. The charges made against it were those of indecency, blasphemy, plagiarism, and subversion. Yet, even by its (male) detractors, it was said to exhibit 'the irresistible energy of Genius'.[77] It was thus no accident that Austen should have had the impudent John Thorpe praise Lewis's romance and set it alongside Fielding's *Tom Jones*, a work also commonly considered to have too much 'warmth of colouring' in its treatment of sexual matters. Both books were held to be unsuitable reading matter for women and the young, but the reputation of *The Monk* was particularly notorious. That this male-authored work should be the *only* novel which Thorpe admits to Catherine to reading is therefore significant. The allusion exposes not only his bad manners but the double standards and hypocrisy with which he is complicit.

For Thorpe, *The Monk* is 'tolerably decent', while Fanny Burney's *Camilla* is 'such unnatural stuff!—An old man playing at see-saw!' As Thorpe proffers common opinion, denigrating female-authored novels which he obviously hasn't read, his careless and complacent use of the epithets 'decent' and 'unnatural' becomes increasingly ironic. The charge of indecency was in fact the most frequent complaint brought against *The Monk*. Thus Austen's satire of male prejudice against women's novels would not have escaped her readers of 1803, had *Northanger Abbey* been published then as scheduled. Only the previous year, *Scots Magazine* had printed a long article, 'On Novels and Romances', in which *The Monk* had been fêted as the ill-famed paradigm of all novels: 'all the faults and immoralities ascribed to novels will be found realized in the Monk: murders, incest, and all the horrible and aggravated crimes which it is possible to

[77] *European Magazine*, 31 (Feb. 1797), 111. Coleridge, in the *Critical Review*, 19 (Feb. 1797), 194, referred to *The Monk* as 'the offspring of no common genius'.

conceive, appear in every chapter, and are dwelt on with seeming complacency.'[78]

The history of *The Monk*'s publication and reception is complex.[79] The first edition, published anonymously in March 1796, attracted little critical attention, although it obviously sold well, as a second edition appeared in mid-September with the author's name and status as MP on its title-page. Before the end of the year, however, only three reviews had appeared and in general these were brief.

According to the June issue of the *Monthly Mirror*, *The Monk* was 'masterly and impressive'. The author had 'availed himself of a German tradition which furnishes an episodical incident, awful, but improbable' and the merit of the work lay in its fine delineation of 'the stronger passions' and their exemplification 'in the progress of artful temptation working on self-sufficient pride, superstition, and lasciviousness'. All was skilfully wrought into a whole, reflecting 'the highest credit on the judgement and imagination of the writer'. More-over, the interspersed ballads indicated 'no common poetical talents'.[80]

The commentary in the October *Analytic Review* was more detailed and stinting in its praise. Although the work 'dis-play[ed] no common powers', it lacked unity; the two plots were 'not indispensably connected' and inevitably had 'the bad effect', of 'splitting the interest'. For this reviewer, the story of Ambrosio's temptation by the beautiful and wily Matilda dominates the interest. He reads it with relish as an amplification and alteration of the French tale of *Santon Bar-sisa* and the only alteration of which he disapproves is Lewis's final contradictory and unnecessary revelation that Matilda was not really a woman after all but a crafty spirit from Hell. Though, he adds,

the gradual discovery of Matilda's sex and person (the evil spirit) is very finely conceived, and truly picturesque; indeed the whole temp-

---

[78] *Scots Magazine*, 64 (June–July 1802), 546.

[79] For a comprehensive account, see André Parreaux, *The Publication of 'The Monk': A Literary Event 1796–1798* (Paris: Librairie Marcel Didier, 1960).

[80] *Monthly Mirror*, 2 (June 1796), 98.

tation is so artfully contrived, that a man it would seem, were he made as other men are, would deserve to be d——ned who could resist even devilish spells, conducted with such address, and assuming such heavenly form.

Lewis's youthful infelicities of sentiment and description notwithstanding, 'the author deserves praise for not attempting to account for supernatural appearances in a natural way'.[81] Radcliffe is not named here, but *Udolpho* is surely the object of this reviewer's comparison. His taste, overall, appears to be for a stronger diet than Ann Radcliffe provided. In fact, the reviewer's masculine levity and emphasis on what he sees as Lewis's convincing portrayal of desire and temptation provides a rejoinder to the sarcastic and peremptory dismissal of *The Monk* by the June issue of the *British Critic*.

In the view of that journal, Lewis's romance was a 'monster', the result of 'good talents misapplied'. Where the *Monthly Mirror* and the *Analytic Review* had praise for Lewis's portrayal of 'the stronger passions', the *British Critic* saw only 'Lust, murder, incest, and every atrocity that can disgrace human nature, brought together, without apology or probability, or even possibility for their introduction'. *The Monk*, it suggested, was sheltering under a spurious morality: 'To make amends, the moral is general and very practical; it is, "not to deal in witchcraft and magic because the devil will have you at last!!" '[82] No mention is made, as in the *Analytic Review*, of pride and repression (terms used by Lewis himself) as factors in the monk's downfall.

Early in 1797, once the second and third editions of *The Monk* had become available, and the author and his status were known, a storm of protest began. The clamour forced Lewis to prepare an expurgated fourth edition. Published early in 1798, *Ambrosio, or The Monk*, as it was now called, was advertised on the title-page as having undergone 'considerable Additions and Alterations'. By the time a (similar) fifth edition appeared in 1800, the scandal had subsided, but the book's fascination and unsavoury reputation continued to live on, surfacing periodically in the comments of such well-known figures as Byron, Carlyle, Hazlitt, and Trollope.[83]

Coleridge, in the *Critical Review*, and 'R.R.', in the *European Magazine*, led the attack on *The Monk* with long and detailed denunciations. So influential were these articles that most later references to *The Monk*'s 'perniciousness' were taken as requiring no justification. Even defences of the work were framed by Coleridge's article, as they usually attempted to refute the points of attack which he had made rather than to advance new arguments in *The Monk*'s favour.[84]

Coleridge had begun by reflecting on the degeneracy of the Gothic Romance, which he placed in the context of contemporary translations of German tales of the 'horrible and preternatural' and the flood of imitations of both English and German works then appearing:

The same phenomenon . . . which we hail as a favourable omen in the belles lettres of Germany, impresses a degree of gloom in the compositions of our countrymen. We trust . . . that, wearied with fiends, incomprehensible characters, with shrieks, murders, and subterraneous dungeons, the public will learn, by the multitude of manufacturers, with how little expense of thought or imagination this species of composition is manufactured.[85]

His choice of the industrial metaphor indicates a hardening of attitude to the Gothic romance in the two-year period since he had reviewed *Udolpho*. In the opening sentences of that review, Coleridge had situated Mrs Radcliffe's work with that of Shakespeare in an English tradition of 'horror . . . and thrilling fears'.[86] Now, it seemed, terror-novels generally were to be seen as 'manufactured' and tainted with Germanic superstition and gloom.

When we look at the numbers of Gothic romances which were appearing on the market between 1794 and 1796, this attitude becomes easy to appreciate. A quick count of those listed in Montague Summers's *Gothic Bibliography* shows that the number published yearly jumped from around twenty

[83] Peck, *Life of Matthew G. Lewis*, 36–7.
[84] Parreaux, *Publication of 'The Monk'*, 90.
[85] *Critical Review*, 19 (Feb. 1797).
[86] Coleridge, *Miscellaneous Criticism*, 355.

in 1791–3 to thirty-five in 1794 and forty-seven in 1796.[87] Among the later English works, we find such titles as Stephen Cullen's *Haunted Priory* (1794), Mrs Eliza Parsons's *The Mysterious Warning, a German Tale* (1796), the anonymous *Count Roderic's Castle, or Gothic Times* (1794), and *Phantoms of the Cloisters: or, The Mysterious Manuscript* (1795), *Austenburn Castle* by An Unpatronized Female (1796), Mrs Isabella Kelly's *Abbey of St. Asaph* (1795) and *Ruins of Avondale Priory* (1796), and John Palmer's *Haunted Cavern* (1795) and *Mystery of the Black Tower* (1796).

Translations of German *Sagen*, convent tales, 'ghost-seer' novels, and minglings of chivalric romance with spirit tales had also begun to gain popularity. Schiller's *The Ghost-seer or Apparitionist* (1795), Cajetan Tschink's *Victim of Magical Delusions, or the Mystery of the Revolution in P——l, a magico-political tale* (1795), Karl Grosse's *The Genius* (1796, also translated and published as *Horrid Mysteries*), Christiane Benedicte Naubert's *Herman of Unna* (1794), Veit Weber's *The Sorcerer* (1795), Christoph Wieland's *Select Tales* (1796), and Lorenz Flammenberg's anonymously published *Necromancer or Tale of the Black Forest* (1794) were all in circulation prior to and/or at the same time as *The Monk*. Like earlier *Ritter-*, *Räuber-*, and *Geisterromane*, the German novels exploited motifs of secret societies, clandestine political organizations, knights, bandit outcasts, wicked clerics, mistaken identity, spirits, castles, vaults, underground passages, caverns, convents, incarceration, and erotica in a varying mix.[88] They were also marked by a strong anti-Catholic bias and a sensuality and coarse materiality, with which *The Monk* had strong intertextual relations.

The German flavour of Lewis's expropriations was not lost on Coleridge. However, the latter's interest in German literature seems to have remained confined to Schiller, as can be seen in his comment on Lewis's interpolation in Ambrosio's story of distinctly Germanic tales of the supernatural:

---

[87] Montague Summers, *A Gothic Bibliography* (New York: Russell and Russell, 1964).

[88] Hadley, *Undiscovered Genre*, ch. 5. See also Manfred W. Heiderich, *The German Novel of 1800: A Study of Popular Prose Fiction* (Berne and Frankfurt: Peter Lang, 1982), 29–43.

The tale of the bleeding nun is truly terrific; and we could not easily
recollect a bolder or more happy conception than that of the burning
cross on the forehead of the wandering Jew (a mysterious character,
which, though copied as to its more prominent features from Schiller's incomprehensible Armenian, does, nevertheless, display great
vigour of fancy).[89]

Twenty years later, in his *Biographia Literaria* (1817), despite
his own expropriations of the Gothic in his poetry, Coleridge
still felt strongly enough to dismiss German novels and plays
as 'Monsters imported from the banks of the Danube'.[90]
    Coleridge's objections to *The Monk* rest on its alleged depic-
tions of brutality, 'ignorance of the human heart', lubricity,
and blasphemy. We have already noted his objection to the
'libidinal minuteness' of many of Lewis's descriptions. He also
contended that Lewis had falsified human nature by having
Ambrosio 'agitated by so fleeting an appetite as lust' in the
face of the marvellous; the monk, according to Coleridge,
should have been overcome with wonder at the magic silver
myrtle which gains him admittance to Antonia's bedroom. It
is difficult to see the justice of this objection, however, as all of
the Monk's actions and feelings in this scene are subsumed by
a compulsive will-to-power which sustains a 'committed im-
personality' towards his own desires and fears, as well as
towards Antonia.[91] How else could he still proceed when 'consciousness of the guilty business on which he was employed
appalled his heart and rendered it more timid than a Woman's'
(*The Monk*, p. 299)? If we read closely, we find that in both this
and the rape scene, Lewis mentions power before lust: 'He
considered [Antonia] to be absolutely in his power, and his eyes
flamed with lust and impatience' (p. 300). Far from introducing a 'moral miracle' as Coleridge claimed, Lewis indulges a
Sadeian fantasy of transgression and domination—extreme,
but arguably convincing in its depiction of sexual pathology.
    Only once, in his initial objection that Lewis gave no com-
fort or pleasure to his readers, does Coleridge suggest that the
work actually registered real-life horrors and uncertainties:

    [89] Coleridge, *Miscellaneous Criticism*, 371.
    [90] Oswald Doughty, 'Coleridge and "The Gothic Novel" or "Tales of
Terror" ', *English Miscellany*, 23 (1972), 126.
    [91] The phrase is that of White, 'Pigs and Pierrots', 65.

The merit of a nòvellist [*sic*] is in proportion . . . to the *pleasurable* effect which he produces. Situations of naked horror, are easily conceived; and a writer in whose works they abound, deserves our gratitude almost equally with him who should drag us by way of sport through a military hospital, or force us to sit at the dissecting table of a natural philosopher. To trace the nice boundaries, beyond which terror and sympathy are deserted by the pleasurable emotions,—to reach those limits, yet never to pass them,—*hic labor, hic opus est*. Figures that shock the imagination, and narratives that mangle the feelings, rarely discover *genius*, and always betray a low and vulgar *taste*.[92]

Here Coleridge may be thought to anticipate the distinction between horror and terror which was to be drawn more sharply by Ann Radcliffe in an introduction meant for *Gaston de Blondville*:

Terror and horror are so far opposite, that the first expands the soul, and awakens the faculties to a high degree of life; the other contracts, freezes, and nearly annihilates them. . . . neither Shakespeare nor Milton by their fictions, nor Mr. Burke by his reasoning, anywhere looked to positive horror as a source of the sublime, though they all agree that terror is a very high one; and where lies the great difference between terror and horror, but in the uncertainty and obscurity, that accompany the first, respecting the dreaded evil?[93]

Radcliffe grounds her distinction in the equivalence forged by Burke between the obscure, the sublime, and the terrible. Although not published until 1826 in the posthumously titled essay 'On the Supernatural in Poetry', her argument was in effect embedded in her novels, and it appears that Coleridge was appropriating it when he contrasted 'pleasurable' terror with Lewis's 'images of naked horror'.

But in so doing, Coleridge was drawing attention to a style of discourse in *The Monk* which we have hitherto not considered. As Robert Kiely points out, 'so much is theatrical and ornamentally grotesque' in *The Monk* that the scenes of violence 'possess an energy and realism for which the reader is not fully prepared'.[94] Witness the straightforward, concrete,

[92] Coleridge, *Miscellaneous Criticism*, 372.
[93] Alan D. McKillop, 'Mrs. Radcliffe on the Supernatural in Poetry', 357.
[94] Kiely, *Romantic Novel in England*, 114.

and at times almost clinical, description of the monk's murder of Elvira:

> He grasped Elvira's throat so as to prevent her continuing her clamour, and with the other, dashing her violently upon the ground, He dragged her towards the Bed. . . . the Monk, snatching the pillow from beneath her Daughter's head, covering with it Elvira's face, and pressing his knee upon her stomach with all his strength, endeavoured to put an end to her existence. He succeeded but too well. . . . She ceased to struggle for life. . . . Her face was covered with a frightful blackness; Her limbs moved no more; The blood was chilled in her veins; Her heart had forgotten to beat, and her hands were stiff and frozen. Ambrosio beheld before him . . . a Corse, cold, senseless and disgusting. (*The Monk*, pp. 303-4)

This is in stark contrast to the 'static and stylistically formal scenes' which have gone before, a point to which Coleridge himself gestures in his allusion to images more suited to 'military hospitals' and the 'dissecting table'. Likewise, the powerful descriptions of the church carnival turned riot have all the horrific realism and immediacy of newspaper and journal reports exploiting the horrors of the September Massacres or other events in France.[95] For some readers, the narrator's claim that 'Lorenzo was shocked at having been the cause, however innocent, of this frightful disturbance', no doubt did little to atone for what they saw as his politically subversive intentions.

'R.R.', for example, in the *European Magazine*, denounced Lewis's 'oblique attack on venerable establishments', arguing that such attacks were misplaced. According to this reviewer, ecclesiastical bigotry paled in significance alongside 'the enormities' perpetrated by the '*democratic enthusiasts*' and '*atheistical devotees*' of the day.[96] *The Monk*, with its climactic scene of the furious mob trampling the prioress to death and setting fire to the Convent of St Clare, not only echoed accounts of those 'enormities', but seemed to be condoning them in the name of a dubious freedom from organized religion.

Indeed, finally, it was *The Monk*'s stance in regard to religion and, more specifically, its irreverence towards the Bible,

---

[95] Harry Thomas Dickinson, *British Radicalism and the French Revolution 1789–1815* (Oxford: Basil Blackwell, 1985), 26.
[96] *European Magazine*, 31 (Feb. 1797), 114-15.

which were most vigorously assailed by critics. Coleridge was not the first to draw attention to the passage in the novel in which the Bible is said to contain 'a greater choice of indecent expressions' than 'the annals of a brothel'.[97] Nor was he the last. Thomas James Mathias, through his lengthy footnotes in successive editions of *The Pursuits of Literature* (1796), continued the attack on the 'blasphemies' of *The Monk* and its author, even to the extent of calling for legal indictment.[98]

Mathias, like Coleridge and many others, made much of Lewis's status as a 'legislator'—'an elected guardian and defender of the laws, the religion, and the good manners of the country'.[99] These categories being so inextricably connected in popular conceptions of British order and stability, it is not difficult to discern political disquiet about Lewis as a youthful MP of atheistic and Whig leanings. 'LITERATURE', wrote Mathias, 'IS THE GREAT ENGINE by which ALL CIVILIZED STATES must ultimately be supported or overthrown.'[100] In a nation whose repressive ministry had been at war with 'regicide' France since early 1793, in which societies for 'Church and King' were springing up all over the country in opposition to British radical groups, and in which (mostly Tory) Church Evangelicals and Methodist leaders were producing anti-Jacobin pamphlets and calling for moral reform among both the upper classes and working poor, critics were very sensitive to the threat posed by the impious teaching of atheists.[101]

Lewis, I have argued, appropriated the daring and anticlericalism of the *Sturm und Drang* and popular German fiction as well as the sensationalism of French drama of the early 1790s. In his private life, he was avowedly most at home with actors, artists, and aristocrats,[102] and he treated religion in *The Monk*

---

[97] Parreaux, *Publication of 'The Monk'*, 92–3, quotes from observations made about this passage by 'Aurelius' in a Dublin periodical called *The Flapper* (17 Sept. 1796).
[98] Mathias, *Pursuits of Literature*, 245–8, 367.
[99] Ibid. 212.　　[100] Ibid. 244.
[101] Parreaux, *Publication of 'The Monk'*, 138–9; Dickinson, *British Radicalism and the French Revolution*, 26–42; Quinlan, *Victorian Prelude*, 68–100.
[102] Peck, *Life of Matthew G. Lewis*, 45; Parreaux, *Publication of 'The Monk'*, 133–4, 159–60.

in a way consonant with eighteenth-century libertarian, aristocratic attitudes and conduct. For all the 'hoo-ha' about *The Monk*, one suspects that few took seriously Lewis's apparent commendation of the virtuous Elvira's expurgation of the Bible on grounds of propriety. In practice, it is likely that institutionalized Bible reading for the young, particularly young women, was from redactions or was at least selective.[103] Thus, far from being genuinely concerned that many biblical narratives 'can only tend to excite ideas the worst calculated for a female breast' (*The Monk*, p. 259), Lewis was merely making explicit the workings of middle-class religious ideology. At all times he seems bent on shocking and mocking those of strict religion and morality, unsettling their pretensions to virtue and an ordered society of their own making. This group, of course, included the ever-moralizing literary critics; so it is perhaps no wonder that they should have found *The Monk* subversive. Nor, perhaps, is it surprising that Ann Radcliffe, in *The Italian*, should have situated her own critique of the Church so carefully.

The Italian *as Fictional Response to* The Monk

Like Lewis, Radcliffe portrays injustice, arbitrariness, and inscrutability as endemic to Catholic institutions. The focus in her novel alternates between the experiences of the lovers, Vivaldi and Ellena, as they are in turn oppressed by both Vivaldi's aristocratic parents, the Church, and the Inquisition. Ellena's family, which 'had never been illustrious', is 'decayed in fortune'. So Vivaldi's mother, the Marquesa, plots with her confessor, Schedoni, to have the orphaned Ellena abducted and confined to the convent of San Stephano, a place which Ellena quickly perceives as 'a prison' run by a tyrannical abbess. However, this oppressive regime is later contrasted with the order of *Santa della Pieta*, which is 'like a large family, of which the lady abbess was the mother'. The abbess of this convent is benevolent and dignified, tempering firmness

[103] Ibid. 97–9; Quinlan, *Victorian Prelude*, 46–7, 228–9.

'with gentleness and grace'; her religion is 'neither gloomy, nor bigotted' and she 'conform[s] to the customs of the Roman church, without supposing a faith in all of them to be necessary to salvation'. Under her guidance, religion becomes a vehicle of happiness, consolation, friendship, interest, and virtue. 'Every innocent and liberal pursuit, which might sweeten the austerities of confinement' is encouraged. Significantly, too, the convent has 'extensive domains', and 'extensive views of the country round Naples, and of the gulf', which nourish sensibility and virtue (*The Italian*, pp. 299–301). It is here that Ellena learns the secrets of her past—that the compassionate nun, Olivia, is really her mother and that the monk, Schedoni, is not her father. Radcliffe's repudiation of the wicked father and recovery of the good mother again foregrounds the strong humanizing role of women as custodians of sensibility, fortitude, and virtue.[104]

With this qualification of her anticlericalism, then, Radcliffe answers Lewis's cynicism about human nature and forestalls any question of her own reverence for Christianity. Innocence and virtue are still meaningful and realizable values;[105] and religion, once reconstituted—linked to nature, domesticated, and given over to the good woman/mother—remains a force necessary to peace and order. It seems no accident that Radcliffe gives to Schedoni a 'secret contempt' of the virtuous and generous of heart, that her proud monk sees 'only evil in human nature', or that he has a freakish appearance and 'habit of intricacy and suspicion' (*The Italian*, pp. 34, 52). These are qualities akin to those which Lewis had claimed for himself, as author, in his Preface to *The Monk*. Through Schedoni, Radcliffe shows the poverty of Lewis's totalizing belief that 'others are treacherous and deceiving', countering his framework of suspicion with a view of her own. Ambiguous as 'feminine' susceptibility to the senses may be, for Radcliffe such aesthetic/moral sensibility is a necessary civilizing force. This is

[104] Morse, *Romanticism*, 73–4, makes the point that the mother 'is supportive of the feminine role; she can supply a strong and clear sense of what it is to be a woman'.
[105] Ibid. 61.

made clear on innumerable occasions, one of the most striking being when Vivaldi's mother attempts to bring Schedoni to the point of suggesting that Ellena be murdered. The Marquesa claims to 'have a man's courage'. But once the decision to dispose of Ellena has been made, she is greatly affected by a requiem being sung in the church and she sees for a time the unnaturalness of her behaviour: 'Oh, wretched, wretched mother! to what has the folly of a son reduced thee!' (*The Italian*, pp. 168, 177). This yielding to 'the united influence of pity and terror' receives only contempt from Schedoni:

'Behold, what is woman!' said he—'The slave of her passions, the dupe of her senses! When pride and revenge speak in her breast, she defies obstacles, and laughs at crimes! Assail but her senses, let music, for instance, touch some feeble chord of her heart, and echo to her fancy, and lo! all her perceptions change:—she shrinks from the act she had but an instant before believed meritorious, yields to some new emotion, and sinks—the victim of a sound! O, weak and contemptible being!' (pp. 177–8)

The narrator's stance in relation to Schedoni's is clear. His 'masculine' values of 'energy', 'firmness', and 'hardihood', admirable as they are, must be domesticated for moral and social regeneration to occur.

In sum, Radcliffe again appropriates the Gothic for feminine, Utopian mythmaking, in which patriarchal power, and aristocratic license and idleness, are exposed. As in *Udolpho* (and disturbingly in the style of Schiller), many aspects of the evil and shadowy Gothic world of *The Italian* remain unexplained. They cannot be subsumed by the novel's 'common-sense' didacticism; yet the final chapter depicts 'a scene of fairy-land'. Here, for the wedding of Ellena and Vivaldi, are gathered not only visitors of higher rank but 'all the tenants of the domain'. The 'style of gardens' is 'that of England', with 'grounds extensive enough to accommodate each rank', while Ellena, the portionless woman who has supported herself by 'embroidering silks', is 'queen' of the environment. Most importantly, 'all are at liberty', with 'no lead in [their] consciences' (*The Italian*, pp. 412–5).

When we reach the 'giorno felice' of the final chapter, it becomes easy for moderns to criticize *The Italian* as 'familial, parochial and conservative';[106] and to contrast it with *The Monk*'s seemingly more honest and realistic acceptance of the ineffectiveness of innocence and virtue in the face of brute power, chaos, and irrationality, both from within and without. But we need to remember that Radcliffe could not completely paper over the energy and infamy which she had depicted, just as Lewis could not conceal the cracks in his myth of revolutionary masculine energy. And read intertextually, with other writers of her time, such as Catharine Macaulay, Mary Wollstonecraft, Edmund Burke, Anna Barbauld, and Hannah More, Radcliffe can appear more progressive than nostalgic. At a time when 'reform or ruin' polemic[107] was mounting among not only reactionaries but reformers of every persuasion in England, her novels seem concerned to recast in women's terms the ethic of the good society and to demonstrate how middle-class women might further it.[108]

Moreover, the historically specific differences in appropriation of the Gothic between Radcliffe and Lewis which I have outlined cannot be mapped on to gender in any general way. As we shall see in the final chapter, Mary Shelley's *Frankenstein*, as a further instance of female-authored Gothic, is also a 'bold' fiction, and it throws familial values and aesthetic/moral sensibility in women more radically into question, while also questioning Romantic notions of the God-like creator: scientist or author. It also reshapes the Gothic in the direction not only of the tale or novella, but of realism and a more subtle use of the fantastic.

[106] Punter, *Literature of Terror*, 93. See Quinlan, *Victorian Prelude*, 68–100, and David Durant, 'Ann Radcliffe and the Conservative Gothic', *Studies in English Literature, 1500–1900*, 22/3 (Summer 1982), 519–30.

[107] See Quinlan, *Victorian Prelude*, 68–100.

[108] For an account of the role of female educators and writers in this movement, see Mitzi Myers, 'Reform or Ruin: "A Revolution in Female Manners" ', *Studies in Eighteenth-Century Culture*, 11 (1982), 199–216.

6

Pseudo-Scientific Gothic: Mary Shelley's Frankenstein: or The Modern Prometheus

Gothic Fiction after 1800

We have seen how, during the 1790s, the Gothic romances of Radcliffe and Lewis in their different ways established a mode which could invest in a variety of sometimes blending, sometimes competing, literary, sub-literary, and non-literary styles and discourses. In these texts we find poems, ballads, travel literature, everyday detail, conduct-book moralizing, discourses of the picturesque and the sublime, dramatic scenes, tragic denouements, and, particularly in the case of *The Monk*, the often fearful elements of myth, legend, fairy-tale, and folklore. Depending on the elements of the text privileged by the reader, this dialogic mix could and did give rise to widely divergent readings and an unsettling sense of ambiguity, even when it did not make an outright assault on the reader's moral and political sensibilities. Read in the climate of political unrest of the late 1790s and early 1800s, the Gothic romance was perceived by many arbiters of literary taste as overwritten, lacking propriety, even subversive. Mrs Barbauld, in her introductory essay to *The British Novelists* (1810), might argue that novels generally had 'had a very strong effect in infusing principles and moral feelings',[1] but negative comment remained dominant. Their very popularity—the eager, rapid way in which novels were passed from one person to the next, particularly amongst the

---

[1] Mrs Anna Laetitia Barbauld, *The British Novelists*, with an Essay; and Prefaces, Biographical and Critical (London, 1810), i. 48.

young—was deemed by some critics to be threatening to public morality.[2]

Wordsworth's Preface to the *Lyrical Ballads*, for example, inveighed against 'frantic novels' which degraded all taste.[3] And according to Hannah More's immensely popular *Strictures on the Modern System of Education* (1799),[4] the Rousseauesque efforts of novelists had become 'the most pernicious source of moral corruption':

Novels, which chiefly used to be dangerous in one respect, are now become mischievous in a thousand. They are continually shifting their ground, and enlarging their sphere, and are daily becoming vehicles of wider mischief. Sometimes they concentrate their force, and are at once employed to diffuse destructive politics, deplorable profligacy, and impudent infidelity.[5]

In particular, the 'swarms of publications ... daily issuing from the banks of the Danube' had replaced the 'writings of the French infidels' as a threat to the nation. 'In spite of strong flashes of genius', these 'distorted and unprincipled compositions' united 'the taste of the Goths with the morals of Bagshot' (*Strictures*, p. 374). The 'grand aim' of these writers and their translators was 'to destroy the principles of Christianity', principles which for the Evangelical More and other reformers were synonymous with social mores and civil law and order.

Apart from this aspect of its reception, however, by 1800 the Gothic romance also seems temporarily to have exhausted itself. Although Lord Byron, in his *English Bards and Scotch Reviewers* (1809), extolled the prose of the popular Gothic

[2] John Tinnon Taylor, *Early Opposition to the English Novel: The Popular Reaction from 1760 to 1830* (New York: King's Crown Press, 1943).

[3] William Wordsworth and Samuel Taylor Coleridge, *Lyrical Ballads*, ed. R. L. Brett and A. R. Jones (London: Methuen, 1963), 249.

[4] Hannah More, *Strictures on the Modern System of Female Education with a View to the Principles and Conduct of Women of Rank and Fortune* (London: T. Cadell and W. Davies, 1799). In the biography by Mary Gwladys Jones, *Hannah More* (Cambridge: Cambridge University Press, 1952), 119, she reports that the *Strictures* went through five editions, three in 1799 alone. Over 19,000 copies were sold in all and the conservative *British Critic* and *Anti-Jacobin* reviews were 'warm in their praise'.

[5] Hannah More, *The Miscellaneous Works of Hannah More* (London: Thomas Tegg, 1840), i. 372. Further references to the *Strictures* from this edition appear in the text.

author Charlotte Dacre ('Rosa Matilda'),[6] in general Gothic romances had begun to be marked by a dull, repetitious formula, as Coleridge noted in 1810 in a letter to Wordsworth.[7] In the novels of authors such as Jane Austen, Maria Edgeworth, William Godwin, and Sir Walter Scott, whose work was recognized as innovative and having literary standing, there was a strong tendency towards realism and a corresponding revitalization of the novel.

This is not to say that Gothic romances ceased to be written or read during these years. Early nineteenth-century magazines, for example, particularly those addressed to women, continued to publish considerable amounts of Gothic fiction. Even if for the most part they eschewed 'Faustian supernaturalism', about twenty reputable magazines offered Gothic novelettes, tales, and fragments, while the *Lady's Magazine* continued its practice of serializing Gothic romances. In fact, as Robert D. Mayo has shown, the Gothic content of this periodical was greater in 1804-6 than it had been in 1791-8.[8] Nor was this later material simply a reprinting of already published stories. The demand for novelty and originality led to the publication of serialized novels, novelettes, and a great many short stories by 'correspondents' whose work was never published in volume form.[9] Indeed, it can be argued that the Gothic short story and fragment (the latter making free use of the unexplained supernatural) began to come into its own only after 1800.[10] By the middle of the century, magazines such as *Blackwood's Magazine* and Dickens's *Household Words* were

---

[6] Writing under the romantic pseudonym of Rosa Matilda, Charlotte Dacre published several Gothic novels in the sensational 'German' style of Matthew Lewis: *Confessions of the Nun of St. Omer* (1805), *Zofloya* (1806), *The Libertine* (1807), and *The Passions* (1811). For a discussion of her work, see Devendra P. Varma's Introduction to Charlotte Dacre, *Zofloya: or The Moor* (New York: Arno Press, 1974), pp. xi–xxx.

[7] Coleridge's formula for Gothic romance is quoted by Doughty, 'Coleridge and "The Gothic Novel" ', 131.

[8] Robert D. Mayo, 'Gothic Romance in the Magazines', *PMLA* 65/5 (Sept. 1950), 773, 778; id., 'The Gothic Short Story in the Magazines', *Modern Language Review*, 37 (1942), 449; id., 'How Long was Gothic Fiction in Vogue?' *Modern Language Notes*, 58 (Jan. 1943), 58–64.

[9] Mayo, 'Gothic Romance in the Magazines', 773.

[10] See Mayo, 'Gothic Short Story in the Magazines', 450–2.

seeking and publishing sophisticated short Gothic fiction from reputable authors, such as Elizabeth Gaskell who, in 1859, republished several of her Gothic tales in two volumes under the title of *Round the Sofa*. The influential *Blackwood's*, with its double audience (a mass and more perceptive, coterie one), also appears to have stimulated writers like the American, Edgar Allan Poe, to include 'sly satire' of Gothicism and German Romanticism in their tales.[11]

Gothic fiction relies for much of its impact on its utilization of the fantastic, but while writers continued to imitate crudely either Radcliffe's 'explained supernatural' or Lewis's 'accepted supernatural', the suspense, tensions, doubts, and uncertainties which had become a feature of the mode were difficult to sustain, and certainly difficult to sustain at length, as Sir Walter Scott noted.[12] So, for this reason as much as any other more sinister ones, after 1800 the three-decker Gothic romance in England was roundly panned or ignored by critics and writers. It was also eclipsed by developments in poetry. In particular, close attention was given to the work of the Romantic poets, Wordsworth, Coleridge, Scott, Southey, Keats, Shelley, and Byron, several of whom in any case had written ballads in the German and old English styles, often appropriating and reworking Gothic motifs. It was not until the publication in 1818 of Mary Shelley's *Frankenstein*, a short novel of inset tales (a structure at odds with its initial three-volume format), and in 1820 of Charles Maturin's *Melmoth the Wanderer*, again a novel of inset tales, that new techniques for incorporating the fantastic in fiction became apparent.

Both works abandon the use of an omniscient narrator in favour of multiple first-person narrators who corroborate each other's stories. Among other things, *Melmoth* utilizes in its framing tale 'an estranged mind-style or world-view',

---

[11] Gary Richard Thompson, *Poe's Fiction: Romantic Irony in the Gothic Tales* (Madison: University of Wisconsin Press, 1973), 16–17; Michael Allen, *Poe and the British Magazine Tradition* (New York: Oxford University Press, 1969), 10, 16, 20–3, 34–5.

[12] Walter Scott, 'On the Supernatural in Fictitious Composition; and particularly on the Works of Ernst Theodore William Hoffmann', *Foreign Quarterly Review* (1827), repr. in Scott, *Sir Walter Scott on Novelists and Fiction*, 314.

constructed by certain complex linguistic devices.[13] *Franken-stein*, through its imagery, also raises doubts at times about the sanity of one of its narrators, Victor Frankenstein. Another striking innovation in *Frankenstein*, however, is its appeal to potential verisimilitude through the appropriation of scientific discourse, while yet drawing on the conventions of the folk-ballad to maintain elements of the supernatural. George Eliot's Gothic novella, *The Lifted Veil*, published by *Blackwood's* in 1859, also presents and maintains fantastic situations in this way.

The continued developments in scientific enquiry during the nineteenth century allowed writers to develop new techniques for introducing and maintaining the fantastic in Gothic nar-ratives, thereby relativizing normative ways of feeling and perceiving in more subtle ways than Radcliffe or Lewis had been able to achieve. At a time when supernatural beliefs of all kinds were under attack, and there was a widespread research interest in psychic phenomena, writers were able to exploit developments in the pseudo-sciences, mesmerism, and psycho-therapy. On one level, the psychic forces these writers invoke seem to have little connection with the ancestral past and so are different from the amoral primitive powers depicted in rural Gothic stories, such as Gaskell's 'The Old Nurse's Story' (1852) and 'The Poor Clare' (1856) or Hardy's 'The Withered Arm' (1888) and 'Barbara of the House of Grebe' (1890). However, pseudo-scientific Gothic tales also continue to draw on folklore, balladry, myth, and legend, alongside their 'scient-ific' references to psychic phenomena, setting up a dialogic interplay of ideas which evoke doubt and fear, and revealing the continuing importance of 'folk' elements for the genre.

For example, the claim of *The Lifted Veil* to Gothic horror lies in its use of folk elements and pseudo-scientific elements to present the narrator's clairvoyance and extreme melan-choly, anxiety, and alienation. These can be given either a scientific or supernatural explanation, but in either case re-main fearful and unnatural. The choice of a shorter form also lends itself to powerfully focused writing, a narrative voice at

---

[13] See Roger Fowler, *Linguistic Criticism* (Oxford and New York: Oxford University Press, 1986), 158–63.

once more intensely personal than that of Walton or Frankenstein or his creature. In *The Lifted Veil* Eliot's narrator,
Latimer, concentrates on and wishes to share, in a direct
address to the reader, guilty secrets about the power of passion
and the irrational side of his mind. His dark visions and
prescience are strongly associated with a Romantic, 'feminine'
sensibility and a poetic aspiration which is denied expression.
Like *Frankenstein*, *The Lifted Veil* is a first-person narration
by a man who 'thirsted for the unknown' but found only
'alienation' and 'repulsion'. Like Walton and Frankenstein,
Latimer reflects with precision upon those elements of his
education and upbringing that have shaped his consciousness.
The domestic affection and insularity of the upper-middle-
class home and its new systematic approach to education
figure largely. As with Frankenstein, too, the dismissal and
denial of the boy's interests lead him into secrecy. In the
manner of Mary Shelley, Eliot combines naturalistic detail
with notions of sensibility, poetic description, and the illicit
yearnings of the *Volksballade* to introduce the fantastic. In
this way the prescience so often ambivalently discredited by
subsequent events in earlier Gothic tales (for example, Emily
St Aubert's intuitions in *Udolpho*) is made into an actuality. Latimer's visions are later verified according to his own
criteria.

What made the claim to actuality possible for Eliot was the
widespread circulation in Victorian society of discussion and
writing about scientific investigations into such phenomena.
Similarly, what made the central idea of *Frankenstein* at least
a dubious possibility was the existence of 'scientific' discussions about galvanism. *Frankenstein* was thus praised by Sir
Walter Scott for its realism, its ability to excite terror 'without
exhibiting that mixture of hyperbolical Germanisms with
which tales of wonder are usually told'.[14] Given the continued
disrepute and waning of the Gothic romance during the first
decade and a half of the nineteenth century, *Frankenstein's*
sudden appearance in 1818 marks a development of the genre
in terms of narration, structure, length, and discursive mix. Its

---

[14] Walter Scott, 'Remarks on *Frankenstein*', *Blackwood's Magazine*, 2 (1818),
repr. in Scott, *Sir Walter Scott on Novelists and Fiction*, 271.

difference in this last respect is announced in a Preface which repays careful reading in the context of the social, cultural, and political struggles of the time.

The 1818 Preface to Frankenstein and Early Nineteenth-Century Cultural Politics

Since its initial publication, *Frankenstein* has been the site of innumerable conflicting readings and theoretical disputes. Its interpretation has been complicated by the fact that the first edition of the novel, published anonymously, contained an unsigned Preface, while the third, a revised edition published in 1831 under Mary Shelley's name (the version now commonly printed), was presented in one volume with a new Introduction by the author herself. Not only are the Preface of 1818 and the Introduction of 1831 markedly different in content and tone; taken individually, each is telling for its own *varied* suggestions about how the tale might be read, a point often overlooked by proponents of supposedly definitive readings of 'the' text.

It is significant that the 1818 Preface was written by a more experienced writer than Mary Shelley—her husband, the poet Percy Shelley, who himself had anonymously published two Gothic romances which had been scorned by the critics when he was only 17 or 18. *Zastrozzi* (1810), which appears to draw on works by Schiller, Radcliffe, Dacre, Godwin, and the American, Brockden Brown, was dismissed by the *Critical Review* as 'execrable' and 'contemptible', 'one of the most savage and improbable demons that ever issued from a diseased brain', while *St. Irvyne; or The Rosicrucian* (1811) was criticized for its wildness, extravagance, and 'description run mad'.[15]

Shelley's Preface to Mary's novel opens with an appeal to empirical possibility in order to announce that, while 'a work

---

[15] *Critical Review*, 3rd ser. 21 (Nov. 1810), 329–31; *British Critic*, 37 (Jan. 1811), 70–1; *Anti-Jacobin Review*, 41 (Jan. 1812), 69–71; repr. in Donald Henry Reiman, ed., *The Romantics Reviewed*, (New York and London: Garland, 1972), 297–8, 204, 31–2.

of fancy', *Frankenstein* is not 'merely [a] weaving of super-natural terrors', not 'a mere tale of spectres or enchantment'. Rather, it is based on a real possibility: 'The event on which this fiction is founded, has been supposed, by Dr. Darwin, and some of the physiological writers of Germany, as not of impossible occurrence.'[16] It is then claimed that although this (unnamed) event is 'impossible as a physical fact'—i.e. at this point in time technically impossible—it 'affords a point of view to the imagination' for the exploration of 'human passions more comprehensive and commanding than any which the ordinary relations of existing events can yield'. Implicit in this are two value judgements: first, that the merit of the fiction lies not in the event on which it is based but in the exploration of the human situations to which this event leads; and, secondly, that such exploration cannot be achieved in fiction which seeks ordinary, everyday verisimilitude.

The passage thus appears to be making a claim for a new or different mode of Gothic. Not surprisingly, 'the event' in the tale—the creation of a man by scientific means—has subsequently become the point of departure for critics who wish to appropriate *Frankenstein* for the genre of science or 'speculative' fiction, to the exclusion of other modes. Samuel Holmes Vasbinder, for example, asserts that the novel 'is at its base built on the monistic, Newtonian science of Erasmus Darwin, Joseph Priestly, and Sir Humphry Davy'.[17]

Now, undoubtedly Mary Shelley's tale appropriates snatches of scientific writings and conversation in circulation at the time of its production, but it does not do so in an unequivocal way. There is also, as we shall see, a strong, continuing appeal to the conventions of the folk- or spirit-ballad, the sublime, and classical myth. It is noteworthy, too, that in his opening sentence Shelley denies any 'serious faith' in the possibility of 'the event'—a disclaimer which Vasbinder, for all his cataloguing of Shelley's knowledge of scientific developments,

[16] Mary Shelley, *Frankenstein: or The Modern Prometheus*, ed. James Kinsley and Michael Kennedy Joseph (Oxford: Oxford University Press, 1980), 13. Further references to this edition appear in the text.
[17] Samuel Holmes Vasbinder, *Scientific Attitudes in Mary Shelley's 'Frankenstein'* (Ann Arbor, Mich.: UMI Research Press, 1984), 2. See also Brian Aldiss, *The Billion Year Spree* (London: Weidenfeld & Nicolson, 1973), 24.

does not seem to notice. Concerned to demonstrate that 'morbid anatomy' was the subject of widespread writing and discussion, this critic mentions the Shelleys' conversations with
Dr Polidori, the work of Johann Wilhelm Ritter and the *Na-
turphilosophes*, Erasmus Darwin on spontaneous vital processes,[18] and the experiments with galvanism carried out by
Giovanni Aldini on the corpses of criminals. He also quotes
from a notice about Aldini's work in the *Edinburgh Review*
(1803).[19] But he fails to mention the acrimonious dispute,
which began in 1814 and was also aired in the journals of the
day, between two London medical men, the famous surgeon,
John Abernathy, and his junior colleague, William Lawrence.
Because the discourses of science and philosophy were not
segregated to the extent that they are now, by 1817 this row
had flared into a full-blown religious and political controversy,
one in which any aspiring young novelist, but especially, perhaps, the daughter of William Godwin and Mary Wollstonecraft, would have needed to intervene with some tact.

Briefly, in 1814 Abernathy had delivered and published a
series of anatomical lectures in which, supposedly drawing on
the work of John Hunter and the chemist Humphry Davy, he
had claimed that life had its own principle: 'it was not the
same as the organization of the body; it depended on a subtle
substance, similar to, though not necessarily identical with,
electricity. Just as life should be thought superadded to structure, so the mind, in turn, should be conceived as superadded
to life.'[20] That same year his lectures were severely criticized
for their lack of clarity, misrepresentation of his authorities,
and the untenability of their content. His critic, writing for the
Edinburgh Review, promoted a chemical explanation of life.[21]
Later, in 1816, William Lawrence also attacked his former
teacher, who had continued his lectures unmodified. Drawing

[18] Samuel Holmes Vasbinder, 'A Possible Source for the Term "Vermicelli"
in Mary Shelley's *Frankenstein*', *Wordsworth Circle*, 12/2 (Spring 1981), 116.
[19] Vasbinder, *Scientific Attitudes in Mary Shelley's 'Frankenstein'*, 79–80.
[20] Owsei Temkin, 'Basic Science, Medicine, and the Romantic Era', in *The
Double Face of Janus and Other Essays in the History of Medicine* (Baltimore
and London: Johns Hopkins University Press, 1977), 346.
[21] *Edinburgh Review*, 23 (1814), 384–98, cited in Temkin, 'Basic Science',
346.

on the *Recherches physiologiques sur la vie et sur la mort* (1800) of the French anatomist, Xavier Bichat, Lawrence's own published lectures argued that life was dependent on organization—'the peculiar composition which distinguishes living bodies'.[22] Lawrence strongly rejected the view that life was dependent on any separate principle or substance, such as electricity. Once the dispute deepened and was read in terms of Abernathy's vitalism versus Lawrence's sceptical and pernicious 'French' materialism, other voices, concerned for God, King, and Country, joined in. Coleridge, for example, defended the vitalist position in one of his philosophical lectures early in 1819.[23] Fear of Jacobinism—for many, easily translated into all things French—again ran high at this time. In 1817 Habeas Corpus was once more suspended,[24] allowing the Government to imprison subjects without trial, and strong measures were directed against any form of sedition. Late in 1817, for example, three men were executed for having led the proletarian Pentridge rising in June.

For this reason it can be hypothesized that Percy Shelley, who at 18 had been sent down from Oxford for publishing his *Necessity of Atheism*, and who was now faced with modifying his radical *Laon and Cythna* for publication, saw the need for a very carefully worded Preface which would 'neutralize' and deflect criticism from Mary's tale if it was to be accepted by a publisher in England. As it was, the manuscript was refused by two publishers before being accepted by Lackington; and one of the first reviewers of *Frankenstein* commented, 'This is a very *bold* fiction; and did not the author, in a short Preface, make a kind of apology, we should almost pronounce it to be *impious.*'[25] In all probability, Shelley had rightly anticipated the following as a typical comment on the tale: 'the expression "Creator", applied to a mere human being, gives us the same sort of shock with the phrase, "the Man Almighty" ... All

---

[22] Quoted in Temkin, 'Basic Science', 347.

[23] Samuel Taylor Coleridge, *The Philosophical Lectures of Samuel Taylor Coleridge*, ed. Kathleen Coburn (London: Pilot Press, 1949), Lecture 12, 341–61.

[24] Habeas Corpus had also been suspended during 1794–5 and 1798–1801.

[25] *La Belle Assemblée*, 2nd ser. 17 (Mar. 1818), 139, repr. in Reimann, *Romantics Reviewed*, 42.

248 FRANKENSTEIN: OR THE MODERN PROMETHEUS

these monstrous conceptions are the consequences of the wild and irregular theories of the age.'[26]

Such responses enable us also to appreciate the strategic value of the avowal, a little later in the Preface, of the author's social concern to present 'the amiableness of domestic affection, and the excellence of universal virtue' (p. 14), and to avoid the 'enervating effects of the novels of the present day'— presumably Gothic fiction. Related to this is the further disclaimer that the tale is a doctrinaire novel—that type of fiction which sets out 'to demonstrate the validity of a political, philosophical or religious doctrine':[27] 'The opinions which naturally spring from the character and situation of the hero are by no means to be conceived as existing always in my own conviction; nor is any inference justly to be drawn from the following pages as prejudicing any philosophical doctrine of whatever kind' (p. 14).

In actual fact, many readers and critics did make connections with the 'Jacobin' fiction of the 1790s, particularly Godwin's *St. Leon* (1799).[28] One hostile critic, for the Tory *Quarterly Review*, saw the novel in political terms as 'piously dedicated to Mr. Godwin and written in the spirit of his school'. 'Mr. Godwin', he continued, 'is the patriarch of a literary family, whose chief skill is in delineating the wanderings of the intellect, and which strangely delights in the most afflicting of human miseries.'[29] Percy Shelley's own review, had he published it, would no doubt have confirmed this critic's view that *Frankenstein* was a 'Jacobin' novel, as Shelley focuses his own reading on the injustice meted out to 'the single Being' created by Frankenstein. He points out that the creature's crimes are not 'the offspring of any unaccountable propensity to evil', but are the result of societal attitudes and injustice:

---

[26] *Edinburgh (Scots) Magazine*, 2nd ser. 2 (Mar. 1818), 253, repr. in Reiman, *Romantics Reviewed*, 823.

[27] Susan Rubin Suleiman, *Authoritarian Fictions: The Ideological Novel as a Literary Genre* (New York: Columbia University Press, 1983), 7.

[28] For example, Walter Scott, in *Blackwood's Edinburgh Magazine*, 2 (Mar. 1818), 614, repr. in Reiman, *Romantics Reviewed*, 74.

[29] *Quarterly Review* (18 Jan. 1818), 382, repr. in Reiman, *Romantics Reviewed*, 765.

In this the direct moral of the book consists; and it is perhaps the most important, and of the most universal application, of any moral that can be enforced by example. Treat a person ill, and he will become wicked. Requite affection with scorn;—let one being be selected, for whatever cause, as the refuse of his kind—divide him, a social being, from society, and you impose upon him the terrible obligations malevolence and selfishness. It is thus that, too often in society, those best qualified to be its benefactors and its ornaments, are branded by some accident with scorn, and changed, by neglect and solitude of heart, into a scourge and a curse.[30]

Such a view of the novel accords with Shelley's political activism on behalf of the poor and oppressed. For example, in his pseudonymous pamphlet of November 1817, *An Address to the People on The Death of Princess Charlotte* (which carried the epigram, 'We pity the plumage but forget the dying bird'), he decried as 'a public calamity' both the events leading to and the execution of the three men convicted of machine-breaking. While he could not condone violence, he argued that the effect of an 'excess of injustice' was 'to provoke that anarchy which is at once the enemy of freedom'.[31] It is, perhaps, because Shelley's views and his connection with Godwin were well known that he was considered by some critics to be the author of *Frankenstein*.[32] Thus his disclaimer that the novel endorsed a philosophical viewpoint again needs to be read in the context of the repressive government and reactionary climate in England.

It is well documented that the first two decades of the nineteenth century had continued to be marked by economic depression, high food prices, hardship, political and social unrest, the preoccupations with the Luddite disturbances of 1811–17, the ambitions of Napoleon, and the long, expensive wars with France.[33] Because of the enormous loss of life and limb, there were continual drives among the poorer classes for recruits to fight in the army and navy and a general war weariness prevailed. During the recessions of 1801–2, 1806–9,

---

[30] Percy Bysshe Shelley, *The Works of Percy Bysshe Shelley*, ed. Harry Buxton Forman (London: Reeves and Turner, 1880), vii. 12–13.
[31] Ibid. vi. 101–14.   [32] Above, n. 28.
[33] See Dickinson, *British Radicalism and the French Revolution*, 8–9, 65–6.

1816–17, unemployment, agrarian riots, ma-
...ing, protest marches, demagogic activities, and
...l insurrection threatened the country with internal
...ion. In these crisis years, a close watch was kept on the
...on's cultural products, and any suspected infringement of
...thority, whether secular or ecclesiastical, was strongly condemned by conservative and reactionary groups.

This included a revival of the intensification of antagonism
to 'French' philosophy and internal movements for reform.
Amongst British proponents of the 'new' philosophy during
the 1790s, the principal targets for vilification had been Thomas Paine, author of *The Rights of Man* (1791–2), and William Godwin, whose *Enquiry Concerning Political Justice*
(1793) and *Things as They Are, or The Adventures of Caleb
Williams* (1794) had made him one of the most famous men of
the decade. Godwin is of particular interest for a number of
reasons, not least of which is that *Frankenstein* was dedicated
to him and has close intertextual relations with his writings.

In the *Enquiry* Godwin had examined human nature, questioned human institutions, and argued that opportunities for
individuals to develop their reason and natural benevolence
were hindered from birth by a myriad of corrupting environ-
mental constraints—legal, social, political, and cultural—all
of which, including marriage, would need to be removed for
the radical regeneration of man to occur. Nevertheless, Godwin was opposed to the idea of redistributing wealth by revolution or legislative measures. His utopian vision of a new
society was based on the perfectibility of man and the achievement of a universal benevolence, that is, the reasoned and
voluntary surrender of wealth and privilege for the good of all.
The *Enquiry* met with some optimistic acclaim when it first
appeared, but as the decade wore on, Godwin's ideals were
denounced by Burke, Mathias, and scores of others in sermons, pamphlets, and fiction.[34] He was even described by
Horace Walpole as 'one of the greatest monsters exhibited by
history'.[35]

[34] B. Sprague Allen, 'The Reaction against William Godwin', *Modern Philology*, 16/5 (Sept. 1918), 57–75.
[35] Ford Keeler Brown, *The Life of William Godwin* (London: J. M. Dent,
1926), 155.

The reaction against Godwin escalated rapidly following his publication in 1798, five months after her death, of both Mary Wollstonecraft's *Posthumous Works* (including her unfinished novel, *The Wrongs of Woman*), and his own indiscreet and ill-timed tribute to his wife, *Memoirs of the Author of a Vindication of the Rights of Woman*. The latter work, published against the advice of Wollstonecraft's friends, quickly became notorious for its unguarded disclosures about her relations with Gilbert Imlay and Godwin, her suicide attempts, pregnancies, and what Godwin perceived as her rejection of Christianity. In the *Posthumous Works* were also Wollstonecraft's letters to the unfaithful Imlay. Thus, as Claire Tomalin points out, Wollstonecraft's personal behaviour, as well as her claims for more liberal divorce laws and sympathy in cases of adultery, were 'publicly established through her own words as well as Godwin's'.[36] Predictably, the Tory press responded by depicting Wollstonecraft as a whore and atheist, Godwin as a pimp, and both as monsters of viciousness.[37] Despite the fact that Godwin publicly modified his views,[38] even as late as 1813 both his and Wollstonecraft's writings were still being parodied in the discursive struggle to impose new standards of correctness, particularly on women. If women were to be given a proper, genteel, religious education, then militant claims for women's rights were proscribed, of course, along with novelistic affectations of sensibility, 'extravagant' Gothic and philosophical or 'Jacobin' novels which dwelt on conflicts between institutions of power and the oppressed, and the 'immoral' German literature with which, via Lewis and others, the Gothic had become associated.

Thus it is not surprising that Shelley's Preface disparages 'supernatural terrors' and aligns *Frankenstein* with the purpose of great tragic poetry and drama—Homer, Shakespeare, and particularly Milton—in its preservation and 'innovative' combinations of 'the truth of the elementary principles of human nature'. The 'humble novelist', Shelley asserts, may

---

[36] Claire Tomalin, *The Life and Death of Mary Wollstonecraft* (Harmondsworth: Penguin Books, 1985), 287–8.
[37] Ibid. 290.   [38] See e.g. his Preface to *St. Leon*, pp. ix–x.

'without presumption' adopt a literary rule which has 're-
sulted in the highest specimens of poetry'. Here, it seems, we
have a modest claim for *Frankenstein*'s respectability as literature for which the paradigm is poetry. Relevant to this
point, too, is the allusiveness of the tale's subtitle, 'The Modern Prometheus', and the epigraph from Milton's *Paradise
Lost*:

> Did I request thee, Maker, from my clay
> To mould Me man? Did I solicit thee
> From darkness to promote me?—

Again, in its final paragraphs, the Preface attempts to give
Frankenstein authority as literature through an account of its
romantic genesis 'in the majestic region where the scene is
principally laid', alpine mountains having become once more
a conspicuous topos for meditations on the sublime in the
poetry of Wordsworth, Coleridge, and Shelley himself. An
allusion is also made to the literary company ('the pen of one
of whom would be far more acceptable to the public') in which
the tale was conceived. The confession that *Frankenstein* was
supposed to have been written, along with tales by others, in
'playful imitation' of some 'German stories of ghosts' and
'founded upon some supernatural occurrence', is put in the
context of pleasant and light-hearted evenings before a blazing
wood fire on cold, rainy evenings—a scene of 'domestic affection' far removed from seditious plotting. Thus, while the
mention of ghost stories here might be read as undermining to
some extent the opening comments of the Preface, it has, as
part of a domestic anecdote, the function of arousing curiosity
in the reader as to the exact nature of the tale.

To sum up, Percy Shelley's cautiously phrased Preface offered several frames for reading *Frankenstein*: a story based on
scientific possibility, a ghost story, a moral or didactic tale
which stresses the value of virtue and 'domestic affection', a
tragic and poetic tale based on classical myth, and (by denial)
a philosophical novel. Indeed, each of these frames has been
utilized in varying degrees by particular critics.[39]

---

[39] For example, see respectively Aldiss, *Billion Year Spree*; Eino Railo, *The
Haunted Castle* (London: George Routledge & Sons, 1927); Kate Ellis, 'Mon-

When, however, we turn to the 1831 Introduction, we find suggested still further contexts of reading. In particular, a lot more is made of the actual genesis of the story in Switzerland in 1816—the conversations at the Villa Diodati about current experimental science and the principle of life, the reading of German ghost stories, and the subsequent 'competition', to write a tale in imitation, between Lord Byron, his physician Dr Polidori, and Percy and Mary Shelley. This autobiographical emphasis has led to many modern psychoanalytic interpretations of *Frankenstein* as a 'birth myth' or a 'psycho-drama' which inscribes the author's female sexual fears, desires, anxieties, suffering, and oppression. What has received little or no attention from critics is the way in which the Introduction also appropriates Romantic discourses about the imagination in order to legitimize the status of Mary Shelley as a female author.

The 1831 Introduction

Mary Shelley's Introduction sets out to answer the question, 'How I, then a young girl, came to think of, and dilate upon, so very hideous an idea?' (*Frankenstein*, p. 5). In so doing it recontextualizes, in the form of a subjective account, the following opening sentences from Percy's own unpublished review of *Frankenstein*, written in 1817:

The novel of 'Frankenstein, or The Modern Prometheus,' is indoubtedly, as a mere story, one of the most original and complete productions of the day. We debate with ourselves in wonder, as we read it, what could have been the series of thoughts—what could have been the peculiar experiences that awakened them—which conduced, in the author's mind, to the astonishing combinations of motives and incidents, and the startling catastrophe, which compose this tale.[40]

sters in the Garden: Mary Shelley and the Bourgeois Family', in George Levine and Ulrich Camillus Knoepflmacher, *The Endurance of Frankenstein* (Berkeley: University of California Press, 1979), 123–42; Leslie Tannenbaum, 'From Filthy Type to Truth: Miltonic Myth in *Frankenstein*', *Keats–Shelley Journal*, 26 (1977), 101–13; Michael Scrivener, '*Frankenstein's* Ghost Story: The Last Jacobin Novel', *Genre*, 19/3 (Fall 1986), 229–317.

[40] Percy Shelley, 'On *Frankenstein*', in Shelley, *Works*, vii. 10.

Reflecting at length on the nature of the creative process and her role as creator, Mary Shelley makes a strong case for *Frankenstein*'s originality, as something which ultimately came 'unbidden' from *within*:

Invention, it must be admitted, does not consist in creating out of void, but out of chaos; the materials must, in the first place, be afforded: it can give form to dark, shapeless substances, but cannot bring into being the substance itself. . . . My imagination, unbidden, possessed and guided me, gifting the successive images that arose in my mind with a vividness far beyond the usual bounds of reverie. I saw—with shut eyes, but acute mental vision,—I saw the pale student of unhallowed arts kneeling beside the thing he had put together. (pp. 8–9)

This statement echoes passages on creation in Percy Shelley's *Defence of Poetry* (1821): 'we are aware of evanescent visitations of thought and feeling, sometimes associated with place or person . . . and always arising unforeseen and departing unbidden . . .'[41] Percy denies any role for the will or conscious choice in the imaginative process, and this absence likewise figures in Mary's descriptions: 'I wished to exchange the ghastly image of my fancy for the realities around . . . I could not so easily get rid of my hideous phantom; still it haunted me . . .' (p. 10).

Confining herself to 'such topics as have connection with [her] authorship alone', she builds up to this statement by first discussing her childhood reading and writing. While writing stories was her 'favourite pastime', at that stage she was 'a close imitator—rather doing as others had done, than putting down the suggestions of [her] own mind' (p. 5). Her dreams, however, 'were all [her] own' and 'at once more fantastic and agreeable than [her] writings'. The writing of her girlhood was 'commonplace', but in the presence of nature—'beneath the trees' or 'on the bleak sides of the woodless mountains' near her home—'[her] true compositions, the airy flights of [her] imagination, were born and fostered'. Here she was 'not confined to [her] own identity' (*Frankenstein*, p. 6).

[41] Thomas Love Peacock, *Peacock's Four Ages of Poetry and Shelley's Defence of Poetry and Browning's Essay on Shelley*, ed. F. H. B. Brett-Smith (Oxford: Basil Blackwell, 1929), 54.

Whatever the difference in 1818 between the Romantic poets' theories of Imagination and Inspiration, by 1830 the importance of an unconscious element and transforming imaginative process in the creation of art was well established, as was the idea of the artist as a solitary figure in the landscape. Mary Shelley's statement about identity can be read as a repudiation of poetic self-centredness or egotism—the habit of which Wordsworth was accused by both Hazlitt and Percy Shelley, of refusing to allow that anything could speak for itself, without the interpretation of the poet.[42]

Having celebrated her imaginative creation of *Frankenstein*, however, Shelley becomes self-effacing about her successful career as a writer:

My husband . . . was, from the first, very anxious that I should prove myself worthy of my parentage, and enrol myself on the page of fame. He was for ever inciting me to obtain literary reputation, which even on my own part I cared for then, though since I have become infinitely indifferent to it. At this time he desired that I should write, not so much with the idea that I could produce any thing worthy of notice, but that he might himself judge how far I possessed the promise of better things hereafter. (p. 6)

From a modern perspective, her avowed indifference to 'literary reputation' simply does not square with her claims for originality and ownership of her work: 'I certainly did not owe the suggestion of one incident, nor scarcely of one train of feeling, to my husband' (p. 10), she asserts towards the end of the Introduction.

This ambivalence towards artistic self-assertion has been most plausibly explained by Mary Poovey, who suggests that family pressure on Mary to be 'original' 'was contradicted by the more prevalent feminine model of propriety, that she be self-effacing and supportive, devoted to a family rather than to a career'.[43] Certainly the 'model of propriety' or domesticity of which Poovey speaks appears to have gained ground in the

---

[42] See James Engell, *The Creative Imagination* (Cambridge, Mass. and London: Harvard University Press, 1981), 209, 257.

[43] Mary Poovey, 'My Hideous Progeny: Mary Shelley and the Feminization of Romanticism', *PMLA* 95/3 (May 1980), 332. See also 'The Model Female', in Quinlan, *Victorian Prelude*, 139–59.

two decades that Mary Shelley was growing to womanhood. At this time even women who earlier had been 'Bluestockings', and championed sensibility and original genius, now took a more conservative stance. Hannah More is a case in point.

In her *Strictures on the Modern System of Female Education*, More speaks severely of the 'romantic girl with a pretension to sentiment, which her still more ignorant friends mistake for genius' (p. 457). Such young women are 'self-taught and self-dependent scribblers' who 'pant for the unmerited and unattainable praise of fancy and genius, while they disdain the commendation of judgement, knowledge, and perseverance, which would probably be within their reach. To extort admiration, they are accustomed to boast of an impossible rapidity in composing . . .' (*Strictures*, p. 458). Although it may appear to be 'a contradiction', it will generally be found to be the case, she continues,

that girls who take to scribble are the least studious, the least reflecting, and the least rational; they early acquire a false confidence in their own unassisted powers; it becomes more gratifying to their natural vanity to be always pouring out their minds on paper, than to be drawing into them fresh ideas from richer sources. The original stock, small perhaps at first, is soon spent. (p. 457)

In educating young women, therefore, 'it will be necessary to combat vigilantly that favourite plea of lively ignorance, that study is an enemy to originality'. Summing up her precepts aphoristically, More writes:

Let it be observed, I am by no means *encouraging* young ladies to turn authors; I am only reminding them that

Authors before they write should read

I am only putting them in mind that to be ignorant is not to be original. (p. 458)

To this end she recommends 'dry tough reading', such as Locke's *Essay on the Human Understanding*, Watt's book of logic, or Butler's *Analogy* as antidotes to 'so much English sentiment, French philosophy, Italian love-songs, and fantastic German imagery and magic wonders' (pp. 420–1).

Having been brought up in an intellectual household, it is unlikely that Mary Wollstonecraft Godwin Shelley needed

Hannah More to convince her of the value of a tough reading programme, as a perusal of her *Journals* reveals.[44] But it is noteworthy that Mary mentions in her Introduction to *Frankenstein* her habit of study and reading while a young wife and mother and 'of improving [her] ideas in communication with [her husband's] far more cultivated mind' (p. 6). By 1831, when the effects on manners of the religious revival were much in evidence,[45] there appears to have been wide acceptance of views on female education and roles like those in More's *Strictures*. That year the *Westminster Review*, for example, summed up the role model for women in the following way:

Woman . . . is formed to obey, and though she have an active and exclusive part to perform, still she must perform it under submission to her lord. Her duties are confined to her home, and consist in ministering to the comfort of her husband, and in educating her children during their early years. To perform these duties well, she must have a docile, patient and submissive spirit, she must possess no elevated description of knowledge; as she is gentle in her temper, so must she be inferior in her attainments.[46]

Such attitudes, combined with the middling status of novels and the dominance of male-authored poetry, seem to have reinforced the old reticence of women to declare publicly their business as writers.

Certainly More's tone and attitude are very different in their emphasis from those of her 'Sensibility' and 'Bas Bleu' days[47] when she delighted in 'discovering' and nurturing unrecog-

---

[44] For lists of Mary Shelley's extensive reading during 1814–17, see Mary Wollstonecraft Shelley, *Mary Shelley's Journal*, ed. Frederick L. Jones (Norman: University of Oklahoma Press, 1947), 32–3, 47–9, 88–90. Similar lists can be found in a more recent work: Mary Wollstonecraft Shelley, *The Shelley Journals*, ed. Paula R. Feldman and Diana Scott-Kilvert (Oxford and New York: Clarendon Press, 1987).

[45] Quinlan, *Victorian Prelude*, 256–7.

[46] 'The Education of Women', *Westminster Review*, 29 (1831), 71.

[47] 'Sensibility' and 'Bas Bleu or Conversation' (a description of the Bluestocking assemblies) were the names of two poems by Hannah More which were published in 1782 and 1786 respectively. 'Bas Bleu', actually written in 1782 and circulated amongst London society first in MS, 'advertised the learned ladies and their assemblies in an easy and pleasing manner'. It also won More extravagant praise from Dr Johnson. See Jones, *Hannah More*, 47–51.

nized female genius. It is true, of course, that even then she asserted the value of further reading for aspiring authors, but she was also far more enthusiastic about 'primitive genius' in Young's sense.[48] Yet by 1799, if anything, she is more severe than the reviewers on the subject of aspiring female authors and novel writing:

Such is the frightful facility of this species of composition, that every raw girl, while she reads, is tempted to fancy that she can also write. . . . a thorough-paced novel-reading miss . . . feels within herself the stirring impulse of corresponding genius, and triumphantly exclaims, 'And I, too, am an author!'

Not only were novel-writers now 'overstocking the world with their quick succeeding progeny'; they were also failing or refusing to write on 'sound Christian principles'. Because novels and romances had been made 'the vehicles of vice and infidelity', and were 'principally directed against the female breast', it was up to women to exercise their considerable moral influence in civil society and halt the downwards spiral in taste and manners.

Given the dominance of such views and the heroic status accorded the poets, Byron, Shelley, Coleridge, and Wordsworth, it is not surprising to find Mary in her Introduction deferring to Byron, whose 'thoughts upon paper . . . [were] clothed in all the light and harmony of poetry' (*Frankenstein*, p. 6), or to Shelley, who was 'more apt to embody ideas and sentiments in the radiance of brilliant imagery, and in the music of the most melodious verse that adorns our language, than to invent the machinery of a story' (p. 7). Each of the poets in his own way had made very high claims for poetry and had conceived of the (male) poet as some sort of prophet. Shelley's statement about poets being 'unacknowledged legislators of the world' is well known. His prejudices can also be gauged from his unpublished review of *Frankenstein*, when he considers the novel first as 'a mere story'. Again, in the 1818

[48] This is evident when she quotes from Shakespeare's *Midsummer Night's Dream* in order to clinch her comparison of genius with 'good sense': 'Genius breaks out in splendid sentiments and elevated ideas; good sense confines its more circumscribed, but perhaps more useful walk, within the limits of prudence and propriety' (More, *Miscellaneous Works*, i. 800).

Preface, he recalls how he and Byron had not completed their stories because they had lost 'all memory of their ghostly visions' during their journey in the Alps.[49] Presumably 'the magnificent scenes' in which they had become 'lost' had called them to a higher order of literary creation than 'mere' story writing could afford.

So Mary (though not, perhaps, without pride) calls her own artistic achievement '[her] hideous progeny', the adjective—already used four times—having been transposed from her conception and description of the creature 'manufactured, brought together and endued with vital warmth' by Victor Frankenstein.

Mary Shelley's choice of the phrase 'hideous progeny' has been seized upon by modern feminist critics to read her novel in terms both of her experience of post-parturition (her first child died within days of its birth and her own mother had died from complications following her birth) and her authorial audacity as a woman in writing or bringing together a text such as *Frankenstein*. Either way, such readings emphasize her nightmarish vision or waking dream of 'the monster' and the depression, guilt, and anxiety which she, on analogy with Victor Frankenstein, is supposed to have felt for her 'crime' or 'frightful transgression' in producing it. I have already commented in Chapter 2 on the problems involved in producing meaning for literary texts in such unmediated, biographical, or experiential terms. In any case, the analogy between the birth of the monster and that of a human infant breaks down when we consider that Frankenstein's 'workshop of filthy creation' is completely isolated from any sort of female presence. It needs also to be remembered that 'progeny' was a common term for novelistic output (as can be seen in Hannah More's use of it, quoted above) and that, in bidding it to 'go forth and prosper', Shelley owns to 'an affection' for her hideous 'offspring', just as 'Monk' Lewis had done for his 'vain' and wayward one. The modesty topos was still employed by novelists of both sexes, but particularly women, and reference to Mary's specifically female 'anxiety of authorship', while certainly not without its point, has perhaps been over-dramatized.

[49] Shelley, *Frankenstein*, 14.

Moreover, 'monster', which has often been taken as a point of departure for psycho-sexual interpretations, needs to be viewed dialogically as a word overlaid with meanings from politics and folklore. Although the term does occur on occasion in the tale, talk about monsters has come, from the beginning, mainly from readers themselves, and this can again be attributed largely to the early nineteenth-century fear of internal revolution.

In this respect the political cartoons of Isaac Cruikshank, James Gillray, and Thomas Rowlandson, the *Cheap Repository Tracts* of Hannah More, and the satirical *Anti-Jacobin* of George Canning[50] had been very successful. Horrifying images of revolutionary France and a Jacobin conspiracy against British Liberty were repeatedly renewed, conflated, and exploited in justification of repressive social and political measures. Following the publication, in 1797, of Abbé Augustin Barruel's conspiracy thesis, *Mémoire pour servir à l'histoire du Jacobinisme*, fears of anything which smacked of atheism or of French doctrine had reached new heights. Barruel, himself a fugitive of the Revolution, had argued that Voltaire was the master-mind of a massive 'Jacobin' plot to overthrow Church and Government, law and order, throughout Europe. The diabolical agents of Jacobinism were supposedly everywhere, insinuating their philosophical notions into the minds of others. In the difficult final years of the decade, the already established stereotype of the atheistic and Jacobinical Frenchman was appropriated by Tory traditionalists, Methodists, and Evangelicals alike. As Gerald Newman puts it, the alleged Gallicism of others became 'a treasury of weapons' for their opponents.[51] Whigs, Methodists, Evangelicals, Dissenters, working-class radicals, and the British aristocracy all in some way at some time were accused of promulgating French values, tastes, and practices, whether new *or* old.

---

[50] *The Anti-Jacobin*, the weekly magazine which appeared from Nov. 1797 to July 1798, was replaced by the *Anti-Jacobin Review and Magazine*, a monthly which continued until 1821.

[51] Gerald Newman, 'Anti-French Propaganda and British Liberal Nationalism in the Early Nineteenth Century: Suggestions Toward a General Interpretation', *Victorian Studies*, 18/4 (June 1975), 391.

In the political caricatures and satires of these years 'French-ness' was aligned with

ideas of destruction, license, abstract political thought, atheism, and impious mockery. 'Philosophy' was perhaps its familiar name. Its face, or faces, were the wizened and triumphantly grimacing coun-tenance of Voltaire, mocker of Christianity and diabolical master-mind of the Revolution, or the face of an ape, which similarly represented destruction and absolute irresponsibility. In either case, a horrible grin appears to have been central to the image.[52]

Even after 1815, when radicalism flourished again in Eng-land,[53] the 'Gallic stereotype'—often a parricidal monster, grin-ning ape, or ghoul—continued to draw 'authenticity and tremendous ideological force from the actual scene of destruc-tion in Europe'.[54] This is clearly evidenced by three cartoons for 1819 by George Cruikshank. In one of these—'Death or Liberty! or Britannia & the Virtues of the Constitution in danger of Violation from the great Political Libertine, Radical Reform!'—Death, wearing a penile arrow, the mask of Liberty, and a *bonnet rouge* with the tricolour cockade, attempts to ravish Britannia, who braces herself against the rock of Reli-gion and holds aloft a flaming sword of Laws. Sheltering under Death's streaming cape of 'Radical Reform' are a crowd of grotesque fiends personifying murder, robbery, starvation, slavery, the Age of Reason, blasphemy, and immorality. Only the staunch British lion, Loyalty, rushes to aid the classically etched Britannia.[55] The year 1819 was one of considerable political excitement and unrest because of severe and wide-spread agricultural and industrial distress. Exaggerated fears of 'mischievous firebrands' and the possibility of 'a bloody and remorseless struggle between property and populace' led Tory paternalists, such as Sir Walter Scott, to defend even the Peterloo massacre.[56]

---

[52] Ibid. 389.

[53] Dickinson, *British Radicalism and the French Revolution*, 77.

[54] Ibid. 388.

[55] Mary Dorothy George, *English Political Caricature 1793–1832* (Oxford: Oxford University Press, 1959), 183–4; pl. 72.

[56] Quoted by David Daiches from a letter written by Scott to his son, Walter, in 1819. See David Daiches, *Sir Walter Scott and his World* (London: Thames and Hudson, 1971), 60.

Mary Shelley's often grinning 'monster' or 'hideous phantom' can, then, also be pressed into service for modern psychopolitical readings of the novel, such as we find in Lee Sterrenburg's account of how *Frankenstein* 'draws on, yet greatly complicates, the revolutionary and antirevolutionary political metaphors of the 1790s'.[57]

A final example should suffice to show that the 1818 Preface and 1831 Introduction are richly diverse and ambiguous as clues to how *Frankenstein* may be read.

One of the most perceptive early readings of the first edition of *Frankenstein* came from John Bell's fashionable magazine, *La Belle Assemblée*. Concerned that so original a work would not be understood, it urged its 'fair readers' to draw from the tale the following meaning: 'that the *presumptive* works of man must be frightful, vile, and horrible; ending only in discomfort and misery to himself.'[58] In summarizing the plot, the subsequent reading stresses both the Prometheus/Frankenstein analogy of the subtitle and Frankenstein's devotion 'to chemistry and his favourite science: the structure of the human frame, and indeed, every animal endowed with life'. The 'event' of the novel is thus described as a form of overreaching:

[Frankenstein] then proceeds to examine *the cause of life and death*—(how vain)—and finds himself capable (we use the writer's own words) 'of bestowing animation on lifeless matter!!!'

This reminds us of the famous philosopher who declared that, give him but matter enough, and he could create a world![59]

Here we have an 1818 interpretation which plays down the didactic aspect foregrounded in the Preface (the monster's delight in 'the picture of social life and its affections' is seen as 'rather prolix and unnatural') in favour of the tale's rewriting of traditional myths in terms of contemporary scientific theorizing and research. This interpretation was also taken up by two dramatizations of the novel staged in London in 1823:

[57] Lee Sterrenburg, 'Mary Shelley's Monster: Politics and Psyche in *Frankenstein*', in Levine and Knoepflmacher, *Endurance of Frankenstein*, 143–71.

[58] *La Belle Assemblée*, 2nd ser. 17 (Mar. 1818), 139, repr. in Reiman, *Romantics Reviewed*, 42–3.

[59] Ibid. 43.

Presumption; or, The Fate of Frankenstein and *Frankenstein; or, The Danger of Presumption.*

The notion that scientific creativity might have unforeseen and dangerous effects is, moreover, suggested again in Mary's 1831 Introduction, in her account of her inspirational vision:

I saw the hideous phantasm of a man stretched out, and then, on the working of some powerful engine, show signs of life, and stir with an uneasy, half vital motion. Frightful must it be; for supremely frightful would be the effect of any human endeavour to mock the stupendous mechanism of the Creator of the world. (*Frankenstein*, p. 9)

This interpretation has remained the dominant one in our own century[60] and certainly speaks to us now in an era of nuclear reactors, test-tube babies, and embryonic implants in males. For our dialogic reading the question thus arises of how 'the orchestrating languages' of Shelley's tale can confirm such an interpretation, and what, too, works to unsettle it.

Scientific Discourse, Balladry, Folklore, and the Sublime in the *1818* Frankenstein

Frankenstein commences with a series of four letters and ends with their continuation. Dated over nine months sometime in the eighteenth century, possibly the 1790s, they are written by Captain Walton in journal form to his 'dear, excellent sister', Mrs Margaret Saville in England, as he sails with his men on an expedition to the North Pole. Thus addressed through this framing device, we are invited to identify with a woman's point of view.

Walton's stated purpose is one of scientific and geographic discovery which will both appease his thirst for knowledge and benefit mankind:

I may there discover the wondrous power which attracts the needle; and may regulate a thousand celestial observations, that require only

---

[60] See Wilfred Cude, 'Mary Shelley's Modern Prometheus: A Study in the Ethics of Scientific Creativity', *Dalhousie Review*, 5/52 (1972), 212–25; also Theodore Ziolowski, 'Science, Frankenstein, and Myth', *Sewanee Review*, 89/1 (Winter 1981), 34–56.

this voyage to render their seeming eccentricities consistent for ever. I shall satiate my ardent curiosity with the sight of a part of the world never before visited, and may tread a land never before imprinted by the foot of man. . . . But, supposing all these conjectures to be false, you cannot contest the inestimable benefit which I shall confer on all mankind to the last generation, by discovering a passage near the pole to those countries, to reach which at present so many months are requisite; or by ascertaining the secret of the magnet, which, if at all possible, can only be effected by an undertaking such as mine.[61]

Prior to this confident espousal of his scientific purpose, however, the proud 'effusions' of Walton's poetic sensibility have been made equally striking; they ironically recall forms of hubris or rash desire in the folk- or spirit-ballad. In a reply which exalts his own vision, Walton counters his sister's common-sense realism about the Pole—what he calls her 'evil forebodings' of 'frost and desolation'—with his poetic imaginings of 'beauty and delight':

I feel a cold northern breeze play upon my cheeks, which braces my nerves, and fills me with delight. Do you understand this feeling? This breeze, which has travelled from the regions towards which I am advancing, gives me a foretaste of those icy climes. Inspirited by this wind of promise, my day dreams become more fervent and vivid. I try in vain to be persuaded that the pole is the seat of frost and desolation; it ever presents itself to my imagination as the region of beauty and delight. There, Margaret, the sun is for ever visible; its broad disk just skirting the horizon and diffusing a perpetual splendour. There—for with your leave, my sister, I will put some trust in preceding navigators—there snow and frost are banished; and, sailing over a calm sea, we may be wafted into a land surpassing in wonders and in beauty every region hitherto discovered on the habitable globe. (*Frankenstein*, pp. 9–10)

Here what is really a poetic vision is given a scientific gloss and rationalization as Walton condescends to Margaret's supposed lack of knowledge and experience. This passage is followed by the one first quoted, and, indeed, we learn that

---

[61] Mary Wollstonecraft Shelley, *Frankenstein: or The Modern Prometheus* (The 1818 text), edited, with variant readings, an introduction and notes, by James Rieger (Indianapolis: Bobbs-Merrill, 1974), 10. All further references are to this edition.

before Walton turned to sailing and the study of mathematics and science, he was for a time a poet, living 'in a Paradise of [his] own creation'. He confesses to having imagined that he 'might also obtain a niche in the temple where the names of Homer and Shakespeare are consecrated'. Subsequent upon his failure and heavy disappointment in this ambition, his activities have transferred to seafaring and discovery. But we may conclude that his pride has remained prodigious, as he boasts of his achievements and acknowledges that he has 'preferred glory to every enticement that wealth placed in [his] path'. His resolutions, too, are 'as fixed as fate' (p. 15). The scene thus seems set for Walton to become the victim of supernatural or daemonic forces.

This expectation is reinforced in his second letter by a specific allusion to the ballad of *The Ancient Mariner*—'I am going to unexplored regions, to "the land of mist and snow;" but I shall kill no albatross, therefore do not be alarmed for my safety' (*Frankenstein*, p. 15)[62]—and furthered by the constant references to polar ice and the ship becoming ice-bound. However, with the sudden appearance of the melancholy, wild-eyed 'stranger', who is taken aboard barely alive, but who lives to tell his story about the 'daemon' *he* is pursuing, we find that Walton has become not so much the mariner as the wedding guest who for some 180 pages must listen and 'make notes' (p. 25). He is also invited to relate the stranger's tale to his own situation and extract some precepts: 'You seek knowledge and wisdom as I once did; and I ardently hope that the gratification of your wishes may not be a serpent to sting you, as mine have been' (p. 24).[63]

[62] This allusion is elaborated upon in the 1831 text; Walton attributes his 'passionate enthusiasm for the dangerous mysteries of the ocean, to that production of the most imaginative of modern poets', and goes on to speak of 'something at work in [his] soul which [he] does not understand . . . a love for the marvellous' (Shelley, *Frankenstein*, 231).

[63] Again, this point receives considerable elaboration in the 1831 text. Drawing an analogy between his pursuit of knowledge and that of Walton, Frankenstein says that he 'may deduce a moral from [his, i.e. Frankenstein's] tale', and warns him that it will contain 'occurrences usually deemed marvellous', but which 'will appear possible in these wild and mysterious regions' (Shelley, *Frankenstein*, 233).

Once we turn to this interpolated tale, we find a mixture of science and folklore converging rather more subtly in the new narrator's consciousness. In explaining how he came to have a 'predilection' for natural philosophy, that 'genius' which 'has regulated [his] fate' (p. 32), the stranger, Victor Frankenstein, at first contrasts the occult sciences of Cornelius Agrippa, Paracelsus, and Albertus Magnus with 'a modern system of science'—'a more rational theory of chemistry' (p. 33). Had his father, Alphonse, not simply dismissed the former as 'trash', but taken the pains to instruct him, he would not have been forced into the solitary and secretive study of the alchemist's and necromancer's 'wild fancies'. As it was, however, he 'entered with the greatest diligence into the search of the philosopher's stone and the elixir of life' (p. 34). Seeking 'glory' rather than wealth, he became fascinated by the essence of life; he also attempted to raise 'ghosts or devils', uncritically following the occultist's prescribed 'incantations'.

To these passages about occult science are juxtaposed those indicating his interest in 'the natural phaenomena that take place every day before our eyes': 'Distillation, and the wonderful effects of steam, processes of which my favourite authors were utterly ignorant, excited my astonishment; but my utmost wonder was engaged by some experiments on an air-pump . . .' (*Frankenstein*, p. 34). It is only when Frankenstein observes a tree blasted by lightning and his father explains the concept of electricity to him, using 'a small electrical machine' and conducting some experiments, that he abandons those authors who 'had so long reigned the lords of his imagination' (p. 35), without, however, pursuing 'the study of any modern system'.[64]

Yet, once at the University of Ingolstadt, the old interest is revived in such a way as to conflate with rather than contrast with the new: the language and methodology of modern science become harnessed to Frankenstein's old visionary yearnings. To introduce this notion and effect the slippage,

---

[64] In the 1818 text, 'some accident' prevents Frankenstein from attending a course of lectures on natural philosophy (36). However, in the 1831 text, Shelley has Frankenstein denigrate the new scientist who 'might dissect, anatomise, and give names; but not to speak of a final cause'.

Shelley uses the technique of presenting two professors whose discourses on modern chemistry are at variance, not unlike those of Abernathy and Lawrence, the London surgeons locked in dispute at the time at which Shelley was writing. M. Krempe ridicules 'the exploded systems' of Paracelsus and company, and although Frankenstein himself has long since 'considered those authors useless', he finds himself contemptuous of 'the uses of modern natural philosophy' advocated by this 'little squat man'. He feels that he is required 'to exchange chimeras of boundless grandeur for realities of little worth' (p. 41). M. Waldman, however, acknowledges the vision of the ancient teachers, and speaks of the 'new and almost unlimited powers' of the 'modern masters' who 'penetrate into the recesses of nature, and shew how she works in her hiding places' (p. 42). He thus describes modern scientific method in the elevated terms which Frankenstein wishes to hear. And the question which Victor sets himself, 'Whence . . . did the principle of life proceed?' (p. 46)—what might be called a 'vitalist' question not unlike the old alchemical one—allows for further glorious discovery, whereas Krempe's position apparently does not. Because the text is not explicit, one can only surmise that Krempe's position is perhaps that of early nineteenth-century materialists, like Lawrence, for whom life is dependent on organization. Frankenstein would want it the other way—that organization is in some way dependent on life, an unknown principle to be discovered as its cause.[65]

Not that this implies a return to the *practices* of alchemy for Victor. The hours he subsequently spends in minute observation of 'the natural decay and corruption of the body' are actually untainted by any form of superstition or magic ritual. His mind, he says, was not impressed with 'supernatural horrors'. A churchyard for him was 'merely the receptacle of bodies deprived of life . . . food for the worm' (*Frankenstein*, p. 47), and when, 'after days and nights of incredible labour and fatigue', he discovers 'the cause of generation and life', finding himself 'capable of bestowing animation upon lifeless matter', this, too has been discovered scientifically: 'Some

---

[65] This difference is made more explicit in a passage in the 1831 text (Shelley, *Frankenstein*, 238).

miracle might have produced it, yet the stages of discovery were distinct and probable' (p. 47). Only in retrospect does Victor see his single-mindedness about this task—that is, his *obsession* with discovery—to have perhaps been tinged with some occult force.[66] He speaks of the 'passion' that arose 'like a mountain river, from ignoble and almost forgotten sources' (p. 32) and later comments: 'Unless I had been animated by an almost supernatural enthusiasm, my application to this study would have been irksome, and almost intolerable' (p. 46). And so once again we are presented with the hubris or immoderate desire which so often attracts a capricious fate in the spirit-ballad. Indeed, breaking off his tale, Frankenstein addresses Walton directly on this point, explaining why he cannot share his discovery:

I will not lead you on, unguarded and ardent as I then was, to your destruction and infallible misery. Learn from me, if not by my precepts, at least by my example, how dangerous is the acquirement of knowledge, and how much happier that man is who believes his native town to be the world, than he who aspires to become greater than his nature will allow. (p. 48)

This is one of the most explicit statements of the dangers of overreaching which we have in the novel[67] and it cues an analogy with the Prometheus of the tale's subtitle.

With Frankenstein's ambition to create a man and the subsequent animation of the Being, the parallel with Prometheus *plasticator*, the Titan from Greek myth who bestowed life on the human race, can be drawn further: 'Life and death appeared to me ideal bounds, which I should first break through, and pour a torrent of light into our dark world. A new species would bless me as its creator and source . . .' (*Frankenstein*, p. 49). Frankenstein recollects the frenetic way in which, working always in his 'workshop of filthy creation' in com-

---

[66] In the 1831 text Frankenstein speaks of the 'guardian angel' or 'spirit of preservation' which attempted 'to avert the storm'. At another point he was aware that his soul was 'grappling with a palpable enemy' as his mind became filled with his 'single purpose'. These passages are strongly suggestive of daemonic possession (Shelley, *Frankenstein*, 239, 241).

[67] See also Shelley, *Frankenstein*, 208: 'All my speculations and hopes are nothing; and, like the archangel who aspired to omnipotence, I am chained in an eternal hell.'

plete isolation and neglect of family and friends, he 'disturbed, with profane fingers, the tremendous secrets of the human frame' to prepare a gigantic body in which to infuse life. While he often turned 'with loathing' from his occupation, he was yet 'urged on by an eagerness which perpetually increased' (p. 50). Once the task was complete, however, he was appalled at the hideousness of the 'wretch' he had created, the 'load that weighed upon his mind', and his life became 'a hell'. At this point he further quotes from *The Ancient Mariner* to help Walton visualize 'his fear and dread' (p. 54). So great was his anxiety that he seemed to see 'the dreaded spectre glide into the room' and seize him. When he struggled violently, he fell into a fit and then into 'a nervous fever', from which he did not recover for several months.

Of interest here is that Frankenstein obviously regrets creating the Being and sees his knowledge and single-minded pursuit as 'dangerous'. Yet the most he can do to express his reservation is to use universal, Godwinian terms:

A human being in perfection ought always to preserve a calm and peaceful mind, and never to allow passion or a transitory desire to disturb his tranquillity. . . . if no man allowed any pursuit whatsoever to interfere with the tranquillity of his domestic affections, Greece had not been enslaved; Caesar would have spared his country; America would have been discovered more gradually; and the empires of Mexico and Peru had not been destroyed. (p. 51)[68]

Despite these references to the misuse of power, Frankenstein never says specifically that it was presumptuous[69] or sacrilegious to bypass natural procreation for an alchemical-scientific one which eliminates or usurps the role of woman. Although, as readers (particularly if we are female), we may

[68] In William Godwin, *St. Leon: A Tale of the Sixteenth Century*, Foreword by Devendra P. Varma, Introd. Juliet Beckett (New York: Arno Press, 1972), 81, the ideal of tranquillity, espoused by Marguerite, is contrasted with St Leon's heroic ideal when St Leon says: 'High heroic feats, and not the tranquillity of rural retirement, or the pursuits of a character professedly literary, had been the food of my imagination, ever since the faculty of imagination was unfolded in my mind.'
[69] In the 1831 version, Shelley added a statement in which Victor calls himself the 'the living monument of presumption and rash ignorance' (Shelley, *Frankenstein*, 245).

well take that particular cue from the repeated allusions to the *Ancient Mariner*—that the Being is his albatross and that he must do penance for his rash and irresponsible act—for Victor it seems rather different. Certainly subconsciously he reacts with guilt or anxiety to his elimination of the woman-mother from the process, as we see from his account of his nightmare[70] in which he kisses his betrothed, Elizabeth, only to find that she is transformed into the corpse of his dead mother, 'the grave-worms crawling in the folds of the flannel'. On the conscious level, however, what leads to his initial rejection of the creature is its horrifying appearance, the reminders of death and charnel houses: the creature's 'yellow skin that scarcely covered the work of muscles and arteries', 'his watery eyes, that seemed almost of the same colour as their dun sockets', and 'the shrivelled complexion and straight black lips' (*Frankenstein*, p. 52).

After this point, Frankenstein's tale becomes itself increasingly like a nightmare, as the Being he has created seemingly moves effortlessly across continents to turn up suddenly to haunt him and murder those close to him, one by one, in retaliation for his absolute rejection and neglect. The creature's presence is uncannily ubiquitous—he is three times seen by moonlight—and can be read as a projection of Frankenstein's guilt. Indeed, there now appears much in Frankenstein's story, as he describes his successive illnesses or fits of derangement, to suggest that he is in some way possessed; and this raises questions about his reliability and his earlier scientific 'positivism'—in particular his supposed lack of superstition or fear of, or communion with, the supernatural.

For example, when he is called home following the murder of his young brother, William, he is filled with the sense of 'a thousand nameless evils' (p. 69). As he approaches the dark mountains near his native town of Geneva, his grief, fear, and gloom and foreboding are overwhelming: 'The picture appeared a vast and dim scene of evil, and I foresaw obscurely that I was destined to become the most wretched of human beings' (p. 70). The spectacular thunderstorm which he then

[70] This point is made by Irving H. Buchen, '*Frankenstein* and the Alchemy of Creation', *Wordsworth Circle*, 8/2 (Spring 1977), 108.

witnesses is described by him at length in terms both geographical and sublime, the former giving a convincing 'scientific' precision and realism to the scene:

the thunder burst with a terrific crash over my head. It was echoed from Saleve, the Juras and the Alps of Savoy; vivid flashes of lightning dazzled my eyes, illuminating the lake, making it appear like a vast sheet of fire . . . The storm, as is so often the case in Switzerland . . . (p. 71)

But, as we found in *The Monk*, the sublime in nature, with its capacity to raise awareness, can be used to prepare the way for the sudden appearance of things or powers preternatural. While we have here no prior mention of ghosts or Gothic castles, but instead an emphatic realism, we find the same technique for introducing the fantastic, even to the ballad-like chant:

While I watched the storm, so beautiful yet terrific, I wandered on with a hasty step. This noble war in the sky elevated my spirits; I clasped my hands, and exclaimed aloud, 'William, dear angel! this is thy funeral, this thy dirge!' As I said these words, I perceived in the gloom a figure which stole from a clump of trees near me; I stood fixed, gazing intently: I could not be mistaken. A flash of lightning illuminated the object, and discovered its shape plainly to me; its gigantic stature, and the deformity of its aspect . . . instantly informed me that it was the wretch, the filthy daemon to whom I had given life. (*Frankenstein*, p. 71)

Like the victim in a spirit-ballad, Frankenstein seems to seek communion with another mode of being. On seeing his creature, he immediately jumps to the correct conclusion that this 'daemon' is his brother's murderer. The creature's sudden appearance and Frankenstein's sudden insight, however, by metonymic slippage, admits of a variety of modern psychoanalytic interpretations of his tale, based on Frankenstein's regressive desires and the notion of the creature as his *alter ego* or *Doppelgänger*.[71] Argued from a 'male' perspective, these readings posit that Frankenstein's familial relationships are at base Oedipal and incestuous, Elizabeth being 'the displaced mother' he cannot marry.

[71] See James B. Twitchell, '*Frankenstein* and the Anatomy of Horror', *Georgia Review*, 37 (1983), 48–55.

However that may be, if the monster *is* but a projection, then it is Frankenstein who is the murderer of William and, later, of Clerval and Elizabeth. Indeed, at this point in his tale, Frankenstein recollects how he 'considered the being . . . nearly in the light of [his] own vampire, [his] own spirit let loose from the grave, and forced to destroy all that was dear to [him]' (p. 72). At other times, too, like the monster, he sees himself as Satan (pp. 158, 208.) But perhaps, as David Ketterer has suggested, 'both murderer and victims, together with the external universe, may be aspects of Frankenstein's mind, or Walton's mind'.[72] Readings such as these, which question the ontological status of the monster, also radically question the status of reality.

Irrespective of what the reader decides on these issues, again and again Frankenstein is found recounting an incident where he himself appears possessed and seeking contact with a spirit world. For example, after the miscarriage of justice in which he had allowed Justine to be executed for William's murder, he had 'wandered', 'like an evil spirit' (*Frankenstein*, p. 85), gnashing his teeth, his eyes 'inflamed' whenever he thought of 'the monster'. He had journeyed to the Valley of Chamounix where he resolved to climb to the summit of Montanvert alone. In viewing the glacier, he had hoped to experience a 'sublime ecstasy that gave wings to the soul, and allowed it to soar from the obscure world to light and joy' (p. 92). Not for Shelley's hero, however, a rhapsodic sense of the 'Deity' such as we find in Radcliffe's romances, or of the 'God' that we find in Coleridge's 'Hymn before Sun-rise, in the Vale of Chamouni'. Rather, as in Percy Shelley's 'Mount Blanc', the alpine mountains signify some primeval, amoral power. Faced with 'the wonderful and stupendous scene' of the 'vast river of ice' and the 'icy and glittering peaks' of Montanvert and Mont Blanc, Victor had called on the 'wandering spirits' to take him as '[their] companion, away from the joys of life' (p. 93). Instantly the creature had approached 'with superhuman speed', this time to tell his own interpolated tale and demand that Frankenstein make for him a female companion.

[72] David Ketterer, *Frankenstein's Creation: The Book, the Monster, and the Human Reality* (Victoria, BC: University of Victoria, 1979), 105.

Again, after the deaths of Elizabeth and his father, Victor had visited the cemetery in which they and William were buried. This time we find all traces of his former positivism gone as he recounts how 'the spirits of the departed seemed to flit around' and he swore by the 'shades' and 'spirits' of the Night to pursue 'the daemon' (p. 199) while the creature's 'loud and fiendish laugh' rang heavily in his ears. Franken-stein, in his obsession with revenge, becomes uncannily like the creature he has created, their positions reversed, the mon-ster leaving clues to keep his creator in pursuit. So, again it can seem that the monster is but a projection of Frankenstein's guilt. When later Victor speaks of his 'guiding spirits' (pp. 201, 206, 214), he claims that he is, even now, visited by his dead friends in dreams (p. 208), and this, too, raises questions about his sanity.

Thus do we find the secular attitudes of science in the novel, both epistemological and moral, at least questioned, if not overturned, by the conventions of balladry and Victor's ad-herence to talk of spirits. There seems no rational explanation for his fall into evil. Moreover, as Michael Holquist argues in his intertextual reading of the novel, Frankenstein regards his creature from the first moment as 'something finished', unique in its 'absolute singularity' and 'cut off from affiliation'.[73] Thus Frankenstein not only fails to nurture the creature. He never makes any attempt to observe and analyse what went wrong with his experiment. As a result, his death aboard Walton's ship can be read in the tradition of the spirit-ballad, as a punishment for his infraction of natural law, especially as he is still not fully repentant.

We learn from Walton's final letters that Frankenstein vacil-lates between warning Walton to desist in his purpose and urging him to press on. At one point Frankenstein even ad-monishes the sailors for their cowardice in turning from the 'glorious expedition'. Read intertextually with the passage from Dante's *Inferno* in which Ulysses rouses his sailors to make their fatal journey of discovery—for which counsel Ulysses was 'consigned to the flaming ditch'—Victor's speech

---

[73] Michael Holquist, *Dialogism: Bakhtin and His World* (London and New York: Routledge, 1990), 92–3.

ironically points again to his own intellectual overreaching.[74] Even as he takes his last breath, he reaffirms the Promethean pursuit: 'Farewell, Walton! Seek happiness in tranquillity, and avoid ambition, even if it be only the apparently innocent one of distinguishing yourself in science and discoveries. Yet why do I say this? I have myself been blasted in these hopes, yet another may succeed' (*Frankenstein*, p. 217). Ever egotistical, while 'examining [his] past conduct' as he lies dying, Franken-stein does not really find it 'blameable' (p. 214). Walton, too, perceives Frankenstein as the archetypal romantic hero: 'a celestial spirit' 'a divine wanderer', 'noble and god-like in ruin' (pp. 23-4, 209). If, as Kiely points out, the reader accepts at their face value (rather than as irony) these eulogies and Frankenstein's admonitions to the mariners, then the question of the immunity of scientific and artistic genius to conven-tional morality is also raised by the novel.[75] Certainly, over the course of Frankenstein's tale as a whole, we find a vacillation 'between rejection and advocacy of modern Prometheanism in science'.[76] It is an ambivalence still further complicated by the novel's qualified endorsement of 'domestic affection', seclu-sion, and sensitivity to nature.

Discourses of Sensibility, Education, and Myths of the Family in Frankenstein

Throughout *Frankenstein* the hero's 'scientific' pursuit of knowledge, power, and glory is interrogated by a Godwinian discourse of human perfectibility, a moral ideal of 'domestic affection' and social benevolence. After the death of Mary Wollstonecraft, Godwin placed much greater emphasis than he had in *The Enquiry* on domestic affection. In the Preface to *St. Leon* he wrote:

I apprehend domestic and private affections inseparable from the nature of man, and from what may be styled the culture of the heart,

[74] See Rieger's note, Shelley, *Frankenstein*, 212.
[75] Kiely, *Romantic Novel in England*, 160.
[76] Aija Ozolins, in 'Dreams and Doctrines: Dual Strands in *Frankenstein*', *Science-Fiction Studies*, 2 (July 1975), 110, finds this true of Frankenstein's story in the 1831 version.

and am fully persuaded that they are not incompatible with a profound and active sense of justice in the mind of him that cherishes them. True wisdom will recommend to us individual attachments; for with them our minds are more thoroughly maintained in activity and life than they can be under the privation of them . . .[77]

Significantly, *St. Leon*, with its self-styled 'eulogium' on 'the affections and charities of private life', also begins with a contrasting ideal of Promethean striving: 'There is nothing that human imagination can figure brilliant and enviable, that human genius and skill do not aspire to realize.'[78] In this novel, however, the secret which sets St Leon apart from his family is his possession of magic gifts, the philosopher's stone and elixir of life, which he has accepted from a mysterious stranger. Though 'brilliant and enviable' secrets of nature, these gifts prove to be destructive of 'domestic and private affections'[79]— honesty, ingenuousness, and true benevolence. Here the novel's qualification of knowledge and power seems less ambiguous than in *Frankenstein*: 'Magic dissolves the whole principle and arrangement of human action, subverts all generous enthusiasm and dignity, and renders life itself loathesome and intolerable.'[80] As we have seen, with 'science' partially substituted for 'magic', *Frankenstein* can be read as re-evaluating the heroic individual's aspiration to knowledge for the supposed benefit of mankind. It does not do so, however, without simultaneously appropriating and testing the Radcliffean and Godwinian family ideals. Certain tenets regarding family affection, friendship, education, seclusion, sensibility, and benevolence are offered as moral norms in the novel but are also interrogated.

We have noted how Victor tells Walton that 'a human being in perfection' is dependent on the preservation of 'a calm and peaceful mind' (*Frankenstein*, p. 51)—the love and tranquillity which accrues from living within the bounds of the normative community of family and friends. Walton, too, though fixed in his purpose of discovery, sees the value of this. He laments his upbringing and yearns for a close and true friend 'wiser and more experienced' than himself, 'to confirm and

[77] Godwin, *St. Leon*, p. x.   [78] Ibid. 1.   [79] Ibid. pp. x, 1.
[80] Ibid. 474.

support' him (p. 23). Walton's experience of education and domestic affection, the first of three models in the novel, is presented as deficient.

Orphaned while yet a child and raised by his uncle[81] (as he reminds his sister), Walton claims to have 'run wild on a common', his education 'neglected'. His passionate fondness for reading set him on a course of self-education isolated from any community, first as a poet, later as a scientist-seafarer, the occupation forbidden by his dying father. Although lonely, he now rejects the notion that he will find a friend 'among merchants and seamen', even though the two men he mentions at length, his lieutenant and the master, obviously have some fine attributes. For him, one is 'unsoftened by cultivation', while the other, though demonstrating 'gentleness', 'generosity', and 'mildness of . . . discipline', 'has scarcely an idea beyond the rope and the shroud'. The sudden insertion of an anecdote about the 'kindliness of heart' of the master summons up sympathy for the crew who, in Walton's final letters, are recorded as threatening to mutiny when it appears that they are doomed if Walton will not turn back. Walton's élitist attitude, too, can qualify for the reader his avowed wish to benefit mankind, especially given his admiration for Frankenstein, who seems to fulfil for Walton all that he seeks in a friend: 'He is so gentle, yet so wise; his mind is so cultivated . . . his words are culled with the choicest art . . .' (*Frankenstein*, p. 22). Thus lack of family affection, proper guidance, and education can be taken as the root cause of Walton's loneliness and admiration for Frankenstein's Promethean determination.

In contrast, Frankenstein, who makes it clear to Walton that he, too, is isolated and loveless—'I have lost every thing, and cannot begin life anew' (p. 23)—appears to have been much more fortunate in his upbringing in terms of affection and education. Early in his tale Frankenstein makes much of the propriety, benevolence, tenderness, and care of his parents. His father, one of a long line of 'counsellors and syndics . . . had filled several public situations with honour and reputa-

---

[81] In the 1831 version, Walton also alludes to 'his best years spent under [the] gentle and feminine fosterage' of his sister (Shelley, *Frankenstein*, 14).

tion' and was much respected for 'his integrity and indefatigable attention to public business' (p. 27). The benevolence of
Alphonse Frankenstein is shown in his compassionate treatment of his merchant friend, Beaufort, who had been thrown
into 'poverty and oblivion'. Having located his friend at the
point of death, not only did he 'come like a protecting spirit'
to Beaufort's daughter—herself a woman of 'uncommon
mould'—but married her two years later.

What Sir Walter Scott called Mary Shelley's 'plain and forcible English'[82] for the most part abjures the overworked words
of the day such as 'sensibility' and 'sentiment'. Nevertheless
we still find here a Radcliffean emphasis on 'the exercise of
domestic virtues' (*Udolpho*, p. 66) and on the retirement from
public life which is commensurate with delicacy of feeling and
the private or 'feminine' sphere. Like Ellena in *The Italian*,
Caroline Beaufort procures 'plain work . . . to support life'.
She is overcome with grief at her father's death and is kneeling
by his coffin, 'weeping bitterly', when found by Frankenstein's
father, who, on marrying her, 'relinquishe[s] many of his public employments, and devote[s] himself to the education of his
children' (*Frankenstein*, pp. 28–9).

In consequence Victor is able to claim that 'no creature could
have more tender parents than mine', that 'my improvement
and health were their constant care' (p. 29) and 'no youth
could have passed more happily than mine' (p. 31). His two
younger brothers, his cousin, Elizabeth Lavenza, and his
friend, Henry Clerval, were all included in the harmonious
'domestic circle', where their studies in Latin and English
'were never forced'. As a result of good planning, structure,
and 'the language of truth and reason', such as Godwin advocated, they 'loved application'.[83] While Victor had a scientific
bent, the gentle Elizabeth 'busied herself in following the
aerial creations of the poets' (p. 30).

[82] Walter Scott, *Blackwood's Magazine*, 2 (1818), repr. in Scott, *Sir Walter
Scott on Novelists and Fiction*, 271.

[83] Again, this section is revised and extended in the 1831 version of *Frank-
enstein*; the bonds of 'devoted affection' are given greater emphasis. For
Godwin's statements about the education of children, see William Godwin,
*Enquiry Concerning Political Justice and its Influence on Modern Morals and
Happiness* (Harmondsworth: Penguin, 1985), 106–12.

It is at this point that we start to find some jarring notes in Victor's account of bourgeois domestic perfection.[84] Not only does there emerge a division of roles in the schoolroom, but Victor's own readings in occult science are 'carelessly' dismissed without explanation by his father, something which Victor regards in retrospect as momentous in the formation of his character and history. Godwin, in *The Enquiry*, speaks of 'the need to get rid of the chilling system of occult and inexplicable causes', but also advocates that a parent show that what is recommended is 'valuable and desirable'.[85] This Alphonse Frankenstein fails to do. As a result Victor is forced into secrecy and solitude, as the loving and dutiful Elizabeth '[does] not interest herself in the subject' (pp. 32–4). Next Victor's mother dies of scarlet fever, having caught the disease from Elizabeth by visiting the latter's sick-bed too early in the recovery stages. Later, Clerval is not permitted by his own merchant-father to accompany Victor to the University of Ingolstadt, even though Victor feels 'totally unfitted for the company of strangers'. As a result, Victor's 'invincible repugnance to new countenances' leads him to reflect on his 'hitherto remarkably secluded and domestic' life as intellectually and socially confining: 'I ardently desired the acquisition of knowledge. I had often, when at home, thought it hard to remain during my youth cooped up in one place, and had longed to enter the world, and take my station among other human beings' (*Frankenstein*, p. 40). Moreover, during his ensuing separation from family and friends, his desire for knowledge becomes an all-consuming passion which effectively isolates him. And despite all its apparent virtues, his upbringing does not help him to regulate his ambition, to consider the possible consequences of his actions, or to live sociably in the broader, public sphere. In sum, we find a myth of family solidarity, affection, and harmony in turn being interrogated by discourses which emphasize the desires, strivings, irrational fears, and fantastic products of scientific genius.

[84] Ellis, 'Monsters in the Garden', 123, has argued that 'Mary Shelley was at least as much concerned with the limitations of [domestic] affection as she was with demonstrating its amiableness'.

[85] Godwin, *Enquiry Concerning Political Justice*, 109–10.

Frankenstein cannot, as Kate Ellis says, take the Monster home[86] as nothing can be permitted to disturb the tranquillity and harmony of the family, whether strong feelings, outsiders, or accounts of strange or unpleasant events. This is evident from the injunction in the letter Victor receives from his father after William's murder: 'Come, Victor; not brooding thoughts of vengeance ... but with feelings of peace and gentleness ... kindness and affection ...' (p. 68). Elizabeth, too, argues: 'We surely shall be happy: quiet in our native country, and not mingling in the world, what can disturb our tranquillity?' (p. 89). Again, when Victor is granted permission to leave Geneva for two years before marrying Elizabeth, his father replies, 'I earnestly desire that period to arrive when we shall all be united, and neither hopes or fears arise to disturb our domestic calm' (p. 150).

That this suppression of feeling and insularity from the public realm renders women abject or ineffectual and men passive or divided is obvious from the reactions of Frankenstein, Elizabeth, Victor, and Justine to Justine's trial and execution for the murder of little William. Justine, a woman who had adored and imitated Caroline Frankenstein in sensibility, gentleness, benevolence, and devotion, and had been a trusted member of the household, is passive and helpless in the face of accusation. As Beth Newman points out, she has no possible explanations for the details of the crime, no story to tell to counter that which, through circumstantial evidence, has been brought against her. Worse, by her appeal to character, she rejects the arguments that might have provided an explanation and so incriminates herself still further.[87] In court Elizabeth, too, can rely only on feminine sweetness, not reasoned and convincing argument, to save her friend, while Alphonse Frankenstein seems uninterested in getting to the bottom of the murder and simply admonishes Elizabeth to 'rely on the justice of our judges, and the activity with which I shall prevent the slightest shadow of partiality' (*Frankenstein*, p. 76).[88] That his

[86] Ellis, 'Monsters in the Garden', 140.
[87] Beth Newman, 'Narratives of Seduction and the Seductions of Narrative: The Frame Structure of *Frankenstein*', ELH 53/1 (Spring 1986), 148–9.
[88] For a fuller discussion of this, see Ellis, 'Monsters in the Garden', 132–3.

only portrait of his dead wife is of her weeping over her father's coffin suggests the claustrophobic and abject nature of the Frankensteins' family life.

In contrast with Victor's description of his family and education are the strivings of the De Laceys, as recounted by the creature to Frankenstein. De Lacey, his son Felix, and daughter Agatha had been forced into poverty and exile after Felix had assisted a Turkish merchant, unjustly imprisoned, to escape from a French prison. They eke out a scant existence on a small farm where, as Kate Ellis notes, their 'relationship . . . to nature significantly differs from that of Victor, for whom nature can only provide occasions for a repeated display of a histrionic sensibility'.[89] The mores of the family are also far less rigid than those of the Frankensteins. For example, the Arabian woman, Safie, daughter of the Turk and beloved of Felix, defies her father after he turns treacherous. When she actively seeks out Felix in Germany, this course of action, unthinkable for Emily St Aubert in *Udolpho*, is accepted as appropriate. Unlike Elizabeth, Safie has been taught by her mother, in the style of Wollstonecraft, 'to aspire to higher powers of intellect, and an independence of spirit, forbidden to the female followers of Mahomet' (p. 119).

Observing the De Laceys in secret from his hovel, the creature constantly emphasizes the family's industry, 'gentle manners', kindness, devotion to their blind father, 'amiability', and 'superior accomplishments' (*Frankenstein*, pp. 103, 105, 106, 108). His own inherent sensibility and benevolence reinforced by their example, he is 'elevated by the enchanting appearance of nature' (p. 111), performs secret acts of kindness, learns the 'god-like science' of language, and resolves to try 'to restore happiness to these deserving people' by delivering them from poverty (p. 110). However, despite their virtue, the De Laceys still reject the creature as monstrous without even learning of his 'gentle demeanour and conciliating words', and this again shows the limitations of the virtues of 'domestic affection' and 'sensibility' which Godwin, in the preface to *St. Leon*, had argued would render people 'more prompt in the service of strangers and the public'.[90]

[89] Ibid. 139.   [90] Godwin, *St. Leon*, p. x.

In that the expulsion of the creature from his 'Eden' (the Miltonic parallels are explicit) causes him to turn to vengeance and violence, we see that, metaphorically, the poor and homeless are ultimately without 'parents' or support. There is no necessary connection between bourgeois tranquillity, with its 'feminine' private affections, and public, disinterested benevolence and justice. Listening to Felix read from Volney's *Ruin of Empires* the creature has

learned that the possessions most esteemed by your fellow-creatures were, high and unsullied descent united with riches. A man might be respected with only one of these acquisitions; but without either he was considered, except in very rare instances, as a vagabond and a slave, doomed to waste his powers for the profit of the chosen few. (p. 115)

'What was I?' he asks, and again the question recurs when he learns about parental care and the differences between the sexes. Having read *Paradise Lost*, he tells his creator, 'I ought to be thy Adam, but I am rather the fallen angel, whom thou drivest from joy for no misdeed. . . . I was benevolent and good; misery made me a fiend' (p. 95). After he has been rejected also by the De Laceys whom he had believed benevolent and good, the creature's anger, born of despair, knows no bounds:

My protectors had departed, and had broken the only link that held me to the world. For the first time the feelings of revenge and hatred filled my bosom, and I did not strive to controul them; but, allowing myself to be borne away by the stream, I bent my mind towards injury and death. . . . unable to injure any thing human, I turned my fury towards inanimate objects. (*Frankenstein*, p. 134)

It is but a step to his vow of 'eternal hatred and vengeance to all mankind' (p. 138). Having been restored to 'gentleness and pleasure' by the advent of spring, 'the loveliness of its sunshine and the balminess of the air', the creature rescues a young girl from drowning, only to be wounded for his benevolence by a man with a gun. Now his 'oppressive sense of the injustice and ingratitude', of the way he is forced continually to suffer, is no longer ameliorated 'by the bright sun or gentle breezes of spring; all joy [is] but a mockery' (p. 138). That sensibility, which he had read about in *Werther*—'the gentle and domestic manners . . . combined with lofty sentiments and feelings, which had for their object something out of the self'—and which he had observed in the De Laceys (pp. 123–4), has failed to prepare people to accept the visually ugly or to overcome oppression and injustice.

Speaking like an eighteenth-century *philosophe*, the creature thus demonstrates of the society of *Frankenstein* what Percy Shelley saw as dominant in British society, a purpose 'to trample upon our rights and liberties for ever, to present us with the alternatives of anarchy and oppression'.[91] When the creature finally mourns over Frankenstein's body aboard Walton's ship, addressing his creator as a 'generous and self-devoted being' and stirring Walton to momentary compassion, he emphasizes his thesis at length: 'No sympathy may I ever find. When I first sought it, it was the love of virtue, the feelings of happiness and affection with which my whole being overflowed, that I wished to be participated' (*Frankenstein*, p. 218). However, 'evil thenceforth became [his] good' when he was rejected and oppressed; 'the fallen angel becomes a malignant devil' (pp. 220–1). The creature, in his Lockean and Godwinian acquisition of knowledge, has passed through stages from an innocent state of nature to that of would-be participant in civilized society. Oppressed at every turn, he has fallen into despair and violence. When he finally disappears rejected and friendless into the sublime 'darkness and distance' to immolate himself, Godwin's ideal of domestic affection leading to public benevolence is again thrown radically into question.

Responses to Frankenstein

In conclusion, on examining the 1818 Preface, the 1831 Introduction to *Frankenstein*, reviews, and the discursive mix and artistic arrangement of the 1818 novel, we have seen its intensely dialogic nature. Making a claim for original authorship, it is a supernatural and tragic tale of overreaching in its appropriation of balladry and pseudo-scientific discourse. It is

---

[91] Percy Bysshe Shelley, 'An Address to the People on the Death of Princess Charlotte', in Shelley, *Works*, vi. 113.

also a political novel and novel of education. In recontextualizing and juxtaposing early nineteenth-century ideals of domestic affection, sensibility, and aristocratic benevolence with
Promethean endorsements of poetic and scientific genius, it
relativizes both these sets of ideals, revealing their contradictions and differing limitations for men and women, for poets
and scientists, and for oppressed groups in society.

From the plurality of the dimensions of reading *Frankenstein*, we have moved to the plurality of different readings
which can be and have been made of it, depending on which
orientation of meaning is privileged by the reader. For example,
we have seen that it was interpreted by some readers of 1818
as a didactic tale about Promethean presumption and by
others as having a more sinister intent. After condemning its
failure to 'inculcate' a lesson of 'conduct, manners or morality', one contemporary reviewer complained that 'it gratu-
itously harasses the heart'.[92] In contrast, in his 1818 review of
Frankenstein, Sir Walter Scott spoke of the author's 'uncommon powers of poetic imagination', his 'high idea of the
author's original genius', and the novel's nature as one 'which
excites new reflections and untried sources of emotion'.[93]

Recently, *Frankenstein* has been said to be a novel which
draws attention to its own intertextuality, its own making
from fragments of other books and discourses. It does this
most prominently by its subtitle, and references to the monster's reading: Volney's *Ruins of Empires*, Milton's *Paradise
Lost*, Plutarch's *Lives*, and Goethe's *The Sorrows of Young
Werther*. This can lead to narcissistic or metafictional readings
currently popular with post-structuralists. On the one hand,
there is a type of feminist, psycho-biographical interpretation,
which sees Shelley's novel as speaking its own 'monstrosity',
its own patching from pre-texts. On the other, there is a
self-reflexive interpretation which places the novel in a frame
of Bakhtinian poetics. For at least one critic, *Frankenstein* is
'not only about the making of a monster', but 'an enactment
of the monstrosity of novelness itself', speaking its own

[92] *Quarterly Review*, Jan. 1818, quoted by Poovey, *Proper Lady and the
Woman Writer*, 122.
[93] See n. 14 above.

dialogism, 'the dilemma of knowing that its constitution is always incomplete and ineluctably other'.[94]

However, *given* the novel's dialogism, whichever way we choose to read in our desires and commitments of the moment, we should remember that *Frankenstein*, like the other Gothic texts we have considered, is unfinalizable. To recall the words of Bakhtin:

Every age re-accentuates in its own way the works of its most immediate past. The historical life of classic works is in fact the uninterrupted process of their social and ideological re-accentuation. Thanks to the intentional potential embedded in them, such works have proved capable of uncovering in each era and against ever new dialogizing backgrounds ever new aspects of meaning; their semantic content literally continues to grow, to further create out of itself. (Bakhtin, p. 421)

Bakhtin has offered us the notion of the novel as a 'microcosm' of dialogized heteroglossia which will always ensure resistance to totalization. With the conjunction of particular discourses at specific historical moments, certain theoretical frameworks and interpretations may strive for and achieve dominance for a time. But no discourse can become totalizing: 'Alongside the centripetal forces, the centrifugal forces of language carry on their uninterrupted work; alongside verbal ideological centralization and unification, the uninterrupted processes of decentralization and disunification go forward' (Bakhtin, p. 272). How one or the other of these forces gains ascendancy at particular moments, Bakhtin does not say.[95] Yet we know that we cannot simply accept that while there is discursive power there is also discursive intervention and resistance and do nothing ourselves. Gramsci has shown that the development of new, anti-hegemonic ways of speaking do not just happen without some committed intellectual spadework and praxis. To adapt a sentence from Robert Young, we cannot rely on the diverse language of social groups to do our politics for us.[96]

[94] Holquist, *Dialogism*, 106.
[95] See Young, 'Back to Bakhtin', 84–6, and Allon White, 'Struggle Over Bakhtin: Fraternal Reply to Robert Young', for a discussion of this.
[96] Young, 'Back to Bakhtin', 86.

Select Bibliography

AERS, DAVID, with COOK, JONATHAN, and PUNTER, DAVID, *Romanticism and Ideology: Studies in English Writing, 1765–1830* (London, Boston, and Henley: Routledge & Kegan Paul, 1981).

AIKIN, JOHN, *Memoir of John Aikin, M.D. with a Selection of his Miscellaneous Pieces, Biographical, Moral and Critical* (London: Baldwin, Cradock and Joy, 1823).

ALLEN, B. SPRAGUE, 'The Reaction against William Godwin', *Modern Philology*, 16/5 (Sept. 1918), 57–75.

ALLEN, MICHAEL, *Poe and the British Magazine Tradition* (New York: Oxford University Press, 1969).

ALTICK, RICHARD D., *The English Common Reader* (Chicago: University of Chicago Press, 1957).

Analytical Review, 19 (1794), 144; 24 (Oct. 1796), 403–4.

ARMISTEAD, J. M., ed., *The First English Novelists: Essays in Understanding* (Knoxville: University of Tennessee Press, 1985).

ARMSTRONG, NANCY, 'The Nineteenth-Century Jane Austen: A Turning Point in the History of Fear', *Genre*, 23 (Summer/Fall 1990), 227–46.

——'The Rise of Feminine Authority in the Novel', *Novel*, 15/2 (Winter 1982), 127–45.

AUSTEN, JANE, *Northanger Abbey, Lady Susan, The Watsons and Sanditon*, ed. John Davie (Oxford: Oxford University Press, 1980).

BAKHTIN, MIKHAIL, *The Dialogic Imagination*, ed. Michael Holquist, trans. Caryl Emerson and Michael Holquist (Austin and London: University of Texas Press, 1981).

——*Problems of Dostoevsky's Poetics*, ed. and trans. Caryl Emerson (Minneapolis: University of Minnesota Press, 1984).

BARBAULD, ANNA LAETITIA (AIKIN), *The British Novelists*, with an Essay; and Prefaces, Biographical and Critical (London, 1810).

——and AIKIN, JOHN, *Miscellaneous Pieces*, 3rd edn. (London: J. Johnson, 1792), 119–27: On Objects of Terror.

BARKER, FRANCIS, *et al.*, eds., *The Politics of Theory* (Proceedings of the Essex conference on the Sociology of Literature, July 1982; Colchester: University of Essex, 1983), 21–2.

BARRETT, EATON STANNARD, *The Heroine, or Adventures of a Fair Romance Reader*, 3 vols. (London: Henry Colburn, 1813).

BARRETT, EATON STANNARD, *The Heroine*, with an introduction by Michael Sadleir (New York: Frederick A. Stokes, 1928), printed from the third edition (London: Henry Colburn, 1815).

——*Woman, A Poem* (London: Henry Colburn, 1818).

BAUER, DALE M., and McKINSTREY, S. JARET, eds., *Feminism, Bakhtin, and the Dialogic* (Albany: State University of New York Press, 1991).

BAYER-BERENBAUM, LINDA, *The Gothic Imagination* (London and Toronto: Associated University Press, 1987).

BELSEY, CATHERINE, *Critical Practice* (London: Methuen, 1980).

——'The Plurality of History', *Southern Review*, 17/2 (July 1984), 138–41.

BIRKHEAD, EDITH, *The Tale of Terror* (London: Constable, 1921).

BLAKEY, DOROTHY, *The Minerva Press 1790–1820* (London: Oxford University Press, 1939).

BLEILER, E. F., ed., *Three Gothic Novels: The Castle of Otranto* by Horace Walpole, *Vathek* by William Beckford, *The Vampyre* by John Polidori, and a Fragment of a Novel by Lord Byron (New York: Dover Publications Inc., 1966).

BOOTH, WAYNE C., 'Freedom of Interpretation: Bakhtin and the Challenge of Feminist Criticism', *Critical Inquiry*, 9/1 (Sept. 1982), 45–76.

BOUTET DE MONVEL, JACQUES M., *Les Victimes cloîtrées* (Paris: Barba, 1803).

BRADBROOK, FRANK W., *Jane Austen and her Predecessors* (Cambridge: Cambridge University Press, 1966).

BREDVOLD, LOUIS, *The Natural History of Sensibility* (Detroit: Wayne State University Press, 1962).

British Critic, 4 (Aug. 1794), 120; 7 (June 1796), 677.

BRONTË, CHARLOTTE, *Jane Eyre* (1847; Oxford: Oxford University Press, 1973).

BROOKE-ROSE, CHRISTINE, *A Rhetoric of the Unreal* (Cambridge: Cambridge University Press, 1981).

BROOKS, PETER, 'Virtue and Terror: *The Monk*', *ELH* 40/2 (Summer 1973), 249–63.

BROWN, FORD KEELER, *The Life of William Godwin* (London: J. M. Dent, 1926).

BUCHEN, IRVING H., '*Frankenstein* and the Alchemy of Creation', *Wordsworth Circle*, 8/2 (Spring 1977), 103–12.

BÜRGER, GOTTFRIED AUGUST, *Gedichte*, ed. Arnold E. Berger (Leipzig and Vienna: 1891).

BURKE, EDMUND, *A Philosophical Enquiry into the Origin of Our Ideas of the Sublime and Beautiful*, ed. J. T. Boulton (London: Routledge & Kegan Paul, 1958).

BUTLER, MARILYN, *Jane Austen and the War of Ideas*, reissued in paperback with a new Introduction (1975; Oxford: Clarendon Press, 1987).

——*Romantics, Rebels and Reactionaries: English Literature and its Background* (Oxford: Oxford University Press, 1981).

CAILLOIS, ROGER, *Au cœur du fantastique* (Paris: Gallimard, 1958).

CAMERON, DEBORAH, *Feminism and Linguistic Theory* (London: Macmillan Press, 1985).

CARRARD, PHILLIPE, 'From Reflexivity to Reading: The Criticism of Lucien Dällenbach', *Poetics Today*, 5/4 (1984), 839–56.

CARROLL, DAVID, 'The Alterity of Discourse: Form, History, and the Question of the Political in M. M. Bakhtin', *Diacritics*, 13/2 (1983), 65–83.

CARTER, ELIZABETH, *Letters to Mrs. Montague between the Years 1755 and 1800*, ed. Revd Montague Pennington (London: F. C. & J. Rivington, 1817).

CAWS, MARY ANN, *Reading Frames in Fiction* (Princeton, NJ: Princeton University Press, 1985).

CHAMBERS, ROSS, *Story and Situation: Narrative Seduction and the Power of Fiction* (Minneapolis: University of Minnesota Press, 1984).

CLARK, KATERINA, and HOLQUIST, MICHAEL, *Mikhail Bakhtin* (Cambridge, Mass. and London: Belknap Press, 1984).

CLIFFORD, JAMES LOWRY, *Hester Lynch Piozzi (Mrs. Thrale)* (Oxford: Oxford University Press, 1957).

COBLEY, EVELYN, 'Mikhail Bakhtin's Place in Genre Theory', *Genre*, 21 (Fall 1988), 321–88.

COLBY, VINETA, *The Singular Anomaly* (New York: New York University Press, and London: London University Press, 1970).

COLERIDGE, SAMUEL TAYLOR, *Coleridge's Miscellaneous Criticism*, ed. T. M. Raysor (London: Constable, 1936).

——*Miscellanies, Aesthetic and Literary*, ed. T. Ashe (London: George Bell, 1885).

——*The Philosophical Lectures of Samuel Taylor Coleridge*, ed. Kathleen Coburn (London: Pilot Press, 1949).

CONGER, SYNDY M., 'Matthew G. Lewis, Robert Charles Maturin and the Germans: An Interpretative Study of the Influence of German Literature on Two Gothic Novels', *Salzburg Studies in English Literature: Romantic Reassessment*, 67 (1977), 1–307.

CONNELL, ROBERT WILLIAM, *Gender and Power: Society, the Person and Sexual Politics* (Sydney: Allen & Unwin, 1987).

Critical Review, 15 (1795), 63–74; 19 (Feb. 1797), 194; 2nd ser. 11 (Aug. 1794), 361–72; 2nd ser. 24 (1798), 236.

CUDE, WILFRED, 'Mary Shelley's Modern Prometheus: A Study in the Ethics of Scientific Creativity', *Dalhousie Review*, 5/52 (1972), 212–25.

DACRE, CHARLOTTE, *Zofloya: or The Moor*, introd. Devendra P. Varma (New York: Arno Press, 1974).

DAICHES, DAVID, *Sir Walter Scott and his World* (London: Thames and Hudson, 1971).

DANOW, DAVID, *The Thought of Mikhail Bakhtin: From Word to Culture* (New York: St Martin's Press, 1991).

DAY, ROBERT ADAMS, *Told in Letters: Epistolary Fiction Before Richardson* (Ann Arbor: University of Michigan, 1966).

DAY, WILLIAM PATRICK, *In the Circles of Fear and Desire: A Study of Gothic Fantasy* (Chicago and London: University of Chicago Press, 1985).

DELAMOTTE, EUGENIA C., *The Perils of the Night: A Feminist Study of Nineteenth-Century Gothic* (Oxford: Oxford University Press, 1990).

DELANY, MARY, *The Autobiography and Correspondence of Mary Granville, Mrs. Delany*, ed. Lady Llanover (London: Richard Bentley, 1861).

DE LAURETIS, TERESA, ed., *Feminist Studies/Critical Studies* (Bloomington: Indiana University Press, 1986).

DERRIDA, JACQUES, 'The Law of Genre', trans. Avital Ronell, *Critical Inquiry*, 7 (Autumn 1980), 55–81.

DE STAËL, MADAME, *Corinne; or, Italy*, trans. Isabel Hill with metrical versions of the Odes by L. E. Landon; and a Memoir by the authoress (London: Richard Bentley, New Burlington Street, 1987).

DIAZ-DIOCARETZ, MYRIAM, 'Bakhtin, Discourse and Feminist Theories', *Critical Studies*, 1/2 (1989) 121–39.

DICKINSON, HARRY THOMAS, *British Radicalism and the French Revolution 1789–1815* (Oxford: Basil Blackwell, 1985).

DONOVAN, JOSEPHINE, 'Women and the Rise of the Novel: A Feminist-Marxist Theory', *Signs*, 16/3 (Spring 1991), 441–62.

DOUGHTY, OSWALD, 'Coleridge and "The Gothic Novel" or "Tales of Terror" ', *English Miscellany*, 23 (1972), 125–48.

DRAKE, NATHAN, *Literary Hours or Sketches Critical and Narrative* (London: T. Cadell, Jr. and W. Davies, 1800; reprint edn. New York: Garland, 1970).

DUFF, WILLIAM, *An Essay on Original Genius* (London: E. and C. Dilly, 1767; reprint edn. New York: Garland, 1970).

——*Letters on the Intellectual and Moral Character of Women* (Aberdeen: J. Chalmers, 1807; reprint edn. New York and London: Garland, 1974).

DURANT, DAVID S., 'Ann Radcliffe and the Conservative Gothic', *Studies in English Literature, 1500–1900*, 22/3 (Summer 1982), 519–30.

——'Aesthetic Heroism in the Mysteries of Udolpho', *Eighteenth Century: Theory and Interpretation*, 22/2 (Spring 1981), 175–88.

EAGLETON, TERRY, *The Rape of Clarissa* (Oxford: Clarendon Press, 1982).

EAVES, T. C. DUNCAN, and KIMPEL, BEN D., *Samuel Richardson: A Biography* (Oxford: Clarendon Press, 1971).

EHRENPREIS, IRVIN, and HALSBAND, ROBERT, eds., *The Lady of Letters in the Eighteenth Century* (William Andrews Clark Memorial Library, Seminar Paper 29, Los Angeles: University of California Press, 1969).

EISENSTEIN, HESTER, *Contemporary Feminist Thought* (London and Sydney: Unwin, 1984).

——*Gender Shock: Practising Feminism on Two Continents* (Sydney: Allen & Unwin, 1991).

ENGELL, JAMES, *The Creative Imagination* (Cambridge, Mass. and London: Harvard University Press, 1981).

English Review, 20 (Nov. 1792), 352–3.

European Magazine, 31 (Feb. 1797), 111.

FAIRCLOUGH, PETER, ed., *Three Gothic Novels*, with an introductory essay by Mario Praz: contains *The Castle of Otranto* by Horace Walpole, *Vathek* by William Beckford, and *Frankenstein* by Mary Shelley (Harmondsworth: Penguin Books, 1978).

FAWCETT, MARY LAUGHLIN, 'Udolpho's Primal Mystery', *Studies in English Literature*, 23 (1983), 481–94.

FEARFUL, FRANK J., 'Satire and the Form of the Novel: The Problem of Aesthetic Unity in *Northanger Abbey*', *Journal of English Literary History*, 32 (Dec. 1965), 511–27.

FIELDING, HENRY, *Tom Jones* (London: Dent, 1962).

FLEENOR, JULIANN, ed., *The Female Gothic* (Montreal and London: Eden Press, 1987).

FORDYCE, JAMES, *Sermons to Young Women* (London: A. Millar and T. Cadell, 1767).

FOSTER, JAMES RALPH, *The History of the Pre-Romantic Novel in England* (New York: Modern Language Association, 1949, and London: Oxford University Press, 1949).

FOUCAULT, MICHEL, *Discipline and Punish: The Birth of the Prison* (Harmondsworth: Peregrine Books, 1979).

——*Madness and Civilization: A History of Insanity in the Age of Reason*, trans. Richard Howard (London: Tavistock, 1967).

FOWLER, ROGER, *Linguistic Criticism* (Oxford and New York: Oxford University Press, 1986).

FRANKL, PAUL, *The Gothic: Literary Sources and Interpretations through Eight Centuries* (Princeton, NJ: Princeton University Press, 1960).

FRITZ, PAUL, and NORTON, RICHARD, eds., *Women in the 18th Century and Other Essays* (Toronto and Sarasota: Samuel Stevens Hakkert, 1976).

FROW, JOHN, *Marxism and Literary History* (Oxford: Blackwell, 1986).

——'Voice and Register in *Little Dorrit*', *Comparative Literature*, 33/3 (Summer 1981), 258-70.

FUGATE, JOE K., *The Psychological Basis of Herder's Aesthetics* (The Hague: Mouton, 1966).

GARLAND, HENRY BURNAND, *A Concise Survey of German Literature* (London and Basingstoke: Macmillan, 1976).

——*Storm and Stress* (London: George Harrap, 1952).

Gentleman's Magazine, 64 (1794), 834.

GEORGE, MARY DOROTHY, *English Political Caricature 1793-1832* (Oxford: Oxford University Press, 1959).

GILBERT, SANDRA M., and GUBAR, SUSAN, *The Madwoman in the Attic* (New Haven, Conn. and London: Yale University Press, 1979).

GILPIN, JOHN, *Observations, relative chiefly to Picturesque Beauty, made in the year 1772, on several parts of England, particularly on the Mountains and Lakes of Cumberland and Westmorland* (London: Blamire, 1786).

GILPIN, WILLIAM, *Three Essays: On Picturesque Beauty; On Picturesque Travel; and on Sketching Landscape: to Which is Added a Poem, On Landscape Painting* (London: R. Blamire, 1794).

GISBORNE, THOMAS, *Enquiries into the Duties of the Female Sex* (London: Cadell and Davies, 1797).

GLOVERSMITH, FRANK, ed., *The Theory of Reading* (Brighton: Harvester Press, 1984).

GODWIN, WILLIAM, *Enquiry Concerning Political Justice and its Influence on Modern Morals and Happiness* (Harmondsworth: Penguin, 1985).

——*St. Leon: A Tale of the Sixteenth Century*, Foreword by Devendra P. Varma, Introd. Juliet Beckett (New York: Arno Press, 1972).

GRABES, HERBERT, with DILLER, HANS JÜRGEN, and BUNGERT, HANS, eds., *Yearbook of Research in English and American Literature* (Berlin and New York: Walter de Gruyter, 1982), 294.

GREGORY, DR JOHN, *A Father's Legacy to his Daughters* (London: W. Strahan, T. Cadell, 1774).

HADLEY, MICHAEL, *The Undiscovered Genre: A Search for the German Gothic Novel* (Berne, Frankfurt, and Las Vegas: Peter Lang, 1978).

HAGGERTY, GEORGE E., 'Fact and Fancy in the Gothic Novel', *Nineteenth Century Fiction*, 39/4 (Mar. 1985), 379–91.

——*Gothic Fiction/Gothic Form* (University Park and London: Pennsylvania State University Press, 1987).

HEIDERICH, MANFRED W., *The German Novel of 1800: A Study of Popular Prose Fiction* (Berne and Frankfurt: Peter Lang, 1982).

HERDER, JOHANN GOTTFRIED, *Werke* (Munich: Carl Hanser Publishing House, 1953).

HILL, BRIDGET, *Eighteenth-Century Women: An Anthology* (London: Allen & Unwin, 1984).

HIPPLE, WALTER JOHN, JR., *The Beautiful, the Sublime and the Picturesque in Eighteenth-Century British Aesthetic Theory* (Carbondale: Southern Illinois University Press, 1957).

HIRSCH, ERIC DONALD, JR., *The Aims of Interpretation* (Chicago and London: University of Chicago Press, 1976).

HIRSCHKOP, KEN, 'A Response to the Forum on Mikhail Bakhtin', *Critical Inquiry*, 11/4 (June 1985), 672–701.

——'The Social and the Subject in Bakhtin', *Poetics Today*, 6/4 (1985), 769–75.

——and SHEPHERD, DAVID, eds., *Bakhtin and Cultural Theory* (Manchester and New York: Manchester University Press, 1989).

HOFFMANN, GERHARD, 'The Fantastic in Fiction: Its "Reality" Status, its Historical Development and its Transformation in Postmodern Narration', in Herbert Grabes with Hans Jürgen Diller and Hans Bungert (eds.), *Yearbook of Research in English and American Literature* (Berlin and New York: Walter de Gruyter, 1982).

HOLLAND, NORMAN N., and SHERMAN, LEONA F., 'Gothic Possibilities', *New Literary History*, 8 (Winter 1977), 279–94.

HOLQUIST, MICHAEL, *Dialogism: Bakhtin and His World* (London and New York: Routledge, 1990).

HORNER, JOYCE M., *The English Women Novelists and their Connection with the Feminist Movement 1668–1797* (1930; Northampton: Folcroft, 1973).

HOWELLS, CORAL ANN, *Love, Mystery and Misery: Feeling in Gothic Fiction* (London: Athlone Press, 1978).

HOY, MIKITA, 'Bakhtin and Popular Culture', *New Literary History*, 23/3 (1992), 765–82.

HUME, ROBERT D., 'Gothic versus Romantic: A Revaluation of the Gothic Novel', *PMLA* 84/2 (Mar. 1969), 282–90.

HURD, RICHARD, *Hurd's Letters on Chivalry and Romance*, ed. Edith J. Morley (London: Henry Trowde, 1911).

HUTCHEON, LINDA, *A Theory of Parody: The Teachings of Twentieth-Century Art Forms* (New York: Methuen, 1985).

JACKSON, ROSEMARY, *Fantasy: The Literature of Subversion* (London and New York: Methuen, 1981).

JACOBUS, MARY, 'The Question of Language: Men of Maxims and *The Mill on the Floss*', *Critical Inquiry*, 8/2 (Winter 1981), 207–22.

JAMESON, FREDRIC, 'Magical Narratives: Romance as Genre', *New Literary History*, 7/1 (Autumn 1975), 135–63.

——*The Political Unconscious: Narrative as a Socially Symbolic Act* (London: Methuen, 1981).

JOHNSON, SAMUEL, *Johnson: Prose and Poetry* (London: Rupert Hart-Davis, 1963).

JONES, MARY GWLADYS, *Hannah More* (Cambridge: Cambridge University Press, 1952).

KAMM, JOSEPHINE, *Hope Deferred: Girls' Education in English History* (London: Methuen, 1965).

KELLOGG, ROBERT, 'Oral Narrative, Written Books', *Genre*, 10/4 (1977), 655–65.

KELLY, GARY, *The English Jacobin Novel* (Oxford: Oxford University Press, 1976).

——'Unbecoming a Heroine: Novel Reading, Romanticism, and Barrett's *The Heroine*', *Nineteenth-Century Literature*, 45/2 (Sept. 1990), 220–41.

KENT, THOMAS, *Interpretation and Genre: The Role of Generic Perception in the Study of Text* (Lewisburg, Pa. and London: Bucknell University Press and Associated University Presses, 1986).

KESTNER, JOSEPH A., *Spatiality in the Novel* (Detroit: Wayne University Press, 1978).

KETTERER, DAVID, *Frankenstein's Creation: The Book, the Monster, and the Human Reality* (Victoria, BC: University of Victoria, 1979).

KIELY, ROBERT, *The Romantic Novel in England* (Cambridge, Mass.: Harvard University Press, 1972).

KIRKHAM, MARGARET, *Jane Austen, Feminism and Fiction* (Brighton: Harvester Press, 1983).

KLAUS, H. GUSTAV, *The Literature of Labour: Two Hundred Years of Working-Class Writing* (Brighton: Harvester Press, 1985).

KLEIN, VIOLA, *The Feminine Character: History of an Ideology* (London: Kegan Paul, French, Trubner, 1946).

KLIGER, SAMUEL, 'The "Goths" in England: An Introduction to the Gothic Vogue in Eighteenth-Century Aesthetic Discussion', *Modern Philology*, 43 (1945), 105–17.

KNIGHT, RICHARD PAYNE, *The Landscape, a Didactic Poem in Three Books; Addressed to Uvedale Price, Esq.* (London: W. Bulmer, 1794).

KOHLSCHMIDT, WERNER, *A History of German Literature 1760–1805* (London and Basingstoke: Macmillan, 1975).

KROEBER, KARL, and WALLING, WILLIAM, eds., *Images of Romanticism* (New Haven, Conn. and London: Yale University Press, 1978).

LACAPRA, DOMINICK, *Rethinking Intellectual History: Texts, Contexts, Language* (Ithaca, NY and London: Cornell University Press, 1985).

LEA, SYDNEY L. W., JR., *Gothic to Fantastic: Readings in Supernatural Fiction* (New York: Arno Press, 1980).

LENNOX, CHARLOTTE, *The Female Quixote, or The Adventures of Arabella*, ed. with an Introd. by Margaret Dalziel, Chronology and Appendix by Duncan Isles (London: Oxford University Press, 1970).

LEVINE, GEORGE, and KNOEPFLMACHER, ULRICH CAMILLUS, *The Endurance of Frankenstein* (Berkeley: University of California Press, 1979).

LÉVY, MAURICE, *Le Roman gothique anglais, 1764–1824* (Toulouse: Association des Publications de la Faculté des Letters et Sciences Humaines, 1968).

LEWIS, MATTHEW GREGORY, *The Monk*, ed. James Kinsley and Howard Anderson (Oxford: Oxford University Press, 1980).

LEWIS, PAUL, 'Gothic and Mock Gothic: The Repudiation of Fantasy in Barrett's *Heroine*', *English Language Notes*, 21/1 (Sept. 1983), 44–52.

LEWIS, WILMARTH SHELDON, *Horace Walpole* (London: Rupert Hart-Davis, 1961).

Limbird's edition of The British Novelist; forming A Choice Collection of the Best Novels in the English Language (London: J. Limbird, 1831), vol. i. There are six novels, paged separately, in vol. i: Ann Radcliffe, *Mysteries of Udolpho* and *Romance of the Forest*; Clara Reeve, *Old English Baron*; Horace Walpole, *Castle of Otranto*; Ann Radcliffe, *Castles of Athlin and Dunbayne* and *Sicilian Romance*.

LITTLE, ANTHONY JAMES, *Deceleration in the Eighteenth-Century British Economy* (London: Croom Helm, 1976).

LITZ, A. WALTON, *Jane Austen: A Study of Her Artistic Development* (New York: Oxford University Press, 1965).

LODGE, JANE AIKEN, *Only a Novel: The Double Life of Jane Austen* (London: Hodder & Stoughton, 1972).

LONGUEIL, ALFRED E., 'The Word "Gothic" in Eighteenth Century Criticism', *Modern Language Notes*, 38 (1923), 453–60.

LOVELL, TERRY, *Consuming Fiction* (London: Verso, 1987).

MacAndrew, Elizabeth, *The Gothic Tradition in Fiction* (New York: Columbia University Press, 1979).

Macaulay, Catharine, *Letters on Education, with Observations on Religious and Metaphysical Subjects* (London: C. Dilly, 1790; reprint edn. New York and London: Garland, 1974).

MacCarthy, Bridget G., *The Later Women Novelists, 1744–1818* (Oxford: Cork University Press, 1947).

McConnell-Ginet, Sally, with Borker, Ruth, and Furman, Nelly, eds., *Women and Language in Literature and Society* (New York: Praeger, 1980).

McIntyre, Clara F., *Ann Radcliffe in Relation to Her Time* (New Haven, Conn. and London: Yale University Press, 1920).

——'Were the "Gothic Novels" Gothic?', *PMLA* 36/4 (Dec. 1921), 646, 652–64.

McKillop, Alan Dugald, 'Mrs. Radcliffe on the Supernatural in Poetry', *Journal of English and Germanic Philology*, 31 (1932), 352–9.

——'Richardson, Young and the Conjectures', *Modern Philology*, 22 (May 1925), 391–404.

Madoff, Mark, 'The Useful Myth of Gothic Ancestry', *Studies in Eighteenth Century Culture*, 8 (1979), 337–50.

Mahl, Mary R., and Koon, Helene, eds., *The Female Spectator* (Bloomington and London: Indiana University Press, 1977).

Malcuzynski, M.-Pierrette, 'Mikhail Bakhtin and Contemporary Narrative Theory', *Revue de l'Université d'Ottawa*, 53/1 (1983), 51–65.

Marks, Elaine, and de Courtivron, Isabelle, eds., *New French Feminisms: An Anthology* (Amherst: University of Massachusetts Press, 1980).

Mathias, Thomas James, *The Pursuits of Literature: A Satirical Poem in Dialogue, With Notes* (London: T. Becket, 1801).

May, Leland Chandler, *Parodies of the Gothic Novel* (New York: Arno Press, 1980).

Mayo, Robert D., 'Gothic Romance in the Magazines', *PMLA* 65/5 (Sept. 1950), 762–89.

——'The Gothic Short Story in the Magazines', *Modern Language Review*, 37 (1942), 448–54.

——'How Long was Gothic Fiction in Vogue?' *Modern Language Notes*, 58 (Jan. 1943), 58–64.

Messman, Frank J., *Richard Payne Knight: The Twilight of Virtuosity* (The Hague and Paris: Mouton, 1974).

Mews, Hazel, *Frail Vessels* (London: Athlone Press, 1969).

Mingay, Gordon Edward, *English Landed Society in the Eighteenth Century* (London: Routledge & Kegan Paul, 1963).

MOERS, ELLEN, 'Female Gothic: Monsters, Goblins, Freaks', *New York Review of Books*, 21/5 (4 Apr. 1974), 35–9.

—— 'Female Gothic: The Monster's Mother', *New York Review of Books*, 21/4 (21 Mar. 1974), 24–8.

—— *Literary Women* (London: W. H. Allen, 1977).

MOI, TORIL, *Sexual/Textual Politics: Feminist Literary Theory* (London and New York: Methuen, 1985).

MONAGHAN, DAVID, ed., *Jane Austen in a Social Context* (London and Basingstoke: Macmillan, 1981).

MONK, SAMUEL HOLT, *The Sublime: A Study of Critical Theories in XVIII-Century England* (New York: Modern Language Association of America, 1935).

Monthly Mirror, 2 (June 1796), 98.

Monthly Review, 9 (June 1792), 198–206: review of Wollstonecraft's *Vindication of the Rights of Woman*; 81 (1789), 563; 2nd ser. 3 (Sept. 1790), 91; 2nd ser. 10 (1793), 224; 2nd ser. 14 (1794), 464–5; 2nd ser. 15 (1794), 280: William Enfield [unsigned review], 'Mrs. Radcliffe's Mysteries of Udolpho'; 2nd ser. 15 (Nov. 1794), 281.

MORE, HANNAH, *The Miscellaneous Works of Hannah More* (London: Thomas Tegg, 1840).

—— *Strictures on the Modern System of Female Education with a View to the Principles and Conduct of Women of Rank and Fortune* (London: T. Cadell and W. Davies, 1799).

MORRIS, DAVID B., 'Gothic Sublimity', *New Literary History*, 16/2 (Winter 1985), 299–319.

MORSE, DAVID, *Romanticism: A Structural Analysis* (London and Basingstoke: Macmillan, 1982).

MORSON, GARY SAUL, and EMERSON, CARYL, *Mikhail Bakhtin: Creation of a Prosaics* (Stanford, Calif.: Stanford University Press, 1990).

—— and ——, eds. *Rethinking Bakhtin: Extensions and Challenges* (Evanston, Ill.: Northwestern University Press, 1989).

MOSS, JOHN, ed., *Future Indicative: Literary Theory and Canadian Literature* (Ottawa: University of Ottawa Press, 1987), 117–36: Sherrill Grace, ' "Listen to the Voice": Dialogism and the Canadian Novel'.

MUDRICK, MARTIN, *Jane Austen: Irony as Defense and Discovery* (Princeton, NJ: Princeton University Press, 1952).

MULLAN, JOHN, 'Hypochondria and Hysteria: Sensibility and the Physicians', *Eighteenth Century: Theory and Interpretation*, 25/2 (Spring 1984), 141–74.

MULLAN, JOHN, *Sentiment and Sociability: The Language of Feeling in the Eighteenth Century* (Oxford: Clarendon Press, 1988).

MURRAY, EUGENE BERNAND, *Ann Radcliffe* (New York: Twayne Publishers, 1972).

MYERS, MITZI, 'Reform or Ruin: "A Revolution in Female Manners" ', *Studies in Eighteenth-Century Culture*, 11 (1982), 199–216.

NAPIER, ELIZABETH R., *The Failure of the Gothic: Problems of Disjunction in an Eighteenth-Century Literary Form* (Oxford: Clarendon Press, 1987).

NEWMAN, BETH, 'Narratives of Seduction and the Seductions of Narrative: The Frame Structure of *Frankenstein*', *ELH* 53/1 (Spring 1986), 141–63.

NEWMAN, GERALD, 'Anti-French Propaganda and British Liberal Nationalism in the Early Nineteenth Century: Suggestions Toward a General Interpretation', *Victorian Studies*, 18/4 (June 1975), 385–418.

OZOLINS, AIJA, in 'Dreams and Doctrines: Dual Strands in *Frankenstein*', *Science-Fiction Studies*, 2 (July 1975), 103–12.

PAGLIARO, H. E., ed., *Studies in Eighteenth Century Culture* (Cleveland: Case Western Reserve University Press, 1973).

PARREAUX, ANDRÉ, *The Publication of 'The Monk': A Literary Event 1796–1798* (Paris: Marcel Didier, 1960).

PASCAL, ROY, *The German Sturm und Drang* (Manchester: Manchester University Press, 1953).

PAULSON, R., *Representations of Revolution, 1789–1820* (New Haven, Conn.: Yale University Press, 1983).

PEACOCK, THOMAS LOVE, *Peacock's Four Ages of Poetry: Shelley's Defence of Poetry: and Browning's Essay on Shelley*, ed. F. H. B. Brett-Smith (Oxford: Basil Blackwell, 1929).

PECK, LOUIS F., *A Life of Matthew G. Lewis* (Cambridge, Mass.: Harvard University Press, 1961).

PIOZZI, HESTER LYNCH (SALUSBURY) THRALE, *Thraliana: The Diary of Mrs. Hester Lynch Thrale 1776–1809*, ed. Katherine C. Balderstone (Oxford: Clarendon Press, 1942).

PITCHER, E. W., 'Changes in Short Fiction in Britain 1785–1810: Philosophic Tales, Gothic Tales, and Fragments and Visions', *Studies in Short Fiction*, 13/3 (Summer 1976), 331–54.

POOVEY, MARY, 'Ideology and *The Mysteries of Udolpho*', *Criticism*, 21/4 (1979), 307–30.

——'My Hideous Progeny: Mary Shelley and the Feminization of Romanticism', *PMLA* 95/3 (May 1980), 332–47.

——*The Proper Lady and the Woman Writer* (Chicago and London: University of Chicago Press, 1984).

PRICE, LAWRENCE MARSDEN, *The Reception of English Literature in Germany* (Berkeley: University of California Press, 1932).

PRICE, UVEDALE, *An Essay on the Picturesque, As Compared with the Sublime and the Beautiful; and, on the Use of Studying Pictures, for the Purpose of Improving Real Landscape* (London: 1794; repr. London: J. Mawman, 1810, and Farnborough: Gregg International, 1971).

PUNTER, DAVID, *The Literature of Terror: A History of Gothic Fictions from 1765 to the Present Day* (London: Longman, 1980).

QUINLAN, MAURICE JAMES, *Victorian Prelude: A History of English Manners 1700–1830* (New York: Columbia University Press, 1941).

RABKIN, ERIC S., *The Fantastic in Literature* (Princeton, NJ: Princeton University Press, 1976).

——'Review of *Fantasy: The Literature of Subversion* by Rosemary Jackson', *Genre* 14/4 (Winter 1981), 523–7.

RADCLIFFE, ANN, *Gaston de Blondville or The Court of Henry III* (London: Henry Colburn, 1826).

——*The Mysteries of Udolpho, The Romance of the Forest, The Castles of Athlin and Dunbayne, A Sicilian Romance*, in *Limbird's edition of The British Novelist; forming A Choice Collection of the Best Novels in the English Language*, vol. i (London: J. Limbird, 1831).

——*The Italian: or The Confessional of the Black Penitents* (Oxford: Oxford University Press, 1981).

——*The Mysteries of Udolpho* (Oxford: Oxford University Press, 1980).

RADCLIFFE, MARY ANNE, *Manfroné: Or the One Handed Monk*, introd. by Coral Ann Howells (New York: Arno Press, 1972).

RAILO, EINO, *The Haunted Castle* (London: George Routledge & Sons, 1927).

RALEIGH, WALTER ALEXANDER, *The English Novel: A Short Sketch of its History from the Earliest Times to the Appearance of 'Waverley'* (London: Murray, 1904).

REED, RONALD LEE, 'The Function of Folklore in Selected English Gothic Novels', Ph.D. thesis (Texas Tech University, 1971).

REEVE, CLARA, *The Old English Baron*, in *Limbird's edition of The British Novelist; forming A Choice Collection of the Best Novels in the English Language*, vol. i (London: J. Limbird, 1831).

REID, IAN, ' "Always a Sacrifice": Executing Textual Unities in Two Stories by Katherine Mansfield', *Journal of the Short Story in English*, 4 (Spring 1985), 77–94.

——'When is an Epitaph Not an Epitaph? A Monumental Generic Problem and a Jonsonian Instance', *Southern Review*, 22/3 (Nov. 1989), 198–210.

REIMAN, DONALD HENRY, ed., *The Romantics Reviewed* (New York and London: Garland, 1972).

RICARDOU, JEAN, *Pour une theorie de nouveau roman* (Paris: Editions du Seuil, 1971).

RIMMON-KENAN, SHLOMITH, *Narrative Fiction: Contemporary Poetics* (London and New York: Methuen, 1983).

RITCHIE, J. M., ed., *Periods in German Literature: A Symposium* (London: Oswald Wolff, 1968).

ROBERTS, BETTE B., *The Gothic Romance: Its Appeal to Women Writers and Readers in Late Eighteenth-Century England* (New York: Arno Press, 1980).

ROBERTS, WARREN, *Jane Austen and the French Revolution* (London and Basingstoke: Macmillan, 1981).

ROGERS, KATHARINE, *Feminism in Eighteenth-Century England* (Urbana, Chicago, and London: University of Illinois Press, 1982).

RUTHVEN, KEN, *Feminist Literary Studies: An Introduction* (Cambridge: Cambridge University Press, 1984).

Scots Magazine, 64 (1802), 470–4, 545–8.

SCOTT, WALTER, *Sir Walter Scott on Novelists and Fiction*, ed. Ioan Williams (London: Routledge & Kegan Paul, 1968).

SCRIVENER, MICHAEL, 'Frankenstein's Ghost Story: The Last Jacobin Novel', *Genre*, 19/3 (Fall 1986), 229–317.

SEED, DAVID, 'Gothic Definitions', *Novel*, 14/3 (Spring 1981), 270–4.

SHELLEY, MARY WOLLSTONECRAFT, *Frankenstein: or The Modern Prometheus*, ed. James Kinsley and Michael Kennedy Joseph (Oxford: Oxford University Press, 1980).

——*Frankenstein: or The Modern Prometheus* (The 1818 text), edited, with variant readings, an introduction, and notes, by James Rieger (Indianapolis: Bobbs-Merrill, 1974).

——*Mary Shelley's Journal*, ed. Frederick L. Jones (Norman: University of Oklahoma Press, 1947).

——*The Shelley Journals*, ed. Paula R. Feldman and Diana Scott-Kilvert (Oxford and New York: Clarendon Press, 1987).

SHELLEY, PERCY BYSSHE, *The Works of Percy Bysshe Shelley*, ed. Harry Buxton Forman (London: Reeves and Turner, 1880).

SHEVTSOVA, MARIA, 'Dialogism in the Novel and Bakhtin's Theory of Culture', *New Literary History*, 23/3 (1992), 747–63.

SKULTANS, VIEDA, *English Madness: Ideas on Insanity, 1580–1890* (London, Boston, and Henley: Routledge & Kegan Paul, 1979).

SMITH, CHARLOTTE, *Desmond* (London: G. G. J. and J. Robinson, 1792; reprint edn. New York and London: Garland, 1974).

SMITH, NELSON C., 'Sense, Sensibility and Ann Radcliffe', *Studies in English Literature*, 13 (1973), 577–90.

SMITH, WILLIAM, *A Dissertation upon the Nerves* (London: W. Owen, 1768).

SOUTHAM, BRIAN CHARLES, *Jane Austen: The Critical Heritage* (London: Routledge & Kegan Paul, 1968).

SPENCER, JANE, *The Rise of the Woman Novelist: From Aphra Benn to Jane Austen* (Oxford and New York: Basil Blackwell, 1986).

SPENDER, DALE, *Mothers of the Novel* (London and New York: Pandora Press, 1986).

SPRINGER, MARLENE, ed., *What Manner of Woman: Essays on English and American Literature* (New York: New York University Press, 1977).

STAM, ROBERT, 'Mikhail Bakhtin and Left Cultural Critique', in E. Ann Kaplan (ed.), *Postmodernism and its Discontents: Theories, Practices* (London, New York: Verso, 1988), ch. 8, pp. 116–45.

STEWART, SUSAN, 'Shouts on the Street: Bakhtin's Anti-Linguistics', *Critical Inquiry*, 10/2 (Dec. 1983), 265–81.

STIMPSON, CATHERINE R., 'Feminism and Feminist Criticism', *Massachusetts Review*, 24/2 (Summer 1983), 272–88.

STUART, DOROTHY MARGARET, *Horace Walpole* (London: Macmillan, 1927).

Studies in the Literary Imagination, 23/1 (Spring 1990), 1–127: Bakhtin and the languages of the novel: evaluations, reconsiderations.

STUKELY, WILLIAM, *Of the Spleen* (London, 1723).

SULEIMAN, SUSAN RUBIN, *Authoritarian Fictions: The Ideological Novel as a Literary Genre* (New York: Columbia University Press, 1983).

SUMMERS, MONTAGUE, *A Gothic Bibliography* (New York: Russell & Russell, 1964).

——*The Gothic Quest* (New York: Russell & Russell, 1964).

TANNENBAUM, LESLIE, 'From Filthy Type to Truth: Miltonic Myth in *Frankenstein*', *Keats-Shelley Journal*, 26 (1977), 101–13.

TARR, MARY MURIEL, *Catholicism in Gothic Fiction: A Study of the Nature and Function of Catholic Materials in Gothic Fiction in England (1762–1820)* (Washington: Catholic University of America Press, 1946).

TAYLOR, JOHN TINNON, *Early Opposition to the English Novel: The Popular Reaction from 1760 to 1830* (New York: King's Crown Press, 1943).

TEMKIN, OWSEI, 'Basic Science, Medicine, and the Romantic Era', in *The Double Face of Janus and Other Essays in the History of Medicine* (Baltimore and London: Johns Hopkins University Press, 1977).

THOMAS, WALTER, *Le Poète Edward Young, étude sur sa vie et ses œuvres* (Paris: Hachette, 1901).

THOMPSON, GARY RICHARD, ed., *The Gothic Imagination: Essays in Dark Romanticism* (Pullman: Washington State University Press, 1974).

THOMSON, CLIVE, 'Mikhail Bakhtin and Contemporary Anglo-American Feminist Theory', *Critical Studies*, 1/2 (1989), 141–61.

——'Mikhail Bakhtin and Shifting Paradigms', *Critical Studies*, 2, 1/2 (1990), 1–12.

THORSLEV, PETER LARSEN, JR., *Romantic Contraries: Freedom versus Destiny* (New Haven, Conn. and London: Yale University Press, 1984).

THREADGOLD, TERRY, and CRANNY-FRANCIS, ANNE, eds., *Feminine, Masculine and Representation* (Sydney, London, Boston, Wellington: Allen & Unwin, 1990).

TODD, JANET, *Sensibility: An Introduction* (London and New York: Methuen, 1986).

——*Feminist Literary History: A Defence* (Oxford: Polity Press in association with Basil Blackwell, 1988).

TODOROV, TZVETAN, *Introduction à la litterature fantastique*, trans. *The Fantastic* by Richard Howard (Cleveland and London: Case Western Reserve University Press, 1973).

——*Mikhail Bakhtin: The Dialogical Principle* (Minneapolis: University of Minnesota Press, 1984).

TOMALIN, CLAIRE, *The Life and Death of Mary Wollstonecraft* (Harmondsworth: Penguin Books, 1985).

TOMPKINS, JANE, *Reader-Response Criticism* (Baltimore: Johns Hopkins University Press, 1980).

TOMPKINS, JOYCE MARJORIE SANXTER, *The Popular Novel in England 1770–1800* (London: Constable, 1932).

TRACY, ANN BLAISDELL, *The Gothic Novel 1790–1830: Plot Summaries and Index to Motifs* (Lexington: University Press of Kentucky, 1981).

TWITCHELL, JAMES B., 'Frankenstein and the Anatomy of Horror', *Georgia Review*, 37 (1983), 48–55.

VARMA, DEVENDRA P., *The Gothic Flame* (London: Arthur Baker, 1957).

VASBINDER, SAMUEL HOLMES, *Scientific Attitudes in Mary Shelley's 'Frankenstein'* (Ann Arbor, Mich.: UMI Research Press, 1984).

VEITH, ILZA, *Hysteria: The History of a Disease* (Chicago and London: University of Chicago Press, 1965).

WALPOLE, HORACE, *The Castle of Otranto*, in Peter Fairclough (ed.), *Three Gothic Novels* (Harmondsworth: Penguin Books, 1978).

——*The Castle of Otranto*, in E. F. Bleiler (ed.), *Three Gothic Novels* (New York: Dover Publications Inc., 1966).

WARD, BERNARD, *The Dawn of the Catholic Revival in England 1781–1803* (London: Longmans, Green, 1909).

WARE, MALCOLM, *Sublimity in the Novels of Ann Radcliffe: A Study of the Influence upon her Craft of Edmund Burke's 'Enquiry into the Origin of our Ideas of the Sublime and Beautiful'* (Uppsala: Lindequist, 1963).

WATT, IAN, *The Rise of the Novel* (Harmondsworth: Penguin Books, 1963).

WEEDON, CHRIS, *Feminist Practice and Poststructuralist Theory* (Oxford: Basil Blackwell, 1987).

Westminster Review, 29 (1831), 71: 'The Education of Women'.

WHITE, ALLON, 'Pigs and Pierrots: The Politics of Transgression in Modern Fiction', *Raritan*, 2/2 (1982), 51–70.

——'The Struggle Over Bakhtin: Fraternal Reply to Robert Young', *Cultural Critique*, 8 (Winter 1987–8) 217–41.

WHYTT, ROBERT, *Observations on the Nature, Causes and Cures of those Disorders which have been commonly called Nervous, Hypochondriac, or Hysteria* (Edinburgh: J. Balfour, 1765).

WILSON, MARGARET BARON, *The Life and Correspondence of M. G. Lewis, with Many Pieces in Prose and Verse Never Before Published* (London: Henry Colburn, 1839).

WOLF, LEONARD, 'Gothic Novels', *New York Times Book Review* (14 Jan. 1973), 2, 28.

WOLLSTONECRAFT, MARY, *A Vindication of the Rights of Woman: With Strictures on Political and Moral Subjects* (London: Source Book Press, 1972).

WOODMANSEE, MARTHA, 'The Genius and the Copyright: Economic and Legal Conditions for the Emergence of the "Author" ', *Eighteenth Century Studies*, 17/4 (Summer 1984), 425–48.

WORDSWORTH, WILLIAM, and COLERIDGE, SAMUEL TAYLOR, *Lyrical Ballads*, ed. R. L. Brett and A. R. Jones (London: Methuen, 1963).

YAEGER, PATRICIA S., ' "Because a Fire was in my Head": Eudora Welty and the Dialogic Imagination', *PMLA* 99/5 (Oct. 1984), 955–73.

——*Honey-Mad Women: Emancipatory Strategies n Women's Writing* (New York: Columbia University Press, 1988).

YOUNG, EDWARD, *Edward Young's Conjectures on Original Composition*, ed. Edith J. Morley (Manchester: Longmans, Green, 1918).

YOUNG, ROBERT, 'Back to Bakhtin', *Cultural Critique*, 2 (Winter 1986), 71–92.

ZAVALA, IRIS M., 'Bakhtin and Otherness: Social Heterogeneity', *Critical Studies*, 2, 1/2 (1990), 78–89.

ZIOLOWSKI, THEODORE, *Disenchanted Images: A Literary Iconology* (Princeton, NJ: Princeton University Press, 1977).

——'Science, Frankenstein, and Myth', *Sewanee Review*, 89/1 (Winter 1981), 34–56.

Index

Herder, Johann Gottfried 187, 220
hermeneutic scepticism 103
heteroglossia 2, 5, 17, 44, 46,
    49–50, 284
Hoffmann, Gerhard 5, 32, 38–40,
    43, 130
Hoffmann, Leopold Alois 212
Holcroft, Thomas 29
Holquist, Michael 273
homogenization 2, 14, 19, 172, 180
Horner, Joyce M. 61–2
Howard, John 102
Howells, Coral Ann 18, 44, 59,
    99, 140, 183
Hume, Robert D. 18, 57
Hurd, William, Bishop 25, 28, 95
Hutcheon, Linda 146–8, 155, 169
hypochondria 71–2, 83, 93, 208
hysteria 71–2, 83, 93, 125–6

ideology 15, 17, 27, 39, 42, 44–5,
    47–50
imagination 9–10, 12, 70, 78, 83,
    91–5, 96–7, 134, 136, 186,
    254–5, 275
Inchbald, Elizabeth 149
intentionality 46–51, 145–8
intertextuality 1, 23, 45, 47–8,
    147, 175, 283
intratextual patterning or framing
    3, 7, 39, 46, 181
Irigaray, Luce 54
irony 100–1, 146–7

Jackson, Rosemary 5, 30, 35,
    39–43, 53, 54, 181
Jacobinism 102, 117, 151, 153,
    167, 233, 247–8, 251, 260
Jacobus, Mary 56–7
James, Henry 15, 22, 37, 44
Johnson, Samuel 70, 86, 89, 163
Joyce, James 55

Ketterer, David 272
Kelly, Gary 157
Kiely, Robert 126, 130, 133,
    171–2, 175, 208, 217, 224,
    231, 274
Kirkham, Margaret 77, 161, 173
Knight, Richard Payne 113–14,
    116–17, 213

Kristeva, Julia 42, 181

Lacan, Jacques 42, 43, 53–5, 224
landscape 111–17, 164, 174, 190,
    203, 209–10, 213, 218–19,
    236, 254–5
    gardening 111, 113–14, 210, 236
Lawrence, William 246–7, 267
Lea, Sydney 220
Leland, Thomas 212
Lennox, Charlotte 98, 148
Lewis, Paul 148, 155, 159
Lewis, Matthew 182–238
libertinism 102, 261
Longinus 27
Luddites 249

MacAndrew, Elizabeth 17–19,
    21–3, 36, 38, 60–1, 65
MacCarthy, B. G. 56
Macaulay, Catharine 31, 237
McKillop. Alan D. 90
Maclean, Marie 42
Madoff, Mark 24, 27, 35, 217, 222
madness 54, 83, 93–4, 102, 136,
    158
Manley, Delariviere 86, 101
Marxist theories 5, 13, 30, 41, 100
Mathias, Thomas James 111,
    149–50, 233, 250
Maturin, Charles 13, 22, 58, 241
Mayo, Robert D. 240
melancholy 71–2, 78, 83, 97, 204,
    242
metadiscourse 45
metafiction 283
metonymy 173, 175, 220, 271
Mews, Hazel 60
Middlemarch 64
Milton, John 25, 132, 133, 140,
    161, 171, 231, 251–2, 281, 283
Mingay, G. E. 108
modesty topos 81–2, 91, 259
Moers, Ellen 58–60, 62, 65
monologism 7, 14, 40, 100
monomyth 14, 24
Montagu, Elizabeth 78, 79, 89
Montagu, Mary Wortley, Lady 74
More, Hannah 70–1, 78, 97, 102,
    237, 239, 256–7, 259, 260
Morley, Edith J. 88–9

Seed, David 67
sensibility, discourses of 44, 67–84,
    90, 93–6, 102, 110, 152,
    163–4, 178–80, 184, 186,
    190–217, 235, 237, 243,
    256–7, 264, 274–83
Sentimental novel, the 22, 71, 73,
    94, 99, 156, 163
sentimentalism 46, 70
Seward, Anna 97, 143
Shakespeare, William 25–6, 91,
    132, 195
Shelley, Percy Bysshe 241, 244–9,
    251–5, 258, 272, 282
Shelley, Mary 54, 59, 97, 237–83
Shepherd, David 51, 103
Smith, Charlotte 80, 98, 110, 149
Smith, Nelson C. 125–6
Smith, William 72
spatial form 22, 63, 65, 66
spirit-ballad, see *volksballade*
Sterrenburg, Lee 262
Stukely, William 71
Sturm und Drang 186, 188–9, 198,
    212, 221, 233
stylization 48, 101, 104, 110, 145,
    147, 167, 172, 181
subjectivity 15, 30, 48, 103, 164,
    219, 222
sublime, the 19–20, 27, 43, 45–6,
    78–9, 95, 104, 121–4, 126–40,
    180, 217–24, 231, 252, 272
subversion 14, 29–30, 39, 41–5,
    51, 53–4, 66, 100, 131, 140,
    169–183, 225, 232, 234
Summers, Montague 18, 30, 228
superstition 16, 29, 43, 46, 93,
    125–6, 129, 130–1, 136, 141,
    205, 214, 216, 226, 267
symbolism 18, 22, 27, 33, 63, 65,
    103, 193, 211, 224

Talfourd, Thomas Noon 126
taste 83, 96, 107, 110–19, 143,
    145, 164, 168
Tayler, Irene 94
Thompson, G. R. 26
Thrale, Hester Lynch, Mrs 79, 89,
    92, 133

Todorov, Tzvetan 5, 15, 36–40
Tomalin, Claire 251
Tompkins, J. M. S. 18, 21, 29, 33,
    35, 60–1, 165
Tracy, Ann B. 13, 18
Tschink, Cajetan 229

unfinalizability 51, 67, 284
utterance, theory of the 47, 49–50,
    101, 145–6

Varma, Devendra 26
volksballade (spirit-ballad) 220,
    222, 242–3, 245, 264, 268,
    271

Walpole, Horace 12–13, 19, 20,
    25–6, 30–6, 80, 89–92, 250
Watt, Ian 61, 68, 74, 75, 87
Weber, Veit 215, 229
Wieland, Christoph 105, 189, 229
Whytt, Robert 72
Wolf, Leonard 58, 60
Wollstonecraft, Mary 96, 102,
    123, 127, 132, 141, 150, 163,
    177, 251, 274, 280
women:
  and authorship 64, 67–97, 190,
      253–9
  and education 56, 60, 62, 69, 76,
      78, 149, 158, 163, 168, 172,
      174, 177, 251, 256–7
  and marriage 69–70, 73, 108–9,
      136
  and their 'proper sphere' 81, 96,
      159, 251
  and writing 53–8, 61–4, 70–84,
      86–9, 94–7, 100–1, 151,
      160–1, 171, 173–4, 251, 254,
      258, 259
Woodmansee, Martha 84–6
Wordsworth, William 239–41,
    252, 255, 258

Yearsley, Ann 87–8
Young, Edward 85, 87–92, 187,
    258

Ziolkowski, Theodore 40